ROUTLEDGE LIBRARY EDITIONS:
INTERNATIONAL SECURITY STUDIES

Volume 14

MILITARY INTERVENTION IN DEMOCRATIC SOCIETIES

MILITARY INTERVENTION IN DEMOCRATIC SOCIETIES

Edited by
PETER J. ROWE AND CHRISTOPHER J. WHELAN

LONDON AND NEW YORK

First published in 1985 by Croom Helm Ltd

This edition first published in 2021
by Routledge
2 Park Square, Milton Park, Abingdon, Oxon OX14 4RN

and by Routledge
52 Vanderbilt Avenue, New York, NY 10017

Routledge is an imprint of the Taylor & Francis Group, an informa business

© 1985 Peter J. Rowe and Christopher J. Whelan

All rights reserved. No part of this book may be reprinted or reproduced or utilised in any form or by any electronic, mechanical, or other means, now known or hereafter invented, including photocopying and recording, or in any information storage or retrieval system, without permission in writing from the publishers.

Trademark notice: Product or corporate names may be trademarks or registered trademarks, and are used only for identification and explanation without intent to infringe.

British Library Cataloguing in Publication Data
A catalogue record for this book is available from the British Library

ISBN: 978-0-367-68499-0 (Set)
ISBN: 978-1-00-316169-1 (Set) (ebk)
ISBN: 978-0-367-71356-0 (Volume 14) (hbk)
ISBN: 978-0-367-71358-4 (Volume 14) (pbk)
ISBN: 978-1-00-315046-6 (Volume 14) (ebk)

Publisher's Note
The publisher has gone to great lengths to ensure the quality of this reprint but points out that some imperfections in the original copies may be apparent.

Disclaimer
The publisher has made every effort to trace copyright holders and would welcome correspondence from those they have been unable to trace.

Military Intervention in Democratic Societies

Edited by Peter J. Rowe &
Christopher J. Whelan

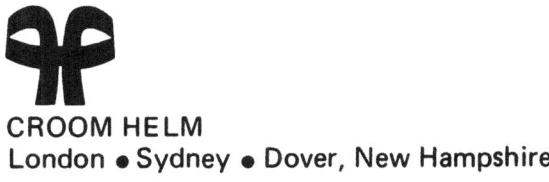

CROOM HELM
London • Sydney • Dover, New Hampshire

© 1985 Peter J. Rowe and Christopher J. Whelan
Croom Helm Ltd, Provident House, Burrell Row,
Beckenham, Kent BR3 1AT

Croom Helm Australia Pty Ltd, Suite 4, 6th Floor,
64-76 Kippax Street, Surry Hills, NSW 2010, Australia

British Library Cataloguing in Publication Data

Military intervention in democratic societies:
    law policy and practice in Great Britain and
    the United States.
    1. Public policy (Law)–Great Britain
    2. Great Britain–Military policy
    I. Rowe, P.J. II. Whelan, Christopher J.
    363.3'0941   363.3'0973   HV6485.G7
    ISBN 0-7099-2241-8

Croom Helm, 51 Washington Street, Dover,
New Hampshire 03820, USA

Library of Congress Cataloging in Publication Data
Main entry under title:

Military intervention in democratic societies.

    Bibliography: p.
    Includes indexes.
    1. Civil-military relations–Great Britain.
2. Law enforcement–Great Britain. 3. Civil-military
relations–United States. 4. Law enforcement–United
States. I. Rowe, P.J. (Peter J) II. Whelan,
Christopher J.
K4720.M55   1985   342.73'0418   85-6650
ISBN 0-7099-2241-8   347.302418

**Printed and bound in Great Britain by
Biddles Ltd, Guildford and King's Lynn**

CONTENTS

Preface
Acknowledgements

1. FOUNDATIONS FOR MILITARY INTERVENTION IN
   THE UNITED STATES David E. Engdahl   1

2. MILITARY AID TO THE CIVIL POWER IN THE
   UNITED KINGDOM - AN HISTORICAL PERSPECTIVE
   Keith Jeffery 51

3. THE PLACE OF THE BRITISH ARMY IN PUBLIC
   ORDER Sir Edwin Bramall 68

4. KEEPING THE PEACE IN GREAT BRITAIN: THE
   DIFFERING ROLES OF THE POLICE AND THE ARMY
   Sir Robert Mark 85

5. WHITEHALL CONTINGENCY PLANNING FOR INDUSTRIAL
   DISPUTES Peter Hennessy 94

6. ARMED FORCES, INDUSTRIAL DISPUTES AND THE LAW
   IN GREAT BRITAIN Christopher J. Whelan 110

7. THE ROLE OF MILITARY FORCES IN PUBLIC SECTOR
   LABOR RELATIONS James B. Jacobs 130

8. ARMED FORCES, PUBLIC DISORDER AND THE LAW
   IN THE UNITED KINGDOM Geoffrey J. Bennett
   and Christopher L. Ryan 166

9. KEEPING THE PEACE: LETHAL WEAPONS, THE
   SOLDIER AND THE LAW Peter J. Rowe 197

10. CONTEMPORARY CHALLENGES TO TRADITIONAL
    LIMITS ON THE ROLE OF THE MILITARY IN
    AMERICAN SOCIETY Edward F. Sherman 216

11. MILITARY INTERVENTION IN DEMOCRATIC
    SOCIETIES: THE ROLE OF LAW
    Christopher J. Whelan 264

Notes on Contributors   294

List of Cases   296

List of Statutes   301

Name Index   303

Subject Index   308

PREFACE

In January 1981, a one-day conference on 'Military Involvement in Civilian Affairs Within the United Kingdom' was held at the Faculty of Law, University of Liverpool. Papers were presented by Colonel Robin Evelegh, Peter Hennessy, Peter Rowe and Christopher Whelan; a paper by Sir Robert Mark was circulated. The idea that this topic had been given only a limited discussion in existing literature and required a more detailed treatment was confirmed by the presence of a large and diverse audience.

In constructing a volume for publication, the editors decided to seek contributions from as wide a range of perspectives as possible in order to provide for the first time a comprehensive treatment of the role of the military within society. We were fortunate to receive permission to reprint two important public statements made relatively recently by very senior police and military personnel. Such perspectives are infrequently available in public. We also sought historical and legal contributions, as well as a review of current government contingency planning. In addition, we invited major contributions from leading experts in the United States in order to broaden the discussion and to show how similar issues have been considered and dealt with in another democratic society. This approach, we hope, sheds light both on the role of the law in democratic societies, and on the way the balance between the state and civil liberties has been struck.

ACKNOWLEDGEMENTS

Keith Jeffery wishes to acknowledge permission to quote copyright material from the Controller of H.M. Stationery Office for papers in the Public Record Office; the Trustees of the Imperial War Museum for the papers of Sir Henry Wilson; and the Earl Haig for the Haig Papers. A version of his chapter was read at the XXth Annual Conference of the Inter-University Seminar on Armed Forces and Society, Chicago, 1980.

An expanded version of Chapter 1 has been published in Vol. 7 University of Puget Sound Law Review 1 (1983). Chapter 3, 'The Place of the British Army in Public Order', has been published in the Royal Society of Arts Journal, July 1980, pp. 480-92. Chapter 4, 'Keeping the Peace in Great Britain: the Differing Roles of the Police and the Army', by Sir Robert Mark, was originally published in his book, Policing a Perplexed Society (London, Allen & Unwin, 1977, pp. 23-33). We are extremely grateful for permission to reprint these. Chapter 7, 'The Role of Military Forces in Public Sector Labor Relations', has been reprinted by permission, from Industrial and Labor Relations Review, Vol. 35, No. 2 (January 1982), copyright 1982 by Cornell University. All rights reserved.

The editors would like to thank the University of Liverpool, the Centre for Socio-Legal Studies, Wolfson College, Oxford and its Director, Donald Harris, for the opportunity of preparing this volume; John Boal (Oxford) for assistance with proof-reading; Doreen McBarnet (Oxford) for commenting on Chapter 11; and Missy Baker and Marian Seitz for assistance while the editors were on their respective 'sabbaticals'. Our greatest debt goes to Jenny Dix without whose constant help this volume would never have appeared in print.

Chapter One

FOUNDATIONS FOR MILITARY INTERVENTION IN THE UNITED STATES

David E. Engdahl

INTRODUCTION

To the conscience of the nation that fancies itself the world's greatest democracy, the idea of military intrusion into the affairs of civil government is profoundly repugnant. In 1972, for example, the United States Supreme Court, through Chief Justice Burger, had occasion to recall the 'traditional and strong resistance of Americans to any military intrusion into civilian affairs. That tradition has deep roots in our history ...' (Laird v. Tatum, 408 U.S. 1, 15). Again in 1974 the same Chief Justice observed on behalf of the Court that even where some form of government force is warranted 'the decision to invoke military power has traditionally been viewed with suspicion and skepticism since it often involves the temporary suspension of some of our most cherished rights ...' (Scheuer v. Rhodes, 416 U.S. 232, 246).
    The enforcement of civilian laws by military means, often but not exclusively associated with riots and other civil disorders, is itself a displacement of civilian process, impermissible per se even apart from any consequences it might entail. In 1866, in Ex parte Milligan (71 U.S. 2) the Supreme Court without dissent rejected the idea that the national military could be used as an alternative to civilian measures to enforce the law, even in times of stress. The Court acknowledged that where civilian authority has actually been overthrown - the civil administration deposed, and the civil courts closed - actual and present necessity compels reliance upon the military until civil authority is restored (id., p. 127). In such circumstances, however, it is some hostile force that has accomplished the displacement of civilian

authority. There is absolutely no lawful power in any branch of the government itself to supersede ordinary civilian law enforcement with military means.

Although the facts of the *Milligan* case involved an individual who had been convicted and sentenced by a military tribunal, the principle proclaimed by the Supreme Court pertains equally to military measures short of trial. During the Civil War, Union troops had been employed on countless occasions in the loyal northern states, superseding regular civilian officials to suppress civil disorders, seizing and confining civilians suspected of supporting the Confederacy. Thousands were detained, many never being brought even to military trial, under the claimed authority of the President as Commander-in-Chief, relying upon an opinion written in 1861 by United States Attorney General Bates (10 Op. Atty Gen. 74, 83-84). The Attorney General had opined that, given the existence of an insurrection in the South, the President enjoyed discretionary power to use the armed forces even in the North to do all he felt necessary to execute federal laws. Bates thought the fact that the President - a civilian - was Commander-in-Chief was enough to satisfy the acknowledged requirement that the military must be kept subordinate to the civil power (*id.*, p. 79).[1]

The thesis advanced by Bates was the same thesis advanced by his successor in the *Milligan* case. The Court's rationale in *Milligan*, rejecting that particular application of Bates' thesis, reaches and discredits the whole. Nevertheless, for several years after *Milligan*, flagrant and wilful disregard of the Supreme Court's principle characterized the process of 'reconstructing' the South. Thus it should not seem remarkable that during the past several years, despite Chief Justice Burger's reminders of the constitutional doctrine, new foundations have been laid for military intervention in the United States.

In 1972 the Nixon administration promulgated a set of new regulations, 'Employment of Military Resources in the Event of Civil Disturbances' (now codified as 32 C.F.R. sec. 215), claiming colour of legality for very substantial military intrusions into the realm of domestic government. The 1972 Regulations took the place of others first devised in 1968 during the Johnson administration (33 Fed. Reg. 9339, June 25) and discontinued in 1971 (36 Fed. Reg. 21339, Nov. 5). The 1968 Regulations themselves had been objectionable on some points of law; but novel provisions in the 1972 Regulations dramatically increased the potential for domestic use of the national military while at the same time substantially reducing prior safeguards against abuse. Then in 1973, at Wounded Knee, the Nixon administration employed the military for law enforcement in a situation which not even those indulgent new Regulations had contemplated. (This episode is discussed later.) The 1972 Civil Disturbance Regulations have remained in force through three subsequent administrations without any modification; Justice Department lawyers still continue to defend those who used the military at Wounded Knee even beyond what those Regulations allow. Moreover, in March of 1982 the Department of Defense issued new regulations entitled 'DOD Cooperation With Civilian Law Enforcement Officials' (32 C.F.R., sec. 213), which reassert the sweeping claims of executive prerogative for military intervention asserted in the 1972 Regulations.

Thus, notwithstanding the statements from the judiciary, within little more than a decade the executive branch of the United States government has consolidated the old, and added several new, foundations for military intervention in the United States. It would be idle for a legal scholar to speculate whether any edifice of oppression is likely to be built upon these foundations, whether sooner or later in time. A sufficient task for the legal scholar is to disclose that the foundations, although faulty, indeed are there; to explain how those foundations came to be laid; and to show that they have no footing on the bedrock of our law.[2]

THE BEDROCK OF CIVILIAN DUE PROCESS

The American colonists of the mid-eighteenth century were British subjects who considered themselves heirs to the liberties that had been won through the struggles of what was then relatively recent English history. Increasingly, however, they came to perceive the King of their time as hostile to the liberties thus claimed. (For a fuller exposition of what follows, see Engdahl, 1971.)

The single most inflammatory mark of the tyranny they perceived was the use of royal military troops contrary to what the Americans believed was allowed by established principles of English law. Increasingly after 1763 British troops were used instead of civil magistrates or the posse to suppress disorders in the colonies, royal military authority thus effectively superseding or suspending ordinary processes of the law. It could have been no comfort to the colonists that on some occasions the King whom they considered a tyrant had indulged similar abuses in the homeland. Even there, the thesis that such use of the military was illegal received some expression (for example, Jones, 1780); in the American colonies, this thesis became an expressed point of rebellion.

In their own written constitutions, adopted after independence, the several American states included various provisions designed to preclude such domestic applications of military force. The weak national government the Americans first created was given no power to maintain an armed force of its own; the Articles of Confederation even prohibited any state from maintaining regular armed forces beyond what Congress might deem indispensable for defense (Art. IV, cl. 4). They desired protection from alien powers, but the Americans would not countenance any risk of military intervention in domestic civil affairs - a risk which their experience in the late colonial period had taught them to associate with standing armies. They were familiar with riots, mobs, and disorders; but they considered any military response to such exigencies intolerable and resolved to rely instead upon civil magistrates, the traditional posse, and the process of civilian law.

The new Constitution proposed in 1787 met with opposition on several grounds; but no feature was more controversial than its provision for a national army, even though the army's maintenance was to be at the discretion of the legislature, exercised at least each second year (Art. I, sec. 8, cl. 12). The specter of military suppression of disorders had not lost its horror. When the Pennsylvania state ratifying convention met, one third of the delegates demanded amendments several of which were aimed at the specter of military law enforcement; voted against ratification when the amendments were refused by the majority; and afterwards published and widely disseminated a pamphlet denouncing the Constitution as countenancing execution of the laws by military force.[3] Hamilton and Madison rushed to answer this denunciation in their <u>Federalist Papers</u>, insisting that no use of military force was contemplated for situations short of armed insurrection.[4] Ratification in Delaware, New Jersey, Georgia, Connecticut, and Massachusetts was accomplished without major excitement over the military law enforcement issue; but in April, May and June, 1788, that issue was partly responsible for the opposition of one third of the delegates in South Carolina and caused several proposed amendments to accompany Maryland's and New Hampshire's ratifications.[5] Madison's own state, Virginia, accompanied its ratification with demands for several amendments aimed at the specter of military law enforcement, as did Hamilton's own state of New York.[6] These demands persuaded Madison that amendments were desirable, and it was he who insistently pressed upon the first Congress the task of preparing amendments to propose to the states. He sought concise phrases to capture the import of those state convention demands he found to have merit. The language which he chose, which Congress approved and the states ratified to assuage the fears of military law enforcement, was that 'No person shall ... be deprived of life, liberty, or property without due process of law'.[7]

No concise set of words could better have comprehended the traditional English prohibition against the use of military force for law enforcement. Long before the rise of a professional army, able Englishmen had been required to keep arms. However, very different rules governed the use of this armed citizenry by the sheriff as a posse and by the constable or Earl Marshal for war. When men in arms in 1381 rose to suppress the mob violence of the Peasants' Revolt using measures beyond those allowed to the civilian sheriff and posse, recourse to such measures (allowable only for war) was a crime; and the crime would have been punishable had not Richard II issued a pardon to the overzealous suppressors. The terms of the pardon are significant: those who had employed measures appropriate only to war were pardoned for their acts done 'sanz due process de loye' (5 Rich. 2, stat. 1, c. 5 (1381)).

The pledge of King John by Chapter 39 of Magna Carta that no free man would be taken, imprisoned, or destroyed except 'by the law of the land', had been demanded at Runnymede specifically because the King had enforced his will by military means in preference to civilian process. Edward II a century later used knights in arms to seize and punish some dissident nobles; when it convened at the accession of that king's successor in 1327, Parliament made explicit reference to Chapter 39 of Magna Carta in denouncing King Edward's resort to military means (Hale, 1847, Vol. I, pp. 343-6; Hale, 1716, pp. 40-1).

Tudors and the first Stuarts nonetheless claimed a prerogative to deal with their subjects by what was then called 'martial law'. This Tudor and Stuart concept of 'martial law' prerogative must be distinguished from the law of military discipline applied in the old Court of the Constable and Marshal or the more modern counterpart rules for the discipline of armed forces; and it must be distinguished as well from what might better be called 'the law of martial rule'. The 'martial law' power claimed by Tudor and Stuart monarchs included the asserted right to intervene by prerogative in the domestic affairs of the kingdom on grounds of purported necessity, suspending or superseding the ordinary law and its processes, whether to require the quartering of troops in private houses; to exact so-called 'ship money' or other assessments or forced 'loans'; to carry out summary trials and punishments; or to suppress civil disorders with military force. As part of this broad 'martial law' prerogative, by the late sixteenth century Lords-Lieutenant under royal commission, with troops assigned to assist them, had become the usual means for suppressing civil disorders in England, superseding the regular civil officials. James I emulated the Tudor example when disorders arose where he had quartered troops awaiting transport abroad.[8] Under Charles I, quartering impositions led to riots and brawls in port towns, which were suppressed with military force under prerogative commissioners on the Tudor model. These events, and the burdens of financial exactions based upon the same claim of a broad 'martial law' prerogative, excited Parliament in 1628 to draw up the Petition of Right, which denounced the whole range of actions taken by virtue of the 'martial law' prerogative as contrary to the law of the realm, and specifically, Magna Carta.[9] Charles' continued claim to prerogative domestic use of troops helped precipitate the civil war which commenced in 1642.

After the Restoration the repudiation of any prerogative 'martial law' power was reaffirmed (Hale, 1716, pp. 39-40). The Bill of Rights of 1689 specifically stated in its first declaration 'That the pretended power of suspending of laws, or the execution of laws, by royal authority without consent of Parliament, is illegal.'

These great events of the seventeenth century firmly settled the principle that the use of the military to enforce law and order is not 'due process of law'. The Riot Act 1714 called for civilian officials and the posse comitatus to disperse mobs and suppress civil disorders, and authorized those civilian personnel to use any force necessary to accomplish the purpose; but that Act made no provision whatsoever for any use of military troops. In notable contrast a different Act passed the very same year (1 Geo. 1, stat. 2, c. 14), dealing not with riots or civil disorders but with 'insurrection' or 'rebellion' as well as 'invasion', authorized the use of militia.[10]

The foregoing was recent history to the American colonists; thus it is not surprising that when British soldiers were used to suppress civil disorders in the American colonies it seemed that King George was making claim to the same prerogative the Tudors and Stuarts had abused. When clashes between troops and disaffected colonists resulted in casualties among the civilians, colonists could claim the authority of Coke and Hale as well as Blackstone to decry those deaths as murders.[11] When the Administration of Justice Act 1774 was applied to prevent local colonial trials of the British soldiers involved in such incidents, the Second Continental Congress enumerated among the causes for taking up arms that Act's 'exempting the "murderers" of colonists from legal trial, and in effect, from punishment' (Ford, 1905, p. 145). In their Declaration of Independence the Americans denounced King and Parliament 'for protecting [British troops] by a mock Trial, from Punishment for any Murders which they should commit on the Inhabitants of these States' (clause 17). By using the military instead of civilian officials and procedures to deal with domestic disorders, the Declaration of Independence maintained (clause 14), the King had 'affected to render the military independent of and superior to the Civil Power'.[12] The Americans saw King George as King Charles, and themselves as asserting the law of the Petition of Right, repudiating the latter-day revival of Tudor-Stuart 'martial law' prerogative, and vindicating the established 'law of the land'. Their adoption of the 'due process' clause of the Fifth Amendment was conditioned in major part by fear of domestic use of the national military force they had newly provided for; they would not have it used, as the British army had been, as a means to suppress civil disorder or execute the laws.[13]

This repudiation of military intervention in domestic law enforcement is the bedrock of due process upon which American government was built. Together with a concept which the early American

statesmen drew from a doctrine propounded by Lord
Chief Justice Mansfield in 1780, after the Revolution but before the Constitution - a doctrine to be
examined later in this chapter - this is the legal
premise upon which the first Congresses under the
Constitution acted when they came to legislate concerning the use of the military in America. That
earliest legislation will be examined below, after
first taking note of the several grounds of authority that the 1972 Civil Disturbance Regulations
claim.

FAULTY FOUNDATIONS, PART ONE: PURPORTED STATUTORY
BASES OF THE CIVIL DISTURBANCE REGULATIONS

The 1972 Regulations[14] articulate at length their
purported legal bases (32 C.F.R. 215.4 (1981)). The
1968 Regulations had some of the same purported
bases (32 C.F.R. 187.4 (1971)); but the bases claimed by the 1972 Regulations are broader, including
sweeping claims of inherent executive power. The
significance of the newly asserted prerogative will
be examined later; the purported statutory bases are
examined first.
 The Regulations rely upon three federal statutes, originating generations apart but presently
codified as Title 10 U.S.C. sections 331, 332, and
333.

10 U.S.C. sec. 331

> Whenever there is an insurrection in any State
> against its government, the President may, upon
> the request of its legislature or of its
> governor if the legislature cannot be convened,
> call into Federal service such of the militia[15]
> of the other States, in the number requested by
> that State, and use such of the armed forces,
> as he considers necessary to suppress the
> insurrection.

This statute is derived from section 1 of
Congress' very first statute pertaining to military
troops and domestic turmoil (Act of May 2, 1792, ch.
28, 1 Stat. 264). The 1792 Act was drafted and
adopted in lieu of a provision that was stricken
from the Senate version of the so-called Militia
Bill[16] a few weeks earlier because of vigorous
opposition in the House. The unacceptable proposal
had provided that the President could call out

8

troops 'to execute the laws of the Union, suppress insurrections, and repel invasion' (3 Annals of Cong. 114-5 (1792), emphasis added). The House debate on that proposal (id., pp. 553-5; see Engdahl, 1971, p. 44) indicates that there was no apprehension over use of the military in circumstances so grave as invasion or insurrection, but that the prospect of its use in any lesser exigency was the subject of serious concern. Section 1 as finally adopted[17] made no reference whatever to executing the laws.

The congressional debates on the 1792 bill (3 Annals of Cong. 574-7) show a clear awareness of the English tradition summarized above. The Riot Acts of 1411 (13 Hen. 4, ch. 7) and 1714 (see note 10) had provided for suppression of riots only with civilian officers and the posse; military measures had been reserved for insurrections. Hale had reiterated that military measures are impermissible so long as civilian institutions remain operable (Hale, 1792, pp. 34-6); and the Americans' most familiar authority, Blackstone, also affirmed that the military may never be used so long as civil courts can function (Blackstone, 1765, p. 152). Congress carefully chose the term 'insurrection' for this reason. Only a handful of 'insurrections' have occurred in American history: for example, the Civil War (1861-5); Shays' Rebellion (1786-7); the Whiskey Rebellion (1794); the Dorr Rebellion (1842); and the civil war in the Territory of Kansas (1856). There is no authority under 10 U.S.C. sec. 331 to use the military except under circumstances thus rare, equivalent to war.

Nonetheless this statute is now commonly cited as if it authorized the use of federal troops merely to suppress riots or other violations of state laws.[18] In 1968 the National Advisory Commission on Civil Disorders in its official Report recommended (GPO ed. at p. 288) that 10 U.S.C. sec. 331 be amended to legalize use of troops in the absence of real insurrection. No such amendment has been enacted; and in any event, amending the statute could not alter the constitutional prohibition which led Congress originally to draft the statute as it did.

The prevalent misconception that this statute can be invoked to deal with riots or disorders not amounting to insurrections is one of the foundations for military intervention in the United States.

10 U.S.C. sec. 332

> Whenever the President considers that unlawful obstructions, combinations, or assemblages, or rebellion against the authority of the United States, make it impracticable to enforce the laws of the United States in any State or Territory by the ordinary course of judicial proceedings, he may call into Federal service such of the militia of any State, and use such of the armed forces, as he considers necessary to enforce those laws or to suppress the rebellion.

This statute derives from a separate section of the 1792 statute already discussed; but it was profoundly altered by amendment during the era of the Civil War. Section 2 of the 1792 Act provided

> [t]hat whenever the laws <u>of the United States</u> shall be opposed, or the execution thereof obstructed, in any state, by combinations <u>too powerful to be suppressed by</u> the ordinary course of judicial proceedings, or <u>by the powers vested in the marshals by [section 9 of] this act</u> ... it shall be lawful for the President of the United States to call forth the militia of such state to suppress such combinations, and to cause the [federal] laws to be duly executed. (See note 17)

In contrast to section 1, discussed earlier, which addressed only insurrection against <u>state</u> governments, section 2 of the 1792 Act concerned execution of <u>federal</u> laws. Like section 1, however, section 2 <u>did</u> plainly contemplate a <u>distinctively military</u> force. Since the House had vigorously opposed the earlier Militia Bill precisely because it would have authorized the use of troops 'to execute the laws of the Union', the enactment of this section would be inexplicable were it not for its careful wording. The recorded debates confirm that the <u>other</u> phrases of section 2 were deliberately crafted and are definitive of its scope.

Section 2 authorized the President to use military force <u>only</u> when federal laws were opposed or obstructed 'by combinations <u>too powerful to be suppressed by</u> the ordinary course of judicial proceedings or by <u>the powers vested in the marshals by this act</u> ...'. This language was absent from the original bill. Vigorous debate ensued and several denounced the original language as far too indulgent of the use of military force (3 Annals of Cong. 574-7 (1792)). Their denunciations spawned amendments to the bill, including not only the language above quoted but also a separate section regarding the powers of federal marshals. Only by examining this separate section 9 can the scope of the authority conferred by section 2 be correctly understood. It declared that federal marshals and their deputies have 'the same powers in executing the laws of the United States, as sheriffs and their deputies in the several states have by law, in executing the laws of their respective states'. If there was no ready explanation for this provision regarding marshals, it would seem anomalous in a statute concerned with the use of military resources. (It would also seem superfluous, because the Judiciary Act of September 24, 1789 (ch. 20, section 27, 1 Stat. 73, 87) had already given federal marshals 'power to command all necessary assistance in the execution of [their] duty'.) Section 9, however, was neither anomalous nor superfluous, but of paramount importance. Its significance, however, cannot be perceived by a modern reader unaware of a doctrine articulated first in 1780 by England's Lord Chief Justice Mansfield, which became a fundamental premise of American law.

British troops had been employed in London during the Lord Gordon Riots in June of 1780 (see Engdahl, 1971, pp. 31-2).[19] Responding to those who denounced this as reminiscent of the 'martial law' prerogative claimed by Tudors and Stuarts, Lord Mansfield distinguished between the use of troops in a military capacity, and their use in a civilian capacity, in the nature of the posse comitatus:

> The persons who assisted in the suppression of these tumults are to be considered mere private individuals acting as duty required ...
>
> ... The King's extraordinary prerogative to proclaim martial law (whatever that may be) is clearly out of the question ... The military have been called in - and very wisely called in - not as <u>soldiers</u>, but as <u>citizens</u>.[20]

As a result of Henry II's Assize of Arms in the twelfth century, a decree of Henry III and the Statute of Winchester in the thirteenth century, and the emergence of the Court of Constable and Marshal in the fourteenth century, the same citizens who for some purposes were a military force under a special system of discipline and specialized tribunals were also, regardless of that other role, subject to call by the sheriff or other civil officers as the <u>posse comitatus</u> under common law obligation enforced by civilian courts (see Engdahl, 1971, pp. 2-5). Lord Mansfield's Doctrine adapted that ancient duality of character to a more modern day.[21]

By virtue of this Mansfield Doctrine sheriffs in the states could call out militiamen in a civilian capacity (even though organized in militia units) as part of their posse. The purpose of section 9 of the 1792 Act, the congressional debates make quite clear, was precisely to affirm that federal marshals could do the same for purposes of executing federal laws.

In 1792 there were no standing federal armed forces, so the immediate impact of section 9 was to enable federal marshals to call up state militia as their civilian posse to execute the laws. Within a few years, however, a modest regular standing federal army had become established, and the amending Act of March 3, 1807 (ch. 39, 2 Stat. 443) authorized use of them as well as militia. Regular soldiers were then commonly used by the marshals <u>as civilians</u>, even though organized in regular army units, in situations where it was well understood that their use as a military force would have been impermissible. The resulting practice, and its basis in the Mansfield Doctrine, was confirmed by the Attorney General of the United States in an 1854 Opinion, declaring:

> the <u>posse comitatus</u> comprises every person in the district or county above the age of fifteen years ... whatever may be their occupation, whether civilians or not; and including the military of all denominations, militia, soldiers, marines, all of whom are alike bound to obey the commands of a sheriff or marshal. The fact that they are organized as military bodies, under the immediate command of their own officers, does not in any wise affect their legal character. They are still the posse comitatus (xxi Parl. Hist., p. 672, 688, per Lord Mansfield). (6 Op. Atty. Gen. 466, 473)[22]

It is only in the light of this practice authorized by section 9 that the import of section 2 can be understood. Section 2 did indeed contemplate a distinctively military force; but it allowed this only where the resistance to federal law was 'too powerful to be suppressed' by civilian means - including the use of military personnel as a civilian force under the command of federal marshals pursuant to section 9.

Two other provisions added during debate over the 1792 Act serve to emphasize the interplay between sections 9 and 2, and the extreme circumstances contemplated by the latter. The first of these required that, before troops could be used pursuant to section 2, the incompetence of judicial proceedings and the failure of the marshals acting under section 9 must be 'notified to the President of the United States, by an associate justice or the district judge'. (This was deleted in 1795; see note 17.) The other, applying alike to section 2 and section 1, required that before the President could use military force he must 'by proclamation, command such insurgents to disperse'. (This provision survives as 10 U.S.C. sec. 334.)

In other words section 2 of the 1792 Act contemplated circumstances equivalent to those of section 1, but involving assaults upon federal rather than upon state authority: rebellions against civil authority, disrupting 'the ordinary course of judicial proceedings', which civilian officials even by exhausting their resources (including troops employed under the Mansfield Doctrine as a civilian posse) could not suppress. So understood, section 2 of the 1792 Act was quite consistent with the rule prohibiting military force against civilians except when civil government is under such assault that civilian institutions are incapacitated: the traditional criterion of insurrection.

By the time of the Civil War, however, Mansfield's subtle distinction, on which American practice had been built, had become obscure. President Buchanan in 1860, explaining his refusal to send troops into the South, said he could not send them as a posse because the federal civilian officials whom the posse should assist had been driven out of the dissident states (Richardson, 1897, p. 634). Actually, of course, Buchanan was faced with a clear case of insurrection, to which the civilian posse use of troops had no application, and in which avowedly military measures were warranted.

President Lincoln promptly discarded Buchanan's inhibitions, and erred on the other side. Under his command, more than 13,000 persons were arrested and confined by military authority in the loyal North. Lincoln's Attorney General, Edward Bates, in a remarkable Opinion delivered to the President within four months of his inauguration (10 Op. Atty. Gen. 74; July 5 1861), provided the rationale on which these outrages were defended. Bates' Opinion asserted (id., p. 79) that the President had inherent power 'to use the army to aid him in the performance of' his duty 'to take care that the laws be faithfully executed'. Although he asserted that this power was inherent and that the doctrine of separation of powers placed it beyond judicial or legislative restraint, Bates viewed the statutes derived from the 1792 Act as recognizing and aiding it (id., pp. 80, 83). The distinction between the use of troops as civilians and their use as a military force was either forgotten or ignored; although he paid lip-service to the requirement that the military be subordinate to the civil power, Bates regarded it as sufficient that the President as Commander-in-Chief 'is a civil magistrate, not a military chief' (id., p. 79).

Bates' thesis was denounced and repudiated not only in Ex parte Milligan but also in other cases, by both federal and state courts.[23] Those judicial declamations, however, came only later, in the slow course of litigation. To Congress, fevered by the internecine war, and looking to the Union Army for the survival of the nation as well as the triumph of a great moral cause, it was no time to respect such constraints. One of the measures enacted during those frenzied first months of the Civil War - within four weeks after Attorney General Bates' radical Opinion - was a revision of section 2 of the 1792 Act, concerning use of the military to enforce federal law.

What survives today as 10 U.S.C. sec. 332 is the substance of that 1861 perversion of the language which originally had been crafted in 1792 to preserve the constitutional standard. The changes wrought by this 1861 Act (of July 29, ch. 25, sec. 1, 12 Stat. 281) and 10 U.S.C. sec. 332 have never been subjected to judicial scrutiny.

The 1861 Act eliminated the requirement that before distinctively military force could be employed the powers vested in federal marshals must be exhausted. This requirement, premised upon the Mansfield doctrine, had limited military force to situations where troops used as civilians in the nature of a posse had been overpowered. The requirement thus was crucial to the measure's constitutionality under the traditional view of due process. Nevertheless, it was now discarded.

Moreover, whereas the prior legislation had allowed recourse to military force only to deal with 'combinations <u>too powerful to be suppressed</u>' by judicial proceedings and the marshals with their posse, the 1861 Act invited such recourse 'whenever ... it shall become <u>impracticable</u>, in the judgment of the President' to rely upon the ordinary course of judicial proceedings to enforce federal laws. Instead of necessity, the statutory criterion for military intervention had now become convenience. With the traditional use of troops <u>as civilians</u> forgotten, and no other federal civilian force of significant manpower available, 'impracticability' or convenience as a criterion virtually assured that there would be military intervention in situations where it would not have been allowable before.[24]

The Civil Disturbance Regulations (32 C.F.R. sec. 215.4(c)(2)(1)(B) (1981)) rely upon 10 U.S.C. sec. 332, essentially unchanged since the 1861 Act, as one basis for the measures of military intervention they contemplate. This statute could not survive judicial scrutiny if historic due process principles were applied. It has escaped invalidation only because there has never been occasion for it to be judicially reviewed. Without any constitutional footing, it remains as another foundation for military intervention.

<u>10 U.S.C. sec. 333</u>

> The President, by using the militia or the armed forces, or both, or by any other means, shall take such measures as he considers necessary to suppress, in a State, any insurrection, domestic violence, unlawful combination, or conspiracy, if it -
> (1) so hinders the execution of the laws of that State, and of the United States within the State, that any part or class of its people is deprived of a right, privilege, immunity, or protection named in the Constitution and secured by law, and the constituted authorities of that State are unable, fail, or refuse to protect that right, privilege, or immunity, or to give that protection; or
> (2) Opposes or obstructs the execution of the laws of the United States or impedes the course of justice under those laws. In any situation covered by clause (1), the State shall be considered to have denied the equal protection of the laws secured by the Constitution.

This statute originated as section 3 of the Ku Klux Klan Act of April 20, 1871 (ch. 22, 17 Stat. 13, 14). The 1871 Act must be viewed in its historical context. The Civil War had ended in April, 1865; and under a presidential plan of reconstruction post-war civilian state governments had been established. None of these, however, granted blacks the vote, and most enacted racially discriminatory statutes. Radical sentiment was inflamed by such evidence of unrepentant attitudes among southern whites. In February, 1866, a bill was passed to enhance the Freedmen's Bureau (created within the War Department a year before), providing that anyone in a former secessionist state accused of infringing rights of a former slave should be tried in accordance with martial law. President Johnson vetoed that measure (Cong. Globe, 39th Cong., 1st Sess. 915-7 (1866)), but four months later another Freedmen's Bureau bill, still providing for military jurisdiction regarding freedmen's rights, was enacted over Johnson's veto (Act of July 16, 1866, ch. 200, 14 Stat. 173).

Meanwhile, also over a presidential veto, Congress enacted the Civil Rights Act of 1866 (April 9, ch. 31, 14 Stat. 27), a beneficient Act marred by two provisions for military intervention: section 5 authorized process servers under the Act to summon for aid not only the posse, but also the military; and section 9 provided that the President or his designee could employ troops 'to prevent the violation and enforce the due execution of this act'. These military means were authorized even though federal civilian authority was then everywhere established. Continuing violence against blacks certainly warranted federal intervention; but there was nowhere such assault upon civilian institutions as could justify intervention military in form.

When ten of the southern states refused to ratify the proposed Fourteenth Amendment the Radicals in Congress, again over a presidential veto, enacted the Military Reconstruction Act of March 2, 1867 (ch. 153, 14 Stat. 428). It established five military districts, each to be governed under martial law by an army general with ample troops. Even granting the Radicals' dubious premise that no legal <u>state</u> governments existed in those recalcitrant states, <u>federal</u> civilian authority had been firmly in place there for almost two years; thus there was no colourable constitutional justification for this military expedient. Rightly doubting President Johnson's will to execute this measure, Congress ordained that all orders regarding military operations were void unless issued through the 'General of the Army', who could not be removed or relieved of command without Senate approval (Act of March 2, 1867, ch. 170, sec. 2, 14 Stat. 486-7). 'General of the Army' was a rank newly authorized seven months earlier (Act of July 25, 1866, ch. 232, 14 Stat. 223) for a sole incumbent 'to command the armies of the United States'; Ulysses S. Grant had been appointed. By immunizing him from presidential removal and requiring all orders to be issued through him, Congress gave Grant rather than the President command over reconstruction.

Under Grant's military command thousands of local officials and six state governors were ousted. The army purged state legislatures, and laws were set aside or modified by military decree. Some 20,000 soldiers constituted the peacekeeping force, aided by black militia recruited after Congress had declared the states' own militia disbanded (Act of March 2, 1867, ch. 170, sec. 6, 14 Stat. at 487). An Act of July 19, 1867, ratified what had been done and provided further that none of the military commanders or persons acting under them 'shall be bound ... by any opinion of any civil officer of the United States' (ch. 30, secs. 2, 4, 10, 15 Stat. 14, 15, 16).

No one really believed that such blatant military intervention could be held constitutional by any civil court. Grant himself said of the Reconstruction legislation: 'much of it, no doubt, was unconstitutional; but it was hoped that the laws enacted would serve their purpose before the question of constitutionality could be submitted to the judiciary and a decision obtained' (quoted in Morison et al., 1977, p. 344). Indeed, the Supreme Court had vigorously reaffirmed the established constitutional rule only four months before the Military Reconstruction Act was enacted in Ex parte Milligan (71 U.S. 2, 127 (1866)). At least one federal court held that since a post-war civilian government had been established in South Carolina a civilian there could not be tried by court martial (In re Egan, 8 F. Cas. 367 (No. 4303) (C.C.N.D.N.Y., 1866)). To prevent further embarrassment by judicial denunciation, Congress declared that no civil court, state or federal, could take jurisdiction of any case arising out of military actions taken between the inauguration of Lincoln and a date fifteen months after the War's end.[25]

Two efforts by states to enjoin this military reconstruction as infringing their rights of sovereignty failed in 1867 because the cases were beyond the constitutional limits of Supreme Court jurisdiction (<u>Georgia v. Stanton</u>, 73 U.S. 50; <u>Mississippi v. Johnson</u>, 71 U.S. 475). A proper case putting the issue did arise when a prisoner held by the district commander in Mississippi sought release by writ of habeas corpus; but when the Supreme Court refused to dismiss the prisoner's appeal and proceeded to hear arguments on the merits (<u>Ex parte McCardle</u>, 73 U.S. 318), Congress over the president's veto repealed the particular jurisdictional statute involved (Act of Mar. 27, 1868, sec. 2, 15 Stat. 44), and that opportunity for judicial denunciation was thus foreclosed (<u>Ex parte McCardle</u>, 74 U.S. 506 (1869)). Other courts did denounce military acts done in the South after the War (e.g. <u>McLoughlin v. Green</u>, 50 Miss. 453, 461 (1874); <u>In re Egan</u>, 8 F. Cas. 367 (No. 4303) (C.C.N.D.N.Y. 1866)), but the Supreme Court was never squarely faced with the issue. Its disposition of related issues leaves no doubt, however, that the Supreme Court would have denounced the legislation had a case within its jurisdiction been made.[26] By mid-1868, new governments had been set up in eight of the states, and the army withdrawn. The General who had directed the whole unlawful enterprise then became President.

Southern blacks suffered extremist retaliation for this outrageous military intervention. Reacting, Congress indulged again the Radicals' penchant for military law enforcement. Although martial law was not reimposed, the Enforcement Act of May 31, 1870 (ch. 114, secs. 10, 13, 16 Stat. 140, 142, 143) like the Civil Rights Act of four years before, authorized military means to execute its terms.

This mad Radical attachment to the expedient of military intervention, repeatedly expressed by the Reconstruction Congress in defiance of the Constitution and evasion of judicial denunciation, accounts for the military enforcement provision of the 1871 Ku Klux Klan Act that now survives as 10 U.S.C. sec. 333. The 1871 Act made no distinction between 'insurrection' and mere 'violence, unlawful combination, or conspiracy'; for all alike it authorized distinctively military force. It was limited to instances where state authorities had failed to protect citizens' federal rights; but it did not require that a <u>civilian</u> federal force (such as marshals with a posse) be considered or employed before taking recourse to military force. In other words, this 1871 Act displayed the very features that Congress in 1792 had eschewed. At that earlier time, lawmakers loyal to the rule of civilian due process had taken great care to tailor their legislation to the constitutional requirement. Among Reconstruction Radicals, however, there was no such respect for the due process tradition, and what now survives as 10 U.S.C. sec. 333 was adopted in disregard of the constitutional rule.

Most of the Reconstruction Era provisions for military intervention have since passed away. Only this and the 1866 Act's authorization of military assistance in executing process concerning certain civil rights offenses (42 U.S.C. sec. 1889) remain, relics of that shameful era when the Congress and a General-turned-President wilfully trampled constitutional principle underfoot in their march on an otherwise noble crusade. This statute, 10 U.S.C. sec. 333, has occasionally been invoked to justify subsequent military interventions, as in the Pullman strike of 1894 and the urban riots of the 1960s; but never has any court had occasion to pass on its constitutionality.[27] It seems impossible that it could survive judicial scrutiny; yet this bastard offspring of the rapacious militarism of Reconstruction days remains on the statute books to serve as a third foundation for military intervention.

FAULTY FOUNDATIONS, PART TWO: OTHER PURPORTED BASES OF THE CIVIL DISTURBANCE REGULATIONS

The three preceding statutes relied upon by the 1972 Civil Disturbance Regulations had been relied upon as well by those promulgated in 1968; but the 1972 Regulations contrive three additional grounds. The first is a sweeping concept of inherent executive emergency power; the second, a purported power of the executive to protect federal property and functions by military means; and the third, an obscure Joint Resolution pertaining to the Secret Service. Each of these are considered here in turn, together with a statute which destroys all three.

The Purported 'Emergency Authority' and the Posse Comitatus Act
The new Civil Disturbance Regulations claim that the Constitution, without need for any statute, confers what they call 'the emergency authority', which authorizes (32 C.F.R. sec. 215.4(c)(1)(i))

prompt and vigorous Federal action, including use of military forces, to prevent loss of life or wanton destruction of property and to restore governmental functioning and public order when sudden and unexpected civil disturbances, disasters, or calamities seriously endanger life and property and disrupt normal governmental functions to such an extent that duly constituted local authorities are unable to control the situations.

The Regulations define 'civil disturbances' broadly to include not only 'group acts of violence' but also other 'disorders prejudicial to public law and order' (id., sec. 215.3(a)). 'Disorder', which is not defined, is a term susceptible of many interpretations. So also is the undefined word 'calamities'. There may be political or economic or social 'calamities', 'disturbances' of the established political order, that do not involve 'group acts of violence' or any of the characteristics connoted by terms such as 'riot', 'tumult', and 'unlawful assembly'.

The reference to 'duly constituted local authorities' indicates that this purported power may be invoked not only when federal, but also when state or local, activities are disrupted. Yet the Regulations do not explain what constitutes 'normalcy' of governmental functions, what constitutes their 'disruption', or what might constitute 'inability' of local authorities to control a situation. What is clear is that federal military intervention in a state may occur without any request from the state itself, even where it purports to be for the sake of enforcing state law; the judgment as to whether state authorities are able to control the situation is to be made by federal, and even by military, officials, as discussed below. Moreover, the role that federal troops are to play is not a subordinate one of assistance to civil authorities in their own law enforcement; instead, on the premise that the local authorities are 'unable to control' the situation, the military is given a free hand to 'restore governmental functioning and public order ...' (id., sec. 215.4 (c)(1)(i)).

All of this would be remarkable enough if the discretion to invoke this purported 'emergency power' were reserved to the President himself; but it is not. The Regulations specifically provide (id., sec. 215.5(a)) that not even a presidential executive order or presidential directive to the Secretary of Defense is required in cases within this purported 'emergency authority'. The critical decisions all may be made by inferior - indeed, by military - officials, as elaborated below.

The 1968 Regulations had contained nothing at all comparable to this purported 'emergency authority'.[28] Although the 1972 Regulations describe it as conferred by the Constitution, that document contains no language expressly conferring such power. The Regulations assert (id., sec. 215.4 (c)(1)) that it is

> based upon the inherent legal rights of the U.S. Government--a sovereign national entity under the Federal Constitution--to insure [sic] the preservation of public order and the carrying out of governmental operations within its territorial limits, by force if necessary.

Since the Regulations acknowledge that this 'emergency authority' has no statutory basis, it plainly is being claimed to exist as an inherent prerogative of the executive branch. Indeed the claim is made in the face of a statute (to be considered below) which specifically negates it.

Even if one were unpersuaded by the argument of the preceding pages that the 'due process' language of the Fifth Amendment originated as a reaction against precisely such claims by English kings, this claim of sweeping inherent executive power confronts an insurmountable constitutional obstacle in the doctrine of the separation of powers. The president's duty to 'take Care that the laws be faithfully executed' (U.S. Const., Art. II, sec. 4) repels any suggestion that he may flout them. The president might invoke the equity powers of the judiciary to protect federal interests from harm (for example, In re Debs, discussed in note 27), and might even take some executive measures without judicial involvement where no statute on point can be found (see Youngstown Sheet & Tube Co. v. Sawyer, 343 U.S. 79 (1952)). Presidential power to act contrary to a statute, however, could be sustained only if the statute were void (id.). While the Constitution makes the President Commander-in-Chief (Art. II, sec. 2), it just as clearly gives to Congress the power 'to make Rules for the Government and Regulation of the land and naval Forces' (Art. I, sec. 8, cl. 14)[29] and to make all laws 'necessary and proper' to effectuate not only the latter but also the President's Commander-in-Chief power (id., cl. 18). Statutes controlling the use of the military therefore have ample constitutional base. It is thus impossible to maintain that the president has authority to use the military in domestic situations in the face of a congressional prohibition.

Congress acted a century ago to negate precisely the same executive 'emergency authority' which the new Regulations now claim. Although military reconstruction of the former secessionist states had been completed in 1870, throughout the presidency of General Grant army troops continued to be used with some frequency to execute federal laws in the South. By the end of Grant's second term, this continued recourse to the military expedient was exacting a substantial political toll. Accusations were made in Congress that the troops were intimidating voters in the South, seizing political prisoners, interfering with civil state governments, and even reconstituting state legislatures (see 7 Cong. Rec. 3849, 3850-2, 4240, 4245, 4248 (1878)).

In the presidential election of 1876, Democrat Tilden had won a popular plurality. His vote in the electoral college, however, was short of a majority so long as four states where returns had been challenged remained in doubt; and in the end, those electoral votes were awarded to Republican Hayes. In two of the states where the vote was in question - Louisiana and South Carolina - unpopular Republican governments were being maintained in power only with federal bayonets. While the outcome of the election was still unresolved, Democrats in Congress charged that had it not been for intimidation of voters by the federal troops, the vote in many districts would have differed enough that an electoral majority for Tilden would have been assured. As a result the House of Representatives passed a Resolution in December, 1876, calling upon outgoing President Grant to account for the use that had been made of troops in the South during the several months preceding the November election. Six weeks before leaving office, Grant sent to the House his reply (both are printed in Lieber, 1898, pp. 4-9).

Grant's reply did not mollify the House, which attached to the 1877 army appropriation bill a substantive rider restricting the domestic use of troops. However, the decision of Hayes at the commencement of his presidential term to withdraw the army from South Carolina and Louisiana diminished the felt urgency of reform. While the House insisted on its rider, the Senate would not agree;

and thus no army appropriation bill was passed until November, when the fiscal year was half over and the House agreed to postpone the reform.[30] The next year, however, those who were determined to curtail military intervention did secure approval in both houses for a similar rider to the Army Appropriation Act of June 18, 1878 (ch. 263, sec. 15, 20 Stat. 145, 152). The terms of that rider, which came to be called the 'Posse Comitatus Act', were directly responsive to the arguments which Grant had put forward in his reply to the House Resolution a year and a half before.

Grant had justified the various instances of military intervention on different grounds. The situation in South Carolina he claimed had amounted to insurrection, so he cited the statute codified now as 10 U.S.C. sec. 331 for his utilization of troops there. With regard to certain instances in several other states, he relied for justification upon the statutes now codified as 10 U.S.C. secs. 332 and 333, and upon a section of the Enforcement Act of 1870, discussed earlier, which has since been repealed. As to certain other situations, Grant claimed simply to have made troops available to be used as a posse in accordance with the traditional practice, although the critical distinction between military and civilian character (the essential feature of that traditional practice) by then had been neglected for many years.

For circumstances not coming within any of the foregoing justifications, however, Grant asserted a 'power as commander of the Army and Navy to prevent or suppress resistance to the laws of the United States ...' (Lieber, 1898, p. 9). 'The companies stationed in the other States,' he declared, 'have been employed to secure the better execution of the laws of the United States and to preserve the peace of the United States' (id., p. 8). In support of this assertion of executive power not derived from any statute, Grant referred to a hodge-podge of historical incidents - all of which, however, were applications either of the statutes or else of the traditional posse comitatus practice. In substance, Grant was making claim to inherent executive power to employ military force to execute the laws and preserve domestic peace.

Congress' response to Grant's assertion of inherent power to enforce the laws by military means was a flat repudiation: the Posse Comitatus Act (Act of June 18, 1878, ch. 263, sec. 15, 20 Stat. 145, 152, emphasis added) declared that

> From and after the passage of this act it shall not be lawful to employ any part of the Army of the United States as a <u>posse comitatus</u>, <u>or otherwise</u>, for the purpose of executing the laws, except in such cases and under such circumstances as such employment of said force may be <u>expressly</u> authorized by the Constitution or by act of Congress.

Currently, wilful violators of the Act are liable to fines up to $10,000 and 2 years' imprisonment (18 U.S.C. sec. 1385). Although its popular name tends to focus attention solely upon the posse concept, it is important to note that the Act forbids the use of the army as a posse, '<u>or otherwise</u>', to execute the laws, except as expressly authorized.

The various existing statutory authorizations, despite the constitutional defects to be found in most of them, were left undisturbed by this Act. Its whole purpose was to put an end to the extra-statutory practices which Grant had sought to justify. The critical word in the Act adapted to accomplish this purpose was the word 'expressly'.[31] The traditional practice of using troops as a posse in accordance with the Mansfield Doctrine <u>had</u> been authorized by Congress; that was the function of section 9 of the old 1792 Act, the substance of which still remained when the Posse Comitatus Act was passed. Nevertheless, that old statutory provision did not 'expressly' authorize any use of troops; consequently, the 1878 Act immediately put an end to the practice of using army troops as a posse.[32]

The Act also excepted from its prohibition such use of the army[33] as might be 'expressly authorized by the Constitution'. The only provision in the Constitution dealing 'expressly' with <u>any</u> domestic use of the military,[34] however, is Article I, Section 8, Clause 15; and that clause only gives to <u>Congress</u> the power to <u>provide for</u> calling forth the militia to execute the laws of the Union, suppress insurrections and repel invasions. This confirms the power of <u>Congress</u> over the matter, and negates any concept of inherent executive authority to use military means to execute the laws. As plainly, therefore, as it prohibits continuation of the traditional posse practice, this 1872 Act prohibits the use of troops 'otherwise' pursuant to 'inherent executive power', relied upon by Grant, and now by the Civil Disturbance Regulations. The Regulations pretend that the purported extra-statutory 'emergency authority' is consistent with this Act, but the pretense is too transparent; in reciting the Act's prohibition, the Regulations notably omit the word 'expressly' (32 C.F.R. sec. 215.4(b)).

The century-old Posse Comitatus Act is no mere relic of history as far as Congress is concerned. Its jealous guard against military intervention was prominent in congressional deliberations in 1981 when section 905 of the Defense Department Authorization Act of 1982 (P.L. 97-86, 95 Stat. 1115) was considered. Section 905 added sections 371 through 378 to Title 10 of the United States Code. These new sections authorize narrowly limited law enforcement use of certain military resources where no such authority existed before; but the new measure is far more notable for Congress' deliberate refusal, in enacting it, to countenance any use of the military such as the 'emergency authority' asserted by the Civil Disturbance Regulations portends.

Certain of the new provisions for the first time authorize the Defense Department to 'make available any equipment ... for law enforcement purposes' (10 U.S.C. sec. 372), and to assign military personnel to train civilian law enforcement officials in that equipment's operation, maintenance and use (id., sec. 373). Administrative personnel testified that in this respect the new legislation merely 'clarifies existing administrative practice' (H. Rep. No. 97-71, Pt. II, pp. 9-10); the practice of loaning equipment, however, actually had lacked any authority in law.[35]

This authorization of loans of equipment (and training in its maintenance and operation), however, is not the most significant feature of the 1982 Act. It also, but very guardedly, makes military assistance available for enforcing a few specified federal immigration, customs and drug laws. What is most significant is that such military assistance as is authorized even for those few specified circumstances is scrupulously cabined with safeguards, and that the unavailability of such assistance for any other law enforcement purpose, even if subject to such safeguards, is reaffirmed.

With reference to the few specified immigration, customs and drug laws only, the 1982 Act provides that in certain explicitly defined 'emergency circumstances' (and then only pursuant to a cabinet-level request for assistance) military personnel themselves may operate or maintain the military equipment made available to the civilian authorities (10 U.S.C. sec. 374). Even in such exceptional situations, however, the new legislation precludes the 'direct participation' of military personnel in law enforcement activities (id., sec. 375). Moreover, military personnel may be used in connection with such equipment 'only to the extent the equipment is used for monitoring and communicating the movement of air and sea traffic' id., sec.374(b)) or when it is used 'outside the land area of the United States ... as a base of operations', 'and to transport such law enforcement officials in connection with such operations' (id., sec. 374(c)). The limitation to activities 'outside the land area of the United States', resulted specifically from Congress' insistence upon 'the traditional opposition to military participation in US law enforcement activities', which 'does not exist in the same extent when that participation occurs overseas'.[36]

It is clear from numerous passages in the relevant committee reports that Congress was acting on the premise that, but for the specific authorization given by this new legislation, even such minimal use of military personnel as having them maintain or operate the military equipment made available to civilian officials for law enforcement would have violated the Posse Comitatus Act. The decision by Congress to grant such authorization only in connection with federal drug, immigration, and customs laws, and even in that connection to require both a cabinet level request and a demonstrable 'emergency circumstance' satisfying a two-part statutory test, and even then to restrict such use of military personnel (except with regard to air and sea traffic monitoring equipment) to places 'outside the land area of the United States' and in any event to ensure against their 'direct participation' in any law enforcement activity, seems rather persuasively to suggest a firm congressional resolve to maintain, with only the most limited and carefully guarded exceptions, the otherwise categorical prohibition of the Posse Comitatus Act.

The will of Congress, however, is not always respected by the executive branch. The regulations on 'DOD Cooperation With Civilian Law Enforcement Officials' added to Title 32 of the Code of Federal Regulations in 1982 (32 C.F.R. sec. 213, 47 Fed. Reg. 14899, April 17 1982), pretend to be consistent with 10 U.S.C. secs. 371-8. Section 213.10 of these newest regulations, however, retaliates against the latest congressional reaffirmation of the prohibition against military intervention with a catalogue, more extensive than any previously published anywhere, of circumstances in which the Posse Comitatus Act allegedly does not apply. Section 213.10(a)(2) lists in four categories, with a total of 22 separately itemized subcategories (in <u>addition</u> to 10 U.S.C. secs. 331-3), activities which according to the Department of Defense 'are not restricted by the Posse Comitatus Act ... notwithstanding <u>direct assistance</u> to civilian law enforcement officials' (emphasis added). By 'direct assistance' the regulation contemplates the use of military personnel in a variety of actions including arrest, stop and frisk, interdiction of a vehicle, pursuit, surveillance, investigation, and interrogation (<u>id</u>., sec. 213.10(3)). These are the very activities which Congress directed that even those military personnel assigned in a defined 'emergency circumstance' to operate loaned equipment used 'outside the land area of the United States' to enforce the immigration, drug, or customs laws must assiduously avoid (10 U.S.C. sec. 375). While Congress regarded its authorization of military aid with respect to the latter few laws as an extraordinary measure for peculiar and chiefly extraterritorial problems, yet still guarded with stringent restrictions, the executive branch treats it as the one circumscribed anomaly among a host of carte blanche authorizations for military intervention in law enforcement affairs.

Some of the circumstances listed in this newest regulation are circumstances in which military assistance indeed has been authorized expressly by Congress. These express authorizations include not only 10 U.S.C. secs. 331-333, but also some very specialized statutes, more specialized and limited than the regulation acknowledges them to be.[37] Several other circumstances are grouped under the heading of 'actions that are taken for the primary purpose of furthering a military or foreign affairs function of the United States, regardless of incidental benefits to civilian authorities' (32 C.F.R. sec. 213.10(a)(2)(i)). Most significantly, however, this newest regulation includes among the circumstances in which even 'direct assistance' of military personnel can be provided purportedly without violating the Posse Comitatus Act, those coming within 'the emergency authority' pretended by the 1972 Civil Disturbance Regulations (<u>id</u>., (ii)(A)).

Thus, although promulgated under colour of implementing Congress' 1982 legislation (by which Congress sought to reaffirm its 1878 repudiation of any executive emergency military law enforcement prerogative), these newest regulations actually reiterate the executive's claim to precisely that same prerogative, asserted under the label 'emergency authority' in the Civil Disturbance Regulations of 1972.

The Purported 'Protective Power'
The 1972 Civil Disturbance Regulations also assert (32 C.F.R. sec. 215.4(c)(1)(ii)) that the Constitution, without the aid of any statute

> [a]uthorizes Federal action, including the use of military forces, to protect Federal property and Federal governmental functions when the need for protection exists and duly constituted local authorities are unable or decline to provide adequate protection.

The 1968 Regulations had provided that military forces could be used to protect federal property and facilities, but had premised such use upon one of the statutes previously discussed, 10 U.S.C. sec. 332 (see for example, 32 C.F.R. sec. 187.5(a)(1) (1971)). That application of sec. 332 was dubious insofar as it failed to acknowledge the incapacitation of civilian means as a necessary precondition; but at least the 1968 Regulations had made no claim to an <u>extra-statutory</u> 'protective power'.

It is upon <u>Congress</u> that the Constitution confers power to make rules and regulations respecting federal property (Art. IV, sec. 3, cl. 2), and to make laws necessary and proper to effectuate federal functions (Art. I, sec. 8, cl. 18); the executive is authorized merely to 'take care that the Laws be faithfully executed' (Art. II, sec. 4). There may be a few things that the executive might do to protect federal property or federal governmental functions in the absence of any relevant legislation; but there is absolutely nothing in the Constitution suggesting that the executive's action in such instances, where the threat is domestic, may take military form. In any event, the power to make laws for the protection of federal property and functions being unequivocally conferred upon Congress, any power the executive might have to the same ends is clearly subject to such strictures as Congress might impose (<u>Youngstown Sheet & Tube Co. v. Sawyer</u>, 343 U.S. 579 (1952)). Therefore, even if the due process clause of the Fifth Amendment were not a categorical prohibition against law enforcement use of the military, such use of the military to protect federal property and functions could not be made in the face of a statutory prohibition.

The Posse Comitatus Act, therefore, is as much a repudiation of the extra-statutory 'protective power' claimed by the 1972 Civil Disturbance Regulations as it is of the broader 'emergency authority' those Regulations claim.

Nonetheless, the 1982 regulations concerning 'DOD Cooperation With Civilian Law Enforcement Officials' boldly reassert (32 C.F.R. sec. 213.10 (a)(2)(ii)(B)) this 'protective power' falsely claimed by the Civil Disturbance Regulations. Indeed, the 1982 regulations repeat (id., paraphrasing 32 C.F.R. sec. 215.4(c)(1)) with new emphasis the 1972 regulations' claim that both the 'protective power' and the 'emergency authority' arise under

> the inherent right of the US Government, a sovereign national entity under the US Constitution, to ensure the preservation of public order and the carrying out of governmental operations within its territorial limits, by force if necessary.

The assertion is that these prerogatives inhere in the national government by virtue of sovereignty and the Constitution: but nothing in either implies that they inhere in the _executive_ branch of that government. On the contrary, the Constitution specifically vests in _Congress_ the power to determine when and how the armed forces may be used. What Congress has said is that it is a felony to make any law enforcement use of the armed forces except as 'expressly authorized by the Constitution or Act of Congress' (18 U.S.C. sec. 1385, the Posse Comitatus Act); nothing in the Constitution 'expressly' authorizes extra-statutory use of the military in _any_ domestic situation, whether there be some 'emergency' or some need for 'protective' action, or otherwise. The boldly defiant thrust of the latest regulations is simply that the executive will use military force whenever the executive deems it expedient to do so, congressional prohibitions notwithstanding.

House Joint Resolution 1292
The sixth and last basis claimed (32 C.F.R. sec. 215.4(c)(2)(i)(D)) for the Civil Disturbance Regulations is House Joint Resolution 1292, adopted June 6 1968. Although this had been adopted before the Civil Disturbance Regulations of 1968 had been

promulgated, those earlier Regulations had not claimed it as authority; but the 1972 Regulations do.

Section 2 of House Joint Resolution 1292 provides (P.L. 90-331, 82 Stat. 170; set out in notes to 18 U.S.C. sec. 3056) that:

> Hereafter when requested by the Director of the United States Secret Service, Federal Departments and agencies, unless such authority is revoked by the President, shall assist the Secret Service in the performance of its protective duties under section 3056 of title 18 of the United States Code and the first section of this joint resolution.

The duties of the Secret Service in connection with which the assistance called for by this Resolution is to be given include enforcement of a variety of laws concerning fraud, counterfeiting, forgery, and funds and obligations of federally chartered and federally insured financial institutions. Far more significant, however, these duties include protection of the persons of the President and Vice President, as well as the President-elect, the families of the President and former Presidents, and major presidential and vice-presidential candidates. In the performance of these duties the Secret Service and its agents are empowered to make warrantless arrests on reasonable grounds of belief with regard to any felony under federal law, and warrantless arrests for any lesser federal offense committed in their presence (18 U.S.C. sec. 3056).

Presidents, past Presidents, their families, and candidates are familiar targets not only for demented eccentrics but also for political extremists seeking to excite or exploit civil turmoil. The fact or reasonable suspicion of some radical plot might easily be taken to justify extensive surveillance or enforcement activities by the Secret Service. Such activities by the civilian Secret Service might not be cause for alarm; but, if the armed forces could then be called upon to aid the Secret Service in its task, a far different situation would be at hand. The new Civil Disturbance Regulations claim House Joint Resolution 1292 as authority for invoking such military aid, even without any personal presidential action, merely on the request of the Secret Service Director.

Reliance upon this Resolution as authority for military aid to the Secret Service, however, is misplaced for the same reason that the old legislation giving federal marshals powers equivalent to state sheriffs could not sustain the traditional posse use of troops after the Posse Comitatus Act: the Resolution does not '<u>expressly</u>' authorize it at all. The Resolution speaks generally of 'Federal Departments and agencies'; and even though this phrase is broad enough to include the Department of Defense, there is no express indication that any of the <u>military</u> resources administered by that civilian department are to be comprehended.[38]

Ironically, the 1982 regulations on 'DOD Cooperation With Civilian Law Enforcement Officials' make no reference whatever to House Joint Resolution 1292, even though they catalogue at extraordinary length all the statutory and purported extra-statutory exceptions to the Posse Comitatus Act prohibition. Among the statutory authorizations claimed by the new regulations to constitute exceptions to that prohibition is Title 18 U.S.C. sec. 3056 (32 C.F.R. sec. 213.10(a)(2)(iv)(E)), the statute cited in House Joint Resolution 1292 as describing the protective duties of the Secret Service. 18 U.S.C. sec. 3056, however, makes no reference whatever to use of any military resources. Whether by virtue of that section itself or House Joint Resolution 1292, therefore, the assertion of authority to employ any military resources to aid in Secret Service protective duties is utterly without any foundation in law, and is a naked affront to the will of Congress declared in the Posse Comitatus Act.[39]

THE BLUEPRINT FOR INTERVENTION: COMMAND AND CONTROL UNDER THE NEW CIVIL DISTURBANCE REGULATIONS

The Civil Disturbance Regulations (32 C.F.R. sec. 215.6(a)) designate the Secretary of the Army (or the Under Secretary of the Army, as his designee) as 'Executive Agent for the Department of Defense in all matters pertaining to the planning for, and the deployment and employment of military resources in the event of civil disturbance'. The Regulations call for this 'Executive Agent' to establish a 'Civil Disturbance Steering Committee', chaired by the Under Secretary of the Army, 'to provide advice and assistance' to the 'Executive Agent' 'concerning civil disturbance matters' (<u>id</u>., sec. 215.8(a)). 'Steering Committee' members include the Army Vice-Chief of Staff, several other uniformed officers, some Defense Department officials, and the Deputy Attorney General of the United States (<u>id</u>.).[40]

The 'Steering Committee', however, does not exercise operational control. The Regulations call (id., (b)) for the 'Executive Agent' to establish 'A Directorate of Military Support ... with a joint service staff under the Chief of Staff, U.S. Army'. With a Director drawn from the Army and a Deputy Director drawn from the Air Force, the Directorate of Military Support is to 'plan, coordinate, and direct civil disturbance operations' (id.). The Regulations further provide (id., sec. 215.7(a)(2)) that, with regard to disturbances within the continental United States, the 'Executive Agent is delegated the authority to exercise, through the Chief of Staff, U.S. Army, the direction of those forces assigned or committed to him by the military departments'. Under the Army Chief of Staff, 'At objective areas, designated task force commanders will exercise operational control over all military forces assigned for employment in the event of civil disturbances' (id., (c)). It is through these 'designated military commanders', responsible to the Army Chief of Staff and his Directorate of Military Support, that the 'Executive Agent' exercises 'the direction of military resources committed or assigned for employment in the event of actual or potential civil disturbances' (id., sec. 215.6 (a)(6); emphasis added). What is contemplated, in other words, as to actual or potential disturbances, is a military chain of command from the Army Chief of Staff (or Vice-Chief of Staff) through the Directorate of Military Support to the task force commanders and their troops. Although co-ordination between military and civil authorities is contemplated (id., sec. 215.5(e)) the only point of civilian control is at the top where the Secretary or Under Secretary of the Army acts as 'Executive Agent' for the Department of Defense.

According to the Regulations (id., sec. 215.5 (a)), the employment of military resources for controlling civil disturbances will

> normally be predicated upon the issuance of a Presidential Executive order or Presidential directive authorizing and directing the Secretary of Defense to provide for the restoration of law and order in a specific State or locality.

Indeed, apart from the Regulations, the statutes (10 U.S.C. sec. 334) require that a Proclamation be issued by the President as a precondition to the use of troops under 10 U.S.C. secs. 331 or 333. The Regulations, however, provide (32 C.F.R. sec. 215.1 (a)(1)) for a major exception to this requirement of presidential involvement: no presidential order or directive is needed, according to the Regulations, for instances within the purported 'emergency authority', to deal with 'Cases of sudden and unexpected emergencies ... which require that immediate military action be taken'. In such instances, no civilian higher than the 'Executive Agent', the Secretary or Under Secretary of the Army, need be involved in the decision. Moreover, since the operational command role resides in the Army Chief of Staff and his Directorate of Military Support, even this minimal civilian role might well be more ephemeral than real. In other words, the 'emergency authority' justification for military intervention, which is the most extraordinary and far-reaching power asserted by the new Civil Disturbance Regulations, may be invoked and implemented by the military itself with only a modicum (if even that) of civilian involvement.

Nor is this all. As the requirement of a presidential order or directive is dispensed with, so also is the accompanying requirement that a 'specific State or locality' be designated (10 U.S.C. sec. 334). Moreover, all of this pertains not only to 'actual' but also to 'potential' sudden emergencies requiring immediate military action (32 C.F.R. sec. 215.6(a)(6)). Although perhaps restricted somewhat by the terms of a Department of Defense Directive which is not available to the public, the Directorate of Military Support under the 'Executive Agent' performs intelligence functions pertaining to planning in readiness for such actual civil disturbances as might sometime occur (id., secs. 215.6(a)(8) and 215.6(a)(13)). Furthermore, the Regulations contemplate (id., sec. 215.6 (a)(6)) that, short of active military engagement, military ground forces may be 'prepositioned' and held at the ready in case disturbances should arise.

Requests for prepositioning are to be made through the Attorney General, and units larger than battalion size are not to be prepositioned without presidential approval (id., sec. 215.5(g)). Any units up to and including a battalion in size, however, may be prepositioned even without presidential approval, whenever a need - even a potential need - might be perceived. The provisions concerning prepositioning represent a particular danger. However efficient prepositioning might seem as a means of facilitating prompt suppression of such disorders as might occur, it is also true that the prepositioning of troops can intimidate citizens and chill the exercise of constitutional rights. It should be recalled that President Grant's arguments in support of prepositioning - solely to prevent riot (Lieber, 1898, pp. 6-7) - had been unpersuasive to the Congress in 1877 and 1878, and that Congress enacted the Posse Comitatus Act in large part because of the intimidation the congressmen believed voters had felt because of soldiers prepositioned to prevent potential disorder at the polls (7 Cong. 3851, 3852).

The alarming import of the Civil Disturbance Regulations should now be quite apparent, even without any imaginative conjuring of 'worst case' scenarios in which an actual military takeover might be conceived. The constitutional rule of due process prohibits any domestic application of military force except in situations of actual insurrection, where assaults specifically against the established institutions of civilian government have accomplished their goal of incapacitating those civilian institutions (Ex parte Milligan, 71 U.S. 2, 127 (1866)). Even though the statutory changes accomplished by Congress during the Civil War and Reconstruction eras compromised that constitutional principle significantly, at least Congress by the Posse Comitatus Act in 1878 had required strict compliance with those amended statutes, which still require personal involvement of the President in every event. The 1878 legislation was, above all, a repudiation of the notion that anyone, even the President himself, could claim any inherent authority to make domestic use of military force, no matter what emergency might be claimed. In the face of all this, the Civil Disturbance Regulations now assert broad extra-statutory authority for the discretionary use of federal troops, not only to protect federal property and functions, but also to deal with any perceived actual or potential 'emergency'. Such an emergency, the Regulations contemplate (32 C.F.R. secs. 215.3(a), and 215.4(c)(1)(i)), might arise in the event of 'calamities', an undefined term; or in the event of 'disasters', another undefined term; or in the event of 'civil disturbances', defined to include not only 'group acts of violence' (whether or not directed at established civilian institutions of government) but also 'disorders prejudicial to public law and order'. The judgment that such an emergency has arisen, or that there is <u>potential</u> that it <u>might</u> arise, need not be made by the President; at most a Secretary or Under Secretary of the Army might be involved, and in any event operational control will be in military hands. Moreover, even when there is no actual deployment of troops, an established Pentagon machinery of intelligence and planning is constantly in operation, watching for occasions for intervention to arise, always prepared to pre-position troops or to take such other actions as might be deemed expedient.

YET ANOTHER FAULTY FOUNDATION

The tiny Indian village of Wounded Knee in South Dakota was the site in 1890 of a notorious episode in the Indian wars accompanying white westward expansion. On February 27, 1973, several score supporters of the activist American Indian Movement (AIM) descended upon this village to call media attention to reservation conditions and grievances. As many of the AIM supporters were armed, and as their commotion disrupted routine in the village, it was a situation of serious law enforcement concern - but hardly an insurrection. By nightfall, however, federal officials had cut off ingress and egress, beginning a seige that would last seventy-one days.

Although the Wounded Knee 'occupation' was publicised worldwide, there was little notice of the use of the military there. Armoured personnel carriers borrowed from the state's National Guard had replaced civilian vehicles at the roadblocks after two weeks; but they were manned by civilians, and no military uniforms were observed. Not until months later, by court ordered disclosure of voluminous records (unpublished, but possessed by this writer), was the extent of military involvement made known.

The Directorate of Military Support had been involved from the very first day. Within three days the 82nd Airborne Division Chief of Staff was at the scene as a DOD 'observer', and an Army colonel was there to coordinate logistics. A brigade of the 82nd Airborne was placed on alert, and alternative operational plans devised by the Directorate were approved by the Army Chief and Vice-Chief of Staff. Several reconnaissance flights were made with Air Force planes, some by crews of Air Force regulars and some by Air National Guardsmen activated to federal duty for the purpose. Ground support for the flights, instruction and maintenance regarding other military equipment, and other functions were performed by Army and Air Force personnel on active federal duty - although they wore civilian clothes. Air Force planes and crews flew military and Justice Department officials between the capital and the remote site of seige. In April, troops at Fort Carson were placed on six-hour alert, prepositioned but never deployed to Wounded Knee. When an accounting was later made, it showed that, apart from the hundreds involved in prepositioning and planning, the parts of the military actually used included a large number of personnel, plus planes, APCs, trucks, jeeps, and sedans, 177 rifles and 190,000 rounds of ammunition, 23,000 flares, hundreds of tear gas grenades, and a wide array of other equipment.

None of the statutory or extra-statutory bases claimed by the 1972 Civil Disturbance Regulations was, or was even pretended to be, present at Wounded Knee. (For a critical assessment by a Judge Advocate in the Marine Corps, see Meeks, 1975.) What heretofore unheard-of authority could justify such use of the military to aid law enforcement?

Acknowledging that Wounded Knee did not constitute a 'civil disturbance' within the terms of the 1972 Regulations, the Department of Defense legal staff with concurrence of the Deputy Attorney General devised a remarkable new foundation for military intervention, relying on an obscure piece of legislation called the 'Economy Act' (31 U.S.C. sec. 686(a)) which provides:

> Any executive department ... may place orders with any other such department ... for materials, supplies, equipment, work, or services, of any kind that such requisitioned Federal agency may be in a position to supply or equipped to render ... <u>Provided further</u>, that if such work or services can be as conveniently or more cheaply performed by private agencies such work shall be let by competitive bids to such private agencies.

Since it deals with allocation of appropriated fiscal resources, administration of the Economy Act is overseen by the Comptroller General of the U.S. who in formal opinions (e.g. 18 Dec. Comp. Gen. 262 at 266 (1938); 23 <u>id</u>., 935 at 937-938 (1944)) has consistently construed it as giving the service rendering agency no authority which it does not have independently of the Act, and as applying only where the service to be performed 'is a normal function of both the procuring and performing agency' (32 id., 392 at 394 (1952)). In the face of the Posse Comitatus Act, and where (as at Wounded Knee) none of the grounds asserted for the Civil Disturbance Regulations is even pretended to be present, it is preposterous to assert that law enforcement is a 'normal function' of the military departments or within their authority apart from the Economy Act.

Even if its administrative construction could be ignored, the Economy Act could not credibly be construed as 'expressly' providing further exception to the Posse Comitatus prohibition: it does not expressly refer to distinctively military resources; it makes no reference to efforts to 'execute the laws'; and it certainly does not specify 'expressly' any 'cases' or 'circumstances' in which law enforcement use of military resources may be made.

In no instance before the Wounded Knee adventure had this fanciful new interpretation of the Economy Act been advanced. No appellate court has yet ratified it; and four criminal trial judges who have considered it disagreed among themselves.[41] A civil damage suit against relevant government officials, by Indians claiming injury from this use of the military, is still pending:[42] the defendants have never claimed any other colourable authority.

CONCLUSION

Good soldiers are patriots. They are worthy of gratitude and praise. They are instruments, however, of war. Riot is not war, nor is civil disorder or even violent disobedience to law. Insurrection, or rebellion, is a case apart, where violence directed at government overthrow has, at least temporarily, attained its goal. The traditional test is whether the courts have been closed. Insurrection, unlike riot, is war.

Events of constitutional dimension in England prior to the mid-eighteenth century had marked this distinction with repeated insistence. The early American statesmen, outraged by the military law enforcement which their tradition decried as unlawful, cited it as a cause for revolution. They would not have their own government repeat the offense; thus they constitutionalised in the Fifth Amendment the traditional English prohibition against military intervention, by providing that no person shall be deprived of life, liberty, or property except by 'due process of law'. Congress, when it first came to legislate with regard to the military, carefully respected that rule.

Seventy years later, a generation of Radicals ravished due process to attain their immediate moral and political goals. When reason and a sense of restraint were restored, Congress sought to curtail military intervention by passing the Posse Comitatus Act. That enactment, however, did not destroy the foundation for such intervention which the Civil War and Reconstruction Congresses themselves had laid. Neither has it proved effective to prevent new foundations from being laid more recently by the executive branch.

We have not for a century experienced quite such egregious military interventions, although numerous more limited instances of military law enforcement have occurred. So long as the victims of such military intervention are relatively few and unpopular, and public support for suppression is strong, such affronts to due process can be survived. But they can be neither forgotten nor excused; the English suffered Tudor and Stuart lieutenancy and commissions for three generations before they took Charles' head. When dissatisfaction becomes widespread, resort to the military expedient serves to kindle rather than quench the fire. Toleration of military intervention in any law enforcement circumstance ultimately portends the sort of military oppression we observe and lament in other countries today.

The promise of 'due process' is empty rhetoric unless those with the requisite authority enforce obedience to what it entails. The judiciary can vindicate the law only in retrospect, as cases are made; and what is needed is the <u>prevention</u> of military intervention, not retrospective redress of its harm. The executive branch, in planning for future exigencies, tends to deprecate and minimize every attempted restraint on its choice of force, and to exploit every pretext to keep available the option of military means. Military officers and executive officials, when a crisis is perceived, will not parse statutes and probe legislative history, or ponder over judicial precedents; their actions will be constrained (if at all) only by their own regulations. If unlawful military intervention is to be prevented, therefore, Congress must be diligent to ensure that those regulations conform to the law.

Consequently, there must be members and committees in Congress willing to make it their business, during periods of quiet when the prospect of crisis seems far away, boldly and persistently to inquire into the relevant regulations of the executive branch, and to insist that those regulations and the executive plans that are made for emergencies conform to the Congress' will. Otherwise, unlawful military intervention will not be deterred.

There must also be determination in Congress to reconsider and revise those few existing statutes which, by virtue of Reconstruction Era excesses and distortions, purport to authorize what the Contitution forbids.

But there is more that Congress must do. The executive branch, although wilful, is not usually wilfully pernicious. It resorts to military expedients because those are the most effective at hand for dealing with exigencies that the executive will not, and should not, ignore. Equally effective civilian expedients for every domestic law enforcement exigency can be provided; some possibilities have been suggested in footnote 34. Congressional action is needed, however, to make such civilian alternatives available. Prohibitions against the military expedient, regardless how insistently maintained, cannot be expected to be effective in preventing military intervention unless adequate civilian alternatives are provided.

With Congress, therefore, rests the question whether this chapter might serve to inspire a revival of faith in, and faithfulness to, due process, or will merely document its demise.

NOTES

1. The historical background of the Commander-in-Chief clause is the struggle between Crown and Parliament for control over the military culminating in Parliament's disavowal of the power of military command after the Restoration, see 13 Car. 2, stat. 1, c. 6, para. 1 (1661). The history of the requirement of military subordination to civilian power is quite different, having to do with claimed prerogative to intrude the military into governance otherwise proceeding according to civilian laws.

2. Some of the material examined in this chapter has been discussed by this author in earlier publications: Engdahl (1971, 1972 (Part One), 1974). The thesis of those earlier articles has been endorsed by some other writers, e.g. Meeks (1975), but criticized in Pye and Lowell (1975). Because of the intervening commentary, the author has carefully

re-examined his views, and has concluded that his thesis is thoroughly sound. Specific response to some of the contentions of Pye and Lowell is made in footnotes herein.

3. 'The Address and Reasons of Dissent of the Minority of the Convention of the State of Pennsylvania to Their Constituents, 1787', in 2 Schwartz, The Bill of Rights: A Documentary History, 662 at p. 671 (1971).

4. Responding in three successive numbers of The Federalist (Nos. 27, 28, 29), Hamilton insisted that the provision for military force was only for 'seditions and insurrections ...' No. 28. By virtue of the necessary and proper clause Congress could provide for the use of citizens as a posse comitatus to assist the officers entrusted with execution of the federal laws, No. 29. The military expedient was only provided for 'times of insurrection ... to guard the public against the violence of faction or sedition', id. Discussing in Federalist No. 43 the 'domestic Violence' provision of the Guaranty Clause, Madison described it as contemplating only 'insurrections in a State'.

5. As to South Carolina, see 2 Schwartz, supra note 3, at 753; New Hampshire, id., at 761; and Maryland, id., at 734-5.

6. As to Virginia, see 2 Schwartz, supra note 3, at 841-3; New York, id., at 911-4.

7. Madison opposed prohibiting a standing army; but it is clear from The Federalist, supra note 4, that neither he nor Hamilton countenanced military law enforcement except in situations of insurrection. As one knowledgeable in the law, Madison must have been aware that the precept of military subordination to civil powers and the prohibition of prerogative suspension of the laws were but corollaries of the more fundamental principle of Chapter 39 of Magna Carta. In the interest of concise statement the redundant verbiage of the Charter provision, elaborately recited in the Virginia and New York proposals, could be excised: to say that neither life, nor liberty, nor property could be touched by military prerogative, was sufficient to say it all. Magna Carta, however, did not foreclose Parliament itself from authorizing military expedients. Madison was resolved to have limitations as effective against the legislative as against the executive branch. See Madison's speech introducing his proposed amendments, 1 Annals of Cong. 453-4, reprinted in 2 Schwartz, supra note 3, at 1028-9. Therefore he chose for his concise

formulation of the anti-military principle of Chapter 39 of Magna Carta the alternative phrase that had been used in New York's proposed provision: 'due process of law'. See 2 Schwartz, supra note 3, at 855-6.

Closing their eyes to this background of the language chosen by Madison and quietly accepted even by those states which had been most insistent upon effective assurances against military law enforcement, Pye and Lowell (1975, p. 657) blandly assert: 'We are aware of no evidence that the due process clause of the Fifth Amendment was intended to deal at all with the subject of military aid to the civil power'. Ignoscunt ut ignarent.

8. An example of the military commissions for riot suppression issued by James I is published in 17 Rymer, Foedera, Conventiones, Literae, et Cujuscunque Generis Acta Publica 647 (2d ed. 1726).

9. The sweeping significance of the Petition of Right is sadly misstated by Pye and Lowell (1975, p. 668). What was declaimed was the whole range of 'martial law' prerogative, explicitly including the issuance and execution of the military commissions. One thing called for by those commissions was the summary military trial and execution of offenders; but another thing equally called for by those commissions was military suppression of the disorders themselves.

10. The 1714 statute was subsequently revived and continued: 9 Geo. 1, c. 8 (1722) and 7 Geo. 2, c. 23 (1734). The latter specifically provided that the lieutenants should have no greater powers than they had under the Restoration statutes of 13, 14 and 15 Charles II, 7 Geo. 2, c. 23, sec. 3 (1734).

11. '... [I]f a lieutenant, or other, that hath commission of martial authority, doth in time of peace hang or otherwise execute any man by colour of martial law, this is murder; for it is against magna carta cap. 29' (Blackstone, 1765, p. 400, quoting E. Coke, Third Institute 52. See also Hale (1716), pp. 39-40).

12. To the same effect, but even more explicitly invoking the due process tradition, the preamble to the South Carolina Constitution of 1776 recited that King George had 'dispensed with the law of the land, and substituted the law martial in its stead ...', S.C. Const. (1776), printed in 2 Poore, The Federal and State Constitutions, Colonial Charters, and Other Organic Laws of the United States, 1615, 1616 (2d ed. 1878).

13. In 1861, Chief Justice Taney explicitly

declared that the due process clause of the Fifth Amendment forbids executive recourse to military intervention for law enforcement. On May 25, 1861, John Merryman had been seized by federal troops at his home in Maryland, a state which had not seceded and where federal (as well as state) civilian authority was intact. Taney declared that he was ruling on the case, not merely as Circuit Justice, but as 'Chief Justice of the Supreme Court of the United States at Chambers', see C. Swisher, The Taney Period 1836-64, vol. V of History of the Supreme Court of the United States, at 848, 849 n. 26 (Holmes Devise, 1974), although the report of his opinion erroneously identifies it as an opinion at circuit, Ex parte Merryman, 17 Fed. Cas. 144 (No. 9847) (C.C.D.Md. 1861). Referring to the 'due process' clause, Taney declared:

> With such provisions in the constitution, expressed in language too clear to be misunderstood by any one, I can see no ground whatever for supposing that the president, in any emergency, or in any state of things, can authorize ... the arrest of a citizen, except in aid of the judicial power. (17 Fed. Cas. at 149)

Although Chief Justice Taney died in 1864, before the whole Court had opportunity to address this same issue, his view was clearly confirmed by the decision of the Supreme Court in Ex parte Milligan, 71 U.S. (4 Wall.) 2 (1866).

14. These Regulations do not govern National Guard troops that have not been federalized. The National Guard in each state is, for practical purposes, the modern successor to the earlier state militia. Each member of each state's National Guard is also - but separately in contemplation of law - a member of the 'National Guard of the United States', which is a reserve component of the federal armed forces. As such they may be called to active duty, or 'federalized', individually or as units. 'Federalized' National Guardsmen are part of the national armed forces, and thus are within the scope of the Regulations.

15. The modern counterpart of the states' militia is the National Guard, which, when called into Federal service, as explained supra note 14, is a part of the national armed forces.

16. The Militia Bill was Congress' first measure under U.S. Const. art. I, para. 8, cl. 16, 'To provide for organizing, arming, and

disciplining, the Militia ...' Act of May 8, 1792, ch. 33, 1 Stat. 271.

17. The 1792 Act expired in three years; but its successor Act of February 28, 1795, ch. 36, 1 Stat. 424, was essentially a re-enactment without change in substance: hence the practice in this chapter of citing only the 1792 Act. An Act of March 3, 1807, ch. 39, 2 Stat. 443, authorized use of the standing federal forces as well as militia.

18. For example, after the urban riots of 1967, Attorney General Clark sent a letter to all governors referring to 10 U.S.C. sec. 331 as authority for the use of federal troops in such instances of 'serious "domestic violence"'; the text of the letter is reproduced in Laird v. Tatum, 408 U.S. 1, at 3, n. 2 (1972).

19. For further accounts, see 3 J. Campbell, The Lives of the Chief Justices of England 402-21 (3d ed. 1874); Proceedings Against Lord George Gordon, 21 State Trials 485 (1781); Rex v. Kennett, 5 Car. & P. 282, 172 Eng. Rep. 976 (1781).

20. The Parliamentary History of England 688-98 (W. Cobbett ed. 1814). Mansfield's doctrine was applied in Rex. v. Kennett, 5 Car. & P. 282, 294, 172 Eng. Rep. 976, 984 (1781), and again in Rex v. Pinney, 5 Car. & P. 254, 263 n. (b), 172 Eng. Rep. 962, 967 n. (b) (1832).

21. Pye and Lowell, 1975, pp. 666-7, suggest that Mansfield addressed not the military or civilian character of the force used, but only its invocation by King rather than local officials. That ignores Mansfield's point that any 'martial law' supervention of civilian process was 'clearly out of the question'. Default by the local officials had required the King to act; but what the King had done, as Mansfield saw it, was to call disciplined army units as the posse, not a military force.

22. Pye and Lowell, 1975, p. 689 n. 361, suggest that the practice of using troops as a posse might have originated with this 'ingenious' Attorney General's Opinion in 1854. An Opinion by a subsequent Attorney General, however, 16 Op. Atty. Gen. 162 (1878), affirms the historicity of the practice.

23. E.g., Johnson v. Jones, 44 Ill. 142, 160-1, 92 Am. Dec. 159, 174-5 (1867); Griffin v. Wilcox, 21 Ind. 370, 388-389 (1863). See also In re Egan, 8 F. Cas. 367 (No. 4303) (C.C.N.D.N.Y. 1866); Milligan v. Hovey, 17 F. Cas. 380, 381 (C.C.D. Ind. 1871).

24. Section 7 of the 1861 Act retained the

provision from sec. 9 of the 1792 Act, that marshals should have the same powers as sheriffs in executing the laws; but eliminating the prerequisite of exhausting those civilian means (including the posse) left this provision without significant function. Section 2 of the 1861 Act retained the requirement of a presidential proclamation ordering 'such insurgents' to disperse; but that Act addressed far more than genuine 'insurrection'. By retaining the term 'insurgents' in the proclamation section while so radically expanding the situations covered, the 1861 Act obscured the distinction, constitutionally crucial, between 'riot' and 'insurrection'.

25. This brazen attempt to foreclose judicial inquiry was ignored by federal courts, see, e.g., Milligan v. Hovey, 17 F. Cas. 380 (No. 9605) (C.C.D.Ind. 1871). In Beckwith v. Bean, 98 U.S. 266 (1879), the Attorney General cited such disregard of the 1867 statute as error; but the Supreme Court majority reversed for a different error and expressed 'no opinion as to the construction of [the jurisdiction foreclosing statute], or as to the questions of constitutional law which may arise thereunder', 98 U.S. at 285. The Court, however, ordered a new trial, whereas the 1867 statute would have required dismissal for lack of subject matter jurisdiction. Two Justices, dissenting as to the different point of reversal, reached the question and pronounced the 1867 Act unconstitutional, id. Other cases suggest that the majority, had they addressed the issue in Beckwith, would have agreed: e.g. Raymond v. Thomas, 91 U.S. 712 (1876).

Earlier Acts, not divesting jurisdiction but immunizing those acting under military orders, were held unconstitutional in state courts, e.g. Johnson v. Jones, 44 Ill. 142, 92 Am. Dec. 159 (1867); Griffin v. Wilcox, 21 Ind. 370 (1863). The Supreme Court noted but did not rule on the issue in Nashville v. Cooper, 73 U.S. (6 Wall.) 247 (1867). A two year limitation statute, see Mitchell v. Clark, 110 U.S. 633 (1884), prevented subsequent adjudication of the immunity feature.

26. See, e.g., Beckwith v. Bean, id.; Raymond v. Thomas, id. In Raymond, to avoid a constitutional ruling, the Supreme Court disingenuously construed the legislation to void a military order that annulled a court decree, explaining, 'It is an unbending rule of law, that the exercise of military power, where the rights of the citizen are concerned, shall never be pushed beyond what the exigency requires', 91 U.S. at 716.

27. *In re Debs*, 158 U.S. 564 (1895), arising out of the Pullman strike, contains a much abused dictum: 'If the emergency arises, the army of the nation, and all its militia, are at the service of the nation to compel obedience to its laws', *id*. at 582. No issue in the case concerned the use of troops, nor did the Court opine whether the Pullman strike was an 'emergency' sufficient to warrant their use; but the context of this dictum was a discussion of the incapacity of civil courts, reminiscent of the classic test of insurrection. See also *id*. at 597.

28. Attorney General Brownell in 1957 postulated a power to use troops without limitation by Congress, but held 10 U.S.C. secs. 332 and 333 sufficient to authorize troops for dealing with a school integration crisis, 41 Op. Atty. Gen. 313.

A similar assertion of unlimitable executive power was made in 1898 by Judge Advocate General Lieber, but without relevant authority. He cited *Ex parte Siebold*, 100 U.S. 371 (1879), which involved only marshals, and *In re Debs*, discussed in note 27.

29. See also cls. 15, 16. Power in Congress to make rules for governing troops negates any notion that the Commander-in-Chief may govern or use them contrary to the rules that Congress has made.

30. Hayes' moderation in the use of troops, despite widespread labour riots, doubtless made the House more willing to postpone repudiation of Grant's prerogative claim until the next year.

31. The Act had originated in the House, with language limiting the use of the Army or Navy to situations 'expressly' authorized by Congress (7 Cong. Rec. 3586). Reference to naval forces was dropped, doubtless because the appropriations bill under consideration was only for the army (*id*., 3877). The Senate approved the measure on the second day of debate (*id*., 4302), but only after Senate Republicans had excised the word 'expressly' (*id*., 4248), and added provision for situations that might be authorized 'by the Constitution' (*id*., 4240). The House, however, refused to accept any weakening of the prohibition they meant to impose. Reference to purported constitutional authorization would be harmless if the word 'expressly' were restored, for the Constitution contains *no* 'express' authorization for such use in the absence of a statute. Restoration of the word 'expressly', however, was crucial, and the House conferees insisted (see *id*., 4648). The Senate yielded, and before enactment the word 'expressly' was restored to the text.

32. See 16 Op. Atty. Gen. 162 (1878); 17 *id*. at 71 (1881), 242 (1881), and 333 (1882); 19 *id*. at 293 (1889), and 368 (1889). The traditional use of soldiers as a posse, however, persisted as to state military forces and state officials, see, for example, *State v. Coit*, 8 Ohio Dec. 62 (C.P. 1897).

33. The language of the original Act specified only the army; but its broader import has long been respected. An Act of August 19, 1956, ch. 1041, sec. 18a, 70A Stat. 626, specifically added the Air Force. The Navy department long ago adopted an equivalent prohibition by regulation, see *United States v. Walden*, 490 F. 2d 372 (4th Cir. 1974). The 1968 Civil Disturbance Regulations (32 C.F.R. sec. 187.4(b) (1971)) acknowledged the policy of the Act as applicable to all forces, including the Navy and Marine Corps – an acknowledgment ominously missing from the 1972 Regulations (*id.*, sec. 215.4(b)).

34. Art. II, sec. 3, does not remotely suggest that the president may use the military in his duty to 'take Care that the Laws be faithfully executed'. Art. II, sec. 2, making him Commander-in-Chief, does not suggest he may use troops for civil law enforcement.

The 'Guaranty Clause', Art. IV, sec. 4, says 'the United States shall guarantee each state against domestic Violence'. This duty, however, is placed not on the president, but on 'the United States', and *Congress* is left to make laws for carrying out this no less than other federal powers, Art. I, sec. 8, cl. 18. Constitutional Convention records suggest that the term 'domestic violence' contemplates only treasonous violence, i.e. insurrection, see Engdahl, 1971, pp. 35-9. Alternatively the framers might have had in mind the Mansfield doctrine for non-insurrectionary violence. As to the 'Guaranty Clause' as well as the militia provision in Art. I, sec. 8, cl. 15, see Engdahl, 1974, p. 588. In any event, nothing in this Clause 'expressly' authorizes military force to suppress domestic violence not amounting to insurrection; indeed it was chiefly to preclude any such construction that the 'due process' clause of the Fifth Amendment was adopted.

Since the demise of the Mansfield doctrine, the militia provision in Art. I, sec. 8, cl. 15, can be applied consistently with due process only to *insurrections* against federal authority. The 'Guaranty Clause', however, can be applied to lesser exigencies because it does not expressly contemplate *military* measures. Under the 'Guaranty' and

'Necessary and Proper' Clauses Congress could authorize the use of federal marshals, or some specialized force of them (like the Special Operations Group') to suppress violence in a state. Likewise Congress could authorise use of Federal Bureau of Investigation or Treasury Department agents, or could create a federal civilian police force specifically for the purpose. Congress could establish a system for interstate lending of police resources, or even provide for 'federalizing' police resources from sister states. The only impediments to such <u>civilian</u> means of federal suppression of violence in the states are limitations of congressional imagination; with the 'Guaranty', 'Necessary and Proper', and 'Supremacy' Clauses, there are no impeding constitutional limitations.

35. The Posse Comitatus Act reaches '<u>any part of</u>' the Army or Air Force. Use of an Air Force helicopter in a search operation has been held proscribed, <u>Wrynn v. United States</u>, 200 F. Supp. 457 (E.D.N.Y. 1961). It was military <u>equipment</u> - red coats and bayonets - that inflamed the American colonists. In old England the posse and soldiers were the same men; the point of the early struggles was that the equippage of war - helmet and breastplate and broadsword and lance - had no place in domestic law enforcement. The legislative history of the Posse Comitatus Act shows that it was military equipment and trappings, more than the persons of the soldiers, that was of concern. One Congressman spoke of the 'moral interference' of military uniforms and arms, 7 Cong. Rec. at 3852. In the Senate it was recognized that some organized body must be available, but not 'a battery of artillery' to deal with civil unrest, 7 Cong. Rec. at 4246.

36. H. Rep. No. 97-71, Part II, p. 17 (Separate views of Rep. John R. Seiberling, regarding language later moved and approved on the floor), 1981 <u>U.S. Code Cong. & Admin. News</u>, p. 1798.

37. Citations to these statutes are set out in 32 C.F.R. sec. 213.10(a)(2)(iv). The irrelevance of House Joint Resolution 1292 is discussed in the text, <u>infra</u>. Two others are discussed in note 39. Some of the others are of dubious validity under the constitutional rule discussed in this chapter, although they might have stood muster under different circumstances of an earlier day. For example, 43 U.S.C. sec. 1064, enacted in 1885 when there were expanses of public land where little or no civil authority prevailed, authorizes either civil or military force to remove unlawful enclosures on the

public lands; and 25 U.S.C. sec. 180, enacted in 1834, authorizes the president to use the military to remove persons settling on lands given by treaty to any Indian tribe. Title 16 U.S.C. secs. 23 (enacted in 1883) and 78 (enacted in 1900) authorize military removal of intruders and pilferers in Yellowstone, Sequoia, and Yosemite National Parks. The regulation also cites 16 U.S.C. sec. 596, which was repealed in 1933.

Title 42 U.S.C. sec. 1989 is a remnant of section 5 of the 1866 Civil Rights Act authorizing military assistance to execute process under certain civil rights laws; the dubious constitutionality of this provision has already been discussed. Secs. 1422 (Guam) and 1591 (the Virgin Islands) authorize territorial governors to request military assistance 'to prevent or suppress lawless violence'; insofar as these provisions are deemed applicable to mere civil disorder, they suffer the same infirmities noted earlier with regard to 10 U.S.C. sec. 332.

Title 50 U.S.C. sec. 220, enacted in 1861 with reference to difficulties encountered at the threshold of the Civil War, authorizes military assistance to prevent the removal of vessels or cargo from the custody of customs officials. It is codified under the heading 'insurrection', and to construe it as applicable in any lesser situation would present the same constitutional difficulties discussed earlier in connection with 10 U.S.C. sec. 331. Title 42 U.S.C. sec. 97, enacted in 1799, requires commanders of 'any fort or station upon the seacoast' to obey state quarantines and health laws, and to aid in their execution 'according to their respective powers and within their respective precincts'; it thus does not authorize any action otherwise outside the military officers' powers, such as enforcing those laws against civilians.

Title 18 U.S.C. secs. 112 and 1116 authorize military assistance to enforce federal laws protecting persons entitled by international law to special protection. The purpose of this 1976 legislation was to ensure that the United States could fulfil obligations under international conventions against terrorism. The legislative history indicates that military assistance should be requested only in such exceptional instances as the takeover of an embassy, H. Rep. No. 94-1614, p. 5, n. 7, 1976 U.S. Code Cong. & Admin. News, p. 4483. Even so, the legality of such military assistance is dubious.

Title 48 U.S.C. sec. 1418 authorizes military protection of the rights of discoverers of extraterritorial guano islands. Title 22 U.S.C. secs. 408 and 461-462 authorize military aid in enforcing the neutrality laws, preventing the illegal export of war material and the launching of expeditionary forces against foreign powers. Title 16 U.S.C. sec. 1361 authorizes use of military aircraft, vessels, personnel, and facilities to enforce the fishery conservation laws at sea. Title 42 U.S.C. sec. 3756 authorizes the Law Enforcement Assistance Administration to use available services, personnel, and facilities of military as well as civilian agencies; but LEAA has no law enforcement authority.

38. Nevertheless Mr Justice Rehnquist, while he was an Assistant Attorney General, did advise the Army General Counsel that the Resolution could be regarded as an express exception to the Posse Comitatus Act prohibition. Unpublished Memorandum from Assistant Attorney General William H. Rehnquist to Hon. Robert F. Jordan III, General Counsel, Department of the Army, Nov. 12, 1968, copy on file at United States Department of Justice.

39. Title 18 U.S.C. sec. 1751, prohibiting assassination and assault against the President and those in line of presidential succession, provides in subsection (1) for investigation by the FBI with assistance from any federal agency, including the military. The legislative history, however, confirms what the face of the statute declares, that such assistance is available only with regard to investigation and not other enforcement activities, Sen. Rpt. No. 498, 89th Cong., 1st Sess., 1965 <u>U.S. Code Cong. & Admin. News</u>, at 2867. Title 18 U.S.C. sec. 351 is a comparable provision regarding members of Congress. The latter originated as a floor amendment and thus lacks any committee history; but its wording, patterned after the former, likewise contemplates assistance of the military departments only with regard to investigation.

40. The Committee members are: Deputy Attorney General of the United States; Assistant Secretary of Defense (Comptroller); Assistant Secretary of Defense (Public Affairs); General Counsel of the Department of Defense; Under Secretary of the Navy; Under Secretary of the Air Force; Vice Chief of Staff of the Army; Vice Chief of Staff of the Air Force; Vice Chief of Naval Operations; Assistant Commandant of the Marine Corps; Representative of the Joint Chiefs of Staff; and the Under Secretary of the Army as Chairman.

41. <u>United States v. Banks</u>, 383 F. Supp. 368 (D.S.D. 1974); <u>United States v. Jaramillo</u>, 380 F.

Supp. 1375, 1381 (D. Neb. 1974), app. dism., 510 F. 2d 808 (8th Cir. 1975); United States v. Red Feather, 392 Fed. Supp. 916 (D.S.LD. 1975) (ruling in limine, later mooted by stipulation to admit the evidence ordered excluded); United States v. McArthur, 419 F. Supp. 186 (D.N.D. 1975); United States v. Casper, 541 F. 2d 1275 (8th Cir. 1976), cert. denied, 430 U.S. 970 (1977).

42. Lamont et al. v. Haig et al., Civil Action No. 81-5048, U.S. Dist. Ct., Dist. of South Dakota.

REFERENCES

Blackstone, W. (1765) Commentaries on the Laws of England, Vol. I, Oxford
Comment (1975) 'Executive Military Power: A Path to American Dictatorship', 54 Nebraska Law Review 111
Engdahl, D. (1971) 'Soldiers, Riots and Revolution: the Law and History of Military Troops in Civil Disorders', 57 Iowa Law Review 1
_____ (1972) 'A Comprehensive Study of the Use of Military Troops in Civil Disorders With Proposals for Legislative Reform', 43 Colorado Law Review 399
_____ (1974) 'The New Civil Disturbance Regulations: the Threat of Military Intervention', 49 Indiana Law Review 581
Ford, W. (ed.) (1905) 2 Journals of the Continental Congress 1774-78
Hale, M. (1716) The History of the Common Law of England (2nd ed.), London
_____ (1792) History of the Common Law (4th ed., C. Runnington), Vol. I, London
_____ (1847) The History of the Plea of the Crown (1st Am. ed.), Vol. I
Jones, W. (1780) Legal Mode of Suppressing Riots
Lieber, G. (1898) The Use of the Army in Aid of the Civil Power
Meeks, C. (1975) 'Illegal Law Enforcement: Aiding Civil Authorities in Violation of the Posse Comitatus Act', 70 Military Law Review 83 (Department of Army Pamphlet 27-100-70, 1975)
Morison, S.E., Commager, H.S. and Leuchtenburg, W. (1977) A Concise History of the American Republic
Pye, A.K. and Lowell, C. (1975) 'The Criminal Process During Civil Disorders', Duke Law Journal 581
Richardson, J. (1897) A Compilation of the Messages and Papers of the Presidents, Vol. 5

Chapter Two

MILITARY AID TO THE CIVIL POWER IN THE UNITED KINGDOM - AN HISTORICAL PERSPECTIVE

Keith Jeffery

It is a truism that the function of an army is to defend the state. In Britain this function has been seen primarily as external, with the army existing to repel any invasion of British territory and to defeat (or attempt to do so) the forces of enemy states. This view is confirmed by historical experience. No major battle has been fought on British soil since Culloden in 1746. There have been only two real threats of invasion since the eighteenth century - in 1805 and 1941. Since 1800, however, the British army has seen active service all over the world in a series of European wars, colonial wars, world wars and what might be termed 'policing operations'. Thus the notion has gained common currency that the British army, when it fights, fights abroad: that the responsibilities of the army, whatever else they may be, are quite evidently not domestic. But domestic security is an inescapable responsibility for any army. The 'defence of the state' must include the capability to assist in the maintenance of public order and the suppression of internal unrest, insurrection, or even revolution. The British army is no different from any other in this respect, but an outstanding characteristic of modern British history (over the past sixty years) is the rarity with which it has been called upon to perform internal security duties. In the United Kingdom since 1918, with the exception of Ireland, most notably in 1919-21 and since 1969, military aid to the civil power (MACP[1]) has been employed in peace-time on only a handful of occasions, and only once actively since the General Strike of May 1926.[2]

The rarity of MACP in Britain stems from two main causes: the comparative lack of violence in British political life and the success of the police alone in maintaining public order (see Critchley, 1980; Benewick and Smith, 1972. For a stimulating introductory essay on the topic, see Crick, 1964). Organized violence, with some notable exceptions (particularly where Ireland is involved), is generally not recognized as either a legitimate or a useful tool of political expression in Britain. This may be ascribed to a number of reasons, including the evolutionary character of the political system, the early establishment of constitutionalism and the relative responsiveness of British parliamentary democracy.[3] On the part of the government, public control has, where possible, been secured with a minimum use of overt force. The style of British policing, reflecting its common-law roots, has tended to be less intrusive than the Roman law mode of policing prevalent in continental Europe (see Bowden, 1978, ch. 9; Chapman, 1971. Histories of the British police vary from the standard, for example, Critchley, 1967, to the critical, for example, Bunyan, 1977). Historically the British police have been highly decentralized with close affiliations to local communities, and also unarmed. Both these characteristics contrast strongly with the army. The latter in particular indicates the degree of force readily available for keeping order and illustrates the gulf between using the police (minimum force) and the army (maximum force). It is a gulf which British governments have been hesitant to cross.

Modern policing in Britain dates from Sir Robert Peel's Metropolitan Police Act of 1829 which established a force in London with the two specific functions of fighting crime and maintaining public order. Since then police forces have had considerably more success with the second, than with the first, of these duties. Although the 'primacy of the police' gradually became established, for some time the army continued to play a significant role in keeping order, so much so that in 1888 the Secretary of State for War laid down 'the effective support of the civil power in all parts of the United Kingdom' as the first principal requirement from the British army (House of Commons Parliamentary Papers (1901), xxxix, pp. 255-7). Between 1870 and 1908 the army were called out to aid the civil power on twenty-four occasions (Report, 1908, p. 369). But the dangers of employing the military were vividly illustrated by the Featherstone Colliery riots in September 1893. Hastily called up by panic-stricken magistrates, a detachment of troops fired on the crowd killing two innocent bystanders. The question was taken up by a parliamentary committee in 1908 which affirmed that the civil authorities were primarily responsible for the preservation of the peace and recommended that police forces should be 'so organised and administered as to obviate to the utmost possible extent any necessity for resorting to military aid' (id., p. 367).

These principles were applied with some success when disorder broke out at Tonypandy, South Wales, during a coal strike in November 1910. Troops were held in readiness, but not used except in one small affray. The local police, reinforced with men from neighbouring forces and the London Metropolitan Constabulary, managed without military assistance. But in August 1911, during a spate of unrest following strikes in the docks and on the railways, troops were called in and opened fire in two places: Liverpool and Llanelli. (For government-side accounts, see Churchill, 1967, pp. 367-86. The 1910-14 period is narrated in detail in Blake, 1979.) In the Llanelli incident two men were killed by soldiers after a train manned by blacklegs had been held up. Along with South Wales, Ireland, that other storm-centre of pre-war British politics, also saw troops called in to aid the civil power. In July 1914, after the nationalist Irish Volunteers' gun-running at Howth, a detachment of soldiers at Bachelor's Walk, Dublin, fired on a hostile, though unarmed, crowd, killing three and wounding thirty-two people (McCardle, 1968, p. 107). This prompted the House of Commons to set up another select committee on the matter, but it met for the first time two days after war had broken out and immediately adjourned for the duration (H.C. Parl. Papers (1914), vii, p. 173).

By 1914, although the army continued to be directly, if intermittently, involved in keeping order, the cardinal principle had been established that if at all possible the police should preserve public order and the army be called in only to meet the gravest emergency. If the army were employed, the government law officers had laid down that they should only use 'such force as is reasonably necessary'. As to the use of lethal weapons, troops should whenever possible 'give sufficient warning of their intention' to fire.[4] The army too had made perfectly clear their extreme dislike of the obligation to discharge 'this most disagreeable and painful duty' (Report, 1908, p. 369). MACP interrupted training and the 'normal' functions of the army –

soldiers themselves regarded their duties primarily as 'external'. It also tended to throw the army into the thick of political controversy, whether hailed as saviours of the state or tools of capitalist oppression. Besides, the army was neither equipped nor trained to deal with public order. The rationale behind military organization is the concerted use of lethal weapons. The army exists to fight other armies, not mobs. From the government's point of view the advantage of the army lies in it being an available and disciplined force. But such advantage swiftly evaporates if discipline breaks down or mistakes are made. This was illustrated all too clearly, and fatally, on a number of occasions. There was, perhaps, just cause, or at least understandable cause, for employing MACP if it seemed acute disorder might escalate to the point of violent revolution. Such was the case after 1918.

Although talk of revolution had been in the air during the industrial unrest of the pre-war years, the possibility and danger of actual revolution were vividly brought home to politicians and generals in Britain by the Russian Revolution and the violent unrest which swept across Europe at the end of the Great War. 'Our real danger now', wrote the Chief of the Imperial General Staff, 'is not the Boches but Bolshevism'.[5] Whether or not there was actually any likelihood of a British revolution - and there is considerable evidence to suggest that it was, at best, a remote possibility (for more details, see Jeffery and Hennessy, 1983) - many members of the government felt that a Bolshevik uprising was just around the corner. These fears tended to outweigh any reluctance they must have had in employing soldiers to keep the peace. Fears of revolution were at their most acute between 1918 and 1921, but they briefly reappeared at the time of the General Strike in 1926, which the prime minister, Baldwin, in particular characterised as a direct attack on the constitution. The weakness of the police confirmed these fears. In 1918 and 1919 there were police strikes which undermined the government's confidence in the force as a whole. From the end of the war until the General Strike the perceived inadequacy of the police and the apparent prospect of violent unrest exactly mirrored the very factors which since the late 1920s have relieved the army in Britain of actual duties in aid of the civil power.

In the post-war years, while the government looked to the army to assume a major role in keeping the peace, politicians were naturally reluctant to commit themselves to an entirely military strategy. The particular dilemma facing them was that if the police alone were unable to keep order (as seemed likely) the only other available force was the army. Thus they were caught between the Scylla of too little force and the Charybdis of too much. One answer was to use troops as police. This was done in Liverpool during the police strike of August 1919 when soldiers patrolled the streets, some armed only with make-shift truncheons fashioned from their entrenching tools. But this could be no more than a stop-gap solution. It was strenuously resisted by senior officers who urged the government to find some other means of reinforcing the police.[6] Various ideas were floated. At one stage in 1920 the cabinet authorized the general staff to concentrate stores of rifles and ammunition at every infantry depot throughout the country in order to arm what would have amounted to vigilante groups of 'loyal' citizens.[7] Enlistment into the Special Constabulary - a part-time police reserve - was encouraged, but the chief method by which the government sought to bridge the gap between civil policing and military control was to experiment with 'third forces' (on 'third force' modes of policing, see Bowden, 1978, pp. 146-7, 234-5). In the British colonies third forces were frequently utilized. Indeed, the empire was largely policed by special quasi-military forces and gendarmeries such as the Burma Military Police, the Cape Mounted Rifles, the Royal Canadian Mounted Police and the Palestine Gendarmerie (see Jeffery, 1978, esp. pp. 78-82, for a discussion of the use of third forces immediately following World War I). They possessed a number of advantages over troops including flexibility and cheapness. The army liked them because they were both administered and paid for by the civil authorities. During a railway strike in the autumn of 1919 the government began recruiting a 'Citizen Guard'. This was little more than the Special Constabulary glamourized with a new title, which, it was believed, would 'prove a stimulus to recruiting'.[8] To meet unrest which never materialized during a coal stoppage in 1921, the cabinet swung towards a more military approach. Not only were the army reserves mobilised, but 80,000 men were also recruited into an armed 'Defence Force', administered by the War Office and commanded by regular soldiers.[9] This force represented an enlargement of the army's civil security duties, but it was accepted by the War Office as a necessary measure to meet the immediate emergency. The army, however, objected vigorously when it was suggested, after the miners had returned to work, that the force be retained to guard explosives and munitions depots. They maintained that such duties were the sole responsibility of the police, and to employ the Defence Force would be to 'admit the principle that the armed forces of the Crown are charged with the protection of civil property'.[10]

Throughout the 1920s police morale recovered from the strikes of 1918 and 1919. In the General Strike the force remained solidly behind the government and was reinforced both by an enlarged Special Constabulary and a new temporary body - the Civil Constabulary Reserve (CCR). Although raised by military recruiting officers, the CCR was under the tactical command of the civil authorities. This marked a victory for the War Office, who after the strike sought to have the CCR established on a permanent basis, arguing the 'clear necessity' in times of civil disturbance for 'some efficient force of semi-military character intermediate between the regular police forces ... and the fighting services'.[11] After protracted negotiations between the War Office and the Home Office, a scheme was agreed for such a third force. But it was never implemented. Nor was the army called in again to assist the police to keep public order. Even during the violence stimulated by the fascist Blackshirt movement in the 1930s, the civil power coped unaided.

The hazards of MACP taken to extremes were highlighted during the post-war years not by events in Great Britain itself, but by the Amritsar massacre in India on 13 April 1919.[12] Following an outbreak of anti-British agitation in the Punjab, General Dyer, military commander in the city of Amritsar, ordered his troops to fire without warning on a prohibited meeting of between ten and twenty thousand people. The crowd was neither hostile nor armed. 1,650 rounds were fired over a period of ten minutes, leaving 379 Indians killed and over 1,200 wounded. The incident had profound political effects in India: public opinion was outraged and it provided the mainspring for Gandhi's non-cooperation campaign. Dyer, however, was commended by his military superiors for his 'strong' measures and in Britain there was considerable approval for his stated objective of teaching a 'moral lesson' to the whole of the Punjab. Dyer was censured by an official enquiry and condemned by the government for applying what Winston Churchill, then Secretary for

War, described as a 'doctrine of frightfulness' (131 H.C. Deb., 5s, cols. 1705-1820). The general had, after all, broken the first rule of MACP: that the minimum amount of force only should be used. The cabinet wanted to dismiss Dyer, but they were strongly opposed by the Army Council who rather approved of his conduct. The general had certainly applied an unequivocally military cure to an epidemic of civil disorder - indeed the immediate effect of the massacre was to stamp out unrest in the Punjab - and the Army Council felt that the civil authorities, having abdicated their responsibilities to Dyer, should stand by his actions. The cabinet view prevailed. Although Dyer was not actually dismissed, he was placed compulsorily on the 'retired list'. The whole affair left opinion sharply divided in Britain. On the one hand, liberals believed that it epitomised the crudity and ruthlessness of MACP. On the other, conservative opinion - widely held among soldiers - was left with the impression that an officer who decided to take resolute action may very well be sacrificed under political pressure.

The Dyer case illustrates an aspect of continuing importance in the use of MACP: the problem of civil control. In a democracy it is generally accepted that the civil power has final authority over the military. In Britain this is secured by the annual approval of Parliament for the maintenance of a standing army. But when the army is called in actively to support the government, both the responsibility and, perhaps more significantly, the initiative for action may shift away from civilians to soldiers themselves. Between the extremes of, for example, troops assisting the police on a 'once and for all' basis, meeting just one particular disturbance, and the full introduction of martial law and military rule, there are a number of stages during which the precise distribution of civil and military power is not at all clear. It is customary in Britain, although not established by statute, for the army to accept the political direction of the civil government as to the circumstances in which they are to use force (de Smith, 1977, chs. 8 and 23; Evelegh, 1978, ch. 1 argues that the civil authority has no right to direct the military use of force). But occasions may arise during emergencies when individual officers may have to act without reference to the civil authority. There is also the possibility of soldiers, who share the common law obligation of every citizen to keep the peace, disagreeing with the civil government's assessment of how force should be applied. Although in a British context the likelihood of the army actually disobeying civil orders is remote, it has not been entirely absent from British political life. The Curragh incident in March 1914, when a number of officers, who had been given the option to resign, did so rather than accept orders which they thought were aimed at coercing Ulster Unionists into a united Ireland, suggests that the principle of civil supremacy might not be absolute (the best account is Fergusson, 1964). This principle presupposes not only an attitude on the part of the army that it is simply an 'instrument' of the civil administration, but also an acceptance of 'government by consensus', which depends upon a relatively high level of trust existing between governing politicians of whatever party, the permanent executive of the state, including the army, and the citizens themselves. Widespread civil disorder may stem from an erosion of trust between a section of the community and the government. It may also strain the mutual confidence of government and army. This is demonstrated by the breakdown in relations between the Liberal prime minister, Lloyd George, and the professional head of the army from 1918 and 1922, Sir Henry Wilson. Wilson was outraged by Lloyd George's reluctance to take strong coercive measures both against what he regarded as 'overmighty' trade unions in Britain, and also, especially, nationalist rebels in Ireland. So upset was Wilson that he refused even to speak to the prime minister from July 1921 until his retirement from the War Office in February 1922 (for a description of the problems Wilson faced, and the relations between him and Lloyd George, see Jeffery, 1977). Wilson was not the only soldier discomforted by Lloyd George. In April 1921, when it seemed civil unrest might arise out of a trade dispute in the coal industry, Lloyd George attempted to remove the general-officer-commanding the London district, General Jeffreys, on the grounds that he was 'lacking the judgment, the calm and the common sense especially needful for such a position'. During a private interview with the prime minister, the general had enquired 'as to whether our officers would be supported in any action they might think it necessary to take, as they had not forgotten the Dyer case'. This was too much for Lloyd George, who was appalled that Jeffreys should consider Dyer's actions and keeping order in London as in any way comparable. 'Premature and unwise action', he wrote later, 'by a light-headed officer with great notions of showing himself to be a strong man may well precipitate a terrible catastrophe'. In the end Jeffreys was not replaced, but a 'steadier' general was temporarily brought in over him.[13]

The use of troops to keep order during industrial unrest raises the possibility that the army might be employed explicitly as an instrument of class conflict. The British officer corps throughout much of this century has demonstrated a striking degree of social exclusiveness. Although in recent years its social base has widened somewhat, it is still principally drawn from the middle and upper classes - what might be termed the 'ruling classes' (for statistical data, see Otley, 1968). It is undoubtedly true that a majority of army officers hold right-wing social and political opinions, but the extent to which these attitudes, except in a very general way, have found expression using MACP is less certain. The War Office seems to have taken into account the inherent conservatism of the officer corps, when in the early 1920s, it issued instructions for intelligence officers performing duties in aid of the civil power. It emphasised that the army took no part in any industrial dispute and that its function was simply to assist in 'disarming all who advocate, prepare or practise violence against law and order, no matter whether they are acting against the Crown Forces or whether they resort to excess of violence in support of the Crown Forces'. Regarding trade unions, it was noted that they had a 'definite, legal, valuable and responsible position in the country' and that the army should not approach them 'as though their existence was illegal or even antagonistic to the national welfare'. 'Intelligence officers', it added, 'must beware of prying into bona-fide Trade Union organisation work and membership, as though they were exploring a conspiracy'.[14] The Manual of Military Law (1929, p. 248) took a similarly 'mechanistic' line on the problem of peacekeeping. The merits or demerits of industrial disputes or unrest, it read, are 'of no concern whatsoever to soldiers, who are solely concerned with the duty and obligation common to all citizens of assisting the civil authority in the maintenance of law and order'.

As for the rank and file, predominantly drawn from the working class, there is little to indicate that they were politicised to any great extent. The available evidence suggests that private soldiers have regarded attempts to excite their class loyalties largely with indifference. In 1912 Keir Hardie, the veteran Labour MP, attempted to amend the Army (Annual) Act so as to make it clear to soldiers when they entered the army that they were not only called upon to defend the United Kingdom but also 'expected to turn out to shoot down strikers if called upon to do so'. This was dismissed by parliament, in the Secretary of War's words, as 'a fantastic proposal' (36 H.C. Deb., 5s, cols. 1305-1338). The same year Tom Mann and four other men were imprisoned for calling upon soldiers not to act against strikers. There were a number of similar cases between the wars (see Young, 1976) and in 1934 parliament passed the Incitement to Disaffection Act, which made it a specific offence 'to endeavour to seduce a member of the forces from his duty or allegiance to the Crown'. The Act applies equally to pacifists as to left-wing activists (de Smith, 1977, p. 470).

Fear of 'revolutionary' unrest within the army early in 1919 prompted the War Office to circulate a questionnaire to the commanding officers of all military units in the United Kingdom to assess the political attitude of their troops. Officers were asked to investigate whether the troops were affected by internal or external agitation, whether they would 'respond to orders for assistance to preserve the public peace' and whether they would 'assist in strike breaking'. The replies indicated that troops could be relied upon to assist the civil power, but the question of strike breaking was more sensitive and commanders believed that it would not be fair to ask troops to do 'black-leg' work (116 H.C. Deb., 5s, cols. 1469-70, 1514-5). The following autumn, when Lloyd George enquired if the army was 'sound', Sir Henry Wilson assured him that it was.[15] The only explicit unrest in the post-war period came not from the regular forces but from the service reserves who were mobilised as part of the government's emergency preparations in the spring of 1921. Many reservists were clearly upset at being embodied to meet unrealised disorder. The most serious incident occurred in a naval reserve battalion, where the men declared that nearly all of them were trade unionists and 'would lay down their arms if called to use them upon their fellow workmen'.[16] On the other hand, an army battalion of Yorkshire miners who had been called up appeared to see 'the funny side of striking and then being called back to the Army to keep order if necessary' (Russell, 1959, p. 76). In one instance fears of military disaffection bordered on the ridiculous. During the General Strike a right-wing employers' organisation reported that the 'Strike Committee' in Newcastle upon Tyne was 'endeavouring to seduce the troops from loyalty to their oath by the subtle means of arranging sports between the soldiers and workers'.[17] Between the wars, however, Sir Henry Wilson was confirmed in his opinion of the army's 'soundness'. Both the War Office in 1919 and political activists throughout the period seem to have underestimated the corporate power and professional discipline of the military.

Ireland demonstrates particular problems of loyalty, resulting not from class affiliations but national sentiment. Within the United Kingdom official opinion, with some reason, has always regarded communal conflict as a more serious threat to military reliability than class conflict. The Curragh incident in 1914 has already been noted. In 1919-21, when the army was extensively committed to assisting the civil power in Ireland, the government specifically decided that regiments recruited in Ireland should not be employed there. Even so there was some unrest among Irish units. A battalion of the Connaught Rangers stationed in India mutinied, apparently 'in sympathy with their country', and declared that they would 'work no more until English troops were withdrawn from Ireland'.[18] The Anglo-Irish war unsettled other regiments too and in November 1921 a sergeant of the Irish guards was discovered to have smuggled two machine guns out of his barracks to Irish nationalists.[19] In the spring of 1920 a senior general refused to accept the post of Chief of Police in Ireland on the grounds that he was an Irish Catholic and it would be distasteful to him to do any work in Ireland 'which was not of a purely military character'.[20] It is an interesting illustration of the perceived relative functions of police and army.

MACP in the United Kingdom has been most frequently applied in Ireland. In policing terms Ireland differs from Great Britain. The Royal Irish Constabulary, for example, was more akin to the Roman law mode of policing than the common law one. It was a para-military force, armed and centrally organized. But the responsibility of the army to assist the civil power when necessary has never been any different in Ireland than in other parts of the United Kingdom. The political constraints regarding the employment of troops are also similar. Between

1919 and 1921 the British government went to great lengths to avoid imposing explicit military control in Ireland. As A.J. Balfour remarked when the use of troops was being discussed in July 1920, 'the Dyer debate has not helped us to govern by soldiers' (Jones, 1971, p. 33). The cabinet were faced with the problem that military 'repression' was not only unpalatable to British public opinion, but it might also, paradoxically, encourage the Irish nationalist guerrillas themselves, whose aims included undermining the British civil administration in Ireland to the point of collapse. At first the government concentrated simply on reinforcing the Irish police. British ex-servicemen (who became known as 'Black and Tans') were recruited into the constabulary and also into the specially-created Auxiliary Division, which formed a 'half-way house' between more conventional police methods and martial law. The Black and Tans, however, failed satisfactorily to fulfil this requirement and the army perforce had to retain their irksome semi-military, semi-police, role. Between December 1920 and the Irish truce of July 1921 martial law was applied, but only over parts of southern and western Ireland - again an index of the government's reluctance to enforce a full-scale military solution. In the end the British cabinet, their martial <u>via media</u> having failed, chose the arguably more effective solution of a complete military and political withdrawal from southern Ireland. The establishment of a Special Constabulary in the newly-created Northern Ireland, however, was to relieve the army of many of its duties there for almost fifty years (there is an excellent account of the Anglo-Irish war in Townshend, 1975).

The involvement of the army in Ireland during the Easter Rising of 1916 and in 1919-21 was in the nature of suppressing open insurrection and, in the later years, guerrilla war. The suppression of riots - a more likely contingency in Great Britain - hardly applied during this period. Before 1914, however, the army had assumed riot control duties frequently enough for the Irish Command to issue a special pamphlet containing tactical instructions for keeping the peace. It covered the two techniques adopted by the British army: the demonstration of <u>potential</u> force and the employment of <u>actual</u> force. The former included the use of military patrols, with the aim not only of apprehending criminals, but also of striking 'a terror in the locality, so as to prevent crime being perpetrated'. The latter dealt particularly with the use of firearms. It emphasised that commanders acted entirely on their own responsibility. If they decided to open fire, they were instructed to 'exercise a humane discretion in deciding both the number of rounds and the object to be aimed at'. Before firing, officers were to make it clear that fire would be 'effective' and it was specifically laid down that under no circumstances should blank ammunition be used.[21] This stipulation was repeated in a similar set of instructions issued by the War Office in 1923 which additionally forbade firing over the heads of a crowd on the grounds that 'it spares the most guilty at the expense of the possibly innocent'.[22]

The question of the degree of force to be applied still remains a crucial problem of MACP. Although armies must clearly plan for the contingency of firearms being used, the preferred technique in Britain is to demonstrate the potential force which can, if necessary, be employed - not so much the 'whiff of grapeshot' as depending upon the moral effect of troops appearing in the streets at all. During a general strike in Glasgow early in 1919, troops occupied the city centre and set up machine-gun posts in the City Chambers. During labour disputes in 1920 and 1921, Sir Henry Wilson ostentatiously moved units, including tanks, into industrial areas. But the most dramatic use of this technique occurred during the General Strike. When the government wished to open the strike-bound docks in London's East End and release food supplies for the capital, the military commander first marched a battalion of guards, 'with drums beating', through the East End to occupy the docks. During the succeeding night he moved four more Guards' battalions to a temporary camp in a local park. 'The inhabitants woke up ... to find a large military camp in being in their midst', recorded the officer. 'There is no doubt that the sudden arrival of so large a force ... had a profound effect'. The advance of military technology added to the available resources. Throughout the General Strike it was found that the use of tanks and armoured cars in militant districts suitably impressed the local population.[23]

But the potential force technique has its drawbacks. The movement or sudden appearance of troops may in itself be provocative and, far from quelling passions, may inflame them. Soldiers are well aware of this. In 1919 Sir Douglas Haig, Commander-in-Chief, Home Forces, directed that troops should be kept concealed as long as possible and should only appear when the civil authorities required their help. 'As soon as the necessity for action was over', he added, 'the troops must at once be withdrawn out of sight'.[24] The War Office took an equally cautious view when in 1927 it outlined the circumstances under which the army might be employed to keep order. Troops should be marshalled in formed bodies 'and there should be a screen of police between them and the civil populace until the military are required to act'.[25] Underlying this War Office opinion was the continuing military belief in the 'primacy of the police' and a deep-rooted aversion to duties in aid of the civil power. It was written, moreover, in the light of experience arising from the General Strike. Although the government had feared the worst, mobilising the army and recruiting more than 200,000 Special Constables, the strike passed off relatively peacefully. The threat of revolution was exposed as a chimera. With the exception of London's dockland, the police by and large managed to cope without recourse to military assistance.

The comparative peaceableness of the General Strike was attributed by one staff officer to 'the sound commonsense of the average citizen and the absence of bitterness, rather than the correct application of the use of force'.[26] His opinion was that, in military terms, the government had over-reacted. But his assessment also indicates an enduring feature of MACP: its incidence to a very great extent depends, not on military action, but political circumstances. Without taking into account the prevailing political culture, any examination of MACP must necessarily be somewhat 'two-dimensional'. The means by which military force is employed are less important than the original decision to deploy it. In the last resort the use of the military can question the legitimacy of the state itself. Tyrants may rule by the sword alone; democrats cannot. 'It will be a bad day for the Empire', wrote a senior general in 1919, 'if the Government of this country has to look to the bayonets of its troops for its support'.[27]

NOTES

1. In Britain three circumstances are recognised when troops may assist the civil government: (1) Military Aid to the Civil Power (MACP), when the police cannot cope with civil disorder such as riots or armed terrorism; (2) Military Aid to the Civil Community (MACC), when the army assists in civil re-

lief measures during natural disasters such as hurricanes or flooding; (3) Military Aid to the Civil Ministries (MACM), when troops are employed to maintain essential services during industrial disputes.

2. Troops have been actively engaged in MACP during the Glasgow general strike, Liverpool police strike, national railway strike (1919); coal stoppages (1920 and 1921); the General Strike (1926); and at the siege of the Iranian Embassy in London (1980). Guards battalions in London were also put on alert, but not used, during the 'Hunger Marches' of the 1930s, plain clothes units of the Special Air Service Regiment and the Royal Military Police have undertaken patrols against IRA bombings in Britain in the 1970s and in 1974 there were four joint police/military 'exercises' at Heathrow Airport, London. In Northern Ireland troops have been used on riot duties in 1932, 1935 and 1947. They were also put on alert during the 1956-62 IRA campaign.

3. One may describe the British as playing a species of 'constitutional cricket', governed not only with written rules, but also many unwritten conventions of 'fair play' and the 'done thing'. Problems arise (to extend the metaphor) when unruly Irishmen attempt to play hurling on the same pitch.

4. 18 August 1911, Opinion of Law Officers, Manual of Military Law 1929, London, HMSO, 1940 printing, p. 269.

5. 10 November 1918, Diary of Sir Henry Wilson, Wilson MSS., Imperial War Museum, London.

6. 2 September 1919, Diary of Sir Douglas Haig, Haig MSS., National Library of Scotland, Acc. 3155, no. 2; 17 October 1919, CinC, Great Britain, to War Office, Public Record Office, London (PRO), W.O. 32/5467 no. 1A.

7. 26 August, 15 September 1920, Wilson diary.

8. 3 and 5 October 1919, Government strike and protection committee meetings, PRO CAB 27/60 & 27/61 S.C. 135.

9. A War Book for the War Office (1927), pp. 64-5, PRO W.O. 33/1147; 28 April 1921, parliamentary answer, 141 H.C. Deb. 5s., col. 371.

10. 3 August 1921, memo. by the Secretary for War, PRO CAB 24/126 C.P. 3189.

11. 5 November 1926, minute by the Adjutant-General, PRO W.O. 32/3456 no. 5A.

12. The best summary of Amritsar from a military standpoint is Sir C.W. Gwynn (1939) Imperial Policing, London, Macmillan, 2nd edn., pp. 34-64. See also the official Hunter Committee Report, London, HMSO, 1920 cmd. 681.

13. 6 April 1921, Wilson diary; Lloyd George to Secretary for War, Lloyd George MSS, House of Lords Record Office, F/16/3/16.
14. 11 June 1921, Notes on the intelligence organisation for emergency home defence, appendix, PRO W.O. 32/5314 no. 23A, appendix A, annex. no. 2.
15. 15 September 1920, Wilson diary.
16. The men also complained about their sub-standard temporary billets. Papers relating to this incident are in the Kennedy MSS (privately held). I am grateful to Dr A. Clayton of the Royal Military Academy, Sandhurst, for this reference.
17. 'Central Council of Economic Leagues Strike Bulletin', no. 3, 6 May 1926, Baldwin MSS, Cambridge Univ. Library, vol. 22f. 28.
18. 18 November 1920, Summary of Connaught Rangers' Mutiny, June-July 1920, India Office Records, London, L/MIL/7/13314. Published accounts of the mutiny are included in Sam Pollock (1969) Mutiny for the Cause, London, Leo Cooper; T.P. Kilfeather (1960) The Connaught Rangers, Tralee, Anvil Books; and H.F.N. Jourdain and M. Fraser (1924) The Connaught Rangers vol. I, London, Royal United Services Institution.
19. Weekly report on UK revolutionary organizations, 24 November 1921, PRO CAB 24/131 C.P. 3500. For examples of unrest in other Irish regiments see 5 August 1920, Sir Henry Wilson to Lord Curzon, Wilson MSS 20B/7 (Royal Irish Regiment), and Sir Charles Bonham-Carter typescript autobiography, ch. 10, Bonham-Carter MSS, Churchill College, Cambridge, BHCT 9/2 (Royal Dublin Fusiliers).
20. 13 May 1920, Churchill to Lord Stamfordham, in Martin Gilbert (1977) Winston S. Churchill vol. IV, companion part 2, London, Heinemann, p. 1096.
21. Orders for the Guidance of Troops in Affording Aid to the Civil Power in Ireland, Dublin, HMSO, 1914.
22. Duties in Aid of the Civil Power, London, War Office, 1923.
23. London District report on the General Strike, 18 November 1926, PRO W.O. 32/3455 no. 1A.
24. 2 September 1919, Haig diary.
25. 30 July 1927, War Office to Home Office, PRO W.O. 32/3456 no. 26A.
26. 28 January 1927, Memo by Col. Dobbie, PRO W.O. 32/3513 no. 26A.
27. 13 October 1919, minute by Adjutant-General, PRO W.O. 32/5611 no. 12.

REFERENCES

Benewick, R. & Smith, T. (eds.) (1972) <u>Direct Action and Democratic Politics</u>, London, Allen & Unwin
Blake, J. (1979) 'Civil Disorder in Britain 1910-39: the Role of Civil Government and Military Authority' (unpub. D.Phil. Univ. of Sussex)
Bowden, T. (1978) <u>Beyond the Limits of the Law</u>, Harmondsworth, Penguin
Bunyan, T. (1977) <u>The Political Police in Britain</u>, London, Quartet
Chapman, B. (1971) <u>Police State</u>, London, Macmillan
Churchill, R. (1967) <u>Winston S. Churchill</u>, vol. II, London, Heinemann
Crick, B. (1964) 'This Peaceable Kingdom', 173 <u>Twentieth Century</u> 51
Critchley, T.A. (1967) <u>A History of Police in England and Wales, 1900-1966</u>, London, Constable
_____ (1980) <u>The Conquest of Violence: Order and Liberty in Britain</u>, London, Constable
de Smith, S.A. (1977) <u>Constitutional and Administrative Law</u>, 3rd edn., Harmondsworth, Penguin
Evelegh, R. (1978) <u>Peacekeeping in a Democratic Society</u>, London, Hurst
Fergusson, Sir J. (1964) <u>The Curragh Incident</u>, London, Faber & Faber
Jeffery, K. (1977) 'Sir Henry Wilson and the defence of the British empire, 1918-22', V <u>Journal of Imperial and Commonwealth History</u> 270-93
_____ (1978) 'The Military Defence of the British Empire, 1918-22' (unpub. Ph.D. Univ. of Cambridge)
_____ & Hennessy, P. (1983) <u>States of Emergency</u>, London, Routledge & Kegan Paul
Jones, T. (1971) <u>Whitehall Diary</u>, vol. III, Oxford University Press
McCardle, D. (1968) <u>The Irish Republic</u>, London, Corgi Books
Otley, C.B. (1968) 'Militarism and the social affiliations of the British army elite', in J. Van Doorn (ed.) <u>Armed Forces and Society</u>, The Hague, Mouton, pp. 84-108
Report of the Select Committee on the Employment of Military in Cases of Disturbance, 16 July 1908 (1908) <u>H.C. Parl. Papers</u> vii
Russell, Lord (1959) <u>That Reminds Me</u>, London, Cassell
Townshend, C.J.N. (1975) <u>The British Campaign in Ireland 1919-21</u>, Oxford University Press
Young, T. (1976) <u>Incitement to Dissaffection</u>, London, Cobden Trust

Chapter Three

THE PLACE OF THE BRITISH ARMY IN PUBLIC ORDER

Sir Edwin Bramall

The British Army has acquired over the years and still has to sustain a wide variety of roles and in 1979, immediately before the Christmas holiday, you saw British soldiers in their inimitably calm, optimistic and uncomplaining way leave the country for Rhodesia in what could be a most hazardous mission trying to maintain the ceasefire and ensure proper elections. Indeed if we pull it off, it will have been due to no little extent to the nerve, sang froid and immaculate professionalism of those few regular soldiers in the bush.
    Of course first and foremost the British Army (together with the other two Armed Forces) is required as a show of confidence and commitment to collective security: an indication that we take the defence of Europe seriously; and this we help to achieve by actually deploying in Western Europe as a credible, flexible deterrent and balance against those who might seek to gain unjustified power, influence and leverage from the mere possession of large military forces. With our inevitable restriction on resources, we are not able to boast that we can 'slug it out' with a numerically superior enemy over an indefinite period and win a clear-cut victory but we do, within the NATO framework, offer the unmistakable option that aggression into the NATO area, however small or large, would mean hard conventional battling with us for a significant period, and that this in turn would lead to a nuclear release as escalation in some shape or form, which one presumes no-one seeks. Thus <u>preventing</u> war is our primary aim, although to do so and deter effectively we have clearly got to be ready to fight within the terms I have mentioned; and we have other commitments too, outside Europe, in areas where we still have responsibilities such as Hong Kong where

literally thousands of immigrants are trying to enter illegally; Cyprus, where amongst other things we contribute to UN peacekeeping forces; Belize where we stand ready to repel any invasion from Guatemala; and Gibraltar - all therefore with their special problems.

But the subject I have chosen covers a different area - an area where hopefully in Great Britain (as distinct from Northern Ireland) the Army would not be needed; that is in the field of public order. And I have chosen the subject not to sensationalise or alarm but indeed the reverse, to reassure and put into perspective.

I say hopefully never be needed because, although the Armed Forces may indeed be considered the ultimate means of upholding Parliamentary authority which any Government, however democratic, must have in the background as an insurance against internal as well as external threats (thus justifying the proper explanation of this subject) it would, in a society like ours, be totally inappropriate to use them in a main public order role, unless disorder was occurring on such a scale that the police could not cope and our whole parliamentary system was threatened or a minority, by violent means and armed force, was attempting to challenge the very authority of Government with a view to changing or overthrowing it.

As long as Democracy as we understand it is allowed to work - and I suppose democracy means in those terms the freedom and flexibility to make gradual changes within a prescribed rule of law; and the manifestations of this are happening - the Queen opening her freely elected Parliament which puts its record and performance and programme for the people to decide every so many years, thus making consensus government possible; and justice being administered impartially by an independent judiciary; as long as all that is being allowed to work, then the only proper people to keep law and order are the Police, who are designed for, suited to (or always have been), constitutionally raised for and, most importantly publicly recognised as, the proper agents for dealing with citizens who are a threat to or are breaking the law, whether as individuals, or members of a crowd; demonstration picket or whatever; and the Armed Forces' only function in this context, is a peripheral one for which their training and equipment may be better suited, such as deterrent to a special sort of terrorism, perhaps in handling violent confrontations with heavily armed hijackers or terrorists; in natural disasters; and of course providing the specialist services and equipment which would be helpful to the police. We seek no other role, which is why our relations with the police are so close and cordial and indeed have never been better, with each respecting the other and knowing where the line of demarcation lies.

But if I left it at that, you might think I was 'begging' the question, and sheltering behind an over-simplistic and too naive an answer. Government by consent can break down; violent demonstrations can border on urban terrorism and insurgency; and police forces can get overwhelmed and exhausted if demonstrations and marches become too violent, widespread and prolonged; and the unhappy events in Northern Ireland since 1969, during which the Army has borne a large part of the burden and suffered considerable casualties, illuminates only too well this progression; here however I must point out that comparison between Northern Ireland and Great Britain can be, and will I hope remain, highly dangerous and misleading.

For in Northern Ireland, <u>unlike</u> Great Britain, consensus government at the Provincial level does not exist because one third of the Province is religiously and culturally divided from the other two thirds, leading to quite distinct political aspirations which are difficult to reconcile within one political system. Then, some sections of the population in Northern Ireland have so far failed to give any support to the police as the impartial legitimate force for law and order. And furthermore in Northern Ireland, <u>unlike</u> Great Britain, there is operating an armed and experienced terrorist organisation dedicated to a confrontation with the administration and to the achievement of political change as to who governs the country through violence - a direct challenge therefore not merely to policies but to the very authority of Government itself.

Such conditions and only such conditions are what forced the Government to deploy the Army in Northern Ireland in the public order role 10 years ago. It is these things which have made it necessary for the Army to act in a police role in some areas where disorderly crowds were too large or too violent and the very fabric of law and order was at risk. This made it essential, if terrorism was to be rooted out, for the Army to assist the police in establishing an infrastructure for the gathering, collation and analysis of intelligence leading to the arrest and subsequent conviction of terrorists in the Courts. This latter of course is best done by the police anyway; and I am glad to say that despite the periodic IRA spectaculars, the number of abnormal areas in Northern Ireland where the Army's assistance is still needed in this way is shrinking.

That then is Northern Ireland where police resources have had to be husbanded, where troops have often been used instead of police to deal with rioting, and where the Army has had to develop its own framework operations, overt and covert, to assist the police in bringing terrorists to justice.

The rule of law still applies, but the special circumstances I have mentioned are happily very different from those that we can expect here for the foreseeable future. But even so I think that you are entitled to a rather more detailed look at the various problems which could confront us over military aid to the civil powers and public order law, in Great Britain, set in some sort of historical perspective.

There are of course a number of ways that the Armed Forces, quite properly and legally, can, and not infrequently have, given aid to the Civil authorities. For example under Section 2 of the Emergency Powers Act of 1964, which allows the Defence Council to authorise the use of the Forces on - and I quote 'urgent work of National importance' and specifically 'on the alleviation of distress, safeguarding of life and property following a disaster, and the maintenance of essential supplies and services' - always providing that this assistance has been asked for by the appropriate civil authority, and that Ministerial approval has been given.

And under these general headings we have experienced such military involvement as the Aberfan tip disaster, the Glasgow Fire Brigade strike of 1973, that same City's dustmen's strike in 1975, and the major firefighting emergency of the winter of 1977/78 which involved some 20,000 servicemen and women.

Once the request for military assistance has been made, Ministers have to take into account certain things before deciding whether the Services should be used. First, whether they can offer the necessary skills (once brought in, after all, they must succeed); and since the Services have no special training for industrial intervention, these will be mostly the general military skills, with a lot of technical activities falling outside their competence and ken. And secondly, and most important, the Government must consider the question of public acceptability; and by public acceptability I do not only mean Union sensitivity, although this is clearly a factor, but the goodwill and support (or lack of it) of the public at large. It was these two factors that made, I believe, all the difference between the first and the second Protestant strike in Northern Ireland in the aftermath of the initiative on Power Sharing.

In the first there was increasingly widespread support for the strike and the troops did not have the expertise to sustain unaided the entire main services. In the second there was far less public support for the strikers. The police dealt firmly with intimidation and the military were able to make a useful contribution by intervention in support of the police only - by doing peripheral jobs, and of course by providing protection for those still at work in the key areas.

Just now, I quoted four instances of the use of the Armed Forces to aid the civil authorities. In the first, at Aberfan, lack of initial public acceptability, because of local prejudice going back over 50 years to an incident at Tonypandy, or more precisely Llanelli, delayed the local authorities asking for what would have been valuable military assistance; but in Glasgow, particularly for its fire brigade strike, the conditions were different and just right.

It was the first ever fire brigade strike in the United Kingdom. It had been condemned by the TUC and the Scottish TUC. There was little support outside; the most important of all, 60 officers remained on duty and the strikers announced that their pickets would not harass either their officers nor those of other fire brigades nor the troops (nor did they).

And on the Services' side, there was ample warning to prepare and gather together the equipment, and there was also proper Service expertise, particularly in the Royal Navy and the Royal Air Force.

The result was that 70 to 80 calls a day were coped with over a 10-day period; and it all ended in something approaching euphoria, with special letters of thanks and free beer all round.

And the more recent firemen's strike, although obviously a great deal larger, followed something of the same pattern. Once it seemed inevitable that the strike would go ahead, the Armed Forces, working through the Army machinery, were given a clear mandate to provide a nationwide fire service from the start of the strike, and this I believe we did, with increasing skill, for nearly nine weeks, coping with an average of 600 calls a day.

It was a not inconsiderable task, but we were helped enormously by the co-operation of County Fire Executives, Chief Constables, Chief Fire Officers and those fire officers who remained on duty, and indeed the whole operation was invaluable in giving us experience of this kind of joint operation. Here too, there was, from the start, public acceptance of the use of the Armed Forces in this way, and indeed from the firemen themselves, so that there were virtually no problems with pickets.

Of course, we could, if asked for, go in and do a job of this sort quite legally, whatever the public view (that would be up to the Government), but acceptability is very important. If there was none, the scope for escalation in severity and geography would be considerable. There would also be a practical danger that if use of the Armed Forces became common in strikes, enjoying Union and substantial public support, and the picketing got rough and the police got into difficulties, soldiers, who would be unarmed, could become victims.

Now none of these uses, MAC(C) and MAC(M) as they are known in the trade, should provide much problem. The greater the degree of acceptability, the smoother will be their passage; but by and large if the national need was there and they can be seen to be serving the community, the general public would I believe approve. But none of them has anything to do directly with public order. The troops are, as I say, unarmed; and would avoid physical contact and arguments with pickets; and should there be violence they would be in the same position as other workers trying to work, with their protection largely in the hands of the police.

If the Armed Forces were ever to be needed for public order - MAC(P), i.e. for dealing with law-breakers - then our legality would come both from that famous obligation under common law 'to come to the aid of the Civil Power when so required', and from the Criminal Law Act 1967 (Section 3) which required, that in so doing, the use of no more force than is reasonable and necessary. I shall return to this later.

In such circumstances the person responsible for maintaining order, and asking for such assistance if he felt unable to do so, would be the appropriate Chief Constable. Although in the Metropolis the special relationship between the Commissioner and the Home Secretary would be bound to mean the Government would to some extent be involved. Indeed you might question whether, if widespread insurgency were to break out, you could deal organisationally in the same way as you would with routine law and order, and whether it would be necessary to have some co-ordinating police authority. But all this is hypothetical. Initially it is the Chief Constable who is responsible, and the police who would be in overall charge. In any precautionary operations they might even specify what tasks the military were to undertake and the military would take their authority, say in stopping cars, from the police. But in a real breakdown of order the police would only say what they were unable to do which was nonetheless essential for the maintenance of public order, and, once called in, command would then devolve to the military commanding officer. And the tactical deployment and exact action to be taken, including whether to open fire and with what, would be for him to decide against the background principle of minimum, or more accurately, reasonable force and he would have to justify his action against that principle.

To make it easier particularly for a small party or individual to make a reasonable force decision, which is not always easy, troops under such conditions are normally issued with routine instructions or a coloured card to give guidance under what circumstances it would be permissible or wrong to open fire. This, of course, is only a guide and has no force of law behind it, rather like the Highway Code.

It is, of course, interesting to speculate that if a soldier refused to help the police when asked, he could, hypothetically at any rate, be proceeded against by the police.

Now, what roles in public order have I in mind? Well, basically and initially the peripheral ones which I touched on at the beginning - the background services, such as helicopters, bomb disposal, special lighting, night vision, which would help the police get on with the job. And then, at the other end of the spectrum, the sporadic armed terrorist attacks or hijacking which are international or eccentric in character and certainly out of the blue. We have had recent examples of these at Lod Airport, the Olympic village, the Scheveningen Prison, and Mogadishu; and it is at such times as these, that upholders of the law may need special skills and equipment over and above those appropriate to the police, if the outcome is to be concluded with the least possible loss of life. But the need has not occurred yet in Great Britain, at least not in a way which cannot be handled perfectly adequately by the police; although Sir Robert Mark did consider that the impression given to the Provisional IRA at Balcombe Street, that the Special Air Service (SAS) were about to be used against them, was instrumental in their early surrender. So our studies in this field are purely precautionary, as at Heathrow Airport, where quite frequently we deploy round the airfield, in conjunction with and under the auspices of the police, to deter those who may have in mind the destruction of aircraft landing or taking off; and also in the earmarking of specially trained and equipped detachments of the SAS for use in the event of attempts to hijack aircraft or threaten airport terminals, embassies and the like, and they are very well prepared to do this.

Strangely enough, although the men working with bomb and gun for political or eccentric ends have always been with us, the British Army in Great Britain (Northern Ireland and Colonial situations have of course been quite different) has practically never been used against them, and I can think of only two incidents, and neither could have been said to have been carried out as effectively and expeditiously as the public had a right to expect.

The first occurred in May 1838 at a place called Bossenden Farm, near Canterbury, where a schizophrenic Cornishman called Sir William Courtney, proclaiming himself the Messiah, had killed a policeman and chased another away with a sword, the Magistrates called out the Army, who went into an assault and killed Courtney and eight of his men but only at the cost of 10 military casualties, six of them fatal.

The other was in June 1911 in what is generally known as The Battle of Sydney Street (Whitechapel not Chelsea), when two members of a Latvian anarchist gang were cornered there by the police. When called upon to surrender they opened fire. Now on the security side there were assembled 750 police under the Commissioner of the City Police, the Head of the CID, Head of the Political Section of Scotland Yard (Special Branch), Lord Knutsford (Colonial Secretary, I think), a Maxim gun from the Tower of

London, and Winston Churchill and 2 NCOs and 17 guardsmen of the Scots Guards. It all led to a bit of a spectator spectacle. In due course the house the terrorists were in caught fire; the fire brigade were instructed, or so it was said, not to go in and the anarchists were suffocated.

Now in both these somewhat bizarre cases, consciences were shocked; there were repercussions in Parliament and the Government of the day got a bad press, which proves that acceptability is still important and that you have got to do the job well and economically if you are not going to have a rumpus. And we are today, as I said, much, much better geared for this sort of thing than we were in 1838 and 1911.

So, although if hostages were involved there would be great public concern, the use of hand-picked military forces in these circumstances would, I think, be publicly acceptable, provided that it was clear that less risk was involved, and less likelihood of casualties if the Army was used, rather than the police; that Ministers authorised it and provided of course the operation was successful. If it was not, whoever did it, there would be criticism on the principle, on the tactics and on the state of training.

So far with the tasks I have outlined, we have not been unduly concerned that public acceptability would not be forthcoming, or that our democratic freedoms were threatened in any way by the use of the military. But we now come to a much more delicate and sensitive form of social breakdown: that is when the police might be in danger of losing control of public order whether due to demonstrations getting too violent (Red Lion Square); to mass picketing (Saltley Coke Depot) where the Chief Constable declined to act against hostile pickets because he didn't have the resources; to riots, or looting, for its own sake (Manchester United losing at home or away); or just everything going on too long and being too widespread.

Now this is still a totally different category from organised terrorism or insurgency as Northern Ireland has experienced, and here the authorities may one day find themselves in a dilemma. No one doubts that the best and most suitable way for our democratic society to deal with civil commotion, short of organised insurrection and an attempt to overthrow a consensus Government, is the traditional police method practised in Great Britain, which is totally different from that practised in Colonial situations, or methods sometimes used in Europe or in the USA; and since 1829 <u>our</u> police have been quietly, almost unnoticed, <u>going</u> about things in this way with great success. Of course, the reason is historical. When the Metropolitan Police were formed by Peel and Wellington, in part to deal with London mobs, they were modelled (by a stroke of genius) not on the militia but on the ancient and local office of Constable and the fact that they wore top hats (which they did) actually emphasised that they in no way posed a threat; that in no way were they the <u>strong</u> arm of the law able to coerce; but were local and unarmed and worked through persuasion, relying on public support.

Now I suppose these traditional methods achieved their greatest triumph in October 1968 in Grosvenor Square after a protest march against the Vietnam War. Just before that, there had been that ugly precedent in Paris, when the 3rd Force or Gendarmerie had dealt violently with a violent demonstration. There was much apprehension. <u>The Times</u> predicted revolution and offices and shops were boarded up. 50,000 turned out to march from Charing Cross to Marble Arch, during the course of which 5,000 broke away to invade the American Embassy in Grosvenor Square. Although they expected acid and shot-guns, the police, backed by mounted police, linked arms to meet them. They got, for their pains, park benches, pickets' banner poles, marbles, pepper, red paint, flints and sharpened pennies, but their techniques worked and the line held, and it ended almost in a carnival atmosphere with the police and demonstrators singing Auld Lang Syne - long may it continue. The Army, with all its discipline and restraint, could never have achieved that, and would be bound to have produced an aggravation of the situation then and in its aftermath.

But it took, I should remind you, 9,000 police, which is greater than the highest operational strength the British Army has ever been able to deploy in the whole of Northern Ireland, except in Operation Motorman in 1972. And how can you keep that up for any length of time and over what area? Although by then perhaps you might say that the Government would be losing consensus and ought to be changing its policy. But public order must be maintained, and if these methods fail we could get into an unfortunate escalating situation, and here, although we have never had to endure it and hopefully we never will, I think you would want me to look at the possibilities dispassionately and objectively. The first stage in the escalation, of dealing with violence, would undoubtedly be the need to issue the forces of law and order special protective clothing, shields, visors, helmets, etc., accompanied by some sort of definite anti-riot drills, such as the Army have developed when in a police role in the particular conditions of Northern Ireland.

The second and third stages, and these may be juxtapositioned depending on the circumstances, would cover first the employment of some sort of missile which will halt or bowl over an offender but which will not kill or wound - fire hoses as favoured by the Continent or rubber bullets favoured by the Army in Ireland. And then, subsequently or alternatively, some sort of incapacitating riot control agent which, for want of a better term, I will call tear gas. Finally, of course, as a fourth stage, there are available, if needed, normal military weapons, for use against those who have taken or are endangering the lives of others.

Now these first three stages represent the grey area met by other countries in various ways. In France by the Gendarmerie or CRS; in Italy by the Carabinieri; in the USA by the National Guard, and not infrequently by the 101st or 82nd Airborne Divisions; but in the past with us really by no one, because we have always avoided, so far, these particular types of confrontation although I suppose, in the Mosley riots in the '30s, the pitched battles in Whitechapel must have come fairly near this category. But the truth of the matter is no one is understandably very anxious to fill it. The Army because it can truthfully say that it is not their job: public support for them and acceptability would be doubtful and the effect on recruiting strains on loyalty and public regard could be serious. On the other hand, the police too must be anxious not to lose the 'bobby', Dixon of Dock Green, image or the public support on which their day to day police work depends, and therefore are not over anxious to incur the enmity and hostility that such a role inevitably attracts.

This then might be the dilemma. Do you dispense with the area of gradual and slow escalation and, as had happened in other countries, if you have to, go straight to the armed military, with the risk that inevitably people may be shot, or at least hurt, who have not been directly endangering the lives of others; or do you, as you have done in Ireland, and would <u>surely</u> have to do in Great Britain if the need ever arose, go for a slowly escalated and more selective use of force; and if so should the police or the Army handle it?

There are, of course, those who criticise gradualisation and say that in the long run it causes more misery and suffering and more casualties, and certainly these arguments would have some substance if one was entering an apparent period of widespread insurrection; but those who do oppose it must think the thing through, and must be entirely certain that 'a whiff of grape-shot' would do the trick and stop the whole thing stone dead. And in Ireland, and certainly in the society we live in in Great Britain, this would be highly doubtful, as well as, incidentally, as I will explain in a moment, probably illegal.

Indeed, if normal police methods and subtle police tactics and democratic processes, and public opinion and Government measures cannot contain the violence, within the scales that we have experienced and coped with up to now, then you could inevitably as I see it, be forced step by step into that grey area and hope that before you emerged from it at the top end, democratic commonsense would have prevailed. I still believe, however, that this grey area represents a police job and not a military one, even in Northern Ireland, where the military have had to do the police job temporarily because of the limited public acceptability of the Royal Ulster Constabulary - a state of affairs which I am glad to say is changing and anyhow as I hope I have made clear does not apply here. And I believe the police now recognise this.

And to put all this in perspective, perhaps it would help to look at the history of the direct use of the military to enforce public order in Great Britain. It goes back a long way and, even in the years before World War I, a year seldom went by without the military being called out in this role. However, <u>the very last time</u> was over 60 years ago in August Bank Holiday 1919. At that time pitched street battles were quite common in Liverpool on a Saturday night between Orangemen and Catholics; and on this particular Bank Holiday half the Liverpool police went out on strike. This was all too tempting for the mobs, and some very bad disorders occurred with the communities combined in looting; and this started up again on Sunday afternoon when the pubs had closed. What police were left were very rough with their truncheons and they then called in the Army. Elements of four battalions and a troop of tanks worked in close conjunction with the police, two rioters were shot and one of them, a gang leader, was killed. The victim's name was Howlett; he was the last person to be killed by soldiers on public order duties in Great Britain. To make the point still further, on Bank Holiday itself, HMS Valiant, carrying 8 x 15 inch guns, steamed up the Mersey. I need say no more, and I stress, it <u>was</u> the last public appearance of the Armed Forces in Great Britain in this role.

And what of the legal position of forces were they to be so employed? Well that is fairly clear. It is governed, as I have said, by the common law and the Criminal Law Act, and guidance to officers who have to act in these circumstances is set out in the Manual of Military Law.

This makes it quite clear that once their <u>men are on the spot</u>, and the need for action is imminent, the receipt or non-receipt of a request for action cannot absolve the Commander from his legal duty, which is to use such force but only such force as is necessary for the restoration of order and the checking of violence.

The Manual of Military Law also makes it quite clear that the force which is used must only be the amount necessary to effect the immediate purpose, e.g. the dispersal of the particular mob which is confronting him.

Ultimately the question whether the force used is reasonable may have to be determined by a jury, and they will doubtless apply their own subjective criteria. It would however require a very abnormal situation for a jury to consider that 'a whiff of grape-shot' was a reasonable use of force; and it would have been difficult for General Dyer for instance, if he had been in the UK, to justify his actions, when at Amritsar in India only a few months before the Liverpool Police Strike, he opened fire on a political meeting and killed not less than 300 people. It has been said that his action stopped the whole Punjab from going up in flames. Be that as it may, a similar action taken over here would never, I am sure you will agree, be regarded as a reasonable use of force.

And how does the Government interpret the law when deciding on whether to use the military. Well, we have an important statement on this legal aspect by Lord Haldane in 1908, when Secretary of State for War (he was later Lord Chancellor). Giving evidence to the Select Committee on Employment of Military in cases of disturbance, he said:

> the soldier is a person who is armed with a deadly weapon and he comes out in a military formation under his own officers. If he appears unnecessarily, he is apt to create an impression of a hostile character. His menacing appearance may lead to the very thing which it is his purpose to prevent - disturbance. It may be perfectly legal for the Army to form up and march along a certain street, but if their doing so will unnecessarily and unjustifiably bring about a disturbance, the military _may_ find themselves breaking the law.

Now Lord Haldane was, of course, talking in a particular context, and it would hardly be correct to suggest that the mere appearance of soldiers on the streets will of itself break the law, and in any case the Army is now equipped and trained in less than lethal weapons. Nevertheless, any _undue_ display of force _may_, and any unreasonable use _would_, amount to an offence, and we can clearly see the principle emerging that public reaction to the use of the military could be said to be a factor in determining the legal propriety of that use.

Then Haldane again:

> In the War Office we are very averse to allowing the military to be employed. We are compelled to do it (to come to the aid of Civil Power): we have no choice, we have to obey the law, but we always insist very strongly that they are called out legally, not illegally; and we are called out illegally if we are called out in any circumstances which admit of being dealt with by a force less menacing than the Military.

In other words so long as the police can cope it is not merely ill-advised, but _may_ be actually illegal to use the soldier.

He meant what he said. Only a month before the City Fathers of Winchester had requisitioned troops to deal with some unruly citizens who were rioting (believe it or not in protest against the removal of some railings around a Russian gun captured in the Crimea). They were beating up the Guildhall. The Mayor appealed to the rifle depot and went to bed.

The Commanding Officer, Colonel Herbert, a no doubt politically aware Green Jacket, sought advice from the Chief Constable of Hampshire. They agreed the troops were _not_ needed and so none was sent and the disturbance died down. The City Fathers complained. The Chief Constable defended his advice on the very interesting and enchanting grounds, that 'Few things would be more detrimental to the interests of the City of Winchester than a collision between the citizens and the Rifles who are and always have been, part and parcel of the City'.

It went to the Secretary of State who said he had not the slightest hesitation in approving the action of the Officer Commanding. So the War Office was averse, and that attitude I am certain has been inherited by the Ministry of Defence, and they are not the only ones. The police have always been averse and have always been confident that, by and large, they can cope for the foreseeable future, even though they may have to change their tactics and methods and to some extent their equipment. And the Army is averse for the reasons I have already given you.

You may say that this is a most extraordinary attitude for a member of a Force, who over the last 50 years has done it again and again in Hong Kong, Singapore, Calcutta, Jerusalem, Bahrain, Aden and Nairobi to name but a few, which for part of the last 10 years has virtually been the civil power in parts of Londonderry and Belfast and which, as a result of all this, is now attuned as never before, and as no other Army, to the law and order role in terms of equipment, training methods, tactical doctrine and, above all, experience.

But we want to be seen as protectors of and not in conflict with ordinary people or as Haldane also said: 'We want the Army to be a popular institution and not a menace to civil liberty'. The first may be a bit optimistic. The Armed Forces are sadly never that popular in peace, although I think they have a greater degree of public support right now than perhaps ever before; but his second wish has been fulfilled despite what the National Council for Civil Liberties say. The police have done without us, or our direct intervention, for 50 years, and I hope that British tradition for comparative non-violence on the streets compared with elsewhere in the world will help us to keep it like that.

And there is a further argument too. Although none of us here would, I am sure, wish the Armed Forces to operate outside the law, the law can indeed be modified for the occasion, if Parliament considers it justified. In other countries martial law has been reverted to quite quickly, and even in this country, Parliament has approved the Emergency

Powers Act for Northern Ireland which allows detention of terrorists without trial, coupled with special powers of search and arrest (although the power to detain without trial has not been used in the last 5 years) and given this is legal under emergency legislation, the military can be of great assistance to the police in mounting intelligence operations and hunting down and arresting those who are known to be involved in terrorism, but on whom insufficient evidence to obtain convictions can, for one reason or another, be produced in a Court of Law. But if society does not wish to change its laws to any great degree (and the public opinion pressures not to do this in a place like Great Britain are all too obvious) then the results which the military can achieve are reduced considerably and they begin to appear a pretty heavy-handed instrument (a sledgehammer to crack a nut) to do the job; which then becomes the painstaking building up of evidence, forensic and otherwise, on which a culprit can be arrested and brought into court for a particular crime. This is essentially police work, and Ireland has shown recently that much as the Army can help on the fringes and in the background, and indeed essential as they are in these roles, the really 'nitty gritty' work of getting evidence on the man with bomb and gun and bringing him to Court must revert to the police, just as soon as they have the strength and morale and public acceptability to deal with it.

So I would return to what I said. Upholding the law and public order is, as long as the Government has a measure of consensus and short of armed insurrection, a police matter. In the years ahead the police will, I am sure, try to maintain traditional police methods. If for a time, and one hopes it will be shortlived, the intensity and scale of violence should reach a certain pitch, they may be forced to move into the grey area and organise their riot control more on the lines of the latest techniques from Northern Ireland; but that is still no reason for unnecessarily calling in the military. If such violence ever developed into identifiable and organised insurrection and terrorism, with armed force being used extensively, and consensus Government and public opinion thwarted, then this would be a different matter.

And of course we are always available at all times to give the police the background administrative and specialist support to enable them to get on with their job effectively and avoid getting exhausted; and the police will never have to turn in vain to us for help of this kind.

And in order to be able to do all these things we must always keep in close contact with each other, exchanging information and ideas and getting to know each other's command and control systems and methods of working and anyone who tells you that sensible cooperation on these lines is a threat to civil liberties is out of his mind.

I leave you with just two quotations by way of a postscript. The first, to justify my perhaps rather 'Softly, Softly' approach, comes from General or Professor Clutterbuck of Exeter University in his book 'Protest and the Urban Guerilla':

> The general effect of violence is to polarise moderate opinion towards the extremes. Why else should urban guerillas use it? Why else should soldiers be trained to bend over backwards to avoid it?

And the second is really for those who hanker for altering our laws too stringently in the face of sporadic violence which our democratic processes can, in the long term, take in its stride. It comes from an essay of 1581 entitled 'Examination of certayne ... Ordinary Complaints' (quoted in 'Critchley's Conquest of Violence'):

> I would not have a small sore cured by a greater griefe; not, for avoydinge of popular sedition, which happeneth very seldome and is soon quenched, to bring in a continuall yoke.

Chapter Four

KEEPING THE PEACE IN GREAT BRITAIN: THE DIFFERING ROLES OF THE POLICE AND THE ARMY

Sir Robert Mark

I would like to take this opportunity to shed some light on a subject about which needless secrecy or reserve is more likely to provoke than allay social disquiet, and on which I think a little plain speaking is long overdue, namely, the extent to which there is, and ought to be, contingency planning between the police and the army in Great Britain for certain limited purposes not involving any threat to, or diminution of, civil liberty.
 I propose to begin by asserting that within Great Britain the police represent government by consent. We are very few in number and we are for the most part unarmed. We live among the communities we serve and our mobility is necessarily limited. Our authority under the law is strictly defined and we are personally liable for the consequences whenever we invoke it. We play no part in determining guilt or punishment and our accountability to the courts both criminal and civil, to local police authorities, to Parliament and to public opinion is unsurpassed anywhere else in the world. In the legal and constitutional framework in which society requires us to enforce the laws enacted by its elected representatives, the most essential weapons in our armoury are not firearms, water cannon, tear gas or rubber bullets but the confidence and support of the people on whose behalf we act. That confidence and support depends not only on the factors I have already mentioned but on our personal and collective integrity and in particular on our long tradition of constitutional freedom from political interference in our operational role. Notwithstanding the heavy responsibilities for the policing of England and Wales given to the Home Secretary by the 1964 Police Act, it is important for you to understand that the police are

not the servants of the government at any level. We do not act at the behest of a minister or any political party, not even the party in Government. We act on behalf of the people as a whole and the powers we exercise cannot be restricted or widened by anyone, save Parliament alone. It is this which above all else determines our relationship with the public, especially in relation to the maintenance of public order, and allows us to operate reasonably effectively with minimal numbers, limited powers and by the avoidance of force, or at least with the use only of such force as will be approved by the courts and by public opinion. It is of course true that the Prosecution of Offences Act and Regulations enable the Director of Public Prosecutions to initiate and control police inquiries and prosecutions, but he is accountable to Parliament through the Attorney General, and those powers are not relevant to operational police decisions in dealing with matters of public order. (Rather different considerations apply in Scotland where prosecutions are undertaken by procurators fiscal appointed by the Lord Advocate.) To sum the position up for you in easily understandable and practical terms, a chief officer of police will always give the most careful consideration to any views or representations he may receive from his police authority, be it Home Secretary or police committee, on any issue affecting enforcement of the law, whether public order or anything else, but in England and Wales it is generally for him and him alone to decide what operational action to take and to answer for the consequences. In the case of the Commissioner of Police in the Metropolis his exercise of those responsibilities will no doubt be all the more scrupulous in that he alone of all chief police officers enjoys no security of tenure and that subject to parliamentary approval he may be removed by the Home Secretary. A provincial chief officer may be retired by his police authority with the consent, or on the direction, of the Home Secretary in the interests of efficiency, but he is entitled to an inquiry by one or more persons appointed by the Home Secretary before suffering that fate.

I emphasise this because whilst the police place great importance on their constitutional freedom the significance of their accountability should not be overlooked as a counterbalance to any improper use of it. Our role, therefore, is that of keeping the peace by the use of old, complex and sensitive procedures and machinery whereby in a democratic society lawlessness is contained and excesses are controlled by methods acceptable to the public as a whole. The law, the courts, the organs of public opinion, our small numbers and above all the limitation of our authority and accountability under the law all contribute to ensure that we are always the servants rather than the masters of the public. That is what I meant when I said that we are in fact the visible manifestation of government by consent.

Now let us consider briefly the rather different role of the army. The soldier, in contrast to the policeman, is the embodiment of the ultimate sanction of force which is necessary to every government, even the most democratic, for protection from external attack or for dealing with revolutionary activities for which the machinery of government by consent is inadequate. A minority which attempts by armed force to prevent government by consent or to usurp the function of government is engaging in revolutionary activity, no matter what euphemisms it employs to describe its activities. If that minority is sufficiently large, sooner or later it will be necessary to decide whether the ultimate sanction of force rather than the ordinary democratic process of law is necessary to contain or suppress it. Northern Ireland is a classic example of this and notwithstanding that it is not part of Great Britain, I clearly ought not to avoid brief mention of it, because of the long-lasting and close involvement of the army in the police function there. I hope I shall be forgiven by Ulstermen, however, for saying on the authority of Lord Cameron amongst others that the Province has never enjoyed government by consent as the term is understood in Great Britain. Its government has always been drawn from one party, increasingly unacceptable to a steadily growing minority. Its inclusion in the United Kingdom suggests to the uninformed that there is little or no difference in our political and social conditions. Even cursory research will show that this is not so and it is, therefore, important that you should not misunderstand the relationship between police and army in Great Britain because of the different conditions which apply to Northern Ireland. The impossibility of maintaining law and order there by ordinary police methods made it necessary in 1969 in the interests of the Province as a whole to invoke military aid to contain the situation until a generally acceptable political solution is found. But the task of the army there, though that of 'keeping the peace' in a literal sense, ought not to be confused with the role of the police on the mainland. The army's task in Ulster is the suppression or containment of force by force or threat of force, even though the degree of force is the minimum sufficient for the purpose. It does not act, as a police force does, on behalf of the community as a whole but on the orders of its political masters to whom it is, through its command structure, accountable. The line of command runs from soldier to battalion, brigade, division, corps, army to the CGS, CDS and of course the Minister of Defence. The ultimate objective of the army is to contain the situation with as little loss of life and destruction of property as possible until return to government by consent permits the resumption of ordinary policing, but it is important to note that the soldier enjoys no immunity from the criminal, civil or military law whilst discharging this duty. It is a thankless task. No one knows better than a policeman the courage and tolerance necessary to stand between opposing extremes so often so unreasonable, and when both sides have recourse to extreme violence the task of containment requires the highest virtues to which man can aspire.

If I may be permitted an aside, never in all its long history has the army better deserved the gratitude and admiration of the nation than during its recent years in Ulster even though its role there lacks the glamour or the glory of the battlefield or the successful campaign of conquest or defence. Even the <u>Washington Post</u>, viewing the scene with a transatlantic eye, traditionally sympathetic to the Irish, is of that view. Its correspondent Alfred Friendly wrote in its pages some time ago: 'Except for Catholics in Ulster, the British see their 14,000 man force there are behaving splendidly (as indeed it is) with courage, incredible restraint and discipline in the face of what would have been thought to be intolerable conditions of insult, provocation and huge physical risks. Television, night after terrible night, has shown the army in a most favourable and even inspiring light.' A tribute which the evidence of your own eyes may suggest is richly deserved.

In Great Britain itself the army was used briefly by Cromwell during the Protectorate for police purposes. This was, of course, long before the establishment of professional police. The scheme was not unlike the deployment of paramilitary police in national socialist Germany. It was unpopular, ineffective and soon abandoned. The army was, thereafter, used intermittently to suppress or contain riots and political demonstrations in the eighteenth and nineteenth centuries and this persisted even after the establishment of the Metropolitan force in 1829, but its occasional use in a police role was always unpopular, sure to arouse public resentment and controversy and steadily diminished as the police increased in numbers and improved in efficiency. The army has not been used in that role in Great Britain since the 1914-18 war. There has thus emerged with the passage of time a firm and deepening conviction, shared by soldiers, police and public alike that the army has no part to play in Great Britain in matters of political and industrial dispute not involving the overthrow of lawful government by force. It is true that there have been occasions in the last half century and in recent years on which either violence or the extreme pursuit of sectional interests during industrial disputes has prompted widespread comment and apprehension about what is loosely called the rule of law. But such incidents, though sometimes provoking understandable misgivings, have generally been countered by the pendulum of public opinion which can and does tend to swing against those who behave in that way. Political change is inevitable in a shifting, turbulent and competitive society. The only such change that could and should involve any reaction from either police or army is that attempted by violence, in the case of the army protracted violence beyond the capacity of police containment, and that has fortunately not so far been our tradition, at least in this century.

It will not, therefore, surprise you when I tell you that the prospect of invoking military force to deal with industrial disputes or political demonstrations has never been contemplated during my thirty-nine years' service and there are, so far as I know, no plans at all for such a contingency. Having made that clear, perhaps I can be equally frank in telling you that there have always been plans for invoking military aid to help us deal with civil disasters such as floods, rescues and so on and that latterly there has emerged a need for contingency plans for military aid to deal with situations in which defensive armour, sophisticated weaponry and specialised training might minimise loss of life in dealing with armed and dangerous men inspired by political motives; in other words political terrorists as distinct from armed criminals. There is nothing mysterious or disquieting about this. The police, mostly unarmed and never armed for routine duties, have in recent years found it necessary to acquire, with the approval of government and police authorities, a limited number of firearms for protection against armed criminals, including political terrorists who are always likely to be comparatively few in number. The extent of police reaction will always be limited, not merely for reasons of economy and safety, but also because the police themselves generally object to carrying firearms except when really necessary. This development poses no threat at all to civil liberties, no matter what radical extremists may say. We are equipped only to deal with armed criminals and political terrorists not posing any extraordinary problem or capable of posing only a limited threat.

Moreover, in doing so without military aid we retain the right to make our own appreciation, decide our own tactics and take such operational action as we think necessary whilst remaining, each one of us, personally accountable to the law for our actions. In doing so, of course, we will avail ourselves of expert advice and maintain close liaison with other authorities likely to be of help. In the case of the Metropolitan Police close liaison with the Home Office ensures a ready availability of every possible kind of assistance. A police officer armed in such circumstances will always be carefully briefed and in a static situation will be led by senior officers, but in the last resort it is he, and he alone, who will decide whether he is justified in using his firearm to protect himself. He does not need the permission of a senior officer. A jury or a police disciplinary inquiry may examine his actions but his use of a firearm does not differ in law from his use of a truncheon. Clearly, however, dangerous situations may arise which, notwithstanding their training, their willingness and their courage, policemen are less likely to resolve with minimum loss of life than the army. In such situations, permission of the Home Secretary is sought by the chief officer of police to invoke military aid and the Minister of Defence, in consultation with the Home Secretary, who will have considered the views of the chief officer of police, will decide whether to authorise the ultimate sanction of force by such troops as he may make available. Such assistance was formerly sought by police from the magistracy rather than from the Home Office, but whatever the legal position the present practice reflects the emergence of a professional, well-organised police service which has inevitably assumed the primary responsibility for law and order. The repeal of the Riot Act is perhaps another indication of that trend. The request to the Home Secretary having been approved, it is clearly desirable that both police and the army should then conform to exactly the same terms of engagement. There is no question of one service coming under command of the other. The police commander would simply indicate to the military commander the problem and the target and offer him whatever support he required whilst playing a containing or supporting role. The army commander would act in accordance with the joint police/army plan. He would not be under the command of the police commander but would act in conjunction with him under his duty at common law to come to the aid of the civil power. The joint objective would, of course, be to bring the operation to a successful conclusion ideally without loss of life. But its achievement would clearly involve a voluntary, if temporary, restriction of the right of the police to complete freedom under the law in their operational decisions and actions. In such circumstances police, army, Home Office and Ministry of Defence must act in complete accord.

The army can also be made available through the same channel of communication in a protective and deterrent role in anticipation of armed terrorist activity and as I am sure you will know such operations at Heathrow Airport are now accepted by the public as necessary and sensible.

There is also what I would call, for want of a better word, the logistical role which the army may be called upon to undertake in civil emergencies as, for example, when it shifted a mass of unemptied dustbins during a dustmen's strike at Glasgow. That assistance was not, of course, invoked by the police but by the Glasgow local authority. It was, however, of direct interest to the police, because if the soldiers had met with violence it would have been the task of the police and not the army to deal with it.

It will be obvious from what I have said that military aid to the civil power in Great Britain will always be restricted to very small numbers of troops, strictly limited in purpose and short-lived in duration. This is perhaps just as well in view of the present size of the army and its other commitments.

Perhaps I should complete the picture for you by brief mention of what is called by the press a 'third force' and of 'private armies' which attracted a great deal of comment recently. A 'third force' is an organisation specifically designed for law enforcement thought to be beyond the scope of the civil police but not requiring the sophisticated weaponry and training of the army. Such forces are to be seen in many countries: the National Guard in America, the Bereitschaftspolizei in Berlin, the CRS and Gendarmerie Mobile in France and special units of the Carabinieri in Italy. The Army High Command, the Home Office and the civil police have always been opposed to a third force and believe that the purposes it could achieve are better fulfilled by the police and the army about whose respective roles and accountability there is no ambiguity and who both enjoy public confidence.

The very term 'private army' provokes a vague feeling of apprehension and suggests a fundamental misunderstanding of the problems posed by social or industrial unrest. You cannot control a free society by force, whether by troops, police or private armies or all three. To do so would require very large numbers of men prepared to exercise arbitrary power in the homeland with a ruthlessness required only of soldiers in war. That destroys freedom, as we know it, polarises society and ensures conflict. That is why a government of any democratic party will avoid confrontation between troops and those engaged in civil or industrial disputes.

I must again emphasise by contrast that the use of force by police to maintain public order can never be arbitrary. It is always conditioned by the factors I have briefly outlined to you. We are unarmed, clearly and locally accountable for our actions by legal procedures, well established and widely understood and we are strictly impartial in that we do not act for the government, for any one party or sectional interest. Any need to enlarge national resources to deal with civil disputes will not be lessened by disregard of those fundamental conditions. Such a disregard would increase, not lessen, civil strife. Well-intentioned public concern on this issue should be channelled to strengthen our well-tried and generally accepted institutions rather than to usurp their functions.

I suspect that there may be some among you in whom the title of this lecture aroused curiosity or even faint apprehension, who now feel disappointed by what I have had to say. Occasional references in the news media to the army at London Airport or at Balcombe Street, where armed men were recently besieged, or elsewhere, naturally attract a good deal of interest, speculation and excitement. If indeed some of you do now suffer a sense of anti-climax perhaps you will, on reflection, feel relieved and reassured to know that the task of preserving liberty and maintaining order in this country is still a police function and that the only circumstances in which military aid is likely to be involved are such as to give no cause at all for anxiety or apprehension to those who take it upon themselves to keep a vigilant eye on our civil liberties.

That may be disappointing to radical extremists and political propagandists, but it happens to be true. It is an important part of the police function to act as a shock absorber in protecting society from violence from any source and it is part of our tradition that we do this with the minimal degree of force necessary to deny the violent the achievement of their objectives, whether criminal or political. Do not underestimate the cost in terms of hardship and physical injury. The uniformed branch of some 17,000 men in London suffers about 3,000 assaults each year, three men having to go sick from their injuries every two days. The expectation of physical injury for policemen in London is very high and will remain so, although an increase in manpower for preventive purposes would undoubtedly reduce it.

It is, however, a price we are willing to pay for the preservation of the English way of life. It is all very well for Voltaire to say: 'I disagree with what you say but will defend to the death your right to say it'. In practical terms these days the defence of that right in this country falls to the police, who protect and will continue to protect demonstrators of the extreme right and the extreme left not less than those who march in the face of a hostile crowd to commemorate what they call Bloody Sunday. [In 1972, troops killed 13 civilians during an unlawful civil rights march in Londonderry - ed.] We, the police, are in fact the most accurate reflection of British society, its tolerance, its strengths and its weaknesses and neither we nor you would welcome or even accept a relinquishment of our role, or any part of it, to the army, other than in the circumstances I have outlined, notwithstanding that both police and army are inspired by the same ideals of service to the people from whom we are drawn and whose well-being is our mutual objective.

Chapter Five

WHITEHALL CONTINGENCY PLANNING FOR INDUSTRIAL DISPUTES

Peter Hennessy

The first week of January 1984 brought two windfalls for the student of emergency planning, one expected, the other not. They complemented each other neatly. The first was a set of Cabinet Office minutes from 1953 released on time, and as a matter of routine, under the 30-year rule. They dealt with the strike in October 1953 of oil and petrol tanker drivers in the London area.[1] It was broken in three days by the use of 6,000 troops brought in under defence regulations left over from World War II (for an account of the strike, see Jeffery & Hennessy, 1983, pp. 223-24). The minutes of the meeting of the Official Committee on Emergencies for October 26, 1953, the last day of the strike, drily record the contingency planners' triumph:

> There has been no signs of hostility towards the troops. Yesterday they had delivered 2.75 million gallons of fuel compared with 2.5 million gallons on an average day of normal distribution.

The second New Year windfall told a different, grimmer story. To mark the fifth anniversary of the opening salvo of the 1979 winter crisis which destroyed the Callaghan administration, Mr William Rodgers, the former Secretary of State for Transport, who had borne the brunt of the haulage strike that year, published a full-page memoir in The Guardian ('A Winter's Tale of Discontent', January 7, 1984, p. 11). It was a story of failure, of personal and political depression.

The Callaghan Cabinet had at its disposal two Emergency Powers Acts, the 1920 statute and the 1964 measure which established some of the World War II defence regulations on a permanent basis, and the

94

resources of the Armed Forces. Yet it felt, and in reality was, virtually impotent in face of a national lorry drivers' strike, as Mr Rodgers' account of a ministerial meeting on January 13, 1979 indicates (id.):

> When ... I urged the need to move vital medical supplies out of Hull docks, defence ministers were adamant and bland: 'It will take days to put a suitable convoy together'. Nor did they have available any detailed plans of the docks to tell them where to go. ... The Home Secretary, advised by the Cabinet Office, was no more eager for the risks involved. The declaration of a State of Emergency had been considered by the Prime Minister but rejected, and it was to be considered and rejected again.

The Callaghan Government did not fall in the technical sense until it lost its vote of confidence in the Commons on March 28, 1979 (the immediate cause of its demise was devolution to Scotland, not trade union power). But neither the country nor Mr Rodgers harboured any illusions about what had brought about its collapse.

> The trade unions had defeated the Labour Government and opened wide the doors to Mrs Thatcher. They had also defeated themselves. A Conservative Government would ensure that they were never the same again.

Mrs Margaret Thatcher took office in May 1979 acutely aware that winter crises, precipitated by the naked application of trade union muscle, had brought down not just Mr Callaghan, but her Conservative predecessor, Mr Edward Heath, as well in 1974. Shortly after becoming Leader of the Opposition, she commissioned Lord Carrington (as Energy Secretary he had been intimately involved in the fuel and power difficulties of 1973-74) to conduct an inquiry in the strictest secrecy into the possibility of a future Tory Cabinet suffering a similar fate and into the countermeasures that might be applied to prevent it.

In so doing, she was placing herself squarely inside a political tradition begun by David Lloyd George, and maintained at periodic intervals by his successors in Downing Street. Before considering the activities of the 1984-model Whitehall emergency organisation - the Civil Contingencies Unit in the

Cabinet Office (CCU), to whose January 1979 discussions we are now privy well short of the 30-year rule thanks to Mr Rodgers (a full account of which is available in Jeffery and Hennessy, 1983) - it is instructive to examine the shifting balance between state power and union power since 1919.

In that year, Lloyd George found himself faced with the spectre of concerted political action from the Triple Alliance, as the labour movement's big batallions - miners, railwaymen and transport workers - styled themselves at the time. He summoned the leaders of the alliance to a meeting and began by telling them the Army was disaffected and could not be relied upon. Lloyd George went on:

> If you carry out your threat and strike then you will defeat us. But if you do so, have you weighed the consequences? The strike will be in defiance of the Government of the country and by its very success will precipitate a constitutional crisis of the first importance. For, if a force arises in the state which is stronger than the state itself, then it must be ready to take on the functions of the state, or withdraw and accept the authority of the state. Gentlemen, have you considered, and if you have, are you ready?

'From that moment on', commented Robert Smillie, the miners' leader, 'we were beaten and we knew we were'.

The most economical way of bridging the gap, in a descriptive sense, between the interwar era, when Baldwin, with the help of the Armed Forces, could break a general strike, and the early 1980s when the Electrical Power Engineers Association (EPEA) could do in a matter of hours what was beyond the grasp of the entire labour movement in 1926 - namely the bringing of the country to its knees by precipitating a collapse of the national grid - the best way of making that leap is to start by eavesdropping on a highly secret meeting in the Home Office on a summer morning in June 1945. It should be remembered that the war in Europe had been over for barely a month. The conflict in the Far East looked like going on for some time as the atom bomb had yet to change the configuration of grand strategy. A Conservative caretaker government was in power and a general election in prospect for the following month. The gathering of June 19 arose from an initiative of Sir Alexander Maxwell, a reforming, liberal civil servant who was, at that time, Permanent Secretary to the Home Office. Eleven days earlier, Maxwell had written to a number of his fellow heads of department about the need to revive the prewar Supply and Transport Organisation (STO), the main bureaucratic, or planning instrument, used by Baldwin to achieve his triumph in 1926. Maxwell said the time had come to consider resuscitating it and, as a first step, a meeting of officials should be called to see what modifications might be needed in the light of modern conditions and to prepare material to be put before ministers.

Around Maxwell's table on that summer morning in June 1945 sat 28 people - about twice as many as attend its present day bureaucratic successor, the CCU, when it meets as a purely Civil Service body with no ministers present. But in its blend of civil servants from various sponsoring ministries, responsible for this essential industry or that, and officers from the Armed Forces, it was very much the same kind of animal.

Opening the meeting Maxwell said that whether industrial trouble was or was not likely, one could not rule out the possibility of large-scale industrial disturbances during the next few years, and it was the business of the Government to be prepared for an emergency of that kind. He had thought, therefore, that this meeting should be called to consider what proposals for dealing with such an emergency should be put before ministers. The kind of organisation which had existed before the War was outlined in the memorandum which had circulated prior to the meeting.

There was general agreement that an emergency organisation should exist, subject to a reservation by the Admiralty representatives that some indulgence in taking part in the organisation should be allowed to Departments which were very busy with the war with Japan. It was also agreed that the general structure of the organisation should be on the same lines as before (PRO T 221/19).

The STO was back in business, or almost. Before moving onto the 1970s, mention should be made of the experience of the Labour Government of Clement Attlee. Its victory at the polls in July 1945 must have given Maxwell a nasty turn. For here he was, preparing a paper asking the Parliamentary representatives of the losing side in 1926 to reinvent the instrument of their demise. He need not have worried. In August 1945, that very effective non-conformist of the old school,

James Chuter Ede, Attlee's Home Secretary, broached the subject with the Prime Minister who recognised the need for a ministerial decision. On October 8 - in the midst of an unofficial dock strike which began in Birkenhead and soon spread around the coasts - Attlee summoned a handful of senior ministers with no civil servants present. They decided to authorise preparation at official level and commissioned Chuter Ede to chair a small committee to work out the details. Next day, the full Cabinet, in ignorance of the work of that very select group which had met in No. 10 Downing Street, took the decision to put the Army into the docks less than three months after taking office.

In a sense, they never looked back. In went the troops in January 1947 during a lorry drivers' strike. Before leaving office, strike-breaking had become second nature to Attlee's ministers with the forces moving into the docks with monotonous regularity in 1948, 1949 and 1950, and even into the London power stations - with decidedly patchy results as Hugh Gaitskell's diary bears witness - in 1950. By the time the Attlee administration left office in 1951, a fully fledged Emergencies Committee, with a Civil Service shadow, had drawn up immensely detailed plans to cope with the consequences of disputes in a whole host of fuel and power, transport and food industries.

In the two decades of consensus politics of the neo-Keynesian variety - commonly known as Butskellism ' - that followed, the contingency planning community enjoyed a period of relative tranquillity, with states of emergency being declared under the 1920 Act only on two occasions - the national rail strike in 1955, and the seamen's strike of 1966. Compare the three and three-quarter years of Mr Heath's government - which saw five of the 12 states of emergency declared in the past 64 years - and you have some measure of the sea-change that took the, by now near moribund, Attlee-model emergencies organisation by surprise, beginning with the December 1970 cuts brought on by 'go slow' in the electricity supply industry.

On December 7, 1970, Douglas Hurd, Edward Heath's Political Secretary, noted in his diary: 'Cold and the electricity go-slow hits harder and quicker than expected'. Next day he recorded: 'A bad day. It is clear that all the weeks of planning in the Civil Service have totally failed to cope with what is happening in the electricity dispute; and all the pressures are to surrender'.

What lay behind Mr Hurd's despair? Two fundamental shifts since 1951, if not since Maxwell's meeting, had tilted the balance of power sharply against the Government and in favour of the wielders of industrial muscle. First there had been a waxing of trade union power following the failure of the Wilson administration to impose its 'In Place of Strife' reforms on the labour movement. Second, and most important of all, technological developments in several key industries made it difficult, if not impossible, to find alternative pairs of skilled hands from the Armed Forces or anywhere else to replace those of striking employees.

But it took more than the electricity go-slow of 1970 to bring these lessons home to Whitehall. That distinction belongs to the miners' strike of 1972, the first national dispute in the industry since 1926. By this stage, the TUC was well on the way to doing to Mr Heath's Industrial Relations Act what it had done to Mr Wilson's White Paper on trade union reform of 1969. The miners' strike of January-February 1972 was preceded by a ten-week overtime ban at the pits which ran down coal stocks. On January 9 1972, the strike began. For an entire month the Government did nothing to conserve coal supplies. Not until February 10 was a state of emergency declared.

On that day an event occurred that has haunted contingency planners ever since. Saltley coke depot in Birmingham was closed after a six-day struggle involving, at peak moments, 800 police and 15,000 massed secondary pickets, many of whom were 'flying pickets' transported from all over the country.

Mr Arthur Scargill, of the Barnsley area strike committee of the National Union of Mineworkers (NUM), had turned flying secondary pickets into a national phenomenon overnight, a demon still to be exorcized in the contingency planning community.

The significance of Saltley was not lost on the principals concerned, as two commentaries, made three years after the event, illustrated: first Mr Brendon Sewill, then special adviser to Mr Anthony (now Lord) Barber, Chancellor of the Exchequer:

> At the time many of those in positions of influence looked into the abyss and saw only a few days away the possibility of the country being plunged into a state of chaos not so very far removed from that which might prevail after a minor nuclear attack.
>
> If that sounds melodramatic I need only

say that - with the prospect of the breakdown of power supplies, food supplies, sewerage, communications, effective government and law and order - it was the analogy that was being used at the time. That is the power that exists to hold the country to ransom: it was fear of that abyss which had an important effect on subsequent policy.

Next Mr Scargill:

You see, we took the view that we were in a class war. We were not playing cricket on the village green like they did in '26. We were out to defeat Heath and Heath's policies because we were fighting a government. Anyone who thinks otherwise was living in cloud cuckoo land. We had to declare war on them and the only way you could declare war was to attack the vulnerable points. They were the points of energy: the power stations, the coke depots, the coal depots, the points of supply.

The failure of the Attlee-style emergencies organisation[2] to deal with the economic consequences of Mr Scargill led to Mr Heath commissioning Lord Jellicoe, the Lord Privy Seal, and Sir John Hunt, a Cabinet Office deputy secretary, to review the whole set-up. Assisting them was Brigadier Richard Bishop, who had recently joined the Civil Service as a direct entrant principal on his retirement from the Forces. A few months after Saltley, responsibility for contingency planning was removed from the Home Office and placed under the auspices of the Cabinet Office, and its new committee, the CCU. Lord Jellicoe became its ministerial chairman, John Hunt its Civil Service chief and Brigadier Bishop its secretary.

During the rest of 1972 Brigadier Bishop, CCU secretary (who died in harness in 1981 to be succeeded by Brigadier Tony Budd), drew up a list of vital services and industries most vulnerable to union action. By early 1973 ministers had detailed estimates of 16 key industries, their capacity for disruption, their importance to the country's well-being and the possibility of using alternative military labour in the event of strikes. Then as now electricity was top of the list. Others have moved up and down as amendments have been made in the light of experience. After the 1979 winter, the haulage industry is somewhat higher than the sixteenth place it occupied in 1972. Water, always in the top ten, moved up to join docks, coal, rail and oil in the group just beneath power, when the docility of its labour force could no longer be taken for granted. Contingency planning since 1972 has been directed towards mitigating the consequences of industrial strength exercised in the direct Saltley manner.

When in the winter of 1973-74 a rerun of the 1972 coal strike seemed certain, there was acute anxiety in Whitehall. Given its limited aims, however, the new civil contingencies organisation stood up well to the test. A prime reason was the successful efforts of the NUM leadership to prevent ugly scenes on picket lines during the February 1974 election campaign for fear of jeopardising Labour's chances at the polls. On top of that, the policy of declaring a state of emergency in plenty of time to conserve fuel supplies paid off.

The difficulties of forecasting, as usual, bedevilled the planners in 1973. What would run short first, electricity itself or raw materials such as steel? Would industrial paralysis come quickly or in stages, or would the bulk of industry suddenly collapse together? To everybody's surprise production during the three-day week was maintained at 75 per cent of normal, even when working hours were cut by 40 per cent, though one official involved remembers 'it was pretty close at the end'.

The main prop of the returning Wilson government for the first 18 months of its life was harmonious relations with the trade unions. With a firm incomes policy and the vivid memory of the 1976 currency collapse haunting them, ministers underwent a sea-change in attitude in late 1977 when faced with a firemen's strike. Why then did the Callaghan government shrink from using the Emergency Powers Act 1964 to deal with the 1979 haulage strike?

The answer was, as Mr Rodgers confirmed five years later, that it had no real counterforce available. A maximum of 20,000 servicemen could have been deployed, fewer than half of whom possessed heavy goods vehicle licences. The CCU estimated there were half a million individual lorry drivers operating in the United Kingdom.

Mr Callaghan's winter was less traumatic and dramatic than Mr Heath's 'Waterloo' of 1972 and 1973-74 but the effect was the same when the country eventually went to the polls. No answers were provided for the country's vulnerability in the face of industrial power wielded with determination on a national scale.

Before turning to the present Government's stewardship of the CCU, it might be useful to look at how two specific contingencies are handled. First, using a reconstruction of CCU meetings during a series of near-misses in the late 1970s in the petrol and oil delivery system, let us see how a dispute in which the Armed Forces can do something, as the experience of October 1953 showed, is planned for inside the heart of the Whitehall machine.

For convenience I have used the names of those who represented their ministries on the CCU in November 1979. Most have been replaced subsequently, and the Ministry of Defence has changed the plan's military codename (latterly to Operation Leadburn).

The unit will meet several weeks ahead of the possible strike, as a civil servants' group initially. Mr Robert Wade-Gery of the Cabinet Office will open the meeting from the chair by summarising the contents of the file labelled 'Operation Drumstick'. It should be possible to maintain about 25 per cent of normal supplies of petrol and oil, he will explain, provided a state of emergency is declared, rationing introduced and the Royal Corps of Transport requisitions oil company vehicles because the Army does not have enough of its own.

He will then invite Mr Ian Hudson and Mr Matthew Wake from the Department of Employment to give the latest intelligence on the position inside the relevant section of the Transport and General Workers' Union. Mr Peter Lazarus, of the Department of Transport, will explain the Department's rationing scheme and the priority to be given to public transport and essential users like the emergency services. Mr Robert Priddle, from the Department of Energy, will convey the oil companies readiness to co-operate with the Government. The Ministry of Defence team, Mr Derek Stephen, Mr Brian Cousins and Brigadier Michael Tillotson, will list the number of troops needed; 5,000 drivers and 10,000 general-duties men to be trained to handle pumps and pipes at the Army's West Moors petroleum centre in Dorset. At least 18 days' notice will be required to get the men back from Germany and through West Moors, particularly if the run-up to the strike spans the Christmas holiday.

With Mr Noel Law of the Home Office, the Ministry of Defence men will emphasise the need to impress upon chief constables their responsibility for securing the safe passage of men and vehicles as they are driven out of company depots to Army barracks and emergency distribution centres. At this point the needs of special interest groups will be raised. Mr Leo Hanson, from the Ministry of Agriculture, might appeal for farmers to be given preferential treatment. Mr David Neville-Jones, from the Department of Industry, could speak up for companies requiring oil to maintain continuous production processes.

Summing up, Mr Wade-Gery will emphasise the need for an urgent meeting of ministers to authorise the drafting of emergency regulations and the proclamation of a state of emergency. Before ministers gather, a handful of officials will receive a special briefing from MI5 on the origins of the possible strike, whether a small group of extremists is manipulating the men or whether it is a straight 'pay and conditions' affair. Invariably, the evidence points to the latter.

A joint meeting of ministers and civil servants, under the Home Secretary Mr Whitelaw's chairmanship, will then prepare recommendations for the full Cabinet. Should the strike materialise, CCU will meet each afternoon to collate reports from the Department of Transport's regional emergency committees and react to events until the strike is ended.

If Mrs Thatcher feels that a purely ministerial forum is necessary to take political decisions arising from the dispute, she may imitate Mr Callaghan by setting up an equivalent of the secret <u>ad hoc</u> committee known as GEN 158, which he established during the winter crisis of January-March 1979. In that case, CCU would meet separately as a mixed committee with Mr Wade-Gery and Brigadier Bishop the only civil servants present at the ministerial group. Once the strike is settled, lessons will be noted for future use and Brigadier Bishop will amend his 'Operation Drumstick' file accordingly.

Strikes in the electricity supply industry have preoccupied the CCU for the past 14 years. They contain the most alarming prospects the unit has to face. In no other sector are the consequences of breakdown so swift, widespread or devastating in their effects on manufacturing industry, sewage and water pumping stations, and households. One insider has described a national power failure as 'the slippery path to hell'.

Technology has moved relentlessly against the government in this area since 1945. It is over thirty years since troops were last sent into a British power station. Hugh Gaitskell, then Minister of Fuel and Power, recorded in his diary for January 27 1950:

> This time without warning, the [unofficial] strike began at four London power stations. We put the troops in at once and made a favourable impression on the public. Unfortunately, however, it proved impossible to get the stations to anything like full capacity owing to the inexperience of the troops and the shortage of people to train them.

The disastrous performance of the troops in 1950 was recalled when members of the Electricity Council told the Department of Energy in March 1978 that they alone, and not the Government, must implement contingency arrangements in the event of industrial trouble. The complexity of modern power stations placed them beyond the capacity of Army engineers. In the autumn of 1977 the CCU commissioned Mr Richard Mottram, of the Ministry of Defence, to investigate the possibility of using troops. The conclusion was that there were not enough of them and that they were not up to it.

There are about 100 Royal Engineers, trained at Brompton Barracks, Chatham, holding a safety certificate from the Central Electricity Generating Board (CEGB) declaring them fit to control a power station. The great 2,000 megawatt coal-burning stations, the backbone of the grid, each need between 90 and 100 engineers to run them on a three-shift system. And such installations would seize up if soldiers, trained to run small power plants at Army depots, were let loose on them. The tolerances on the boilers are so fine that the danger of overload, or even explosion, is immense if control is in unskilled hands.

The Electricity Council has insisted, and the CCU accepted, that members of the 28,000-strong EPEA are indispensable and irreplaceable. What Royal Engineer and Royal Electrical and Mechanical Engineer technicians could do is to help power engineers to keep more equipment going - three rather than two 500 megawatt generators in a large coal-burner is the estimate - if EPEA men agreed to supervise them on maintenance and monitoring tasks in place of striking manual workers.

The Electricity Council and the EPEA are adamant, however, that they would not welcome military help. The council and the CEGB have drafted detailed contingency plans to protect the country from disaster. They are based on computer simulations of how the grid can shed its load in an orderly fashion without the danger to switching equipment, industrial appliances and household goods that an uncontrolled degradation of the system would bring. The authorities believe that with EPEA support they could sustain half of normal supplies, well above the 30-40 per cent range where run-down could become unstoppable, for a substantial time without manual workers' or military help.

Their estimate was tested on November 4 1977 when the 10 pm shift walked out at the four huge S. Yorkshire coal-burning stations of Drax, Ferrybridge C, Eggborough and Thorpe Marsh. Other stations in the Midlands suffered similar disruptions. Engineers used to working in the control room took over, with some trepidation, such unfamiliar tasks as monitoring the pumps, fans and boilers and even unloading coal. Most important of all, the handful of chemists at each station who maintain the critical purity of water supply for boilers stayed at work.

In sustaining half of normal output until the unofficial action ended on November 11, engineers at the stations and the National Grid Control Centre, with the five regional control centres, demonstrated great resource and stamina as the nation teetered closer to a three-day week than was appreciated outside the industry and the government at the time.

Power engineers are the most powerful group of workers in the country. The Government has no alternative but to rely on them to keep a sense of public responsibility. A senior EPEA official said:

> If we decided to come out, that is it. We would beat any government. But I would not frighten people too much. There is no way that our members would come out and take on the Government unless there was extreme pressure. To shut the whole system down is not a strike, it is a catastrophe. I do not think it is a power that ought to be used. It does not matter how many the Army have got, if we will not let them in. ... If we were going to do the job of keeping the stations going we would stop anybody else. Technically, we could run a good half of the system by ourselves for a long time, almost indefinitely. However, it is virtually inconceivable that we would run the system against an official strike of manual workers.

If the grid did collapse, danger to public health would be the greatest worry. The water system can withstand rota power cuts of up to six hours. The Thames Water Authority, and many others, have standby generators at all their pumping stations. If those failed and mains supply became contaminated, households without power would find it very difficult to make supplies safe by boiling. Sodium hypochloride tablets are an effective disinfectant in trained hands, such as the Royal Engineers, but in untrained hands they are useless.

Short of ultimate disaster, the CEGB has become increasingly diligent since the early 1970s in strengthening its hand against lesser but still worrying contingencies like a miners' strike, with secondary pickets preventing the movement of supplies into power stations. Apart from coal, power stations need other strategic supplies like chlorine for water treatment, hydrogen for cooling activators, furnace oil for starting the boilers and oxy-acetylene for maintenance staff. Two months' supply of those are kept on site.

The British national grid is the strongest in the world, with more alternative routes for bringing power into conurbations than, say, the United States. If the unthinkable did happen, the damage would be enormous but the blackout would not be perpetual. Up and down the country the CEGB has placed in sheds alongside the boilers clusters of jet engines designed for Concorde and the Vulcan bomber. The gas turbines can be started from cold within two and a half minutes. Between them they can add almost 2,500 megawatts to the grid, enough to get the pumps, fans and boilers started again. Their unit cost is high, but as an insurance policy they are worth every penny.

On taking office, Mrs Thatcher, unlike several members of her Cabinet, was not privy to the details of Whitehall contingency planning for the electricity supply or any other industry. As Secretary of State for Education in the Heath Administration she had had nothing to do with the CCU and its works. She did possess, however, a general perspective afforded by her membership of the Cabinet in 1970-74 and a more precise appraisal from her close study of the Carrington report of 1975.

Opening her 1979 election campaign, she had adopted a misleadingly insouciant air on the subject. At the official launching of her manifesto on April 11, she was asked by a foreign journalist: 'Do you think you have enough policemen, soldiers, whatever it takes, to have a confrontation with extremists on an issue of face?' 'I don't think we are on the same wavelength', came the brisk reply.

The Conservative strategy for altering the balance of industrial relations was quickly made plain. In the short-term, the Government would stand aloof from pay bargaining - except where the Civil Service, its direct labour force, was involved or those state industries where, in the last analysis, the Exchequer had to carry the financial consequences of pay settlements. In the long-term, there would be action on trade union law.

Very privately, the short-to-medium term was being taken care of by the CCU whose chairmanship fell to Mr Whitelaw. A number of reviews were put in hand, on the Prime Minister's instructions, with ad hoc Cabinet committees - or MISCs - examining the fuel, power and water industries. Ministers also looked at the possibility of the Territorial Army (TA) being used to strengthen the ranks of regulars in future operations involving the provision of alternative labour under the Emergency Powers Acts.

Nothing came of the idea. Mr Francis Pym, then Secretary of State for Defence, eventually persuaded Mrs Thatcher that, while drawing on the 70,000-strong TA could more than double the 20,000 regulars available, at a pinch, for strike-breaking, their introduction could jeopardise the main reserve function of the TA. The Ministry of Defence pointed out that many territorials were trade unionists in civilian life. Straining their loyalty would be improper and probably counterproductive. Nor should TA drill halls be used as mustering points for civilian volunteers during strikes - another old chestnut of the contingency planning community which was revived in 1979-80 to no visible effect as yet.

Other re-evaluations bore fruit, however. The CEGB was asked by the Government to stockpile still more coal inside the perimeters of its power stations. Though nobody had any illusions about the services running the national grid, the object was to buy more time, the supreme art of the contingency planner. The CEGB obliged and managed to get an easing of its cash limit to finance the operation.

On the water side, the Government backed down in 1981 rather than risk the first national strike in the industry's history. In 1983, however, it stood firm and a month-long stoppage ensued. The worst fears contained in the contingency files did not materialise, however, and ministers were peeved at the National Water Council for its over-gloomy forecasts. Thanks to the unseasonably mild weather in January and February 1983, moderate behaviour on the water worker's picket lines, the willingness of NALGO supervisory staff to perform manual tasks and the increased automation of the system since Brigadier Bishop first rejigged the file in 1972-73, the country survived without widespread breakdown or health hazard. The contingency plan for introducing up to 15,000 troops did not need to be activated.

At the turn of 1983-84, there was a feeling in the country that the sting of trade union power had been drawn. Mrs Thatcher had survived four winters and had been re-elected with a huge majority. With unemployment over three milions and inflation curbed, a 'new realism' in industrial relations was detected by commentators. The statute outlawing secondary picketing - the Saltley weapon - had been vigorously applied against the National Graphical Association in its dispute with Messenger Newspapers. The NGA, at least for the time being, had backed down. At the Department of Employment Mr Tom King was considering ways of achieving 'no-strike' agreements in essential industries and services as pledged by the 1983 Conservative manifesto. The prospect of privatisation in some of the public utilities raised the possibility that the grip of monopoly unions in state enterprises might be further weakened.

Yet inside the CCU there was no trace of premature euphoria. The 1984 team of Mr Leon Brittan (who had replaced the ennobled Lord Whitelaw as Home Secretary), Mr David Goodall (who had succeeded Mr, now Sir, Robert Wade-Gery, just in time for the railway disputes of 1982) and Brigadier Budd had no illusions. The apparent gains of 1979-83 could evaporate in a single day. As one insider put it, the law banning secondary picketing would be to no avail 'if the lads just turned up en masse one day' and stopped an essential service or industry. Though local chief constables were far better placed than in 1972. Arrangements for rapid assistance from one force to another had been demonstrated on a number of occasions during the 1981 summer riots and during the NGA-Messenger dispute in 1983. But the spectre of Saltley remained unexorcised. 'In this area, government is largely a matter of bluff', said one member of the Thatcher administration.[3]

Emergency planning since 1919 - the hidden history of British industrial relations - shows that the country depends on government and trade unions recognising that a final showdown, an answer to the 'Who rules?' question posed by Lloyd George to the Triple Alliance, is in nobody's interests. Should such a 'High Noon' occur, the balance of social and institutional forces in the nation, the kind of checks and balances that preserve our liberties, could be tilted permanently in favour of one side or the other, changing the political and constitutional landscape of the country beyond recognition.

NOTES

1. For meetings of the Churchill Cabinet's Official Committee on Emergencies in 1953 see Public Record Office CAB 134/858. For its sub-committee on priorities during the October 1953 oil strike consult CAB 134/861.
2. This interpretation is strongly challenged by veterans of the Home Office Emergencies Organisation. They regard it as black propadanda disseminated by the Cabinet Office and claim the root of the problem lay in the difficult relationship between Mr Heath and his Home Secretary, Mr Reginald Maudling.
3. This chapter was written in January 1984 before the miners' strike of that year which became a test-bed for the improvements in contingency planning and the changes in police tactics since Saltley.

REFERENCES

Jeffery, K. & Hennessy, P. (1983) States of Emergency: British Governments and Strike-breaking since 1919, London, Routledge & Kegan Paul

Chapter Six

ARMED FORCES, INDUSTRIAL DISPUTES AND THE LAW IN GREAT BRITAIN

Christopher J. Whelan

In Great Britain, the civilian role of the military is nowhere more apparent than in the industrial arena. Industrial action and its consequences have prompted the use of service personnel both to provide substitute labour and to control disorder. Indeed, that the civilian role of the military has expanded significantly in the recent decade is due for the most part to the increased willingness of governments to pursue 'military' solutions to 'industrial' crises and threats, and to undertake the substantial contingency planning necessary to achieve this. The main objective of this chapter is to outline the law relating to military intervention in industrial disputes and to place this law in its modern context. Although service personnel have been used, since the Second World War, as a 'labour' rather than a 'military' force, the same law which facilitated a significant public order role for the military in industrial situations in the nineteenth and early twentieth centuries remains today.

USE OF TROOPS IN INDUSTRIAL DISPUTES

Since 1945, service personnel have replaced striking employees in at least thirty disputes (Table 6.1). The military role has increased substantially in the last decade and a half. Twelve of these thirty disputes occurred since 1970 (and nine since 1975). These figures become more significant, as does the military role itself, if one adds to it the number of disputes in which the military have been standing-by, ready to intervene, within 72 hours. Since 1970, the military have been standing-by in fifteen disputes, thirteen of which occurred since 1976, ten since 1979 (Table 6.2).

Table 6.1: Military Intervention Since 1945*

Employees involved

Dockers	8	(July & Oct., 1945, 1946, 1947, 1948, 1949, 1950, 1972)
Meat-handlers	3	(1946, 1947, 1950)
Railwaymen	2	(1955, 1982)
Seamen	2	(1960, 1966)
Dustmen	2	(1970, 1975)
Firemen	2	(1973, 1977-78)
Ambulance drivers	2	(1979, January 1981)
Industrial civil servants	2	(1978, 1981)
Min. of Works employees	1	(1948)
Electricity manual workers	1	(1949-50)
Gas maintenance workers	1	(1950)
Petrol tanker drivers	1	(1953)
Postal workers	1	(1955)
Air traffic assistants	1	(1977)
Prison officers	1	(1980-81)

* Tables 6.1-3 exclude N. Ireland. The military have intervened there since 1970 in at least five disputes: electricity supply (1970, 1971), the Ulster Workers Council stoppage (1974), prison guards (1978), transport (1979); see generally, Creighton, 1983, pp. 9-32.

Table 6.2: Military Standing-by Since 1970

Employees

Water workers	3	(1979, 1981, 1983)
Local authority manual workers	2	(1970, 1979)
Petrol tanker drivers	2	(1978, 1979)
Ambulance drivers	2	(June 1981, 1982)
Dockers	1	(1970)
Seamen	1	(1976)
Nuclear power workers	1	(1977)
Road hauliers	1	(1979)
Civil service computer staff	1	(1979)
Firemen	1	(1980)

The revival and growing sophistication of government contingency planning, together with the increased predilection, which contingency planning facilitates, to use service personnel, has led, inexorably perhaps, to a significant growth in the role of the military in recent industrial disputes. Table 6.3 charts this trend.

Table 6.3: Military Involvement in Industrial Disputes 1970-1983

Year*	1970	1971	1972	1973	1974	1975	1976
Number	3	0	1	1	0	1	1

Year	1977	1978	1979	1980	1981	1982	1983
Number	3	2	7	2	4	1	1

* Year in which involvement commenced.

Since 1970, military personnel have been 'involved' in no less than twenty-seven disputes, twenty-two since 1975. Even if no actual intervention took place (and on several occasions, for example, in ambulance drivers' disputes in 1981 and 1982, military involvement was avoided by the successful use of police as alternative labour: see Morris, 1980), the industrial parties and the military will have been affected. Civilians bargaining in the shadow of threatened military intervention on the one hand and the military preparing to undertake civilian tasks on the other ensure that normal operations on both sides are 'disrupted'. One can glean a sense of this from Table 6.4 which shows how many and for how long service personnel between 1977 and early 1981 had their military tasks disrupted by their industrial 'duties'.

The scale of military intervention in industrial disputes and, indeed, the scope of these disputes themselves have varied enormously, even in recent years. Major national disputes have led to a substantial military involvement. For example, 20,000 service personnel (which, according to Hennessy (The Times, 8 January 1981, p. 2), is the maximum number which could be deployed without recalling personnel from the British Army of the Rhine or from the security forces in Northern Ireland) undertook striking firemen's duties over a nine-week period in 1977-78.[1] They have also led to the undertaking of relatively minor tasks, for

Table 6.4: Number of Military on Stand-by 1977-1981*

Year	Number	Period (weeks)	Number
1977-78: Firemen	20,000	9	20,000
1978-79: Oil tanker drivers Ambulance drivers	150,000	1 4	350 300
1979-80:	-		
1980-81: (to 29 Feb. 1981) Prison Officers	60,000	17	1,000

* 72 or less hours notice to deploy. Derived from Defence Estimates.

example, during the merchant seamen's dispute in 1966, the RAF was used to supply foodstuffs to remote Scottish Islands; in the railwaymen's dispute in 1982, troops laid wire netting in London parks on which cars could park. Similarly, disputes which were limited and local in scope have, on occasion, led to significant military involvement (dustmen: Tower Hamlets (London) 1970, Glasgow 1975; firemen: Glasgow 1973). The nature of some of the tasks actually performed by the military in industrial disputes will be considered later.

The increasing role of the military has been the result of similar attitudes by both Labour and Conservative parties when in government: both have readily invoked military intervention almost entirely in disputes in which they, as financier of the direct employer involved, or during a period of incomes policy, have a major interest in the outcome. At the same time, there has also been an increased willingness, particularly on the part of the public sector trade unions, to engage in industrial action in 'essential' services.[2] The possibility of a government conflict of interest (if this is not a tautology), the impact of military intervention on labour relations, the duty placed on government to protect public health and safety and the major constitutional questions raised are all factors which make the legal criteria for use of the military so important in democratic societies. At a time when government, yet again, is considering what to do about so-called 'emergency' strikes and has begun work on legislation to reduce the risk of essential service strikes (see, e.g., The Times, 12 December 1983, p. 22; Financial Times, 20 February 1984, p. 1) but still maintains a veil of secrecy over the military role (see Chapter 11), it is highly appropriate to set out the existing state of the law, a law whose basis is the combination of wartime expediency and nineteenth-century concepts.

LEGAL CRITERIA FOR MILITARY INTERVENTION

Although the most commonly invoked legal authority for use of the military in industrial disputes is now the Emergency Powers Act 1964, other sources of legal authority, which have a much longer history, are also of importance. In this chapter, the variety and scope of all legal authority for military intervention will be analysed.

Military commanders, and indeed service personnel generally, will look to two sources for a statement of the law: the Queen's Regulations for the Army 1975, Chapter 11, 'Military Aid to the Civil Authorities' and the Manual of Military Law, Part II, Section V, 'Employment of Troops in Aid of the Civil Power'. They may also turn to 'related publications': Land Operations Volume III, Internal Security Doctrine and Instructions and other Defence Council Instructions. All of these are 'restricted' and not available for public scrutiny.[3] According to the Queen's Regulations (QR), and using what has become Ministry of Defence parlance, there are three potential 'recipients' of military aid (within the UK and in peacetime): the Civil Community, Civil Ministries and the Civil Power.

Military Aid to the Civil Community (MACC) in Emergencies in Peacetime
'Where there is no proclamation the Defence Council may ... authorise the temporary employment of Service personnel on work which the Council have approved as being urgent work of national importance' (QR for the Army 1975 (1976) J11.004b).[4]

Section 2 made permanent the Defence (Armed Forces) Regulations (S.R. & O. No. 1304 (1939)). This empowered the Admiralty, the Army Council or the Air Council by order to authorise officers and men of HM naval, military or air forces under their respective control to be temporarily employed in agricultural work or such other work as may be approved in accordance with their instructions as being urgent work of national importance. Thereupon, every person subject to the Naval Discipline Act, military law or air-force law is under a duty to obey any command given by his superior officer in relation to such employment, and every command shall be deemed to be a lawful command within the meaning of the Naval Discipline Act, the Army Act, 1955, or the Air Force Act, 1955, as the case may be. It can readily be seen that the wartime regulation had been made to clarify the position regarding lawful orders to soldiers, where tasks were being performed outside normal military duties and not following a proclamation of emergency; it was, according to Henry Brooke, then Home Secretary, a 'safeguard and a necessary safeguard' (H.C.Deb., Vol. 689, col. 1414) against the possibility of a challenge to a command.

Since the Defence (Transfer of Functions) Act 1964, the functions of the three Councils have been taken over by the Defence Council. The Council was established under the royal prerogative and has both statutory and prerogative functions. The latter give to the Council administration and command over the armed forces. Since 1982 (Q.R. Amendment No. 6) the Council comprises the Secretary of State for Defence (who chairs the Council and is responsible to Parliament for its business), the Ministers and Parliamentary Under Secretaries of State for the Armed Forces and for Defence Procurement, the Chiefs of the Defence, Naval, General and Air Staffs, the First Sea Lord, the Vice Chief of the Defence Staff (Personnel and Logistics), the Chief of Defence Procurement for the Ministry of Defence (MOD), the Chief Scientific Adviser of the MOD, and the Permanent Under Secretary of State of the MOD (Queen's Regulations Annex A(J) to Chapter 1, p. 1A-1).

Between 1940 and 1964, the regulation had been approved annually by Parliament without controversy. It was made permanent in the 1964 Act without 'any objection in principle' (H.C. Deb., Vol. 689, col. 1417) being offered by Frank Soskice for the Opposition. The Act was presented by Henry Brooke as 'a wide exercise in foresight. It is an insurance policy against contingencies ...' (id., col. 1414). The regulation had been invoked on thirteen occasions between 1947 and 1964 (id., col. 1440). Since then, the Act has been invoked on at least ten occasions between 1970 and 1983. Indeed, with the exception of the dockers dispute in 1972, and the industrial civil servants disputes in 1978 and 1981, all military intervention in industrial disputes since 1970 has been authorised by this statute. It is, therefore, the major instrument by which military intervention is authorised. Most recent examples of civilian tasks performed by the military include firefighting, refuse collection, air traffic control, prison duties and ambulance driving. The problem for most legal commentators who consider the 1964 Act is that very little is stated in terms and no procedures are outlined. No accountability, legal or political, has been built into the regulation or into the statute. The most noteworthy comment which can be made is that a relatively obscure regulation made permanent can be the source potentially of such a major intrusion into civilian affairs and yet be made virtually without comment or objection (see Chapter 11). It is the lack of parliamentary control and the operative procedures which need to be emphasised here.

The fact that no proclamation of emergency nor any formal consultation with Parliament is required means that there is no immediate control over the exercise of these powers. Furthermore, the Defence Council and their predecessors have had a very wide discretion to interpret what constitutes 'urgent work of national importance'. Work which has been so defined has included supplying food to the Western Isles during an unofficial seamen's strike (1960), removing refuse in Tower Hamlets (1970) and in Glasgow (1975). There is no definition in the Act of 'urgent work' nor of 'national importance'. The war-time regulation enabled Buckingham Palace boilers to be stoked by the military in 1948 during a strike by Ministry of Works employees. There is no immediate legal or political check on this discretion, and this lack of external control is most disturbing. Furthermore, the powers of the Defence Council and of the Army, Air Force or Admiralty Boards which might be appointed 'may be exercised and their duties performed by any two of their numbers and any document may be signed on behalf of Our Defence Council or any of the said Boards by any two of their members or by the Secretary' of the Council or Board (Q.R. 1975, Amendment No. 6, 1982). Clearly then, members of the Defence Council enjoy what is, in a democratic society, an extraordinarily wide discretion.

Military Aid to Civil Ministries (MACM) in Emergencies in Peacetime

'If a national emergency is proclaimed under the Emergency Powers Act 1920 in a situation where the supply and distribution of the essentials of life to the community are extensively threatened, the powers of the authorities will be regulated by Order in Council' (J11.004a).

The 1920 Act, like the 1964 version, was enacted to remove doubts that an order to servicemen to carry on vital services during a strike might not be a lawful command (Jeffery and Hennessy, 1983, p. 51). Under the 1920 Act, a definition of emergency, a set of procedures and some political controls have been laid down. Under section 1 (as amended by the Emergency Powers Act 1964, s. 1), if at any time it appears to Her Majesty that 'there have occurred or are about to occur, events of such a nature as to be calculated, by interfering with the supply and distribution of food, water, fuel or light, or with the means of locomotion, to deprive the community, or any substantial portion of it, of the essentials of life' Her Majesty may, by proclamation, declare that a state of emergency exists. Following such a proclamation, under section 2, regulations may, by Order in Council, be made 'for securing the essentials of life to the community', including 'such powers and duties as Her Majesty may deem necessary for the preservation of the peace, for securing and regulating the supply and distribution of food, water, fuel, light, and other necessities, for maintaining the means of transit or locomotion, and for any other purposes essential to the public safety and the life of the community'. Of the twelve proclamations of emergency made under the 1920 Act (mines, 1921, 1926, 1972; docks, 1948, 1949, 1970, 1972; London tramwaymen and busmen, 1924; railwaymen, 1955; seamen, 1966; power workers, 1970; and mines, railwaymen and Middle East oil, 1973-4), regulations have been made on ten occasions (the exceptions being 1924 and 1948). Troops have been used under these regulations during six proclamations (mines, 1921, 1926; docks, 1949, 1972; railwaymen, 1955; seamen, 1966) and under the wartime regulation discussed above in the 1948 docks emergency.

Detailed legal analysis has revealed a number of shortcomings in the legal controls over the government's powers under the 1920 Act (Morris, 1979; Whelan, 1979). The definitions contained in the Act are sufficiently elastic to enable the government not only to proclaim an emergency whenever it so wishes, but also to make wide-ranging and extensive regulations. Parliamentary supervision has not led to any effective control over the exercise of these powers and legal review is practically impossible. These failings will be considered briefly in turn.

Definition: The government have proclaimed emergencies in three 'local' disputes - London tramwaymen and busmen 1924, and unofficial docks disputes in London in 1948 and 1949. Whether or not a 'substantial portion of the community' was threatened is questionable. No reference in the statute is made to threats to the national economy; indeed, one major rationale for the enactment of emergency procedures in the Industrial Relations Act 1971 was to extend safeguards to such threats.[5] Yet in the 1966 seamen's strike, the two reasons given by Harold Wilson, then Prime Minister, for the proclamation of emergency were firstly, 'to accept this demand would breach the dykes of our prices and incomes policy' (The Times, 8 June, 1966, p. 1) and secondly,

> The reason for the Proclamation was that the main volume of imports into this country - not only food, but also raw materials - is becoming progressively and more damagingly disrupted. This is bound to affect employment fairly quickly, and is also affecting our export trade. (H.C. Deb., Vol. 729, col. 37)

In other words, the basic reason for the proclamation was danger to the national economy, not within the definition of emergency contained in the 1920 Act. Quintin Hogg (later Lord Hailsham) took up this point for the opposition, stating that 'As the Act stands, it would not be a legitimate motivation to take those circumstances into account in declaring an emergency', that is, the 'import and export trade' (id., col. 752). He did not argue that such factors could not create an emergency, but that, on technical grounds, the 1920 Act did not cover them. He accordingly proposed that the time may have come 'to examine the phraseology of the Act in the light of contemporary economics' (id.).

Regulations:[6] Governments have 'deemed necessary' an enormous array of regulations and given themselves a wide range of powers. Although the full extent of these have not been utilised, they have been available in reserve. Powers which have been exercised have included the requisitioning of land and property, control of public services, transport and supply, imposing 'three-day weeks', and public order control. The claim made by Colonel Wedgwood that these powers give the executive 'an absolute right of dictatorship' (id., Vol. 198, col. 315) is hard to refute. Despite the fact that regulations only remain in force for seven days at a time (s. 2(2)), in practice, emergencies have often been lengthy - the longest being the miners' dispute in 1926 which lasted seven and a half months. Since 1966, the regulations have rarely been debated; discussion has been limited to isolated regulations which have been added to the general 'corpus' (id., Vol. 842, col. 1592, Robert Carr) following 'the well-established precedents for Regulations of this sort' (H.L. Deb., Vol. 346, col. 762, Lord Champion). There has been virtually no recent consideration therefore of what amounts to very extensive authority indeed.

In terms of the use of service personnel, regulations under the 1920 Act would enable other provisions to be invoked which would make military intervention effective. Thus, if civilian vehicles had to be requisitioned in a lorry drivers' dispute, in order that the military could drive them, a proclamation of emergency would be required.[7] In the 1948 docks dispute, servicemen began unloading food supplies five days before an emergency was proclaimed. The Prime Minister announced that regulations would be made under the 1920 Act 'giving powers to the Government to do all that is necessary both by deploying Service personnel whenever required for the maintenance of essential food supplies, and by the requisition of equipment for the maintenance of the life of the community' (H.C. Deb., Vol. 452, col. 1840). In the 1949 docks dispute, a regulation was made to allow troops to do work normally restricted to registered dockers under the dock labour scheme (id., Vol. 467, col. 2288; reg. 2, The Emergency Regulations 1849, S.I. 1949, No. 1300); while in the 1966 seamen's dispute, Sir Elwyn Jones, the Attorney-General, stated that the armed forces would need to requisition civilian port facilities (id., Vol. 729, col. 848). Without such regulations the military have no power to requisition vehicles; intervention under the 1964 Act in the 1979 ambulance drivers' dispute amounted to 'army ambulances with troops to drive and supervise' (The Guardian, 20 January 1979, David Ennals, Secretary of State for Social Services) and in the 1978 firemen's strike to use of civil defence equipment.

Parliamentary Control: Parliament must be informed of a proclamation of emergency 'forthwith' or within five days if it is not due to meet (section 1(2)). Proclamations last for one month at a time and can be extended (section 1(1)). Regulations must be laid before Parliament 'as soon as may be after they are made' (section 2(2)). These procedural requirements have always been adhered to and rarely have opposition parties dissented significantly from a government's actions. Yet the Parliamentary control which has been exercised has not in practice made much difference. Morris, for example, describes it as 'limited and compliance with the procedure is more a matter of form than an effective method of restraining the excesses of the executive' (1979, pp. 333-34). Although the potential for political control does exist, the absence of any effective legal control (id.) and the failure of Parliament to provide a check has left the government with a relatively free hand both to use the military and to support their intervention with other measures.

Military Aid to the Civil Power (MACP)
'To maintain peace and public order' (J11.002). MACP is a combination of common law and royal prerogative powers which, in recent years, has been used only in 'non-industrial' circumstances - anti-terrorism and 'natural' disasters being the most common examples. However, the common law and royal prerogative powers upon which MACP is now authorised were invoked in numerous industrial disputes in the nineteenth and early twentieth centuries (see Chapters 2 and 11). They could have a role to play today to facilitate military intervention to deal with circumstances, such as public disorder, not covered by the Emergency Powers Acts. However, although the Defence Council, which exercises statutory functions under the Emergency Powers Act 1964, also exercises the prerogative functions of 'command and administration' over the armed forces (J1.001, J1.003), unlike MACM and MACC, MACP is lawful without government or Defence Council authority. Indeed, if a local chief officer of police requested military aid to quell industrial disturbances in a situation where the government, through the Defence Council, attempted to reject such an approach, a constitutional crisis could easily emerge (Marshall, 1979, p. 278). In these circumstances, the military commander would turn for guidance to the Queen's Regulations and to the Manual of Military Law. If he did so, however, it would most likely be in vain.

The 'main object' of the Manual as a whole is 'to provide officers in general with a readily available means of acquiring such legal knowledge as they may need for the performance of their duties' (Part I, Section I). The object of Section V 'is to give an explanation of the law relating to the duty of the soldier in case of riot and other disturbances of the peace' (para. 1). In fact, the terms of Section V are extremely ambiguous, and officers could have great difficulty understanding the law. Part of the reason for this is that the law is in a form which is best described as 'elusive'. This theme is taken up at length in Chapter 11 of this book. The terms in which the Manual 'explains' the law are contradictory and confusing. According to paragraph 2 (and based upon <u>Charge to the Bristol Grand Jury</u> (1832) 5 C. & P. 261), there is a common law obligation 'which governs soldiers and other citizens alike ... to come to the aid of the civil power when the civil power requires his assistance to enforce law and order'. Earlier this century, the view was expressed that this was a blanket duty allowing the military no discretion but to aid the civil power (Marshall, 1979, p. 278). The Manual does not accord with this view. Paragraph 3 states that the law is 'clear that a soldier must come to the assistance of the civil authority where it is necessary for him to do so but not otherwise'. Thus, a soldier is legally liable for an excessive use of force 'unless the circumstances are such that he has no opportunity of ascertaining and judging the facts of the case for himself and is therefore compelled to accept the opinion and appraisal of the situation of the civil authority concerned' (para. 3). Similarly, military commanders must, if they have time to do so, investigate and acquaint themselves with the facts and judge for themselves whether to intervene: a commander 'on the spot, while attaching great weight to the opinion of the magistrate, must decide whether military intervention is necessary to deal with the circumstances in which he has been requisitioned' (para. 4). This point is emphasised in relation to 'military matters' particularly the use of force (para. 5), which of course is the raison d'être of MACP. It is only if the magistrate demands 'immediate intervention before the commander has had time to investigate for himself' that he must intervene and will be 'protected by the law' (para. 4). Thus, although the primary obligation for the preservation of order and for the suppression of disturbances rests with the civil authority (paras. 4, 5), and a commander, in all cases where it is practicable, should place himself under the direction of a magistrate (para. 5), it is left both to the soldier and to the commander to judge for themselves and to be responsible for the action to be taken. That this places the military in a confusing position is well illustrated by this part of paragraph 5: the commander 'would incur considerable responsibility if he were to fire without a request to take action from the magistrate or if he were to refuse to fire when requested to do so, but circumstances which he sees before him might justify a commander in firing, or not firing, notwithstanding the request which he receives from the magistrate'. In the 1911 railwaymen's strike, when two men were killed, the military commander involved in disturbances ordered his troops to shoot without any formal consent from the magistracy. Moreover, military commanders have refused calls for help, for example on the grounds that they feared military intervention would make the situation worse (see Bramall, Chapter 3). There is no doubt that a similar responsibility applies to the use of force short of firing. As paragraph 3 states: 'Even though the civil authority should give directions to the contrary the Commander of the troops, if it is really necessary, is bound to take such action as the circumstances demand'.

In MACP therefore, the military assume under the common law a combination of roles - that of assistance and subservience and that of independence and responsibility. When royal prerogative powers are added, it is the independent role which comes to the fore. The Queen's Regulations, which adopt the modern parlance of the police rather than the magistracy as the civil power (even though the 1973 edition of <u>Stones Justice Manual</u>, at p. 2972, still refers to the magistracy calling out the military), outline the procedures which will be invoked should the assistance of the armed forces be called for (J11.002). The officer to whom the application is made is at once to inform the Ministry of Defence and his immediately superior authority. Assistance will normally be requested by the chief of police and should be confirmed in writing. Where a request is received from another source, the Service commander on the spot is to refer the request to the chief officer of police and report it to his superiors. However, both the Regulations and the Manual of Military Law make it clear that though there is no difference under common law between soldiers and other citizens in respect of their duty to respond to the call of the civil authority, there is, 'in cases of disturbance where the civil authority has not asked for help' (para. 3) and 'in very exceptional circumstances for grave and sudden emergencies' (J11.002) which have arisen 'a duty to take action laid upon military commanders by Queen's Regulations which is not laid upon other citizens, except magistrates and peace officers (QR 1182)' (para. 3). In such emergencies the commander is to act on his own responsibility and is to report as early as possible the matter and the action he has taken to the Service authorities and to the chief officer of police (J11.002).

Although this interpretation of Queen's Regulations in the Manual has been described by Evelegh as 'startling' (1978, p. 8), there is a precedent. In August 1911, during a railwaymen's strike, military commanders sent troops to protect strike breakers following the suspension of an army regulation that required a requisition from a civil authority and despite objections from local authorities. An accusation that illegal or extra constitutional action had been taken was rejected by Winston Churchill, the Home Secretary: 'The military authorities always enjoy power to move troops in their own country ... wherever it is found to be convenient or necessary' (H.C. Deb., Vol. 29, col. 2286). The important question which is raised is how far the military are indeed empowered to act contrary to or independently of the wishes of the civil power (see Marshall, 1979, p. 278). The vagueness of terms such as 'when it is really necessary' or 'in the opinion of the commander' are not merely fodder for the constitutional law technician. To the military commander passing by Saltley Coke Depot in 1972 and seeing 6000 pickets and demonstrators defeat police attempts to clear gates or by the St Paul's district of Bristol in 1981 and seeing the police retreat in the face of civil disturbances, these are important questions. Just as important, both to the military and to those affected by their prospective involvement, would be the commander's response to requests to 'ride shotgun' through picket lines - that is, to escort supplies for example into a nuclear power station or to distribute food supplies with orders to 'get through at all costs' as in the General Strike of 1926 (see Jeffery, Chapter 2).

The other main legal ambiguity is - who takes command when the military come to the aid of the civil power? It is quite clear that both the police (<u>Albert v. Lavin</u> [1981] 2 W.L.R. 955), magistrates (<u>R. v. Kennett</u> (1781) 5 C & P 282; <u>R. v. Pinney</u> (1832) 3 St. Tr. 11) and central government have legal authority to request military aid. It is equally clear that the legal responsibility for such intervention falls both on the civil power (Greer, 1983) and the military themselves (see above). There is a difference of opinion between the police and the military, however, as to which 'branch' should exercise command and control following intervention. In the 1910-11 industrial disturbances, the military commander, Sir Nevil Macready, took full control of military tactics. More recently, Sir Robert Mark has stated, in contrast, that following military aid,

> it is clearly desirable that both police and the army should then conform to exactly the same terms of engagement. There is no question of one service coming under command of the other ... In such circumstances police, army, Home Office and Ministry of Defence must act in complete accord. (Chapter 4, p. 91)

Sir Edwin Bramall, however, believes that 'in a real breakdown of order ... once called in, command would then devolve to the military commanding officer' (Chapter 3, p. 74).

MILITARY-POLICE RELATIONSHIPS

The two major forms of state intervention in major industrial disputes are the use of the military and the use of the police. Historically, the two agencies have, in the context of many industrial disputes, acted in parallel or in direct collaboration. In ambulance drivers' and firemen's disputes, the police have acted as 'filters' to ensure that only 'emergencies' were handled by service personnel. In the air traffic control assistants' dispute in 1977, RAF fuel tankers, accompanied by sixty police officers, broke through picket lines at West Drayton air traffic control centre (<u>The Times</u>, 14 October 1977). Moreover, contingency planning builds upon an existing and ongoing relationship between the military and the police. Thus, in the 1983 water dispute, eight regional emergency committees were established comprising police, military, Manpower Services Commission, local authority, Department of Industry and Central Office of Information representatives. Co-ordination of this kind is not, of course, restricted to industrial disputes. Indeed, it is likely that much greater collaboration takes place in the context of terrorism. In this section, the relationship between the police and the military is analysed in terms of legal theory and of the current practice.

Law
In terms of strict legal theory, the two main forms of state intervention in industrial disputes - provision of substitute labour and maintenance of public order - are separate and distinct, in terms both of the legal standards and constitutional procedures which apply. Thus, in terms of substitute labour, until very recently, the military have undertaken this task exclusively under the direction of the Defence Council and its predecessors. The military, as Crown employees, are subject to a chain of command which rises, ultimately, to the Secretary of State for Defence; the military are thus subject to governmental orders. In terms of public order, the police have taken the primary responsibility. Police officers are not servants of government, central or local; chief officers of police are not subject to governmental instructions regarding the operational use of police. If military aid was sought in public order situations then it was the magistracy or, in London, the Metropolitan Police Commissioner who would request assistance (QR 1164, 1165(b) (1955 version)). Thus, in order to preserve police impartiality and their independence of the government, suggestions that they be used for 'industrial' purposes have always been rejected. Even during the general strike in 1926, a proposal to use police vans to convey medical supplies to hospitals was dropped when Sir John Anderson, Permanent Under-Secretary to the Home Office, objected that it would contravene the 'very big principle ... that in a dispute the police do not help either side' (Wheeler-Bennett, 1962, p. 106). By contrast, the armed forces have never had such an impartial and independent reputation (Marshall, 1979, p. 274).

In the last decade, the traditional role of the police and the modern procedure to invoke military assistance in aid of the civil power have both changed. In the 1979, 1981 and 1982 ambulance drivers' disputes, the police maintained an emergency service where ambulancemen refused to provide cover. Police resources were also relied upon in the 1979 social workers' dispute. According to Morris (1980, p. 1), the 1979 ambulance drivers' dispute was the 'first occasion on which the police have undertaken jobs normally performed by strikers during an industrial dispute'. Not only did this raise 'some interesting legal problems' (can the police refuse to 'strikebreak'; what is the scope of police 'duty'; what are the risks of urging policemen to disobey such orders?), but Morris was told by the Home Office that 'The assistance provided was at the discretion of the police' (id., p. 1). This represents a major undermining of the traditional responsibility for industrial dispute policy, particularly as it can be argued that the police were used <u>instead</u> of service personnel.

Practice
Further undermining of traditional legal and political accountability for intervention in relation to the public order context of industrial disputes has also occurred, but in a paradoxical way. While the use of police as an alternative labour supply represents a 'decentralising' and less accountable form of intervention, the procedure to invoke military assistance in public order situations has been centralised and taken away from the magistracy, and even, to an extent, from the chief officer of police. 'Modern' practice has been outlined by Sir Robert Mark (Chapter 4, pp. 92-3):

> Permission of the Home Secretary is sought by the chief officer of police to invoke military aid and the Minister of Defence, in consultation with the Home Secretary, who will have considered the views of the chief officer of police, will decide whether to authorise the ultimate sanction of force by such troops as he may make available. Such assistance was formerly sought by police from the magistracy rather than from the Home Office, but whatever the legal position the present practice reflects the emergence of a professional, well-organised police service which has inevitably assumed the primary responsibility for law and order.

This change of procedure, and indeed the use of police as an alternative labour supply, calls into question the independence and impartiality of the police. At the very least, as Marshall points out (1979, p. 274), consideration should be given to the question whether these are assets worth preserving. Questioned about the new procedure for invoking military aid outlined by Sir Robert Mark, the Home Secretary, Roy Jenkins, not only endorsed it but 'thought it would be more satisfactory ... that the circumstances ... in which the military is required to assist the civil power should be determined by a Minister responsible to the House rather than purely by the magistracy' (H.C. Deb., Vol. 909, col. 617). Moreover, in the 1982 health service workers' dispute, the MOD stated that military aid would only be provided if requested by health authorities (The Times, 8 June 1982). While these matters have not been publicly debated, the issues involved are not dissimilar to those raised during the miners' strike in 1984 regarding accusations that government directed or influenced the police response to mass picketing: how far should the police and military role in industrial disputes be centrally co-ordinated and the responsibility of government; how far can the public order and 'industrial' roles be divorced in practice; and what are the implications more generally of different forms of state intervention?

CONCLUSION

The recent and growing willingness of governments to use the military in industrial disputes is a phenomenon of major importance. To lawyers, the minimal legal and political control of government discretion, the ambiguities in the law and, indeed, the very lack of legal constraints are all most disturbing. To trade unionists, even those with a short historical memory, the implications of military intervention are obvious, particularly in the public sector. One union response to government contingency planning (as reported by Peter Hennessy, The Times, 25 November 1980) has been to mirror such plans from the union side by establishing a 'rival headquarters'. Thus, in the civil servants' dispute in 1981, specific targets were singled out for industrial action such as the Inland Revenue, Customs and Excise (as well as GCHQ Cheltenham). Yet it remains true in practice that the military role is not unconfined. Certain tasks are not susceptible to effective intervention by the military, particularly where technological or specific industrial skills are required. Very often, the military could not intervene without civilian guidance; alternatively, as in the firemen's disputes, they have to rely upon their own and other old equipment which is not too complex or dangerous. Moreover, there is ample evidence that use of the military can exacerbate disruption since the task of safeguarding essential supplies is indistinguishable in practice from strikebreaking (see Jeffery and Hennessy, 1983).

It is to be hoped that this chapter, and indeed this book as a whole, will, together with other 'airings' of these issues (such as Morris, 1983 and NALGO, 1984), lead to a more open debate concerning the law, policy and practice of military and police roles in industrial disputes and in the maintenance of 'essential' services.

NOTES

1. Note however that the manning of 1000 'Green Goddesses' nationwide still left many areas with the barest of fire cover. Thus, the county of Cornwall had only two fire engines and Suffolk only one. Over 20,000 troops were used during the 41-day dock strike in 1945.

2. For example, in 1975 there were 19 industrial disputes involving 13 branches of the Prison Officers' Association. In 1976, 34:23; 1977, 44:21; 1978, 119:63 (Sunday Times, 26 October 1980).

3. Extracts of Land Operations Vol. III were published in Time Out, 10 January 1975, and are outlined in T. Bunyan, The History and Practice of the Political Police in Britain, London, Quartet, 1977, pp. 277-78.

4. The phrase 'and the emergency is limited and local' was deleted in Amendment No. 3, January 1979.

5. According to the Industrial Relations Bill: Consultative Document (1970), para. 165 (Department of Employment and Productivity), 'the Emergency Powers Act 1920 cannot be invoked solely on the grounds that the national economy is endangered'.

6. The statute expressly prohibits regulations which (a) impose compulsory military service or industrial conscription; (b) make it an offence to strike or peacefully persuade others to do so; (c) alter any existing criminal procedure or confer any right to punish by fine or imprisonment without trial (s. 2(1)(3)).

7. Note though that the government can also alter the law by regulation to increase the scope

for military intervention. Thus, the Motor Vehicles (Drivers' Licences) (Amendment) (2) Regulation 1980, and the Heavy Goods Vehicle (Drivers' Licences) (Amendment) 1980 gave troops under the age of 17 the power to drive vehicles over three and a half tonnes in weight.

REFERENCES

Creighton, W.B. (1983) 'Emergency Legislation and Industrial Disputes in Northern Ireland', in J.C. Wood (ed.) Encyclopedia of Northern Ireland Labour Law and Practice, Belfast, Labour Relations Agency

Greer, S.C. (1983) 'Military Intervention in Civil Disturbances: the Legal Basis Reconsidered', Public Law 573

Jeffery, K. & Hennessy, P. (1983) States of Emergency: British Governments and Strike-breaking Since 1919, London, Routledge & Kegan Paul

Marshall, G. (1979) 'The Armed Forces and Industrial Disputes in the United Kingdom', 5 Armed Forces and Society 270

Morris, G.S. (1979) 'The Emergency Powers Act 1920', Public Law 317

_____ (1980) 'The Police and Industrial Emergencies', 9 Industrial Law Journal 1

_____ (1983) 'The Regulation of Industrial Action in Essential Services', 12 Industrial Law Journal 69

NALGO (1984) Government Activities Against Trade Unions, London, NALGO

Wheeler-Bennett, J.W. (1962) John Anderson, Viscount Waverley, London, Macmillan, quoted in Marshall, 1979, p. 274

Whelan, C.J. (1979) 'Military Intervention in Industrial Disputes', 8 Industrial Law Journal 222

_____ (1983) Industrial Conflict: the Role of Government and the Law in the US and UK, Centre for Socio-Legal Studies Bibliography in Socio-Legal Studies, No. 2, Wolfson College, Oxford

Chapter Seven

THE ROLE OF MILITARY FORCES IN PUBLIC SECTOR LABOR RELATIONS*

James B. Jacobs

The intervention of military forces in labor-management disputes is highly controversial in a democracy committed to solving labor-management disputes through collective bargaining mechanisms and to keeping the military out of domestic politics. It is therefore quite remarkable that the repeated use in recent years of National Guard forces, and in two cases of federal troops, to replace striking public employees has attracted so little attention. There does not appear to be a single scholarly article on the subject in either the labor relations or civil-military relations literatures, despite a substantial number of such deployments since the 1970 postal strike.

This chapter is intended to call the use of military forces as replacements to the attention of scholars and practitioners in collective bargaining. This practice raises important questions concerning the suppression of public sector strikes and the proper role of military forces in civilian governance.

HISTORY OF MILITARY FORCES' REPLACEMENT ROLE

Despite the controversy it often provoked, military intervention in labor conflicts was common from 1875 to 1925 (Dulles, 1966). Military forces, usually state militia, were frequently called upon during that period to preserve law and order in violent strike situations. In theory the militia's role was to keep peace, but in fact the military often used force, sometimes wantonly, to break strikes (Hofstadter and Wallace, 1970, pp. 109-86). During the great railroad strike of 1877, for example, 45,000 militiamen were called up in eleven states and more than 100 strikers were killed and several hundred were wounded. In fact, between 1877 and 1892 at least 30 percent of the militia's active duty assignments involved strikes (Riker, 1957, p. 55). And in a particularly notorious case, President Cleveland sent federal troops to 'preserve order' in Pullman, Illinois in 1894 despite the protests of Governor Altgeld, who argued against the use of troops.

The role of the military, particularly the National Guard,[1] as an industrial police force persisted into the twentieth century, but strike duty subsided by the late 1920s and all but disappeared after World War II (id., p. 65). In recent years the National Guard has been called upon for such duty only in unusually violent situations, such as the 1974 truckers' strike, during which troops were called up in Pennsylvania, Ohio, Minnesota, Tennessee, Kentucky, Iowa, West Virginia, Illinois, Maryland, Indiana and Alabama.

A less common form of military involvement in labor conflict throughout most of our history is the deployment of military personnel as <u>replacements</u> for striking employees. Blackman's history of presidential seizures (Blackman, 1967, pp. 294-8, on which information in this and the succeeding paragraph is based) traces the first such intervention to June 1863, when, in response to a strike by longshoremen, the government used federal troops and civilians to load and unload vessels at New York piers. During a 1917-18 loggers' strike that interrupted the supply of spruce wood for army aircraft, federal soldiers were assigned to logging camps where, under contract with private firms, they constructed and operated a logging railroad and a large sawmill. Twice in 1919, troops loaded, unloaded and moved military cargo ships and troops ships. In 1941, the Navy Department recruited civilians to replace machinists whose wildcat strike disrupted work at ship-repair yards in San Francisco. In August 1944, a few hundred sailors and soldiers cleaned out debris from government vessels in Bethlehem Steel Corporation's struck ship-repair yards in New Jersey and New York. On several occasions in the ensuing thirty years, the military, directly or with civilians, was called upon to load and unload strike-bound ships and to assume clerical functions related to the movement of military cargo. All these deployments appear to have been linked to military or national defense activities.[2]

Until 1970 troops had not been used to replace striking public employees, except for one instance - the 1919 Boston police strike, during which 4,500 members of the State Guard were called upon to maintain order in the face of looting and threatened mob violence. The Guard's capacity to carry out the police function effectively broke the strike and few of the strikers were rehired. It is said that the Guard's success was responsible for catapulting Calvin Coolidge, then the Governor of Massachusetts, into the vice-presidency (Russell, 1975).

Table 7.1: Military Call-Ups in Labor Disputes, January 1970-August 1981

Dates	Place	Government Employees on Strike
1970:Mar 24-30	New York City	Postal Workers
1971:June 25	Nashua, New Hampshire	Firefighters
1973:Jan 3	Milwaukee, Wisconsin	City Employees
1973:July 6-12	Puerto Rico	Firefighters
1973:Sept 1-3	Texas	Traffic Safety
1973:Sept 12-13	Texas	Prison Guards
1973:Nov 5-10	Milwaukee, Wisconsin	Firefighters
1974:Mar 12-13	Warm Springs, Montana	Mental Health
1974:Mar 18-20	Galen-Boulder, Montana	Hospital Workers
1974:July 12-13	Lucasville, Ohio	Prison Guards
1974:July 16-17	Cranston, Rhode Island	Prison Guards
1974:July 18-19	Lima, Ohio	Mental Health
1974:Nov 10-12	Cranston, Rhode Island	Mental Health
1974:Nov 27	San Juan, Puerto Rico	Water Works Employees
1975:May 13	Lucasville, Ohio	Prison Guards
1975: Aug 13-Sept 8	Pine Bluff, Arkansas	Firefighters
1975: Oct 3-9	Kansas City, Missouri	Firefighters
1976:Nov 11-16	Warm Springs, Montana	Mental Health
1976:Nov 12-19	Springfield, Illinois	Public Employees
1977:July 3-22	State, Wisconsin	Prison Guards

Date	Location	Group
1977:Sept 2-12	St Croix, Virgin Islands	Prison Guards
1978:Mar 12-13	Rhode Island	State Employees
1978:July 1	Memphis, Tennessee	Firefighters
1978:July 14	Louisville, Kentucky	Firefighters
1978:Aug 17	Memphis, Tennessee	Police
1978:Sept 6	Mach, New Hampshire	Firefighters
1978:Sept 14	Wichita, Kansas	Firefighters
1978:Nov 18-23	St Bernard Parish, Louisiana	Firefighters
1978:Dec 1-6	Huntsville, Alabama	Police and Firefighters
1979:Feb 5-Mar 14	Montana	State Employees
1979:Feb 1-10, and Feb 6-Mar 6	New Orleans, Louisiana	Police
1979:Apr 18-May 7	New York	State Employees
1979:June 27-29	Cape Girardeau, Missouri	Firefighters
1979:May 2-4	Birmingham, Alabama	Police and Firefighters
1979:Sept 12-20	Cranston, Rhode Island	Mental Health
1979: Oct 21-Nov 16	Hawaii	State Employees
1979-80: Dec 27-Jan 3	Kansas City, Missouri	Firefighters
1980:Mar 18-23	Kansas City, Missouri	Firefighters
1980:May 8-16	Nashville, Tennessee	Firefighters
1980:July 14-25	Mobile, Alabama	Firefighters
1980:Nov 24-25	Marion, Indiana	Firefighters
1980:Dec 6-7	Boston, Massuchusetts	Commuter Transit
1981:Mar 1-2	Milwaukee, Wisconsin	Firefighters
1981:Mar 20-21	Milwaukee, Wisconsin	Firefighters
1981:June 23-25	Concord-Manchester New Hampshire	State Employees
1981:July 10-14	Boston, other locations, Massachusetts	Mental Health
1981:August	Nationwide	Air Traffic Controllers

Source: National Guard Bureau, Washington D.C.

For the most part, however, until the 1960s public employees were not unionized and did not strike. Those few public employee strikes that did occur apparently did not affect critical government functions, or at least not severely enough to provoke the call-up of military personnel as replacements. Perhaps important political and philosophical inhibitions prevented politicians from turning to the military to assure the continuation of struck public service.

From 1970 to the middle of 1981, however, military forces have been used as replacements for striking public employees on forty-six occasions (see Tables 7.1 and 7.2). The precedent-setting action was the postal strike in March 1970 during which President Nixon sent 30,000 regular and reserve federal troops and National Guardsmen to replace striking postal employees in New York City. The strikers capitulated just two days after the troops assumed the task of sorting and delivering mail.

Table 7.2: Yearly Summary of Recent National Guard Call-Ups in Public Sector Labor Disputes

Year	Number
1970	1
1971	1
1972	0
1973	4
1974	7
1975	3
1976	2
1977	2
1978	9
1979	8
1980	5
1981*	5

* This covers the period through August 1981, including the use of federal troops during the air traffic controllers' strike.

The postal strike and the recent air traffic controllers' strike are the only occasions during recent years when federal troops have served as replacements for striking public employees. As Table 7.1 shows, however, National Guardsmen have been called upon at the state and local levels to work as firefighters, policemen, prison guards, and mental health attendants, among other jobs. While it may be premature to speak of a trend, it is worth noting (in Table 7.2) that the number of National Guard interventions increased from seventeen in the six-year period 1970-75 to twenty-five in the five-year period 1976-80. The largest deployment was in April 1979 when New York State Governor Hugh Carey activated over 12,000 Army and Air National Guardsmen to replace striking state prison guards (Zimmer and Jacobs, 1981, pp. 531-44).

LEGAL CONSTRAINTS

We need to ask when a governor (or a President in the case of striking federal employees) can and should call up troops to replace striking public employees. What justifies the use of military forces? Must there be a serious threat to public health and safety? An imminent catastrophe? Or are we only dealing with an executive 'judgment call'? To answer these questions requires, in part, an examination of federal and state law, particularly constitutions and statutes.

All but two instances of military personnel replacing public employees since 1970 involved state or local employees. Federal troops were used only in the 1970 postal strike and, to a limited extent, in the 1981 air traffic controllers' strike.[3] This analysis begins, nevertheless, with the postal strike because President Nixon's use of military personnel in that situation set the precedent for subsequent gubernatorial actions. The fact that Nixon's action was not seen as significant by scholars at the time is partially explained by its having been overshadowed by the Vietnam War and other controversial uses of the armed forces. In hindsight, however, the postal strike was crucial; since then - in just a decade - military deployments for public sector strikes have become unexceptional and are taken for granted. If one views the 1970 postal strike deployment as an extraordinary event in American history, based as it was on questionable legal authority, the whole issue of using troops in this way becomes problematic.

The 1970 Postal Strike
On March 19, 1970, thousands of postal workers around the country walked off their jobs over a salary dispute.[4] The strike was most severe in New

York City, where mail service came to a virtual halt. After an injunction failed to bring the strikers back to work,[5] President Nixon declared a national emergency and sent 2,500 regular military personnel, 15,300 Army, Navy and Marine reservists, and 12,000 New York State Army and Air National Guardsmen to New York City to sort and deliver the mail.[6] Within two days, the union capitulated and the strikers returned to work. The domestic use of troops to break the postal strike enjoyed widespread popular support, even in the liberal press,[7] in contrast to the furor that developed over the secret bombings and the invasion of Cambodia at about this time. Perhaps this support explains why, in contrast to massive legal literature on the President's actions in Southeast Asia, not a single scholarly article on the postal strike deployment ever appeared in the law reviews.

Despite the lack of objections at the time, presidential deployment of troops domestically raises profound questions about the proper role of the armed forces in a constitutional system and about the respective powers of the executive and legislative branches of government. The Constitution does not specifically provide for domestic deployment of troops, but to the extent that the text of the Constitution deals with this power, it entrusts it to the Congress, not the President. Congress is given the power to organize the militia (U.S. Const., art. I, sec. 8, cl. 16) and to provide for calling it forth to execute the laws (id., cl. 15). Congressional control over the regular armed forces is inferable from the powers to 'raise and support' armies and to maintain the navy (id., cls. 12, 13), and to 'make rules for the government and regulation of the land and naval forces' (id., cl. 14). When Congress uses its authority to regulate the use of the military, the President must conform his actions to the terms of such regulation.[8] The Executive's power to deploy troops domestically, if any, must come either from congressional authorization or from the President's own constitutional powers as Commander in Chief,[9] as executor of the laws,[10] or from whatever inherent authority vests in the President as Chief Executive.[11]

<u>Inherent powers</u>. President Nixon's declaration that the postal strike was a national emergency may have been an attempt to justify the troop deployment on the basis of inherent presidential power to act in times of grave national crisis.[12] Most

constitutional scholars would accept the idea that a President can use troops when the survival of the country is at stake. There is little doubt that the Executive, acting on his own authority, can mobilize the armed forces to repel a sudden attack by a foreign enemy or to quell a domestic insurrection. This has been referred to as a raison d'état, but it is almost always raised only in hypothetical discussions of national security.

Whatever the President's inherent authority to prevent the nation's military defeat or the demise of the republic, a postal strike is another matter. Disruptions of mail delivery cause inconvenience, even hardship, to be sure; but other countries have weathered postal strikes without collapse (Canada, for example[13]). In any case, at the time of the emergency proclamation the strike had achieved only partial success in most cities around the country. Postal officials had not yet had an opportunity to see how well service could be maintained with supervisory personnel and other replacements. Certain agencies, like Selective Service and welfare, had contingency plans they did not even get the opportunity to test.[14]

It is possible to speculate that President Nixon's concerns went beyond the disruption of mail service. He spoke of the 'survival of a government based upon law' (N.Y. Times, March 24, 1970, p. 16). His argument, in effect, was that the sovereignty of government itself was challenged by the postal workers' illegal strike.[15] Perhaps the President and his advisors saw the strike, or at least wanted to portray it, as a challenge to the national administration and to 'law and order'. Their reasoning may have been that if the postal workers were able to force a settlement through an illegal strike, governmental authority would be seriously undermined. But this surely overstates the case. Even if the postal strike enjoyed some initial success, the government could still have enforced criminal and civil penalties against the strikers, or it could have fired them and hired replacements. It seems a gross distortion to have defined the strike, especially in its early stages, as a national calamity. Using the President's hazy, inherent authority to prevent national collapse to justify breaking the strike with military personnel was, at best, a drastic and unprecedented expansion of presidential powers. The very nature of constitutional government precludes the use of inherent executive power in all but the most compelling circumstances.

Commander in Chief. The President's power as Commander in Chief is a war power and does not apply to internal affairs.[16] As the Court noted in Youngstown Sheet and Tube Co. v. Sawyer, '[e]ven though "theater of war" be an expanding concept, we cannot, with faithfulness to our constitutional system, hold that the Commander in Chief of the Armed Forces has the ultimate power to take possession of private property in order to keep labor disputes from stopping production' (343 U.S. 579, 587). The wide indulgence granted to the President when the nation is fighting a foreign enemy is not granted when the President acts domestically. When Congress authorizes domestic use of troops, the President assumes the role of Commander in Chief, but this power as 'first general' cannot serve as a substitute for congressional action.

Executor of the laws. In the postal strike deployments, President Nixon explicitly relied on his powers to execute the laws, reasoning that since Congress provided for the establishment and operation of the postal system, military force could be used to ensure fulfillment of the postmaster's statutory obligations.[17] But this argument proves too much. Following it to its logical conclusion, all federal employees could be replaced by military personnel if, in the judgment of the President, their statutory duties were not being satisfactorily discharged. The authority to execute the laws could be transformed into a charter for military rule.

Fortunately, the Constitution's 'faithfully execute' clause does not provide the basis for military dictatorship. When executing the laws, the President may take only such actions as are not prohibited or pre-empted by Congress; he cannot violate the laws in order to execute them (Corwin, 1978, p. 91). The question therefore is whether use of troops in the postal strike was authorized or prohibited by Congress.[18]

The Posse Comitatus Act. In 1878, reacting to President Grant's frequent use of the regular military forces in labor disputes and other circumstances,[19] Congress passed the Posse Comitatus Act (20 Stat. 152). As amended in 1956 (70a Stat. 626), it provides:

> Whoever, except in cases and under circumstances expressly authorized by the

> Constitution or Act of Congress, wilfully uses any part of the Army or the Air Force as a posse comitatus or otherwise to execute the laws shall be fined not more than $10,000 or imprisoned not more than two years, or both. (18 U.S.C. sec. 1385 (1976))[20]

The Act is the most significant legislative restriction on executive use of troops. On its face, this law clearly prevents the President from assigning military personnel[21] to strike replacement duty unless there is another law that expressly permits it.

A law adopted in 1861 is the one most relevant to the use of troops in a domestic crisis; it provides, as one would expect, that troops may be deployed domestically in grave situations of insurrection and disruption, when civil authority has broken down:

> Whenever the President considers that unlawful obstructions, combinations, assemblages, or rebellions against the authority of the United States, make it impracticable to enforce the laws of the United States ... by the ordinary course of judicial proceedings, he may ... use such of the armed forces as he considers necessary to enforce those laws or to suppress the rebellion. (10 U.S.C. sec. 332 (1976))[22]

Other statutes empower the President to deploy the armed forces when there is an 'insurrection in any state against its government' (id., sec. 331) and to suppress unlawful combinations or conspiracies that 'obstruct the execution of federal law' (id., sec. 333). These statutes also presuppose the inability or unwillingness of civilian institutions to perform their lawful functions. These statutes were not cited, however, in President Nixon's executive order deploying federalized National Guardsmen to deliver mail.[23]

Instead, the President pointed in his executive order to 10 U.S.C. sec. 3500, which authorizes the President to use Army National Guardsmen for domestic peacekeeping 'whenever [he] is unable with the regular forces to execute the laws of the United States'.[24] The statute provides for the use of the National Guard as a last resort; presumably, the regular force must first attempt, and fail, to execute the laws. As in the case of the emergency proclamation, neither President Nixon in his executive order, nor Assistant Attorney General (now

Justice) William Rehnquist in an internal memorandum on this subject, elaborated on the unprecedented decision to use Guardsmen as a replacement for strikers.[25]

Gubernatorial Authority
The majority of public employees work for state and local government; most public sector strikes occur at these levels. To determine when troops can be called up to play a replacement role at these levels, we must look to state constitutional and statutory law.[26] State statutes or constitutions, or both, specify the conditions under which the National Guard may be activated.[27] None of the states that have adopted comprehensive public sector collective bargaining statutes have included provisions for use of Guardsmen as replacements. These laws are sufficiently flexible, however, to leave largely to the governor's discretion the decision whether or not to deploy the Guard in public sector strikes. While the courts, in theory, can review such deployments, in practice they are unlikely to second-guess the governor.[28]

A sampling of constitutional and statutory authority for gubernatorial deployment of the National Guard is presented in Table 7.3, which shows that several states permit the governor to use troops 'to execute the laws of the state'. Read broadly, this formulation could justify the use of troops in any illegal public employee strike. Since no-strike provisions are usually part of the law of the state, the Governor could deploy troops to enforce the ban on public employee strikes. Alternatively, it could be argued that troops are justified to maintain public services that are authorized by law. The latter justification would apply even to states in which public employee strikes are permissible, unless one interprets the acceptance of public sector strikes as a permissible exception to the requirement that executive agencies maintain their operations.[29]

A number of states authorize the governor to call out the National Guard in case of 'emergency'. Since almost anything can be labeled an 'emergency', a governor is free to deploy National Guardsmen in almost any strike by state and local employees. While every public sector strike creates severe problems for some governmental operations, sometimes adjustments can minimize service disruption and hardships for service beneficiaries; in other circumstances substantial disruptions are difficult, if not impossible, to avoid.

So far there have been no reported judicial decisions on challenges to the governors' use of troops as replacements in public sector strikes.

Table 7.3: Gubernatorial Authority to Activate the National Guard in Selected States

State	Authority (Emphasis added)
Alaska	Alaska Constitution, Article III, sec. 19. The governor is commander-in-chief of the armed forces of the State. He may call out these forces <u>to execute the laws</u>, suppress or prevent insurrection or lawless violence, or repel invasion.
Colorado	Colorado Constitution, Article IV, sec. 5. The governor shall be commander-in-chief of the military forces of the state ... He shall have the power to call out the militia <u>to execute the laws</u>, suppress insurrection or repel invasion. Colorado Rev. Stat., secs. 28-3-104. The governor shall be the commander-in-chief of the armed forces ... and may employ the same for the defense or relief of the state, the <u>enforcement of its laws</u>, and <u>the protection of life and property therein</u>.
Louisiana	Louisiana Constitution, Article 4, sec. 5(J). The governor shall be commander-in-chief of the armed forces of the state ... He may call out these forces <u>to preserve law and order</u>, to suppress insurrection, to repel invasion, or <u>in other times of emergency</u>. Louisiana Rev. Stat. Ann. Chapter 1, sec. 7 (West). The governor may call into the active service of the state any part of the militia that is necessary in the event of insurrection, invasion, or riot, or imminent danger thereof, or in the event of public disaster from flood, fire, storm, or earthquake, or to assist civil authorities in guarding prisoners.

New Jersey	New Jersey Stat. sec. 38A:2-4 (West). The governor may, in case of insurrection, invasion, tumult, <u>riot, breach of peace</u>, natural disaster or <u>imminent danger to public safety</u>, order to active duty all or any part of the militia ...
New York	New York Military Law, Article I, sec. 3. The governor of the state shall be the commander-in-chief of the militia of the state ... New York Military Law, Article I, sec. 6 (McKinney). The governor shall have power, in case of invasion, disaster, insurrection, <u>riot, breach of the peace or imminent danger thereof</u>; to order into active service ... the organized militia.
Ohio	Ohio Constitution, Article 9, sec. 4. The governor shall have power to call forth the militia, <u>to execute the laws of the state</u>, to suppress insurrection, to repel invasion, and to act in the event of a disaster within the state.
Rhode Island	Rhode Island Gen. Laws, sec. 30-2-6 (1968). In case of martial law, war, invasion, rebellion, insurrection, riot, <u>tumult, public calamity</u> or catastrophe, <u>or other emergency, or imminent danger thereof, or resistance to the laws of this state</u> or the United States the governor shall order into service all or any part of the militia.

This may be due to the fact that such suits would have little chance of success, given the record of judicial deference to executive authority in this area (see note 28). In the federal courts, such suits would be unlikely to survive a motion to dismiss, since no federal statutory or constitutional rights are involved. A disgruntled Guardsman would have standing in state court to challenge an allegedly illegal call-up, but, as Table 7.3 shows, the constitutional and statutory authority for executive discretion to activate National Guard forces is so broad that such a suit would have little chance before a state judge faced with an illegal strike and disrupted governmental services.

NONLEGAL CONSTRAINTS

The decision-making process leading to a call-up of the National Guard in strike and strike-threat situations has not been analyzed in case studies. In the absence of such a literature, it is useful to speculate on the factors local leaders and the governor consider in making a decision to call up the Guard.

The Capacity to Serve: Practical Constraints

The National Guard is better suited to some replacement duties than others. Whether or not the Guard can play an effective replacement role depends upon the complexity of the operations to be performed and on the consequences of faulty performance. We may hypothesize that where operations are very complex and where the consequences of faulty performance are severe, there will be a greater reluctance to call upon the National Guard.

The 1980 strike by New York City transit workers is an example. An informant who was close to the negotiations admits: 'We never seriously considered using the Guard. The transit system was simply too complex; the potential for a cataclysmic accident was too great'. It was feared, in addition, that angry workers might sabotage the system. Thus, although the decision to close down the transit system enormously inconvenienced New Yorkers and cost businesses millions of dollars in losses, a call-up of the National Guard was never considered a viable option.

At the other end of the continuum lies a postal strike. Postal operations, especially mail delivery, require only low-level skills.[30] National Guardsmen can be briefed and sent into action in a few hours. If their performance is poor, the mail may be lost or go undelivered, but there will be no loss of life, serious property damage, or catastrophe.

The job of prison guard lies somewhere in between. It has major responsibilities, but it really requires little training (Jacobs and Retsky, 1975, pp. 5-29). Most guards are trained 'on the job' and much of their duty involves little more than watching prisoners. In a strike situation, the role can be even further narrowed by confining the prisoners to their cells around the clock. Under such a 'lockdown', the danger of violence or escape is greatly reduced and the replacements' main task is to serve food in the cells.

The National Guard has been very successful at providing vital services and maintaining security during prison guard strikes. The Guard served without apparent incident, riots, killings, or escape during lengthy strikes in Wisconsin (1977), Montana (1979), and New York (1979) (see League of Women Voters, 1978; Jacobs and Zimmer, 1980; Zimmer and Jacobs, 1981). In fact, in all three there was a honeymoon period of mutual respect and cooperation between Guardsmen and prisoners. Some of the regular prison activities were resumed as the Guardsmen gained enough confidence to handle various situations. Part of the success of the Guardsmen in the New York prison guard strike may be attributable to the fact that the number of Guardsmen far exceeded the regular complement of prison guards.

Institutions for the mentally ill and retarded and nursing homes are probably even easier than prisons for replacements to operate, since there is less need to worry about violence or escape. In addition, family members and other volunteers who are interested in the patients or inmates in these institutions may help if replacement Guardsmen need assistance.

Modern day firefighting, on the other hand, is a complex task involving the use of sophisticated equipment. Some fires, such as those in chemical plants or oil storage facilities, are extremely dangerous. Negligent performance by firefighters can result in the loss of life and property. Firefighting is thus not the easiest role for Guardsmen to fill; yet, as Table 7.1 shows, firemen's strikes account for the greatest number of replacement call-ups. Government leaders no doubt believe that the risks in not providing any protection against fire outweigh those incurred by a National Guard call-up.

How have Guardsmen performed when called upon to replace striking firefighters? A review of newspaper reports on National Guard deployments for such strikes reveals that the troops, with the help of civilian supervisory personnel, have learned to use most of the equipment and have performed adequately. In some instances, however, delayed reaction to alarms is reported to have 'caused' major property damage.

In Great Britain, a nationwide firefighters' strike in 1977 led to the activation of 20,000 military replacements. They were outfitted with outdated firefighting equipment, apparently to soften the strikebreaking symbolism (Whelan, 1979a, b). Nevertheless, the military personnel performed adequately, according to Geoffrey Marshall (1979, p. 277):

> The strike ended on January 12, 1978, having lasted for three months. Susbsequently published insurance figures have shown that the cost of fire damage to property was roughly twice that of the corresponding period in the previous twelve months. The evident unpopularity of the strike, together with the lack of sympathetic action by other unions or support by the Trades Union Congress, were factors that helped to bring about a settlement. <u>But a major part was undoubtedly the size and effectiveness of the effort by which the strikers were replaced.</u> (emphasis added)

Police strikes pose less of a challenge than firefighters' strikes. Troops are often already trained for police action and they can without difficulty present a highly visible and mobile patrol. In fact, military forces on the streets may be a more effective deterrent to crime than civilian police.

As studies of police have emphasized, police work often involves responding to simple requests for assistance, getting to hospitals, and settling disputes (Wilson, 1972). Many of these functions can be performed by untrained personnel or referred to other agencies, friends or neighbors. Military personnel may not be able to respond as quickly to emergency calls as regular police, but most serious offenses occur before a phone call is made to the police. Investigative functions can usually be suspended during a short strike and plainclothes investigators may well remain on the job in spite of a strike by the uniformed forces.

With the National Guard patrolling the streets, it is unlikely that widespread looting and an increase in individual acts of violence will result from a police strike. The greatest concern is rather that the troops themselves will cause damage and possibly the loss of life by reckless acts. In several of the riots of the 1960s, National Guard units showed poor judgment in exercising force.[31] Improved training and increased concern for general safety and peace-keeping would probably lead to a more effective performance by the Guard during police strikes.[32]

Political Impediments

Calling up troops to act as replacements obviously involves political risks: the potential for violent confrontations between strikers and Guardsmen, the possible opposition of uninvolved unions, and the spectre of sympathy strikes. Some politicians and most trade unionists sharply criticized, for example, the use of troops in the 1970 postal strike.[33] For the most part, though, organized labor's response to troop activations has been surprisingly restrained. The official position of the American Federation of State, County, and Municipal Employees (AFSCME), for example, supports legislation that 'provides access to legislated interest arbitration for public safety employees as an alternative to the unlimited right to strike ...'. Where the public safety is not involved, AFSCME supports legislation allowing strikes but prefers 'voluntary binding arbitration' as an alternative.[34]

The leaders of public sector unions probably believe that opposition to the use of National Guardsmen to maintain essential services would be unpopular and might jeopardize the acceptability of public sector collective bargaining.[35] The public is not apt to tolerate both illegal strikes and a ban on the use of replacements. If troop deployment in public sector strikes were to become more prevalent, however, union opposition might intensify.

The Financial Costs

The financial cost of calling out of the National Guard pales in comparison to strikers' demands for wage increases, although much depends upon the number of employees affected by the settlement and on the number of strikers. Deployment of the National Guard during the 1979 New York prison-guard strike, for example, cost about a million dollars per day, but state officials estimated that even a one percent permanent wage concession to state employees would have been more costly.

In making financial assessments, it is important to determine who will bear the costs of military deployments. In the case of state employee strikes, the money saved by not paying the strikers can be set off against the cost of the National Guard. In strikes by local employees, the city may not only save money by not having to pay the strikers but, in addition, the state usually pays for the Guard. This might create an incentive for fiscally pressed cities with severe labor difficulties to request National Guard personnel. New York State has addressed this problem by requiring the county, city, or municipality that requests the Guard to pay half the costs of mobilization and deployment (New York State Military Law, sec. 212 (McKinney Supp. 1980)).

Resistance to Strike Duty
'The primary motive for the revival of the militia [in the 1870s]' according to Riker (1957, p. 5), 'was a felt need for an industrial police'. This need gave the militia the ability to attract support from influential economic interests. But the industrial peace-keeping role was controversial and the unpopularity of strike breaking among the working class created serious recruitment problems. It was crucial for the National Guard's survival to de-emphasize its strike-breaking role and find a different raison d'être.

The problem was solved when the Guard became the bona fide reserve component for the United States armed forces in 1903.[36] This change was desirable for several reasons. First, the federal government assumed an ever increasing share of the cost of operations and payroll. Second, the National Guard gained prestige as a 'real military force' with national defense responsibilities. Third, service was not suspect in any way; indeed, it was popular and prestigious.

The 1903 Dick Act, which established the National Guard as the Army reserve, provided that training and equipment would be paid for in large measure by the federal government. The Guard was used in 1916 on the Mexican border and in 1917 in the First World War. Guard forces also saw extensive service in World War II and in Korea. Under the 'total force' policy developed by the Department of Defense in 1970-72, reservists rather than draftees are currently the primary source of personnel for augmenting active forces in military emergencies (Coffey, 1979, p. 78). The National Guard is thus, by law, the nation's first line of military reserves (10 U.S.C. sec. 263 (1976)). While the army reserve is oriented toward support and training, the National Guard's mechanized, armor and infantry divisions are oriented toward combat involvement (Coffey, 1979, p. 97).

Service as a replacement force in public sector strikes is thus no longer relevant to the National Guard's mission or self-concept. One might ask, then, whether this does not also hold true for emergency humanitarian deployments for floods, snow storms, and blizzards. Those traditional duties have a long history, however, and enjoy public support. They enhance the Guard's political strength and even its recruitment efforts.

Given the history of the National Guard, however, its leaders may well have doubts about becoming too involved in labor conflicts. In addition, service in public sector strikes is likely to become more controversial. The Guard may eventually have more actual clashes with strikers, as they did in New York's 1979 prison guard strike, and any such clashes may prod the ire of organized labor, as they did in the 1970 postal strike and the 1979 Montana prison guard strike. Guardsmen may be injured, as in the 1978 St Bernard Parish (La.) firefighters' strike. The presence of the Guard may trigger sympathy strikes, as was suggested when Mayor Lindsay proposed that the Guard be called out during the 1968 sanitation workers' strike in New York City (N.Y. Times, February 22, 1968, p. 30). Such duty takes time away from training for military responsibilities. For all these reasons, it would not be surprising to learn that the National Guard itself accepts its replacement role with great reluctance.

POLICY ISSUES

Nearly all states that have extended collective bargaining to public employees have also denied public employees the right to strike. To enforce the ban, they provide for a variety of deterrent and punitive mechanisms. In New York State, for example, striking public employees incur a fine equal to the day's wages (in addition, of course, to losing a day's pay) for every day on strike (Peterson, 1981, pp. 545-62). The union whose members are on strike faces the possible loss of checkoff privileges and, in addition, the employer is authorized to seek an injunction against the strikers and their union and to enforce the injunction through contempt proceedings (New York Civil Service Laws, secs. 210-211 (McKinney Supp. 1980).

This study shows that the National Guard can also be viewed as a weapon for deterring and defeating illegal strikes. In a variety of contexts in which the Guard could play a replacement role effectively, it is already an implicit factor in contract negotiations. As bargaining by police, firemen, and correctional officers reaches an impasse, both sides begin to consider the role that could be played by the state's military forces. Indeed, state negotiators could alert and preposition the National Guard to increase their bargaining leverage.[37]

If the military forces are already a part of public sector collective bargaining, the issue that must be faced is whether the role of the military should be made explicit and, if so, whether it should be enhanced or diminished.

Legitimizing and Enhancing the Military Role
Since public sector strikes are illegal, one might well ask why we should not recognize and encourage the deployment of military forces as effectively as possible in all illegal strike situations. Why not develop policies to make the Guard as effective a replacement force as possible? Would it not make sense, for example, to train individual units to take over various agency operations? Why not have the National Guard account for the civilian skills of its personnel so that they can be deployed in public sector strikes as individuals rather than as units?

To legitimate and enhance the Guard's replacement role in the ways just suggested might strengthen the governor's hand in preventing strikes. Such a policy would not be without a price, however, for it might disrupt both the labor relations process and civil-military relations.

Most states do not permit public employees to strike, but neither do they choose to punish illegal strikers with the state's full criminal powers. While it would be a mistake to conclude that we have a de facto practice of tolerating public employee strikes, it would also be wrong to conclude that we unequivocally oppose them. In a country in which workers have the right to bargain freely over the terms and conditions of employment, there is considerable ambivalence about how to treat public employees who strike.

To a degree, strikes in the public sector, like strikes in the private sector, are a test of strength. But in the public sector the state's strength has been augmented by a variety of legal enforcement mechanisms including injunctions and strike penalties. This gives the state an advantage but not necessarily a decisive one. To 'unleash' the National Guard as a public sector strike-breaking force might eliminate many strikes, but perhaps at the cost of weakening collective bargaining. One has to ask if a strike threat, even a remote one, is necessary to make public sector collective bargaining effective. The potential for a strike may be necessary to keep the public employer bargaining in good faith. Otherwise public sector bargaining, without interest arbitration, might be substantially undermined.

Another argument against enhancing the National Guard's replacement role is that it would increase conflict between labor and management. Unions would react bitterly to an explicit move to make the National Guard part of the state's negotiating team. Strikes might be more protracted and violent; to overcome the state, a union would have to take extreme action. To turn labor-management disputes in the public sector into battles would weaken the morale and commitment of public employees and destabilize the controlled conflict that may be necessary for public sector labor relations to work.

To enhance the National Guard's replacement role would also be too costly in terms of civil-military relations. Keeping the military at arm's length, out of entanglement with civilian affairs, has been a key feature of the American political system. Greater reliance on the military to help control workers may lead to weaker and weaker civilian governments. It is not healthy for a democracy to rely on the military to cure domestic ailments. The present need for the National Guard to moderate labor-management relations in the public sector underscores the need for more effective 'institution building' in state and local government.

Diminishing or Eliminating the Military's Role
If one sees the use of military forces as replacements for striking public employees as at least a potentially serious problem in labor and civil-military relations, it is worth considering whether it would be advisable to diminish or even eliminate the military's role as a strike replacement force.

The role of replacements. This is not the appropriate place for a full-scale analysis of the role of replacements in the public sector collective bargaining framework. Briefly, though, private employers are free to continue operations in a struck plant by using replacements and there seems to be no reason why public employers should not have the same right. The question then arises: what replacements are available to public employers?

In the past, supervisors, personnel from other agencies, trainees, units from other communities, and even volunteers have all been used to keep government agencies operating. In addition, during most public sector strikes, some employees have continued to work. If one were firmly committed to using the National Guard sparingly, all other replacement and alternative services options would be utilized before resorting to the military trump card.

Even in the uniformed services - police, fire, prisons - it has not always been necessary to call on the National Guard. In the majority of strikes, public employers have either ceased operations or found ways to maintain services. Consider the following examples taken from Keith Ocheltree's Six Strike Stories (1969). In response to a 1967 strike by 217 social workers in Sacramento, California, the Board of Supervisors authorized new positions, thus permitting replacements to be hired; strikers who did not return to work were fired. In November 1968, 2800 New York State mental hospital attendants went out on strike; the department continued essential operations by cancelling leaves, providing overtime for supervisors and nonstrikers, subcontracting for certain institutional services, and reducing the number of patients at the affected institutions. Seventy-five percent of the sanitation workers in Atlanta walked off the job in September 1968; with police protection, the remaining workers maintained essential services.

Even in police, fire, and prison strikes, there appear to be alternatives to military forces (Gentel, 1979). The police struck in Tucson in September 1975. Thirty-three patrolmen and fifty-nine supervisors, working on twelve-hour shifts, were able to maintain services. In October 1975, Oklahoma City experienced a police strike; 140 highway patrolmen and 434 nonstrikers carried on; and private security guards were hired to protect police headquarters. In February 1976, police and firefighters went on a protracted strike in Los Cruces, New Mexico; nonstriking police officers went on twelve-hour shifts, sheriff and highway patrol departments were placed on alert, and trainees stepped in to assume firefighting responsibilities. Two weeks after the strike started, the city began firing the strikers and hiring replacements.

Even in the nation's largest cities, it has proved possible to weather strikes without National Guardsmen. Despite Mayor Lindsay's repeated requests for help during the 1968 sanitation workers' strike in New York City, Governor Rockefeller refused to activate troops. San Francisco's Mayor Joseph Alioto refused, despite intense pressure from the Board of Supervisors, to ask for National Guard assistance in an August 1975 police strike. In 1980, Mayor Jane Byrne of Chicago rode out a turbulent firefighters' strike by relying on supervisors and a variety of other personnel. Even in prison strikes it is not always necessary to turn to the National Guard. In 1973, correctional administrators operated the infamous Walpole, Massachusetts prison for seven weeks with the help of state police, front office personnel, guards from other prisons, and replacements hired off the streets.

It is clear that every strike by police, firefighters, prison guards, sanitation workers, or school teachers does not present an 'emergency' requiring activation of the National Guard. The greater the commitment to solve civilian problems by civilian means, the greater will be the effort to rely on civilian replacements in public sector strikes or, better still, to avoid such strikes in the first place.

Most effective legal constraints. It would be possible to make constitutional and statutory changes to limit the kinds of strikes for which it would be permissible to activate military forces. The law might provide, for example, that military forces could not be used as replacements except in strikes by members of the uniformed services, that is, police, firefighters, and prison guards. But this kind of formulation carries potential problems. It might legitimize and make call-ups routine for strikes in the uniformed services. It might deny to the governor the option of using troops in situations in which health and safety are threatened, such as certain strikes against hospitals, nursing homes, and sanitation departments. Using the term 'essential services' to delimit those activities for which the activation of troops would be permissible could raise similar problems. Some services are central to the state's governing role - police, courts, and prisons - and their cessation could create a problem or crisis in governing. Other services the state has chosen to undertake - hospitals, transportation, fire protection, sanitation, and welfare - and their cessation could cause severe inconvenience and hardship for beneficiaries.

To anticipate those strike situations in which the threat to life and property is sufficiently grave to require military forces as replacements, a standard such as 'emergency' suggests itself. It is possible to refine the emergency trigger by adding requirements like 'clear and present danger to life and property'; but this leaves enormous discretion to the executive branch. One determined to use troops could find a 'clear and present danger to life and property' in any public sector strike.

If enhanced legal constraints are necessary to prevent an excessive reliance on military forces, rewriting the standard that governs the executive's authority to deploy troops will not be sufficient. A more stringent substantive standard will have to be complemented by stronger structures and procedures - most notably by relying on the popular American division-of-powers formula. The judiciary could be empowered to review the situation in a procedure similar to that provided by the Taft-Hartley Act, which authorizes the President merely to seek an injunction from the courts against a strike that threatens national health or safety. Of course, judges are likely to show great deference to the Chief Executive in times of purported crisis: only twice have federal courts refused a presidential request for a Taft-Hartley injunction. Still, twice may be better than never, particularly if these precedents have given Presidents pause in other cases. In addition, having to appear before a non-involved decision-maker would force an executive to articulate a justification for the use of troops. Such a justification would then be available during and after the strike for scrutiny and criticism. A legislative veto is another possibility that could be explored.

CONCLUSION

The problems associated with formalizing policies for the use of military forces as replacements make it worth considering whether the current nonpolicy should be preserved in the short run. Today's legal constraints on the use of military forces as replacements are weak, indeed almost non-existent. Yet certain practical and political constraints continue to present some resistance to automatic activation of troops in public sector labor disputes. These constraints may dissipate over time if the tide of public opinion hardens against public employee strikes and if government develops more confidence in the capacity of troops to serve effectively.

The temptation is to emphasize legal constraints. But the danger is that any formal standard will have the ironic effect of legitimating the use of military forces as replacements in a vaguely defined class of cases. Troops may then be used when the threat to life and property is minor or when other alternatives are available.

In the final analysis, the use of troops to back up civil institutions is a political problem. The best solution would be for wise leaders to make public sector collective bargaining work. But if civil institutions cannot govern themselves effectively, the attraction of a 'military solution' may prove irresistible. There is a need to bring this subject into the open. Examination of the proper use of the military in labor conflicts will help constrain unreflective and excessive use of troops to solve civilian problems.

NOTES

* Reprinted by permission, from Industrial and Labor Relations Review, Vol. 35, No. 2 (January 1982), 1982 by Cornell University. All rights reserved.

1. The National Guard, as the state militia were called after the 1870s, is a military force under dual federal and state control. See U.S. Const. art. I, sec. 8, cl. 18. The governor of each state has constitutional and legislative authority to call out the state's National Guard in a variety of emergency circumstances. Since the beginning of the twentieth century, however, the National Guard has increasingly come under federal domination. Congress has organized the National Guard as a reserve component of the federal armed forces. Under current Defense Department planning, the National Guard is a crucial linchpin in a 'total force concept' that requires American armed forces to be ready to fight several wars at the same time. See Colonel William Shaw, 'The Interrelationship of the United States Army and National Guard', Military Law Review, vol. 31 (January 1966), pp. 39-84; and Melvin L. Wulf, The National Guard and the Constitution (New York: A.C.L.U., 1971), pp. 1-3.

2. When the military was used, the scope of the intervention was restricted. In the New York harbor strikes, for example, the military moved only military passengers and supplies, 'leaving the private cargoes and passengers under the strike

bans': Blackman, 1967, p. 228.

3. By the end of the first week of the controllers' strike, 521 military air traffic controllers were filling in for strikers at airports around the country. The Defense Department authorized the use of 2,800 military personnel. These replacements are expected to be on duty from six to twenty-one months, until civilian replacements can be trained. President Reagan's authority to use military air traffic controllers comes from The Federal Aviation Act of 1958, 49 U.S.C., sec. 1343(i)(1976), which provides for the Federal Aviation Agency Administrator to 'use ... the available service, equipment, personnel and facilities of other civilian or military agencies ...'.

4. Work stoppages occurred nationwide - Philadelphia, San Francisco, Chicago, Denver, Pittsburgh, Cleveland - affecting about half of all mail service in the country. Hardest hit were banks, public utilities, credit agencies, and government agencies.

5. Two federal judges issued injunctions ordering the president of Branch 36 of the National Letter Carriers Union to direct the carriers to go back to work. The president complied, but the rank-and-file did not. The Assistant U.S. Attorney pressing the government's case did not seek criminal punishment of the strikers, noting that '[r]epressive measures will not get the mail delivered'. <u>N.Y. Times</u>, March 20, 1970, p. 40. The government <u>did</u>, however, seek fines against the union and seven of its officers. <u>N.Y. Times</u>, March 21, 1970, p. 12.

6. President Nixon's Declaration of National Emergency stated:

> [A]s a result of [the postal employees'] unlawful work stoppage the performance of critical government and private functions ... has wholly ceased or is seriously impeded ... The continuance of such work stoppages ... will impair the ability of this nation to carry out its obligations abroad, and will cripple or halt the official and commercial intercourse which is essential to the conduct of its domestic business ... [T]herefore, I, Richard Nixon, President of the United States of America, pursuant to the powers vested in me by the Constitution and the laws of the United States and more particularly ... Section 673 of Title 10 of the United States Code, do hereby declare a state of national emergency, and

direct the Secretary of Defense ... to use such of the Armed Forces ... [and] any or all of the ... Army National Guard and of the Air National Guard [to maintain postal service and to execute the postal laws].

Pres. Proc. No. 3972, 3 C.F.R. 473 (1970) (1966-1970 Compilation).

7. The administration even had the support of the New York Times. On the second day of the walkout an editorial defined the work stoppage as an affront by those 'bent on paralyzing the essential functions of government', N.Y. Times, March 20, 1970, p. 46. A later editorial stated: 'More than the mail ... the future of a government based on law is in the balance', N.Y. Times, March 22, 1970, p. 16. Two days later the President used the same words. On March 23rd, the Times editorialized: '[t]he contagion spreads from ghetto to campus to agencies of government, sweeping aside all respect for law. The mood of the postal rebels was well reflected in this city. "We have them by the throat - It's Now or Never." The "them", of course, is the Government of the United States', N.Y. Times, March 23, 1970, p. 40.

8. Note, 1973, pp. 137-8. Legislative limitations on executive use of the military in domestic affairs go back to 1792, when Congress refused to grant the President the power to execute the laws with military force. Engdahl, 1974, p. 584. The Civil War and Reconstruction statutes that allowed domestic military deployments, 10 U.S.C., secs. 331, 332, and 333 (1976), restrict executive use of the armed forces to specific types of emergency situations. See text accompanying notes 22-3 infra. In the Posse Comitatus Act of 1878, 18 U.S.C. sec. 1385 (1976), Congress specifically prohibited the use of the army to execute the laws, unless expressly provided for in other legislation. See text accompanying notes 19-23 infra.

9. U.S. Const. art. II, sec. 2, cl. 1 provides '[t]he President shall be Commander in Chief of the Army and Navy of the United States ...'.

10. Id., sec. 3 charges the President to 'take care that the laws be faithfully executed'.

11. Id., sec. 1 provides '[t]he executive power shall be vested in a President of the United States of America'.

12. President Nixon never explicitly claimed reliance on inherent powers to justify deployment of troops in the postal strike; his emergency

proclamation and executive order were vague and ambiguous. (See note 6 above.) There is no doubt, however, that President Nixon had an expansive view of inherent powers, particularly with respect to the military. In 1972, the Nixon Administration promulgated new regulations concerning the use of federal troops in civil disorders. The regulations incorporate the theory that the President has an inherent, constitutional right to use troops in a variety of vaguely defined domestic crises. See 'Employment of Military Resources in the Event of Civil Disturbances', 32 C.F.R. sec. 215.4(c)(1)(i) and (ii) (1980).

13. After forty-two days, the 1981 Canadian postal strike was ended by a negotiated settlement. The Canadian government did not find it necessary to take legal action against the strikers, nor to rely on extraordinary measures to restore mail delivery.

14. President Nixon did not elaborate on his conclusion that the postal strike had created a national emergency. However, in his television address to the nation he stated:

> The United States postal system is a vital element of our entire communications system. The poor depend heavily upon it for medical services and also for Government assistance. Veterans depend upon it for their compensation checks. The elderly depend upon it for their Social Security checks.
> The nation's business is dependent upon it as a way to stay in business so they can meet their payrolls. And our men in Vietnam depend on mail calls as their only link with their loved ones.

N.Y. Times, March 24, 1970, p. 16. One has to wonder how difficult it would actually be to find alternatives to the postal service for each of these beneficiary groups. Military personnel, veterans groups and volunteers, for example, could presumably have collected and delivered letters to and from those in Vietnam.

As for the criteria for declaring a national emergency, one recent commentator notes: 'the test for when a national emergency exists is completely subjective - anything the President says is a national emergency is a national emergency'. See the note, 'The National Emergency Dilemma: Balancing the Executive's Crisis Powers with the Need for Accountability', Southern California Law Review, vol. 52, no. 5 (July 1979), pp. 1458-1511. There were four declared national emergencies between March 1933 and September 14, 1978. In addition to the postal strike, President Nixon also declared a Balance of Payments Emergency in 1971. In 1976, Congress enacted the National Emergency Act, 10 U.S.C. secs. 1601-1651 (1976), establishing guidelines for both the declaration and termination of future emergencies. Only one national emergency has been declared since passage of the 1976 act. In 1979, President Carter declared a national emergency in order to freeze the assets of the Iranian government. Executive Order 12170, 3 C.F.R. 457 (1979 Compilation and Parts 100 and 101).

15. 18 U.S.C. sec. 1918 (1976) makes it a crime for federal employees to strike.

16. Youngstown Sheet and Tube Co. v. Sawyer, 343 U.S. 579, 587 (Opinion of the Court), 632 (Douglas J., concurring), 644 (Jackson J., concurring), 650 (Burton J., concurring), 660-61 (Clark J., concurrinng) (1952).

17. President Nixon's Executive Order began as follows:

> Whereas certain employees of the Postal Service are engaged in an unlawful work stoppage which has prevented the delivery of the mails and the discharge of other postal functions in various parts of the United States; and
> Whereas, the laws of the United States ... require that the business of the Post Office Department, including the expeditious processing and delivery of the mail be regularly carried on; and
> Whereas the aforesaid unlawful work stoppage has prevented and is preventing the execution of the aforesaid laws relating to the Post Office Department; and
> Whereas the breakdown of the postal service in the numerous areas affected by the said unlawful work stoppage is a matter of grave national concern; and
> Whereas I am charged by the Constitution of the United States to take care that the laws be faithfully executed ...

Executive Order 11519, 3 C.F.R. 909 (1966-1970 Compilation).

18. In seeking to resolve the question of the President's authority to deploy troops to replace

federal workers, I am drawn to the Supreme Court's landmark decision in <u>Youngstown Sheet and Tube Co. v. Sawyer</u>. The Court held that the President had no constitutional authority to seize the nation's steel mills; such authority had to come from Congress, 343 U.S. at 587-9. Since Congress had just defeated a proposed amendment to the Taft-Hartley Act that would have given such power to the executive, this was an implied prohibition of seizure. <u>Id</u>. at 586 (Opinion of the Court), 598-603 (Frankfurter J., concurring), 657 (Burton J., concurring), 663-4 (Clark J., concurring).

Justice Jackson's concurring opinion has achieved greatest prominence. Jackson argued that the President's power is at its maximum when he acts pursuant to an express or implied authorization of Congress. It is in a 'zone of twilight' when he acts in the absence of congressional authority and can rely only on his own independent powers. It is at its lowest ebb when he 'takes measures incompatible with the express or implied will of Congress, for then he can rely only upon his own constitutional powers minus any constitutional powers of Congress over the matter'. <u>Id</u>. at 637 (Jackson J., concurring). Nixon's use of the regular armed forces and reservists during the postal strike clearly fits Justice Jackson's third category as Congress has expressly prohibited such use of troops in the Posse Comitatus Act. See text accompanying notes 19-23, <u>infra</u>.

19. An excellent review of the history of the Posse Comitatus Act finds that its framers fully intended to limit the President's use of military forces in peacetime to those circumstances expressly provided for in the Constitution of the United States or in federal statutes. Deanne Siemer and Andrew Effron, 'Military Participation in United States Law Enforcement Activities Overseas: The Extraterritorial Effect of the Posse Comitatus Act', <u>St Johns Law Review</u>, vol. 54, no. 1 (Fall 1979), pp. 1-54 (quotation from pp. 44-45).

> The context of the debate further underscores development of a common theme. Debate focused on opposition to use of the military in situations where the organized discipline and factors of a military force were not required, as, for example, in the collection of taxes, service of process, supervision of elections, and in response to labor strife, when the task was within the existing or potential capability

of state forces.

20. 'Posse Comitatus' literally means the power or force of the country, referring to the power of a sheriff to summon the entire population of a county above the age of fifteen to his assistance in certain cases.

21. There is no doubting that the Posse Comitatus Act applies to active duty Army and Air Force Reserves and to the Army and Air National Guard when in federal service. Major H.W.C. Furman, 'Restrictions Upon the Use of the Army Imposed by the Posse Comitatus Act', Military Law Review, vol. 7 (January 1960), p. 99. At the time of the strike, the Defense Department regarded the Act as an expression of policy applicable also to the Navy and Marine Corps. Major Clarence Meeks, 'Illegal Law Enforcement: Aiding Civil Authorities in Violation of the Posse Comitatus Act', Military Law Review, vol. 70 (Fall 1975), p. 101. In 1972, the Nixon Administration broke with traditional policy by asserting that the Navy and Marine Corps were outside the ambit of the Act. Note, 1973, pp. 130, 144, note 1.

22. History indicates that the lawmakers who passed this statute in 1861 believed it permitted the use of federal troops only when civilian institutions were incapacitated in the course of a rebellion, insurrection, or riot. Engdahl, 1974, pp. 581-617. Further, even had the statute been applicable, it would seem to authorize no more than firing or jailing strikers who disobeyed the court injunction, not establishing military operation of the postal system. When Arkansas state officials actively impeded the implementation of school desegregation in the 1950s, President Eisenhower relied on this statute (as well as on 10 U.S.C. sec. 333 (1976)) to send the National Guard to Little Rock. Executive Order 10730, 3 C.F.R. sec. 389 (1954-1958 Compilation). The Guard's military presence was used only to prevent violence and to ensure that nothing obstructed the integration of the schools. The Guard did not assume the administrative, clerical, or educational duties of school officials.

23. The Armed Forces Reserve Act of 1952, 10 U.S.C. sec. 673 (1976), authorizes the President to order members of the Ready Reserve to active duty in times of war or national emergency. President Nixon relied on this statute to utilize reservists, but invoked 'the powers vested by the Constitution' to

justify their domestic deployments. In its subsequently formulated administrative regulations, the Nixon administration did not interpret this statute as an exception to the Posse Comitatus Act. See 'Employment of Military Resources in the Event of Civil Disturbances', 32 C.F.R. sec. 215.4 (c)(1)(i) and (ii) (1980). Indeed, it would be absurd for Congress to grant the President authority to deploy the reserves domestically, while not allowing him to deploy the regular forces.

24. President Nixon also relied in his executive order on 10 U.S.C. sec. 8500 (1976), which contains the same provisions as sec. 3500, except that it is applicable to the Air National Guard.

25. In an unpublished internal White House memorandum to Assistant to the President, John Erlichman, Rehnquist stated:

> I have been unable to locate any square precedent for the use of 10 U.S.C. sec. 3500 to authorize the Guard to actually perform a federal function, rather than simply guard or protect others who are performing that function, but the statutory language is broad enough so that a reasonable argument can be made in support of such use.

'Memorandum to the Honorable John D. Erlichman', from Assistant Attorney General William Rehnquist, March 22, 1970.

26. Each state constitution confers executive power upon the governor or names him the state's chief executive; designates him the commander-in-chief of the state's military forces; and charges him with the faithful execution of the laws (Massachusetts and New Hampshire implicitly, from the oath of office). Thirty-six state constitutions specifically provide the governor with authority to call out the National Guard. National Association of Attorneys General (hereinafter NAAG), Committee on the Office of Attorney General, Legal Issues Concerning the Role of the National Guard in Civil Disorders (Raleigh, N.C.: The National Association of Attorneys General, 1973), pp. 10-20, Table 3.

In every case but New York, this enabling power is governed by constitutional provisions strictly subordinating the military to civil authority. Id., pp. 10 and 12, Table 4. Moreover, under nineteen constitutions only the legislature can suspend the operation of civil law; these provisions are meant to avoid a situation where the governor might use a public emergency as an excuse for using the military irresponsibly. Also, in 1973 over half of the states had civil defense statutes granting the executive wide discretion in emergencies. Id., p. 13.

27. Only one constitution, Tennessee's, places any legislative check on the governor's power to call out the militia. Notably, the legislature has circumvented that limitation by defining 'militia', Tenn. Code Ann., sec. 7-106 (1970), not to include the National Guard. Some states limit the use of the Guard in emergencies by defining emergency narrowly enough to exclude labor strife. See, Cal. Military and Veterans Code, sec. 1505 (West 1955). Others establish a civil defense advisory council that may limit the governor's emergency powers. See, N.C. Gen. Stat. sec. 166-4 (1976); Vt. Stat. Ann. tit. 21, sec. 4 (1958). Although most states require a proclamation or executive order to be issued when these powers are claimed, few have any specific criteria for issuing a justificatory proclamation. A governor has even broader legal discretion than the President over whether, how, and when to call up the Guard. NAAG, Role of the National Guard, pp. 17-19.

28. There is a strong tradition of judicial non-involvement in executive decisions involving deployment of the militia. See, e.g., Luther v. Bordon, 48 U.S. (7 How.) 115 (1845); Gilligan v. Morgan, 413 U.S. 1 (1973).

29. In Montana, for example, prison guards are allowed to strike after they exhaust impasse procedures and give notice. In 1979, the guard union announced its intent to strike if wage demands were not met. State negotiators met with National Guard officers, devised a plan for sending troops to the prisons, and arranged to have Guard officers meet prison officials and tour their facilities. In effect, the Guardsmen were activated and prepositioned before the prison guards walked off the job. The justification was not maintenance of prison operations but rather anticipation of a likely emergency: when the strike occurred Governor Thomas Judge issued a 'state of emergency' proclamation.

30. The pigeon-holing of letters by zip codes could be done by an experienced clerk at a piece rate of 1200-1500 per hour; the marines sorted at a rate of 600 per hour. N.Y. Times, March 24, 1970, p. 2.

31. National Advisory Commission on Civil Disorders, Report (New York: New York Times Co.,

1968), pp. 497-506.

32. By planning, officer education, practical exercises, attention directed to abuse of force, and other measures taken since Detroit, Newark and Kent State, the National Guard has developed tactics thought to be substantial improvements over those previously used. NAAG, Role of the National Guard, pp. 81-4.

33. Democratic political figures were virtually unanimous in condemning President Nixon's emergency actions in the postal strike. George Meany condemned it but urged the employees to return to work. Jerry Wurf termed the use of troops a 'shocking piece of strike-breaking'. John DeLury, president of New York City's Uniformed Sanitation Men's Association, said 'the use of troops in New York City is a step backward to the Stone Age of labor-management relationships with federal employees'. N.Y. Times, March 24, 1970, p. 35. There were, however, several unions that supported the President, including the United Electrical, Radio and Mechanic Workers of America, the New York State chapter of the AFL-CIO, the Newspaper Guild, and the District Council 37 of AFSCME. N.Y. Times, March 24, 1970, p. 35.

34. American Federation of State, County, and Municipal Employees, 'Public Sector Dispute Resolution', adopted at the 23rd AFSCME International Convention, June 1978. Similarly, the AFL-CIO's Public Employee Department resolved at its Fifth Biennial Convention in June 1981 that it

> ... supports and will urge the Congress to provide federal legislation so that public safety employees of states and political subdivisions thereof, shall be subject to a national public safety employees collective bargaining law providing binding arbitration as an impasse procedure for settling labor disputes between employers and their employees. [and that it] ... recognizes the inalienable right of public employees in other work sectors, other than the areas of public safety, to withhold his or her services in any collective bargaining legislation provided for those employees.
> [and that] for the purposes of this resolution, public safety officers shall be those uniformed employees in the fields of firefighting, fire protection and law enforcement.

35. In the AFSCME resolution cited id., for example, that union acknowledged that public sector strikes are often counterproductive, adversely affecting the cause of public sector trade unionism and, in the case of public safety workers, affecting the health and safety of a community.

36. Act of January 21, 1903, 32 Stat. 775, as amended, 35 Stat. 399 (1908). See also National Defense Act of 1916, 39 Stat. 166, as amended, 41 Stat. 759 (1920).

37. When another postal strike appeared likely in July 1981, Pentagon officials prepared to mobilize over 100,000 military personnel - regular forces, reservists, and National Guardsmen - to move 90% of the mail, Chicago Tribune, July 21, 1981, pp. 1, 16.

REFERENCES

Blackman, J.L. (1967) Presidential Seizure in Labor Disputes, Cambridge, Mass., Harvard University Press

Coffey, K.J. (1979) Strategic Implications of the All-Volunteer Force: The Conventional Defense of Central Europe, Chapel Hill, The University of North Carolina Press

Corwin, E.S. (1978) The Constitution (revised by H.W. Chase and C.R. Ducat), 14th ed., Princeton University Press

Dulles, F.R. (1966) Labor in America, 3rd ed., New York, Thomas Y. Crowell

Engdahl, D.E. (1974) 'The New Civil Disturbance Regulations: the Threat of Military Intervention', 49 Indiana Law Journal 584

Gentel, W.D. (1979) Police Strikes: Causes and Prevention, International Association of Chiefs of Police, Washington D.C.

Hofstadter, R. & Wallace, M. (1970) American Violence: A Documentary History, New York, Knopf

Jacobs, J.B. & Retsky, H. (1975) 'Prison Guard', 4 Urban Life 5

Jacobs, J.B. & Zimmer, L. (1980) 'The 1979 Montana Prison Strike: A Case Study', unpublished paper, Cornell University

League of Women Voters (1978) Changing of the Guard: Citizen Soldiers in Wisconsin Correctional Institutions, Madison, Wisc., League of Women Voters

Marshall, G. (1979) 'The Armed Forces and Industrial Disputes in the United Kingdom', 5 Armed Forces and Society 277

Note (1973) 'Honored in the Breach: Presidential Authority to Execute the Laws with Military Force', 83 Yale Law Journal 137

Ocheltree, K. (ed.) (1969) Six Strike Stories, Chicago, Public Personnel Association

Peterson, A.A. (1981) 'Deterring Strikes by Public Employees: New York's Two-for-One Salary Penalty and the 1979 Prison Guard Strike', 34 Industrial and Labor Relations Review 545

Riker, W. (1957) Soldiers in the States: the Role of the National Guard in American Democracy, Washington D.C., Public Affairs Press

Russell, F. (1975) A City in Terror: 1919 - The Boston Police Strike, New York, Viking Press

Whelan, C.J. (1979a) 'The Law and the Use of Troops in Industrial Disputes', Working Paper No. 2, Centre for Socio-Legal Studies, Wolfson College, Oxford

────────────── (1979b) 'Military Intervention in Industrial Disputes', 8 Industrial Law Journal 222

Wilson, J.Q. (1972) Varieties of Police Behavior: the Management of Law and Order in Eight Communities, New York, Atheneum

Zimmer, L. & Jacobs, J.B. (1981) 'Challenging the Taylor Law: New York Prison Guards on Strike', 34 Industrial and Labor Relations Review 531

Chapter Eight

ARMED FORCES, PUBLIC DISORDER AND THE LAW IN THE UNITED KINGDOM

Geoffrey J. Bennett and Christopher L. Ryan

The objectives of this chapter are to explain the application of certain (sometimes basic) legal rules to the problems in issue and to consider some of the most important aspects of relevant constitutional considerations. For example, the word 'riot' appears frequently, but what in law is riot? This essay will be an attempt not only to examine certain key legal terms and concepts but also to clarify the role of the military in the maintenance of public order. It is hoped that the reader will be left with a general view of the circumstances in which the use of troops to quell disorder may become a reality and of the potential dangers, the legal difficulties and the necessary safeguards to allow for the efficient use of the military without jeopardising the democratic social order as we know it.

Clearly the use of the military to contain disorder has been and should always be an extreme measure of last resort. This fundamental principle is proclaimed strongly and constantly by military (Bramall, Chapter 3; Perkins, 1973, p. 10), ex-military (Evelegh, 1978), police (Alderson, 1979) and politician (Enoch Powell, The Times, October 4th, 1977) alike. Because of this, the circumstances in which the military are so employed are likely to be atypical of the law's normal response to public disorder. Although in what follows the main attention will be focussed on such relatively major incidents, it would clearly be misleading if some allusion was not made to what one might call the standard case of civil disorder.

In Great Britain there is no entrenched or constitutionally guaranteed provision for the maintenance of free speech or freedom of assembly. Such freedoms only exist where they are not curtailed by law or constitutional convention. The

United Kingdom is a signatory to the European Convention on Human Rights which <u>inter alia</u> provides for freedom of speech and assembly in Articles 10 and 11, but any obligation under this Convention is, in the final analysis, only of persuasive value in so far as our courts are concerned.[1] The question of whether it is now time to establish in this country an authoritative, entrenched constitutional instrument guaranteeing such freedoms and controlling the exercise of executive power is an issue which has been widely debated elsewhere (Scarman, 1974; Fawcett, 1976; Jaconelli, 1976, 1980). Nevertheless, the present constitutional position is that in law certain liberties exist subject to specified legal restraints. For example, freedom of speech exists subject to the restraints imposed by the laws of defamation, obscenity, blasphemy, contempt, official secrets and confidentiality. Even so, the present existence of certain freedoms does not ensure that they will not be encroached upon, emasculated or abolished completely in the future.[2] Moreover, because of the lack of a single written constitution and the piecemeal development of the law which has traditionally proceeded on a largely <u>ad hoc</u> case by case basis, there is no clear and comprehensive code from which the law's attitude to civil disorder can be extracted. Cases have been decided and legislation passed as a specific response to pressing current political or social problems. The result is that the law is to be found spread amongst a wide range of judicially decided cases, and often disconnected and disparate statutes which, it might be said, do little to assist those in authority and the citizen in or out of uniform to ascertain even the most basic constitutional rights and duties. It is, however, vital to appreciate how far one may legitimately go in the exercise of freedom of speech and assembly to support, protest about or demonstrate for or against those things one feels strongly about. Only then is it possible to know when the line has been over-stepped so as to permit appropriate counter measures.

COMMON 'ORDER' OFFENCES

In an age bedevilled with faceless bureaucrats, remote politicians and mass media controlled (not disinterestedly) by a very few who have access to such media far beyond the reach of the ordinary man's financial resources, the ability to assemble and to demonstrate is vital to the expression and communication of democratic opinion. For most practical purposes the greatest restraint on the liberty of the individual in the context of public order is to be found in the Public Order Act 1936 as amended by the Race Relations Act 1976.[3]

Although not all of its provisions were completely novel in their scope, the original 1936 Act was passed as a direct response to the serious threat of civil disorder posed by the fascist followers of Sir Oswald Mosley in the 1930s. Its provisions (as amended) permit the re-routing or even the banning of public processions (s. 3) if there is a risk of 'serious public disorder'; the prosecution of members of para-military organisations (s. 2); and also the outlawing of uniforms showing political allegiance in public (s. 1). In the context of public order the two most important provisions of this Act are s. 5 which creates the offence of using 'threatening abusive or insulting words or behaviour' which may lead to a breach of the peace and s. 5A (introduced by the Race Relations Act 1976, s. 70) which introduced the new offence of inciting racial hatred by the use in public of 'threatening insulting or abusive' words in circumstances where 'hatred is likely to be stirred up against any racial group in Great Britain'. In this instance no breach or potential breach of the peace need be proved nor any intent to stir up racial hatred.

In the context of public order these two statutory provisions together with those pertaining to obstruction of the highway (Highways Act 1980, s. 137 and Town Police Clauses Act 1847, s. 28), constitute the most commonly exercised restraint on an individual's freedom of speech and assembly so that by far the majority of offences against public order will be dealt with under those statutes or else under the common law offences of assault or breach of the peace. All of these offences are in the main not such as would ever justify the intervention of the military forces. There are, however, some more serious offences where such intervention might be envisaged but, at least on the mainland of Great Britain, the number of recorded cases in that category is very small as a proportion of the offences against public order as a whole (Criminal Statistics for England and Wales, 1981, Cmnd. 8668).

A situation which does not readily fit into the well-worn categories of public order offences arose in a case of large-scale passive resistance (R v. Chief Constable of the Devon and Cornwall

Constabulary, ex parte Central Electricity Generating Board (CEGB) [1981] 3 All E.R. 826). A number of objectors obstructed the work of the CEGB by entering a site which it was proposed to develop, although without using any violence. The Court of Appeal held that the police could, at the invitation of the Board, assist in removing the trespassers, even though this was a peaceful demonstration, in order to prevent actual or apprehended breaches of the peace. The CEGB maintained that the police had a duty to remove the passive protestors from in front of the CEGB's excavation machinery and that the protestors were committing a criminal offence under section 281(2) of the Town and Country Planning Act 1971 by preventing the CEGB from carrying out their statutory duty. That Act, however, provides no power of arrest. The Chief Constable took the view that he could intervene only if he honestly believed that the protestors' conduct was likely to cause a breach of the peace (which he did not), and that he had no power to move peaceful protestors from private places unless he could reasonably anticipate a breach of the peace (which he could not given that for six months the passive physical protest had generated no violence).
The Court of Appeal felt that the Chief Constable was under 'a definitive legal mandate' to act but the Court refused to grant an order for mandamus to force the Chief Constable to perform his duty because the authority of R v. Metropolitan Police Commissioner ex parte Blackburn ([1968] 2 Q.B. 118 at 186) established clearly that the decision whether or not to act was one for the Chief Constable alone.
If a similar protest on a much wider scale were ever encountered, would it justify military intervention? Although it is not easy to fit these circumstances into any of the traditional categories for summoning military assistance, they could clearly impose excessive demands on police manpower. Nevertheless it is suggested that military involvement in such a demonstration could rarely, if ever, be justified. There must surely be more than inconvenience, even gross inconvenience, before the use of troops is appropriate.

OCCASIONS FOR MILITARY FORCE

Nevertheless there are certain less common but more serious circumstances which the law has recognised as justifying the intervention of troops in support of the civil authority. These are conveniently set out in paragraph 7 of Part II of the Manual of Military Law, section V, under the title 'Employment of Troops in Aid of the Civil Power'. This provides at most a synopsis of the situations when military forces might be used, but it could hardly be regarded as a comprehensive statement of the present law (see Rowe, chapter 9).

The occasions it states when troops may be called to give assistance are:
  (i) A National Emergency (Emergency Powers Acts 1920 and 1964);
  (ii) Intimidation of Workers (Conspiracy and Protection of Property Act 1875 as amended by s. 5(11) of the Criminal Law Act 1977);
 (iii) Unlawful assembly;
  (iv) Riot;
   (v) Insurrection.

The circumstances surrounding (i) and (ii) and the law relating to them are dealt with fully in chapters 5 and 6 of this book. The situations envisaged in (iii)-(v), though frequently alluded to in earlier chapters, require further explanation.

INSURRECTION

Insurrection is simply a convenient shorthand for the offence of 'levying war against our Lord the King in his realm' which is declared to be treason by the Treason Act 1351 together with such things as 'compassing or imagining' (falsely publicising) or intending the death of the King, violating his wife, giving aid within the realm to his enemies and killing his chancellor, treasurer or justices while in the course of their duties.[4]

Treason in the form of insurrection or 'levying war against the King' encompasses today the forcible resistance to the authority of the government in some public or general way such as an attempt to usurp the role of the government or to instigate a coup d'état or perpetrate some act of a general public nature in which the insurgents have no peculiar interest.[5] Treason of this type would seem to be distinguishable from riot and unlawful assembly only by the generality of its purpose (R v. Dammaree (1710) 15 State Tr. 521). If the public disorder invoked is confined to a private or local purpose then it would not amount to treason but would be encompassed by one or other of those two lesser common law offences. Today treason based upon insurrection like rout, another common law offence which stands between unlawful assembly and riot and which was committed when an unlawful assembly began some move towards the execution of its common purpose, has fallen into disuse (Criminal Statistics for England and Wales, Cmnd. 8376). The result is that public violence and disorder amounting to either offence in law is now prosecuted as unlawful assembly, riot or one of the lesser common law offences like affray, which will be discussed below. Until treason by insurrection and rout are abolished by law, and abolition of rout was proposed by the Law Commission in 1982 (Working Paper No. 82), it is unsafe to assume that they will never be used against those involved in public disorder. There is no doctrine in English law similar to that found in Roman Law and now peculiar to continental jurisdictions, as well as to old Scottish statutes, that laws wither away and 'die' if not applied or enforced for a period of time (desuetude). Indeed, the offence of affray was vigorously reintroduced in the 1960s after a long period of disuse; blasphemy is another offence to have been recently revived (R v. Lemon [1979] A.C. 617).

UNLAWFUL ASSEMBLY

Both riot and unlawful assembly have certain features in common, but the distinction between them is still relevant especially as regards the paying of state compensation to the victims of public violence (Riot (Damages) Act 1886) and also, according to the Manual of Military Law (Part II, Section V), in relation to the response which might be made by the military. Neither substantive offence in its present form has received a statutory definition with the result that the ingredients of both have to be extracted from numerous decided cases scattered through the common law.[6]

An unlawful assembly is an assembly of three or more persons having a common purpose either to commit a crime of violence or to achieve some other object (whether lawful or unlawful) in such a way as to cause reasonably courageous persons to apprehend a breach of the peace. Breach of the peace is itself a common law offence which is difficult to define shortly with precision but clearly it must include riot and affray and may include assaults and batteries committed in public (Coward v. Baddeley

(1859) 4 H & N 478; <u>Lewis v. Arnold</u> (1830) 4 C & P 354)[7] and it includes the situations where there are reasonable grounds for believing that any such event may occur (<u>R v. Light</u> (1857) D & B 332). The gist of unlawful assembly is the display of a common purpose to disturb the peace and actual violence is not necessary (<u>R v. Vincent</u> (1839) 3 St. Tr. N.S. 1037; <u>R v. Hunt</u> (1820) 1 St. Tr. N.S. 171). There are other features of the crime which also give it a wide ambit. A gathering of people in a private house preparing for a poaching expedition (<u>R v. Brodribb</u> (1816) 6 C & P 575) or the occupation of private premises (Sierre Leone High Commission) by students as a form of protest (<u>Kamara v. DPP</u> [1974] A.C. 104) have been held to amount to unlawful assemblies.

Even a gathering which starts innocently enough can subsequently become an offence once the appropriate common purpose manifests itself. This point was affirmed by the so-called Garden House Hotel affair at Cambridge where a large number of students beseiged a hotel to object to the holding of a dinner there as a part of a 'Greek Week' (<u>R v. Caird and Others</u> [1970] 54 Cr. App. R. 499). This led to charges of unlawful assembly and riot, Sachs L.J. saying:

> the moment when persons in a crowd, however peaceful their original intention, commence to act for some shared common purpose, supporting each other in such a way that reasonable citizens fear a breach of the peace, the assembly becomes unlawful. (<u>id</u>., p. 504)

It is well to note that heavy sentences (described by Sachs L.J. as 'stern but correctly so') were imposed on the student demonstrators and affirmed by the Court of Appeal.

Finally, although it is necessary to prove in the alternative either that the participators intended to use or support the use of violence or to show that, irrespective of the object or goal, the assembly, in attempting to attain their end, excited terror and alarm in the neighbourhood, it is not necessary to show that those assembled intended a criminal purpose or end (<u>R v. Hunt</u>, <u>supra</u>). A person who is present at and does not leave the scene of what was originally a peaceful demonstration but who has no wish to take part in subsequent violence would not be guilty of participating in an unlawful assembly. It is different if he took part, helped or encouraged. This is a question of fact for the jury to decide, but clearly mere presence without encouragement should not make that person liable (R v. Atkinson (1869) 11 Cox. C.C. 330; R v. Coney (1882) 8 Q.B.D. 534). He must be shown either to intend to use violence or to perform or assist acts which he knew would be likely to lead to a breach of the peace.

Demonstrations by minority political interests which excite widespread or vehement public reaction pose an obvious dilemma. The nice constitutional law question that arises in this situation, and especially in relation to the exercise of freedom of speech, is whether primacy should be given to the desirability of free speech and association or to the demands of public order and police manpower? If by gathering together or by speaking in public other members of the community are so incensed, possibly through their own bigotry (leaving aside any issue of incitement by the speaker or the assembly), that they breach the peace, should the assembly be prevented from gathering together or the speaker prevented from speaking? Should those who actually breach the peace be controlled with force and charged with criminal offences or should public order be maintained by curtailing our freedom to gather or to speak out in public?

The legal response to this difficulty is somewhat ambivalent. In Beatty v. Gillbanks ((1882) 9 Q.B.D. 308) members of the Salvation Army marched through the streets of Weston-super-Mare knowing, from past experience, that they would be violently opposed by a rival faction known as the 'Skeleton Army' which represented the brewing interest. Nevertheless, they proceeded and the Court made clear that they committed no offence of unlawful assembly. That which a man does lawfully cannot be rendered an offence by the unlawful opposition of others. Although this represents a general legal principle, which is referred to in the Manual of Military Law, as a guide to practical action the case needs to be approached with some caution. Even if the participants in such a demonstration are not guilty of unlawful assembly, there are a number of other ways in which they may be restrained under pain of some criminal sanction aimed at preventing or punishing a breach of the peace. For example, in O'Kelly v. Harvey ((1883) 15 Cox. C.C. 435) a magistrate who considered that a meeting to be addressed by Parnell was likely to be violently broken up by Orangemen was held not to have committed an assault in dispersing the prospective audience. Likewise the Constable was not liable for assault when, anticipating a breach of the peace, he plucked an orange lily from the bodice of a Protestant lady who insisted on walking through a Catholic area causing a hostile crowd to gather about her (<u>Humphries v. Connor</u> (1864) 17 Ir.C.L.R.I.). Indeed failure to 'move on' in such circumstances can amount to the offence of obstructing a police officer in the execution of his duty (<u>Duncan v. Jones</u> [1936] 1 K.B. 218). And a person who habitually uses language or gestures at public meetings which are calculated, or likely, to cause a breach of the peace, may be bound over by court order to keep the peace under pain of punishment for contempt of court (Magistrates Court Act 1952, s. 91).[8]

Accordingly, even though there may be no question of unlawful assembly, the police in such circumstances have a wide range of other common law as well as statutory powers which provide for the suppression of public disorder. Among the common law offences available for application in these instances are breach of the peace; criminal libel; blasphemous libel; sedition; public nuisance; assault; affray, rout and riot; and the armoury of statutory offences include obstructing a constable in the execution of his duty (Police Act 1964, s. 51(3)); obstructing the highway (Highways Act 1980, s. 137; Town Police Clauses Act 1847, s. 28); the use of threatening or abusive language with intent or likely to cause a breach of the peace (Public Order Act 1936, s. 5 as amended by the Race Relations Act 1965, s. 7) or likely to stir up racial hatred (<u>id</u>. s. 5A introduced by the Race Relations Act 1976, s. 70); conspiracy (Criminal Law Act 1977, s. 1); statutory assaults (Offences Against the Person Act 1861, ss. 18, 20 and 47; and Police Act 1964, s. 51(1)); criminal damage (Criminal Damage Act 1971, ss. 1-3); the offence of entering and remaining on property (Criminal Law Act 1977, ss. 6-10); treason (The Statute of Treasons 1351; Treason Act 1702, s. 3; Treason Act 1795, s. 1; Treason Felony Act 1848; and Treason Act 1945); and sundry other offences (see the Tumultuous Petitioning Act 1661, s. 1; Seditious Meetings Act 1817, s. 23; Metropolitan Police Act 1839, s. 52 (all of which relate to petitioning and assembling in the vicinity of Parliament)); Shipping Offences Act 1793; Vagrancy Act 1824, s. 4 (dealing with being armed with intent); and Metropolitan Police Act 1839, s. 54(13) and City of London Police Act 1839, s. 35(13)).

RIOT

A riot is an aggravated form of unlawful assembly. The difference was explained in a leading case by Alderson B. when he said:

> An unlawful assembly differs in this respect from a riot, that a riot must go forward to the perpetration of some act which the unlawful assembly is calculated to originate and inspire. Something must be executed in a turbulent manner to execute a riot. (R v. Vincent, supra)

Like unlawful assembly, riot is a product of judge-made law which, in practical terms, means that the punishment for both is imprisonment or a fine without any fixed maxima being set.

The classic description of riot is found in Field v. Metropolitan Police Receiver ([1907] 2 K.B. 853). There are five elements which are stated to be necessary: (1) at least three persons; (2) a common purpose; (3) the execution or inception of the common purpose; (4) an intent to help one another by force if necessary against any person who may oppose them in the execution of their common purpose; (5) force or violence not merely used in demolishing, but displayed in such a manner as to alarm at least one person of reasonable firmness and courage. The judges in the case produced this formulation from a distillation of the earlier authorities and its facts provide a good example of how the test is applied. More than three youths together carried out their common purpose of demolishing a wall. As soon as it fell, the caretaker of the premises came out into the street and the youths then ran away. It was held that this did not constitute a riot as elements (4) and (5) were missing. There was apparently no evidence that the youths intended to help one another by force against any person who might oppose them, and the conduct of the youths was not such as would alarm persons of reasonable firmness and courage.

In most cases it is likely that the 'common purpose' will be an unlawful one, such as the destruction of property or the infliction of personal injury on others. If the purpose is prima facie lawful, then it would seem that conviction for riot could only be justified if the violence displayed is gratuitous. It was not apparently considered that, notwithstanding the opposition likely to be encountered, the Salvation Army marchers in Beatty v. Gillbanks (supra) were guilty of riot. As regards the requirement of alarm, the case of Langford ((1842) Car & M 602; 174 E.R. 653), on which element (5) of the definition in Field's case (supra) is based, held that it was sufficient that only one person was terrified. More recently, in Devlin v. Armstrong ([1971] N.I.R. 13, 38) it was stated by the Court of Criminal Appeal of Northern Ireland that alarm might be inferred from the circumstances without calling an actual witness to say that he was alarmed.

AFFRAY

Closely related to the offence of riot is the common law offence of affray. The sudden and rejuvenated appearance of this crime after nearly a hundred years of desuetude (see Button v. DPP [1966] A.C. 591) is a further example of the courts' ability and willingness to apply arcane common law principles to modern conditions. The essence of the offence is an unlawful display of force or violence whereby a reasonably courageous bystander might be terrified. Its great attraction to prosecutors is the absence of any necessity to prove a 'common intent' which can be a difficulty in establishing the existence of a riot. Typically, it might be charged in the case of, for example, a serious brawl on licensed premises, but in many cases it may be a reflection of prosecuting convenience that the charge brought is affray rather than riot.

There is a similar difficulty to that which exists in riot regarding what has to be proved to establish the element of terror. In R v. Sharp and Johnson ([1957] 1 Q.B. 552) two men fought in the street watched by a large crowd. There was no evidence that any person was put in fear but the judge's direction that it was sufficient if the fight might have frightened reasonable people was upheld. Lord Goddard C.J. said: 'it might be enough for a witness to say that persons appeared to be alarmed ...'. Subsequently in Taylor v. DPP, Lord Reid said ([1973] 57 Cr. App. R. 915, 928) that in order to prove the element of 'terror' in the circumstances where people are present 'it is not necessary to prove by their evidence that they were terrified. It is enough if the circumstances are such that ordinary people would have been terrified. I say "would" not "might" have been'. In that case, however, the judges were in agreement that where the events occur in a private place it would be surprising if the offence (of affray) could be complete without the actual presence of onlookers to be frightened by sight or sound. This view has been confirmed by the recent decision in R v. Farnill ((1982) Crim. L.R. 38) which involved a brawl in the dark in the car park of a public house with no evidence of any other person being present or within earshot or reasonably likely to appear on the scene. The court held that it was not necessary to prove that any other person was actually present or frightened but because the offence was designed to protect the public it must at least be proved that there was a reasonable likelihood of a third person coming on the scene.

CRITICISMS

Clearly the problem which presents itself to the civil authorities and military alike concerns the identification of a riot. Is the legal definition a clear and adequate guide? The view has been expressed by Evelegh that it is not. He states:

> This is far too vague and too easily disputed to allow the security Forces to act with confidence against rioters. Particularly in a somewhat diffused situation, it is hard on such an uncertain authority for the individual non-commissioned officer or junior officer, the most likely ranks to have to make critical decisions, to take firm action early enough to prevent disorder from developing. (Evelegh, 1978, p. 79)

Given that a decision as to the existence of a riot may have to be made quickly and often in difficult circumstances, the requirement of being satisfied (and perhaps able to prove) a common purpose is likely to be problematic. What if a youth, photographed holding a brick in the middle of a disturbance, claims that he was merely ensuring that the missile would not fall into the hands of those with malevolent intent (id., p. 78)? Of course, if this is correct, he is rightly entitled to an acquittal. However, given that the onus rests on the prosecution to prove its case beyond reasonable doubt (Woolmington v. DPP [1935] A.C. 462), it is arguable that some cases of dubious merit will result in an unjust acquittal. These considerations, together with recent disorder in the large industrial cities, have prompted renewed debate over the desirability of legislation to fill the vacuum left by the abolition in the Criminal Law Act 1967 of the Riot Act 1714.

THE RIOT ACT 1714

The origins of the 1714 Riot Act lay in the popular tumults following the Hanoverian succession, but its terms remained substantially unaltered in its more than 250 year history. The rationale behind the Act depended on the fact that greater force was thought to be permissible in preventing a felony than a mere misdemeanour.[9] At common law, riot was merely a misdemeanour and the effect of the Riot Act was therefore to convert it under certain circumstances into a felony. In an age when it was known that the authorities would be likely to react with considerable force against anyone committing such a felony, the deterrent effect of the Riot Act may well have been considerable. As one authority puts it:

> Severe as it is, it has been many times productive of most beneficial consequences. The timely warning given by it brings many to a sense of their danger, and as far as possible ensures the speedy vindication of the law, or at least the separation of the innocent from the guilty. (Wise, 1907, p. 107)

Contrary to the impression sometimes given in recent discussion of a new Riot Act, the effect of a proclamation under the 1714 Act was not that anyone remaining in the vicinity thereby automatically became guilty of riot. The Act required that a proclamation be made calling upon the rioters, who had to number at least twelve, to disperse peacefully in the name of the Sovereign. Only after the lapse of an hour did those who remained riotously assembled together thereupon become guilty of a felony (R v. Fursey (1833) 6 C & P 81; 172 E.R. 1155, 1158). Although aimed at rioters, it would seem that once the Riot Act had been read everyone present after one hour had elapsed was bound to disperse or suffer the consequences whether or not actively engaged in the riot.

If the Riot Act was not read at a scene of disturbance, the mere presence of a person amongst the rioters would not make him guilty of riot unless it could be shown that he had taken part in an assembly for an unlawful purpose and had helped, or encouraged, or incited the others in the prosecution of that purpose (R v. Atkinson, supra).[10] If mere presence at the scene of a disturbance was itself to be made an offence, it would be a considerable departure from previous or existing law as outlined above.

A NEW RIOT ACT?

Strong support for a return to the concept of the 1714 Riot Act is given by Evelegh who argues that 'to have been able to say, as the Riot Act would have allowed, "disperse in one hour or be shot dead", would have quickly put an end to all rioting in Northern Ireland' (Evelegh, 1978, p. 159). One does not necessarily need to agree with such a judgment to see, nevertheless, the force of the argument for a clarification of the law. If society wishes to retain a law of riot, and expects those obliged to disperse rioters to resort to extremes of force, doubtless a claim could be made for the clear and relatively simple expedient of a public declaration that a state of riot exists. Such a view might be supported by reference not only to the desirability of the police and the military being aware of their duty, but to the arguably even more important consideration that civilians should not find themselves unexpectedly and suddenly exposed to extreme and perhaps even lethal force. But to see a simple public declaration as an absolute solution belies the real complexity of the issue. It cannot be denied that there are difficult problems associated with any attempt to re-introduce statutory prohibitions and controls over rioting. For example, should mere presence at the scene of disorder constitute an offence? Should 'innocent' and 'guilty' alike automatically be liable? Should persons accused of rioting be denied trial by jury? Should any particular warning be given to rioters of impending counter measures? Should the area in which such measures might be employed be precisely defined? Should the counter measures be prescribed or ad hoc? All these are problematic but the most difficult issue which existed under the 1714 Act would still remain even if modern legislation could satisfactorily deal with the other issues. This problem is highlighted by what occurred during the

Gordon Riots of 1780. There six days of rioting ensued before the proclamation under the Act was made because the Justice of the Peace and Mayor whose job it was to 'read' the Riot Act could not, owing to the legal uncertainty as to the amount of disorder that would justify the proclamation, decide when a riot existed.[11] Clearly any new legislation aimed at containing riot must define that subject with a good deal more precision than at present, and likewise the circumstances in which extraordinary measures might be taken should be clear beyond peradventure.[12]

An example of the way this might be done may be obtained from the Law Commission Working Paper No. 82 'Offences Against Public Order'. It talks of codifying the common law definition of riot which differed in some respects from that used by the Riot Act 1714. For example, the common law offence of riot requires that only three people need be involved in public violence whereas the old Act specified twelve. Despite such differences of detail, the offences were essentially similar. Mere codification of either, or of an amalgamation of both, will not alone alleviate the fundamental problem. This can only be overcome by a clear and precise definition of a riot and of the related aspects such as the authority responsible for containing such conduct; the area within which it is to operate; the time within which such authority may operate; the type or level of force which may be utilised and the responsibilities of those making the necessary decisions.

To date the only official view which has been made known is the pronouncement by the then Home Secretary, Mr Whitelaw, that new legislation to control rioting is something which the Government should consider carefully (H.C. Deb., Vol. 8, col. 1404). Because of this declaration, the Law Commission in their 'Offences Against Public Order' (Working Paper (No. 82), para. 1:14) refused to discuss the issue.

Lord Scarman received from the Commissioner of the Metropolitan Police proposals for new and increased power to contain public order situations in the form of a suggested offence of failing to disperse after a warning subject to a defence for an accused if he could show that he had reasonable excuse to be where he was in the circumstances. Lord Scarman rejected this proposal partly because he thought its introduction was unnecessary in the sense that the police already have wide powers

(Report of an Inquiry by the Rt. Hon. the Lord Scarman OBE, 'The Brixton Disorders 10th-12th April 1981', para. 7.32 <u>et seq</u>.) or powers that are too wide (Legal Action Group Briefing Paper, <u>The Times</u> 17th July 1981) under the present law pertaining to riot, rout, unlawful assembly, breach of the peace and the like, mentioned above. Secondly, Lord Scarman foresaw certain practical difficulties. For example, in order to establish the offence it would have to be proved that the warning to disperse had been heard and since a riot is generally a noisy occasion such proof might not be easy. Defining the defence of 'reasonable excuse' and the area to be cleared by the order appeared to him to be fraught with difficulty. Arguably, any proposed legislation can be rejected on the basis that it constitutes a serious threat to civil liberties in that (drug offences aside) such proposals would introduce into our law the novelty of a serious absolute or strict liability offence. If arrested in the area after the warning one would be liable and therefore the traditional right to a jury trial would be lost. Also, such an offence giving such wide power to the police would affect innocent and guilty alike and consequently could give rise to the sort of resentment which developed against the notorious 'sus' law (Vagrancy Act 1824, s. 4, repealed by the Criminal Attempts Act 1981, s. 8).

In so far as there is opposition to the reintroduction of riot legislation on the historical ground that in the past a proclamation more often than not resulted in bloodshed, it is important to realise that the bloodshed resulted largely from the limited options available to the military - rifle fire and bayonet charge. Today the control and dispersal mechanisms available are more sophisticated and less lethal although some are no less controversial (for example, dogs, mounted men, armoured vehicles, water cannon, tear gas, rubber and plastic bullets, and batons).

Indeed, recently, an application was made to the European Commission on Human Rights by a woman who complained that her son died after having been struck on the head by a plastic bullet in Northern Ireland. She asked that the Commission rule that the United Kingdom Government was in breach of Article 2 of the European Convention on Human Rights - The Right to Life. The Commission heard the parties' submissions on 10 July 1984 (<u>S v. The United Kingdom</u>, application No. 10044/82). If the Commission considered an application admissible it would consider its merits and place itself at the disposal of the parties with a view to securing a friendly settlement of the matter on the basis of respect for human rights (Art. 28). If a friendly settlement is achieved the Commission would send to the Committee of Ministers a report containing a brief statement of the facts and of the solution reached (Art. 30). If no such settlement is reached, the Commission would draw up a report on the facts and state its opinion as to whether the facts disclose a breach by the State concerned of its obligations under the Convention (Art. 31). The report will be transmitted to the Committee of Ministers of the Council of Europe, who will take a decision unless the case is referred, by the Commission or the contracting party concerned, to the European Court of Human Rights. Such remedies, however, were not available because in this instance the application concerning plastic bullets was declared inadmissible and no appeal is possible from such a finding by the Commission.

DEGREE OF FORCE

Major General Sir Charles Gwynn in his book <u>Imperial Policing</u> (1939) specifies three situations involving military aid to the civil authorities. In the small war situation aimed at re-establishing civilian control it was legitimate that there be no limitation upon the amount of force employed, the military being in complete command. But maximum force was not to be employed either where the civil power had temporarily collapsed or was in such disarray that it had involved the military in sharing the authority of government, or where the civil authority while under stress was still in sole command and the army was required to aid the civil police power. In both the latter cases minimum force only should be applied by the military and not some form of preemptive military strike.[13]

The modern law, however, seems to be entirely contained within s. 3 of the Criminal Law Act 1967. The mere existence of a riot appears to bestow no special authorisation or indemnity for the use of force outside the somewhat brief terms of the section.[14] Quite apart from the cryptic unhelpfulness of that section there is no clear recognition of the various states of disorder graduated by way of seriousness from affray through unlawful assembly, rout and riot to insurrection and ultimately to such a state of disorder that martial law might be said to exist.

The result of the present law is therefore uncertain as to what state of legal disorder exists, combined with little real guidance as to what degree of force can be used against it (Bennett and Rowe, 1981, p. 991).

MARTIAL LAW

Martial law is a situation in which the civil disorder is of such a might and magnitude that order can only be restored by giving power over to the military authorities or by it being assumed by them. If such a state can be said to exist, then it is generally thought that the general officer commanding the forces will become all powerful and his actions 'non-justiciable and, for the time being, absolute, subject only to consultation (if this is feasible) with the civil power' (de Smith, 1981, p. 511). The difficulty lies in discerning when martial law comes into operation since it is defined in terms of a state of affairs and not a precise and settled body of rules. It would seem that the preconditions are, first, a civil authority unable to contain widespread disorder or armed conflict and secondly the authorisation or acquiescence by it in the imposition of military government upon civilians in order to restore order. Thirdly although martial law may be proclaimed such a proclamation is of no legal effect if martial law was not justified by absolute necessity. The Irish Cases (R v. Allen [1921] 2 I.R. 241; R v. Strickland [1921] 2 I.R. 317) maintain that the ordinary courts have jurisdiction to decide whether the state of disorder is such as to warrant martial law. If they decide it is, then nothing the military does will be reviewable by the law courts, at least until the courts decide that the disorder has been pacified. Then, however, proceedings may be brought against the military at least for such conduct as was manifestly unreasonable in the circumstances but possibly also for any unnecessary use of force against persons or property. Again the law is not precise on this point (de Smith, 1981, p. 512; Dicey, 1967, pp. 289-91; Keir and Lawson, 1967, p. 231). Although legislation should clarify this uncertainty, it is largely academic because whether it does or not, as de Smith says, 'in practice an Act of Indemnity is almost certain to be passed (assuming that the disturbances are quelled), exonerating from liability persons who were acting in good faith for the suppression of the uprising' (de Smith, 1981, p. 514). The prospect of martial law ever coming into operation in this country is so remote as to preclude any further discussion of it. The reason for this lies in the fact that troops can be used under prerogative and statutory powers. The use of troops under those powers should put an end to the disorder long before any question of a state of martial law existing could arise. However, where troops, having been committed to the fray, have experienced prolonged difficulty in quelling widespread resistance and chaos martial law might take precedence.

LEGAL BASIS OF MILITARY OPERATIONS

Once a decision has been reached, if that is possible at all in the circumstances, as to whether or not a state of civil disorder exists of such magnitude or ferocity that it should be suppressed by military force, other questions of constitutional law immediately arise. For example, by what right under our constitution may military forces be established, maintained and deployed (particularly in quelling public disorder)? Given that the law permits such matters, does the military have to obey the directions of central government or the police in suppressing disorder or may the military operate independently? None of these issues is as straightforward as it might seem.

First, the legality of establishing and maintaining standing armed forces by the monarch was ostensibly curtailed by Article 9 of the Bill of Rights 1688 which states:

> the raising and keeping of a standing army within the Kingdom in time of peace, unless it be with the consent of Parliament, is against the law.

Subsequently, Parliament did authorise the existence of a standing army. Initially by way of a Mutiny Act passed annually, disciplinary powers were given to military commanders and the existence of the Army was legalised for a year at a time. From 1881 until 1955 that annual Act was called the Army Act and it continued to confirm the authorisation contained in the 1881 Act for a further year with whatever amendments Parliament considered necessary each year. In this way the requirements of Article 9 of the Bill of Rights were thought to be satisfied.

The Army Act 1955 provided an innovation which departed from that established pattern. That Act was to give a maximum life of five years to the Army, subject to annual renewal by Order in Council which must be laid in draft before Parliament and which is subject to affirmative resolution by each house.

An opinion has been expressed that since 1954 the armed forces have been maintained illegally in that neither the Army Act 1955 nor any of the successive armed forces enactments renewed quinquenially has granted 'explicit annual Parliamentary authorisation for the existence of a peacetime standing army as required by the Bill of Rights 1688' (letter of Professor Colonel G. Draper in The Times, 17 June 1981, p. 15). That view argues that the ancient provision requires the positive consent of Parliament by the passage of legislation and not simply its passive and unrecorded consent.

The words of Article 9 are not that explicit. Just as express and implied repeal of legislation are recognised as constitutional[15] so are express and implied consent on affirmation. This is a consequence of the doctrine of sovereignty or supremacy of Parliament. Provided the procedures for the creation of the law are complied with, the laws so produced are unimpeachable before a court of law no matter how harsh, fantastic or inconsequential.[16] A further concomitant is the ability to delegate the power to make law. Such a delegation may be complete so that the delegatee has the ability to produce law without more being done or, as in the case of the armed forces Acts, the delegation may not be absolute and may require some further element of approval or disapproval either by positive act or by silence on the part of Parliament. If the procedure is complied with, law is produced. Besides, the armed forces Acts expressly provide every five years for the bringing forward of the authorisation contained in the respective 1950s legislation. For example, quinquennially the Army Act 1955 is brought forward for a further twelve months to expire unless continued in force for a further series of twelve month periods up to a limit of five years by annual Order-in-Council affirmed in each House of Parliament. Irrespective therefore of Parliament's ability to specify any procedure whatsoever, the current one in this instance involves an affirmative resolution. Furthermore the schedules to the annual appropriations Act empower payment to the members of the armed forces and could be said either to be a positive annual affirmation in accordance with Article 9 of the Bill of Rights or else to amount to an implied repeal or a superceding of the prohibition contained in that document.

The conclusion must be that the consent of Parliament to the maintenance of the armed forces has been and continues to be granted and that the armed forces are legally constituted.

ARMAMENT AND DEPLOYMENT

Given that the armed forces are legally established and maintained, what of their armament and deployment? Short of a state of martial law coming into existence the government, which is clearly the civil power primarily responsible for containing and suppressing uprisings (de Smith, 1981, p. 511), having made the decision to intervene, may through Parliament pass emergency legislation authorising virtually anything as a counter measure. Alternatively the government, through its ministers acting as advisers to the Crown, may exercise prerogative power.

In Heuston's view (1964) the consequence of Chandler v. DPP [1962] 3 W.L.R. 694 was that the armament and disposition of the military are part of one of the oldest prerogatives of the Crown[17] and its exclusive discretion in such matters cannot be challenged in a court. In this case, Chandler, a disarmament protester, was convicted of conspiracy to enter a prohibited place. It was held that the trial judge rightly refused to allow him to call evidence to show that nuclear disarmament would be beneficial not prejudicial to the state. Deployment abroad is not the concern of this paper although constitutionally the authority for use at home or abroad is basically the same in that, legislation aside, both are legitimate exercises of prerogative power. That power, which was referred to by Heuston (id., p. 64) as arcana imperii, is a mystery and arguably in so far as it relates to the deployment of the military by central government to control disorder, it is a dangerous mystery unwarranted in a democratic society. It is exercisable, largely without check, by the executive.

Clearly the existence and scope of prerogative powers are matters of common law for the courts to decide. Secondly, the discretion whether or not to exercise these powers, once verified, is not reviewable (Heuston, id.; cf. dicta of Lord Denning M.R. in Laker Airways Ltd. v. Department of Trade [1977] 2 All E.R. 182 at 192ff.). So, for example, once it is recognised that the power to arm the military is part of the prerogative then the actual decision to arm with any particular weapons or none at all is beyond the review of the courts of law. Administrative law cases have held that where a discretion exists the courts can compel that rules be obeyed and can check that everyone acted reasonably in making the decision, but that power applies only where a statute confers a discretion (for example, Padfield v. Minister of Agriculture [1968] 1 All E.R. 694). Thirdly, the prerogative does not permit the executive by fiat to make lawful what is otherwise unlawful and should not permit it to make unlawful what is currently lawful: 'The pretended powers of dispensing laws or the execution of law by regal authority as it hath been assumed and exercised of late is illegal' (Bill of Rights, 1688, Article 2).

THE PREROGATIVE

The prerogative is made up of those exceptional powers and privileges inherent in the Crown at common law. These include command of the armed forces; the treaty making power; the appointment of military officers, senior civil servants, judges and other functionaries and dignitaries; the creation of peers; the conferring of honours; the giving of assent to legislation and the summoning and prorogation of Parliament. Both historically and factually it is simply 'the residue of arbitrary power or authority which at any given time is legally left in the hands of the Crown' (Dicey, 1967, cited by Lord Dunedin in Attorney General v. De Keyser's Hotel [1920] A.C. 508, 526). Such authority once belonged to the monarch but now in almost every instance the monarch acts on the 'advice' of Ministers. As Jennings (1959, p. 87) puts it, the effective decision is that of Cabinet, Prime Minister or Departmental Minister concerned. This was the result of the Glorious Revolution of 1688 which was the culmination of the process whereby the monarch was stripped of his arbitrary or discretionary powers. These prerogatives passed into the hands of his ministers responsible to Parliament. Henceforth the monarch was to act on their advice unless 'he could find another set of ministers' who could keep a majority in the House of Commons' (id.). Jennings stated (id.) that although the bulk of Cabinet decisions are concerned with statutory functions, 'foreign affairs, matters relating to the Commonwealth and a few matters relating to the army and navy and the control of the civil service are still exercised under prerogative power ...'.

Today, it is often difficult to state whether any particular prerogative still exists and even the scope of those prerogatives that do exist has always been difficult to define. Legislation and delegated legislation has encroached on the prerogative and the effect of this adds to the uncertainty and confusion. Obviously the use of prerogative powers enables the government to act quickly. For instance, in the case of insurrection or widespread disorder: 'It is the last resource provided by the Constitution to guarantee its own working' (Keir, 1969, p. 496), but it hardly seems justified that such arbitrary power should be available for use against the citizen, albeit the unruly citizen, in a democratic society. The ability to translate emergency powers into legislative form with rapidity indicates that reliance on obscure prerogatives is not a vital or necessary power of government.[18]

The power of central government, or of any other authority for that matter, to intervene in public disorder should be clearly codified in statutory form so that those asked to act, and citizens generally, may not be uncertain, confused or misled as to their rights, their duties and as to the consequences of their acts.

KEEPING THE PEACE

Finally, are the military bound to act on the order or request of central government and of any other authority within the community? The then Chief Constable of Devon and Cornwall writing in 1979 took the view that in all respects the military should be subservient to Parliament and that therefore the military can never come to the aid of the civil power without the permission of the government of the day (Alderson, 1979, p. 78). This, however, is not in law the reality of the situation. As indicated above, it is true that central government may order or request intervention by way of the prerogative or some emergency statutory power but those, at present, are not the only ways in which the military may become involved with public order.

Primarily it is the function of the police (who are duty bound) to maintain the Queen's peace. Yet it is well established in law that every citizen (military personnel included) in whose presence a breach of the peace is being, or reasonably appears about to be, committed, has the right, and indeed the duty, to take reasonable steps to prevent that breach of the peace by detaining the offender against his will (<u>Albert v. Lavin</u> [1981] 2 W.L.R. 955).

Lord Diplock has described this duty which is incumbent upon all citizens as a duty of imperfect obligation in that it does not place the citizen under any obligation to do anything which would expose him to personal injury (<u>Attorney General for Northern Ireland's Reference</u> [1977] A.C. 105). This would apply to members of the military acting individually. On the other hand, the military <u>per se</u> may come into the same category as the police officer who, by reason of his oath and office, has the function of preserving peace and public order. Under common law there are very few circumstances in which an omission to act is punishable, but this is one of them. Because of his duty a police officer cannot stand by passively and watch robbery or statutory assault or breaches of the peace or potential breaches occur (<u>R v. Dytham</u> [1979] 3 W.L.R. 467, in which the accused was a police officer who, having seen a man ejected from a club, and then beaten and kicked to death, had done nothing). Mayors, magistrates and army officers would seem to fall into this category where failure to maintain public order is concerned (see note 11).

Police, mayors, magistrates and army officers are not the only persons in society however with absolute or perfect obligations in this area. Every citizen at common law has a duty (of 'perfect obligation') to assist a police officer who has seen a breach of the peace committed by two or more persons or who has been assaulted or obstructed in making an arrest and has with reasonable necessity called other persons to assist him (<u>R v. Brown</u> (1841) Car. & M. 314).

The Manual of Military Law (Part II, Section V) simply reiterates the common law as stated by Tindal C.J. (<u>Charge to the Bristol Grand Jury on January 2nd</u> (1832) 4 C & P 261) to the effect that 'every citizen is bound to come to the aid of the civil power when the civil power requires his assistance to enforce law and order ... when called to aid the civil power soldiers in no way differ in the eyes of the law from other citizens ...'. This being so both are placed in a dilemma in that if the police officer seeking assistance is in the process of arresting a suspected offender the citizen has no immunity from civil liability if the arrest is unlawful (and there is always the possibility of sustaining severe physical injury) if he goes to the policeman's aid; and on the other hand if he refuses to assist, without a lawful excuse (such as inability due to physical or mental handicap), when two or more persons are actually committing a breach of the peace, he is committing an offence (R v. Brown, supra).[19]

Clearly one way, but not the only way, in which the military may become involved in suppressing public disorder is by request or order. The procedure for seeking or ordering such aid would seem to be that 'the Chief Constable, or in London the Commissioner, seeks military aid ... by applying to the Home Secretary who in turn seeks agreement from the Minister of Defence and the Cabinet' (Alderson, 1979, p. 80). According to Bramall, 'the police will never have to turn in vain to (the army) for help' (Chapter 3, p. 84). He also stated that it would be 'totally inappropriate to use (the armed forces) in a main public order role, unless disorder was occurring on such a scale that the police could not cope and our whole Parliamentary system was threatened ... and the Armed Forces' only function in this context is a peripheral one for which their training and equipment may be better suited'. Given that the military has the ultimate but restricted public order function and given that there is no special force in this country for dealing with such problems Bramall concluded that this is a police function into which the military should be drawn as a last resort and he concludes that it might be illegal to use soldiers when the police can still cope with the disorder.

Under the old riot legislation (Riot Act 1714, ss. 1-4) there was no provision specifying when a request for military assistance might be made.[20] However s. 3 of the 1714 Act, for instance, stated that '... such ... person or persons as shall be commanded to be assisting unto any ... justice of the peace, sheriff or under-sheriff, mayor, bailiff or other head officer ... to seize and apprehend, and they are hereby required to seize and apprehend, such persons so unlawfully, riotously and tumultuously continuing together after (the) proclamation ...'. History and the cases mentioned earlier show that both under this Act and at common law the civil authorities as specified in s. 3 above are entitled to, and did, summon military assistance as the situation demanded it but it would be wrong to suggest that this was or is the only way (individual involvement by soldiers or citizens aside) that the military can come to play a role in maintaining order. Likewise it would be misleading to give the impression that the military cannot intervene in these matters where the police are coping if this implies that the military is excluded until the civil authority decides the police cannot cope then formally requests military involvement. It is part and parcel of the rule of law that every citizen is duty-bound to prevent breaches of the Queen's peace so that members of the military may lawfully intervene to restore order. Evelegh (1978, p. 8) correctly states this view when he says: 'it is startling to reflect that, in strict constitutional theory, a corporal, with ten privates in a lorry, who happens to drive through Grosvenor Square in London when a crowd of demonstrators had burst through a police cordon and were attacking an embassy, would have not merely a right to intervene and suppress disorder with lethal weapons if necessary but an absolute duty to do so ...'.

Greer (1983), on the basis of historical analysis and a consideration of the implications of the various legal theories which might be used to justify military intervention, suggests that the 'prerogative theory' precludes not only judicial review but also 'the local civil authorities (the police and magistracy) from independent legal authority to summon the regular army'. He goes on to argue that the common law 'posse comitatus' power imposing a duty on magistrates to deploy troops was terminated by the advent of the doctrine of ministerial responsibility, but, as his analysis shows, this area of constitutional law is confused both on the questions as to who may summon military assistance and as to whether or not the military may intervene on its own initiative. At times, the fear of the army and concern for democracy and civil liberties has prevailed and at other times the fear of disorder has influenced the views held in society. Greer states (p. 586) that it is clear that the decision to call in the military 'has once again become ministerial and is no longer 'magisterial'. Later he argues that the military has a duty to come to the aid of civil powers when instructed to do so by the government and that the military has no authority to take the initiative. The historical review and the arguments put forward by Greer, while persuasive, are not necessarily conclusive.

The Queen's Regulations for the Army 1975 state (1976, ch. 11, para. J11002a):

> Should the assistance of the armed forces be called for in order to maintain peace and public order the officer to whom the application is made is at once to inform the Ministry of Defence and his immediately superior authority. Assistance will normally be requested by the chief officer of police and should be confirmed in writing ...
> Where a request is received from a source other than the chief officer of police, the Service commander on the spot is to refer the request to the chief officer of police and report it to his superiors. It is, however, possible in very exceptional circumstances for grave and sudden emergencies to arise which in the opinion of the commander demand his immediate intervention to protect life and property. In such emergencies he is to act on his own responsibility and is to report as early as possible the matter and the action he has taken to the Service authorities mentioned above and to the chief officer of police.

Further paragraphs (J11004, J11005, J11007) provide for intervention in the case of national disasters, to maintain essential services and supplies and to assist in national agricultural crises. Clearly the Queen's Regulations envisage requests for military aid coming from sources other than central government and also the possibility of the military acting on its own initiative.

Again the only conclusion possible is that the law as it stands is unsatisfactory either because it is confusing or simply because it has not developed since the mid-nineteenth century. For example, in law it was and still is (central government aside) the mayor and magistrates who may request aid from the military to quell disorder (see note 11). It was not, and still is not, the police and yet in reality today they are the body most likely to want or need assistance. Must the police request the mayor or a magistrate to request the local military commander to intervene? Must the request whatever its origins be sanctioned by central government? These matters are not clear and can only be made so by statute. Not only should the question of which civil authority or authorities are able to request military aid be so clarified but also the opportunity should be taken to state whether and how the military might intervene on its own initiative and what its liabilities are both if it fails to act and if it reacts excessively.

One principle which should not need such clarification but which sadly from the evidence (Evelegh, 1978, p. 10) does seem to require reiteration is that nobody may suspend or dispense with the law. That power has been denied formerly to Kings (Bill of Rights 1688; see Bowles v. Bank of England [1913] 1 Ch. 57 at 84), a President (Nixon v. Sirica, 487 F. & M. 700 (D.C. Cir. 1973), a Prime Minister (Fitzgerald v. Muldoon and others [1976] N.Z.L.R. 619) and Ministers (R v. Commissioner of Police for the Metropolis [1968] 2 Q.B. 118, 137) as an infringement of fundamental constitutional law. Political directions of this sort should be clearly refuted or else clearly authorised by statute as exceptional.

CONCLUSION

The inescapable conclusion to be drawn from the foregoing discussion is that certain areas of the law relating to disorder need clarification. In particular, legislation should make clear when a disturbance is to be classified as a riot or some other offence. This could form the basis of further legislation which would indicate at whose behest, request or authority, for how long, and by what means the military might intervene. Even if one were to accept the argument that it is not possible to spell out accurately how much force is to be used in every particular situation, it does not follow that nothing can be done to define and accurately describe the circumstances in which any force, especially military force, can be employed. Such legislation is essential if our constitution is not to be undermined. In the present state of the law, how can we expect the military and civil authorities, or the citizen, to know their respective rights, duties and liabilities in a situation where clarity of thought and certainty of action may be paramount requirements?

NOTES

1. Malone v. Commissioner of Police of the Metropolis (No. 2) [1979] 2 All E.R. 620. Telephone tapping, even if in breach of Article 8, did not give a plaintiff a direct right in an English Court.
2. But see Lord Denning MR in Hubbard v. Pitt [1975] 3 All E.R. 1 at p. 10.
3. There are other restraints contained for example in the laws governing obstruction of the highway and public nuisance.
4. See also the Treason Act 1702, s. 3; and the Treason Act 1795, s. 1 together with the Treason Felony Act 1848.
5. See East, 1 P.C. cited in Smith and Hogan, Criminal Law, 5th edition at p. 778.
6. See Law Commission Working Paper No. 82, Offences Against Public Order (1982), for current codification proposals.
7. See Salmond on Torts, 15th edition at p. 170 which states: 'a breach of the peace takes place when either an assault is committed upon an individual or public alarm or excitement is caused. Mere annoyance or insult is not enough ...'. More recently, see R v. Howell [1981] 3 All E.R. 383 and the discussion in R v. Chief Constable of the Devon and Cornwall Constabulary, ex parte CEGB [1981] 3 All E.R. 826.
8. See Wise v. Dunning [1902] 1 K.B. 167 and Lansbury v. Riley [1914] 3 K.B. 229.
9. A felony was an offence made such by statute or which, at common law, carried the penalty of death or forfeiture of property. All other offences were misdemeanours. With the proliferation of criminal statutes in the nineteenth century this division became increasingly technical, but certain other procedural and administrative rules still made the distinction significant. For the classification of criminal offences today and the procedure relevant to each, see C. Hampton (1977), Criminal Procedure (London), 2nd edition at p. 292ff. The distinction between felonies and misdemeanours was finally abolished by the Criminal Law Act 1967.
10. See R v. Coney (1882) 8 Q.B.D. 534 at 541 for reference to 'taking part in the matter' or 'concurring in the act' by merely being present.
11. See R v. Kennett (1781) 5 C & P 282 in which the Lord Mayor of London was convicted of neglect of duty in relation to the Gordon Riots; and R v. Pinney (1832) 3 St. Tr. 11 in which the same charge was levelled against the Mayor of Bristol and

two army officers as a consequence of the Bristol Riot of 1831, and see n. 19 below.

12. Despite the close affinity of riot to the offence of affray, the Manual of Military Law makes no reference to the latter presumably because it is not considered serious enough to justify military intervention. This highlights again the problem - where is the line to be drawn between a fight, brawl or mêlée and an unlawful assembly or riot?

13. The Hunter Commission Report of the 1920 Committee of Inquiry into the events of Amritsar especially Brigadier Dyer's Statement to the Army Council, Cmnd. 771 (1920) and the Inquiry into the Punjab Disturbances, Cmnd. 705, 681 and 534.

14. Section 3 reads:
(1) A person may use such force as is reasonable in the circumstances in the prevention of crime, or in effecting or assisting in the lawful arrest of offenders or suspected offenders or of persons unlawfully at large.
(2) Subsection (1) above shall replace the rules of the common law on the question when force used for a purpose mentioned in the subsection is justified by that purpose.

15. Implied repeal has been challenged in the courts but without success, Scrutton L.J. said in Ellen Street Estates Ltd. v. Minister of Health [1934] 1 K.B. 590: 'Parliament can alter an Act ... by repealing in terms the previous Act ... and ... also, by enacting a provision which is clearly inconsistent with the previous Act'.

16. A.V. Dicey, The Law of the Constitution: 'Parliamentary sovereignty means ... the right to make or unmake any law whatsoever ...', confirmed in Edinburgh and Dalkeith Railway v. Wanchope (1842) 8 CC & F 710 [H.L.]. See more recently, Manual v. Attorney General [1982] 3 All E.R. 822.

17. The term 'the Crown' is simply the personification of the State and in reality is synonymous with the government of the day. See Diplock L.J. in Town Investments Ltd. v. Secretary of State for the Environment [1977] 1 All E.R. 813 at p. 818ff.

18. See, for example, the Emergency Powers (Defence) Acts 1939-40; the Defence of the Realm Acts 1914-15 and especially the Emergency Powers Act 1920 and 1964 together with the Reserve Forces Act 1966 and the Army Reserve Act 1950 (S.10(1)) which vest in the Secretary of State power to call out the reserve forces if required to assist the civil authorities in preserving public order.

19. R v. Brown (1841) Car. & M 314. A police

officer tried to stop a prize fight and called upon the accused to assist him. The accused was sitting on the box of his carriage and refused saying that he had to mind his horses, which were in the care of two grooms. The refusal to help was held to be criminal by Alderson J. on the basis that there was a breach of the peace by two or more persons; there was a reasonable need for assistance and the accused had the ability to render such assistance.

20. See ss. 88-89 of the English Draft Criminal Code 1879 which, although not adopted in the UK, formed a model for Commonwealth jurisdictions.

REFERENCES

Alderson, J. (1979) *Policing Freedom*, Plymouth, Macdonald & Evans

Bennett, G.J. & Rowe, P. (1981) 'Reflections on the Law and Lethal Force - A Shot in the Dark', *New Law Journal*, vol. 131, no. 6019

de Smith, S.A. (1981) *Constitutional and Administrative Law*, 4th edn., London, Penguin/Longmans

Dicey, A.V. (1967) *Introduction to the Study of the Law of the Constitution*, London, Macmillan

Evelegh, R. (1978) *Peace-Keeping in a Democratic Society*, London, Hurst

Fawcett, J.E. (1976) 'A Bill of Rights for the UK', 1 *Human Rights Review* 5

Greer, S.C. (1983) 'Military Intervention in Civil Disturbances', *Public Law* 573

Gwynn, Major General Sir Charles (1939) *Imperial Policing*, London, Macmillan

Heuston, R.F.V. (1964) *Essays in Constitutional Law*, 2nd edn., London, Stevens

Jaconelli, J. (1976) 'The European Convention on Human Rights - The Test of a British Bill of Rights', *Public Law* 226

_____ (1980) *Enacting a Bill of Rights: The Legal Problems*, Oxford, Clarendon

Jennings, Sir W.I. (1959) *The Law and the Constitution*, 5th edn., University of London

Keir, D.L. (1969) *The Constitutional History of Modern Britain Since 1485*, 9th edn., London, Black

_____ & Lawson, F.H. (1967) *Cases in Constitutional Law*, 5th edn., Oxford, Clarendon

Perkins, Brigadier K. (1973) 'Soldiers or Policemen?', *British Army Review*, 7

Scarman, Lord (1974) *English Law - the New Dimension*, London, Stevens

Wise, E. (1907) *The Law Relating to Riots and Unlawful Assemblies*, London, Butterworths

Chapter Nine

KEEPING THE PEACE: LETHAL WEAPONS, THE SOLDIER AND THE LAW

Peter J. Rowe

The use of troops to aid the civil authorities in time of disturbance is not a recent phenomenon. Before the growth of an organised and mobile police force the army was the only body that was capable of being directed to a particular place and there to concentrate sufficient numbers of armed men, ready to defend life and property (Radzinowicz, 1956, pp. 115 et seq.; Bramall, Chapter 3). In 1893, for instance, 2000 miners rioting at a colliery near Wakefield were faced by twenty-eight soldiers who, fearing that they would be surrounded, opened fire and killed a number of them (Parliamentary Papers 1893-4, C. 7234, Report of the Committee on Featherstone Riots).

More recent events demonstrate that even an armed police force may be unable to control violence that occurs on a large scale. It is then that the army may be called upon for assistance. This may occur when a cohesive section of the population has become alienated, for whatever reason, from the police force or government. In Ireland during the nineteenth and early twentieth centuries troops were employed to restore order; in the United States in the 1960s, race riots occurred in a number of cities (see generally, Murray, 1971); and since 1969 Northern Ireland has been the focus of attention. In Great Britain, however, recent experience points to the deployment of soldiers to assist the local police when a group of armed men take hostages and threaten to kill them. The tactical skill of the soldier and the traditional reluctance of the British police to use firearms explains the reliance on the army in this type of case. The question of when soldiers may be requested to assist the police is not entirely free of doubt and it is discussed elsewhere (Chapters 6 and 8; see Wade and Phillips,

1977, p. 506; Evidence of the Secretary of State for War (Haldane) H.C. Papers 236 (1908) paras. 103-04). In practice the army will only be called out after consultation at government level following a request from the chief officer of police for assistance.

Lethal weapons form part of the normal equipment of the soldier[1] and their use will almost certainly cause death or severe injury. If liability is imposed it will be either for a serious criminal offence or for an award of substantial damages. This chapter will examine the legal status of the soldier, the uncertain boundary between the lawful and the unlawful use of force and the individual liability of the soldier.

THE STATUS OF THE SOLDIER WHEN ASSISTING THE CIVIL POWER

Apart from powers given to soldiers by statute (such as the Northern Ireland (Emergency Provisions) Act 1973) many older authorities state that a soldier is merely a citizen in uniform. In 1911 the Law Officers stressed that '[a] soldier differs from the ordinary citizen in being armed and subject to discipline but his rights and duties in dealing with crime are precisely the same as those of the ordinary citizen'.[2] Indeed, two centuries earlier, Lord Mansfield said, 'Whether the citizen's coat be a brown one or a red one' the duty is the same.

However, this simple analogy disguises a more involved position. It is true that a soldier is subject to the law of the land, and in particular he, like all citizens, has a duty to come to the aid of a police officer if called upon to assist (R v. Brown [1841] Car. & M. 314); indeed, every citizen, 'in whose presence an actual or reasonably apprehended breach of the peace was being or about to be committed' is under a common law duty 'to make the person ... refrain from so doing, and, in appropriate cases, to detain him against his will'(Albert v. Lavin [1981] 3 All E.R. 878; but see Grunis, 1978, p. 417, n. 74). However, the soldier is also accountable under military law, breach of which may entail imprisonment, detention or a fine (Army Act 1955 as amended).[3] In particular he has a duty, under s. 34 of the Army Act 1955, to obey all lawful commands. Lord Diplock in Reference under s. 48A of the Criminal Appeal (Northern Ireland) Act 1968 (No. 1 of 1975) ([1976] 2 All E.R. 937 at 946) took this point:

In theory it may be the duty of every citizen when an arrestable offence is about to be committed in his presence to take whatever reasonable measures are available to him to prevent the commission of the crime; but the duty is one of imperfect obligation and does not place him under any obligation to do anything by which he would expose himself to risk of personal injury, nor is he under any duty to search for criminals or seek out crime. In contrast to this a soldier who is employed in aid of the civil power in Northern Ireland is under a duty, enforceable under military law, to search for criminals if so ordered by his superior officer and to risk his own life should this be necessary in preventing terrorist acts. For the performance of this duty he is armed with a firearm, a self-loading rifle, from which a bullet, if it hits the human body, is almost certain to cause serious injury if not death.

In addition, it might be argued that a soldier, like a police constable, holds a 'public office', and wilfully, without reasonable excuse, to neglect a duty he is bound to perform by law, is the criminal offence of misconduct in a public office (R v. Dytham [1979] 3 All E.R. 641).

When it comes to the actual use of force the status of the user is not decisive of itself, since s. 3 of the Criminal Law Act 1967 (in Northern Ireland a similar provision applies) provides that '[a] person may use such force as is reasonable in the circumstances in the prevention of crime, or in effecting or assisting in the lawful arrest of offenders or suspected offenders or of persons unlawfully at large' [emphasis added]. This section is further stated to replace the common law position as to the justification for the use of force. Yet, a view has been put forward by a former Assistant Director of Army Legal Services that the law as just outlined is deficient since it does not distinguish between those who use force in a purely private capacity and those seeking, at the state's direction, to restore peace in the land as part of their professional duty and armed by the state with lethal weapons for that purpose (Wakerley, 1975).[4]

The main jurisprudential problem with lethal weapons is not their use but control of their use. If those who use force on behalf of the state are to be given greater latitude from the outset than those who act in a purely private capacity, problems of limits on the use of weapons become apparent. Would a soldier, as opposed to a private citizen, be liable under military law only for the 'unnecessary' use of force? Unless he is to be the sole judge of when to use force, an ex post facto assessment will have to be faced. It would seem to make little difference, at the moment when he makes the decision to fire, whether this inquiry is to be subsequently conducted by a court-martial or before a jury. It is the very notion of an inquiry and of personal accountability that is the safeguard against arbitrary action. As Nichols (1976, p. 190) observes, 'It is no longer a credible position for a civilised society to take that a soldier in time of urban guerrilla warfare should be regarded as a special constable and in time of conventional warfare as an extra-legal being. A soldier is a soldier is a soldier.'

Once the decision is taken to place soldiers outside the law durante bello a situation, in effect, of martial law will prevail (see generally, Dicey, 1960, chapter VIII; Evelegh, 1978, p. 107, who argues for the statutory abolition of this concept; a soldier would, however, remain liable under military law). As a result of 'the troubles' in Ireland in 1920, martial law was imposed in certain areas by the General Officer Commanding. Anticipating that the acts of individual soldiers might precipitate legal action, Parliament in the same year passed an Act of Indemnity in order to exonerate retrospectively those who took part in suppressing the 'state of war'. The advantages (from a military point of view) of a wider power of search, arrest and punishment available under martial law have to some extent been achieved by emergency powers granted by statute. In addition, an effective intelligence network can direct the army against the law-breakers rather than the community as a whole.[5]

Criminal Liability
The civil police are responsible for investigation into the circumstances of alleged criminal conduct by soldiers if the trial is to be held in a criminal court. It is the function of the courts, emphasised a Northern Ireland judge, 'to stand between those who use force and those against whom it is exercised to ensure that it is not used excessively to cause unlawful harm'.[6] It is not, however, for the soldier to prove his innocence. He is entitled to be acquitted if the prosecution cannot prove that the

force used was unreasonable. So where there is doubt as to whether or not he should have fired, or used the force he did, he is entitled to an acquittal.

Northern Ireland provides a useful paradigm within which to apply the very general standard contained in s. 3 of the Criminal Law Act 1967 (see generally, Boyle, Hadden and Hillyard, 1980).[7] The balance between the lawful and the unlawful use of force is illustrated to some extent by the fact that between 1970 and 1979 a total of 186 people had been killed by the army in Northern Ireland in the course of anti-terrorist operations (H.C. Deb., Vol. 968, col. 369). On the other hand between 1972 and 1976, 28 soldiers have been charged before courts in Northern Ireland with offences involving shooting, of whom 13 were convicted (id., vol. 918, col. 278). Only one soldier has been convicted of manslaughter, but his conviction was subsequently quashed on appeal (R v. Foxford [1974] N.I. 181).

In 1974 a soldier shot and killed a person whom he suspected of being a member of the IRA. He had been ordered to bring the man, who was walking away, back for questioning. When the soldier called upon him to halt, he ran off and was then shot. Following acquittal of the soldier on a charge of murder the Attorney General for Northern Ireland referred the case to the House of Lords seeking guidance as to the use of force in similar circumstances (Reference under s. 48A of the Criminal Appeal (Northern Ireland) Act 1968 (No. 1 of 1975) [1976] 2 All E.R. 937). The House felt that the 'reasonableness' of force was a question of fact and not of law; it was a matter to be decided by a jury (where one is sitting). In subsequent cases it would be proper for the judge to emphasise factors to the jury that might be relevant to their decision, but he could not direct them to decide that the force was unreasonable if they found certain facts proved. Lord Diplock did, however, point out that a jury ought to take into account, inter alia, that a soldier may be faced with a split-second decision as to whether he ought to open fire or not.

As a general principle the criminal law ought not to be stated in vague and uncertain terms. It should be possible, in Evelegh's vivid phrase (1978, p. 77), for 'the 18 year old "kid" of modest intelligence in uniform in Northern Ireland' to discover what the law allows him to do. To throw the whole issue into the jury's lap makes it an unpredicable matter and one that may vary from jury to jury.

Reasonable force would seem to involve two issues: first, was the force necessary to achieve the prevention of crime (or were there any alternative means to achieve this); and secondly, was the force used proportionate to the crime to be prevented? In theory equal considerations apply where the force used was in order to effect the arrest of the offender, or suspected offender, but the balancing of gains and losses, implicit in the second issue, may be much more difficult. To some extent this explains a desire to consider what future crimes the alleged offender might commit if he were permitted to escape (see the dictum of Lord Diplock, Reference, supra, 947).

In Northern Ireland a useful by-product of the power given by s. 2 of the Northern Ireland (Emergency Provisions) Act 1973, to try without a jury what are broadly described as terrorist offences, is that judges, in the process of reaching a verdict, have been able to discuss in depth 'the circumstances' that would make the use of force reasonable: '[I]f the force the ... soldiers used was reasonable in the circumstances in which they used it, the defects, if ... any, in the planning of the operation would not ... render the force used unreasonable' (Farrell v. Secretary of State for Defence [1980] 1 All E.R. 166, 172, Viscount Dilhorne). In R v. MacNaughton ([1975] N.I. 203), for instance, the Lord Chief Justice tried (and acquitted) without a jury a sergeant who shot a man whom he suspected of being concerned with an explosion that had recently occurred. The man had been arrested by the sergeant but was shot when he attempted to escape. In assessing the reasonableness of the accused's action his Lordship stated, '[T]he patrol was working in active service conditions and I do not refer to the mere mounting of roadblocks or the undertaking of routine patrols. ... [There was] the possible presence of an ambush. These facts make a great difference, to my mind, in assessing whether shooting at an escaping prisoner was a reasonable way of dealing with the situation. There was the danger of booby-traps. There was ... the possibility of masking a line of fire. This created a situation quite different from the escape of a person from prison or an escape in some place where conditions are comparatively peaceful. ... [T]here must have been the likelihood that if [the man] escaped he would undertake terrorists' acts' (id., 209). Clearly, it would seem that in assessing the reasonableness of the force used it is not vital to categorise the crime to be prevented as an insurrection, riot or unlawful assembly. There can, for instance, be no general right to use lethal force to quell an insurrection or a riot.[8] The statements concerning the permissible degree of force outlined in nineteenth century official reports or in charges to juries are of little value in assessing the liability of the soldier in a situation similar to Northern Ireland.

In order to give some guidance on the meaning of 'reasonable force', the Ministry of Defence produced the 'Yellow Card' which has been issued to soldiers and declares, in perhaps more cautious terms than the law actually demands, when fire may be opened. Since the card emanated from the Ministry and not from Parliament or a court of law, it cannot be definitive of a soldier's legal position. Rule 3, for example, stipulates that warning shots are not permitted, yet McGonigal L.J., in a case in 1975, thought this to be too sweeping.[9] The practice of prosecutions in Northern Ireland suggests, however, that soldiers will only be charged if the guidelines in the Yellow Card have not been followed.

The Soldier Who Makes a Mistake. The test in s. 3 is partly objective in the sense that in considering whether the use of force was 'reasonable' the court will have to ask itself what a reasonable soldier would have done in the circumstances, as they presented themselves to the accused and in the light of his belief at that time.[10]

In R v. Bohun and Temperley (unreported, Judgment 4 July 1979),[11] two soldiers were charged with murder when they shot a sixteen year old youth. A cache of weapons had been discovered in a graveyard and the two accused were sent to watch over it and to arrest anyone coming to collect the weapons. The youth came to the graveyard, picked up an unloaded rifle, probably pointed it in the direction where, unknown to him, the two soldiers were, and both soldiers fired, killing him.

The Lord Chief Justice of Northern Ireland, trying the case without a jury, acquitted the soldiers of murder since they reasonably, though mistakenly, believed their own lives were in danger when they fired. Lord Lowry L.C.J. went on to say that 'in looking back it is sad to say, the Army and the two soldiers gravely mishandled the operation because they shot an innocent boy who, whether he was holding the gun or not, had no capacity to harm them'. His lordship considered, but in fact dismissed, the option of finding a verdict of manslaughter.

<u>The Effect of Superior Orders</u>. Enough has been said so far to show that a soldier's liability is personal. Whilst in other countries a soldier may avoid liability in civilian courts by pleading that he was merely carrying out an order, and that the order was not manifestly illegal (see Nichols, 1976; Keijzer, 1978; Hughes-Morgan, 1977; Green, 1976, pp. 17 <u>et seq</u>.); in England the Manual of Military Law (Part I, paras. 156-7) states 'the better view' to be that a superior order 'can never of itself excuse the recipient if he carries out the order, although it may give rise to a defence on other grounds'. The Manual, like the Yellow Card, is not definitive of the soldier's legal position and there are in fact decisions which suggest that a soldier would be guilty only if the order were manifestly or plainly illegal.[12] On the other hand, support can be found for the stance taken by the Manual. In <u>R v. Taylor</u> (1940) (quoted in Keijzer, 1978, p. 175; see also <u>R v. Trainer</u> (1864) 4 F. & F. 105) a soldier was ordered by his sergeant to fire at a motorist who would not comply with the orders of an air-raid warden to dim and extinguish his lights during an air-raid. In his summing up the judge directed that there were circumstances in which the use of a weapon would be justified, but that if its use were not so justified by the circumstances, it could not be legitimated by the order of a superior. The accused clearly believed it was his duty to obey the sergeant's orders. He was, however, subsequently acquitted. If the order of the superior leaves discretion in the subordinate as to the means of carrying out the order, <u>a fortiori</u> the order cannot be raised as a defence; although, no doubt, it would be a material factor to be taken into account. This is illustrated by <u>R v. Thomas</u> (4 M. & S. 441 (1816)). In that case, a Royal Navy ship lay in the Medway and her crew was being paid off. To avoid inconvenience from people coming to meet the sailors, Thomas, a marine, was placed as a sentinel with orders to keep all boats away unless officers were present. A musket was given to him, with three blank cartridges and three bullets. Boats did approach and Thomas repeatedly bade them to keep off. One boat, however, persisted and came close under the ship. Thomas fired and killed a man who was in it. He was tried and convicted of murder despite

the fact that he believed that it was his duty to fire.

In <u>Reference</u>, <u>supra</u>, the soldier, it will be recalled, was ordered by his sergeant to bring a man back for questioning. When he called upon him to halt the man ran off and he then fired. In the Court of Criminal Appeal in Northern Ireland, McGonigal L.J. (who dissented on the main issue) thought that even if the soldier's action conformed to the directions in the Yellow Card (and therefore a 'superior order') he would not be able to escape liability because his actions were 'so manifestly extreme that it could not be set up as a matter of justification or exoneration'.

The law as stated in the Manual clearly places the soldier in a dilemma since he may be 'faced with legal difficulties to be solved in a flash which could take a trained lawyer hours to consider' (<u>R v. MacNaughten</u> [1975] N.I. 203, 208, Lord Lowry L.C.J.). The training and discipline to which a soldier is subject turns him from an individual with a rifle into a member of a group (whether regiment, company, platoon or section) possessing collective fire power under the command of an individual (see <u>R v. Bohun</u>, <u>supra</u>, and the case of soldier B). The superficial attraction of the view that he is protected if the order is not manifestly illegal is that it encourages obedience to orders and therefore promotes military discipline, but on the other hand, it derogates from the principle of the personal liability in law of the actor and it subordinates civilian to military law or civic liberty to military necessity (see Kenny, 1966, p. 68). The person who gives an illegal order would also be guilty of the offence of murder or manslaughter if death resulted (<u>Kinder v. U.S.</u> (1954) 14 C.M.R. 742, quoted in Murray, 1971, p. 157), and s. 3 of the Criminal Law Act may not be available as a defence to him (<u>Farrell v. Secretary of State for Defence</u> [1980] 1 All E.R. 166, 172).

It must not be supposed however that military orders only compel a soldier to do acts that might amount to crime. In fact such orders may offer greater protection to the civilian population since a commanding officer may direct that weapons are only to be used in very limited circumstances. Further, any other conduct of the soldier that is considered to be worthy of punishment, but would not amount to a criminal offence, could be charged as 'conduct or neglect, prejudicial to good order and military discipline' under s. 69 of the Army Act

1955. However, as Evelegh points out (1978, pp. 85-86), when civilian police are investigating an incident the military hand is stayed and military punishment cannot be inflicted.

The soldier's dilemma could be solved in practice by not prosecuting, before the civil courts or by court-martial, a soldier who obeyed an order that was not plainly, but was in fact, illegal. Alternatively, if a prosecution were commenced a nolle prosequi might be entered by the Attorney General or the soldier could be pardoned, as the jury recommended in Thomas (supra). If the act was not criminal but the soldier honestly thought it was and therefore refused to obey an order, discretion might be exercised by the military authorities in not charging him under s. 34 (failing to obey a lawful order).

Reform of S. 3 of the Criminal Law Act. We have seen that s. 3 produces no real guidance to those who have a duty to enforce it. The court is left to 'feel' its way to a solution, and as Lord Devlin, a distinguished former Lord of Appeal put it (in another context), '[j]udgment by feel is government by men and not by laws' (1979).[13]

Uncertainty of the legal position may result in inaction by the army, as it did in a spectacular way in the Gordon Riots in 1780. Evelegh has suggested (1978, pp. 94 et seq.) that the military authorities might invoke the 'declaratory judgment' and obtain a declaration by a court of a particular legal point. But the House of Lords in Reference (supra) appeared to scotch all ideas of judicial guidance by emphasising that what is reasonable in the circumstances is essentially a question of fact and not of law. As to the limits of s. 3, the 14th Report of the Criminal Law Revision Committee (1980) failed to offer any guidance to judges, juries, and magistrates on the principles they should apply when considering whether reasonable force was used. Ashworth (1980, p. 563) regretted this approach and stressed that

> [i]t is simply not true to say that every case is different and must be taken on its own facts: facts vary indefinitely, but the principles applied in judging the reasonableness of the defendant's actions are often general ones. Nor is it true to say that occasions for justifiable force always arise suddenly, with no time for considered choice: some do, and proper

indulgence should be shown towards 'spur of the moment' or 'crisis' reactions, but others do not. Nor is it true to say that detailed legislation is bound to lead to inflexibility and injustice: a variety of legislative techniques is available.[14]

Such a legislative technique can be traced in the American Law Institute's Model Penal Code (1962, 3.07 (iii-iv) which states that the use of deadly force will be justifiable by a peace officer if he 'believes that the force employed creates no substantial risk of injury to innocent persons and the actor believes that: (i) the crime for which the arrest is made involved conduct including the use or threatened use of deadly force; or (ii) there is substantial risk that the person to be arrested will cause death or serious bodily harm if his apprehension is delayed.'

The Criminal Law Revision Committee in 1980 considered this provision but decided against recommending something similar to it. English law is likely to continue therefore on the basis of an <u>ex post facto</u> rationalisation of soldiers' actions. The English soldier, at least, has the benefit of the Yellow Card to help him.

<u>Liability to Pay Damages</u>
A number of claims for damages in Northern Ireland have been brought against the Ministry of Defence in respect of the actions of soldiers. According to the Defence Secretary in 1973 (H.C. Deb., Vol. 855, col. 388) there were 150 civil claims against the Crown. In 1977 the then Secretary outlined that an 'out of court settlement had been made when the Ministry accepted that a particular person was innocent of involvement in the shooting incident which led to his death' (<u>id</u>., Vol. 930, col. 329). The first reported instance of such a claim reaching a court was <u>Farrell</u> (<u>supra</u>; see also <u>Lynch v. Fitzgerald</u> [1938] I.R. 382; <u>McGuigan v. Ministry of Defence</u> [1982] 19 N.I.J.B.) in 1977, which arose out of an incident where soldiers shot three men who they believed were about to place a bomb in a bank. It was all a mistake. In fact they were attempting to rob a person who intended to place a bag in the night-safe of the bank. One of the widows claimed damages from the Ministry of Defence as being responsible for the actions of the soldiers.

Two interesting features were present in this case. First, unlike most cases involving soldiers, trial of the plaintiff's claim was before a jury, and secondly, there was an attempt (though unsuccessful) to make the Ministry liable for the officer who sent the soldiers to the roof-top overlooking the bank and was responsible for handling the operation. Unfortunately (at least for those keen to learn what view the House of Lords would have taken on liability in negligence in these circumstances), the plaintiff lost on this issue because it was not pleaded in her statement of claim. The jury found that the soldiers had acted within s. 3 (which applies to civil as well as criminal cases) and therefore the Ministry was not liable.

A more recent case, Doherty v. Ministry of Defence (House of Lords, 1980, unreported; see Rowe, 1981) shows that the Ministry may have to pay damages to a person shot by a soldier when there is no legal justification for the shooting. The plaintiff was awarded £15,000 for trespass to the person when he was, as the court found, wrongfully shot and wounded by a soldier who had himself been fired at by a gunman a short time before.

A vital issue is left undecided by both Farrell and Doherty and on which the law is quite uncertain - that is, would an action in negligence lie against a soldier? This tort is concerned with negligent acts or omissions and is much wider in scope than trespass to the person, which is based on direct injury. Examples of negligent conduct might be an officer who negligently 'set up' an operation where the risk to an innocent suspect was a high one (as in Bohun or Farrell) or where a soldier shot at a legitimate target, missed and hit an innocent person instead.

It is really an issue of public policy for the courts to decide. It boils down to the question: do members of the security forces owe a duty under the law of negligence to take reasonable care to guard against risk of injuring actual or suspected terrorists? If the courts were to decide that no duty is owed, liability to pay damages, although not entirely denied (because a soldier who causes direct injury will remain liable), is nevertheless curtailed.

One of the principal arguments for this view might be that the threat of a claim for negligence (especially as to the planning of an operation) would so inhibit the security forces that it would not be in the public interest to impose such a duty. On the other hand the Lord Chief Justice in Northern Ireland said in 1979 in Bohun, 'I do not intend to give any currency to the view that the Army are above the general law in the use of weapons or are in any way beyond its reach'.[15]

Suppose the courts ultimately decide that there is no good reason in policy why a duty to take reasonable care should not be owed: what standard of care would be applied? In <u>Doherty v. Ministry of Defence</u> (<u>supra</u>) the trial judge had said that (even if the account of the shooting given by the soldiers was correct) 'he would have held the soldier who fired liable in negligence on the grounds that his marksmanship fell below the standard which was desirable or reasonable in anyone discharging a lethal weapon'. The House of Lords declared, without giving any reasons, that in their view that statement was wrong. It might be wrong for two possible reasons:
(i) it assumed a duty to take reasonable care towards actual or suspected terrorists upon which as we have seen there is doubt, and
(ii) the standard of care required of the soldier as suggested by the trial judge might be considered to be too high. A soldier might have only a split second in which to spot a target, aim and fire at it. The law would require too much if it were to ignore the realities in which he must act. Moreover, a relevant factor when considering whether a soldier (or a police officer) has acted reasonably must be the object that he desired to achieve. With the level of violence as high as it was in Northern Ireland in 1972, it might be argued that the risk to members of the community from terrorist attacks was considerable and this justified a lesser standard of care from the soldier than would be sufficient in less highly charged circumstances.

<u>Preventing Terrorists Claiming Damages</u>. The case of <u>Doherty v. Ministry of Defence</u> shows that it is possible for a person who is shot by a soldier to claim damages in circumstances where the latter is unable to rely on s. 3 of the Criminal Law Act. Apart from the difficulty of assessing damages to a terrorist (see <u>Burns v. Edmen</u> [1970] 2 Q.B. 541), there is a rule of public policy that a person may have his claim for compensation barred if it is grounded on a criminal or immoral act. This is sometimes known by the maxim, <u>ex turpi causa non oritur actio</u> (see, e.g. <u>Ashton v. Turner</u> [1980] 2 All E.R. 870; <u>Murphy v. Culhane</u> [1976] 3 W.L.R. 458). The limits of this defence are not yet settled, but it would clearly not apply as a defence if the person shot, although suspected, was in fact

innocent. Strictly, to apply it at all in the circumstances of Northern Ireland would mean that a soldier who used more force than was reasonable would never be liable in a claim for damages for the use of excessive force if the person shot was in fact a terrorist; as McGonigal L.J. emphasised in Farrell (supra), 'excessive force would be excusable'. Other defences that might be invoked would be that the victim knew the full extent of the risk he was running and willingly took the risk of being shot (see Lane v. Holloway [1967] 3 All E.R. 129).[16] In such a case no damages would be awarded. Damages, on the other hand, might be reduced if the court were to find that the plaintiff was partly responsible himself for being shot.[17]

Who Pays the Damages? Damages awarded to a person shot by a soldier will normally be paid by the Ministry of Defence, but whether the Ministry is in law liable at all for the civil wrongs of soldiers is not entirely clear if war-like operations are in progress.[18] It is unthinkable that the Ministry would refuse to pay damages awarded to a plaintiff by a court if the soldier, while believing himself to be acting within his duty, in fact crossed the Rubicon and was adjudged liable. The effect on the morale of soldiers would be serious if an individual soldier had to pay damages from his own pocket, but this could happen, in theory. Perhaps some form of insurance ought to be arranged by the Ministry to cover this eventuality, especially as there is no trade union in the armed forces to look after the interests of its members (see Ward, 1979).

International Law. By Article 2 of the European Convention on Human Rights a state guarantees to everyone within it the 'right to life' (from which there can be no derogation under Article 15).
However, the Article goes on to provide that a killing will be justified if the use of force is no more than is absolutely necessary:
(a) in defence of any person from unlawful violence,
(b) in order to effect a lawful arrest or to prevent the escape of a person lawfully detained,
(c) in action lawfully taken for the purpose of quelling a riot or insurrection.
The Convention does not apply as a part of English law (Malone v. Commissioner of Police in the Metropolis (No. 2) [1979] 2 All E.R. 620 although for Northern Ireland see The Protection of Human Rights by Law in Northern Ireland, Cmnd. 7009

(1977)) but the United Kingdom clearly has an international obligation to bring its law into line with the terms of the Convention.

An individual may bring a claim before the European Commission of Human Rights against the United Kingdom alleging that he is a victim of a breach by the State of the Convention's obligations.[19] Similarly, one state may bring a complaint to the Commission against another. In 1972 Ireland brought a complaint under Article 2 against the UK concerning the events of 'Bloody Sunday' on 30 January 1972, when 13 people were killed during a civil rights demonstration. It was claimed that the British authorities had failed to protect the lives of civilians. The Commission refused to consider this part of the complaint since claims for compensation had not been pursued in the Northern Irish courts before the application was made. There is no power, however, in the Court of Human Rights to compel a state to prosecute offenders under their national law (<u>Ireland v. The United Kingdom</u>, Eur. Court H.R., Series A. Judgment of Jan. 18th, 1978).

CONCLUSION

The law is in an unsatisfactory state since the soldier may be placed in an impossible situation, operating under conditions in which a mistake might lead to serious legal complications. The law on which he must act was hardly designed to make his task any easier. It may indeed be quixotic to suggest that more legal guidance might be given since views may well differ as to the degree of force that may be used. Nonetheless, it is essential in a democratic society that the soldier's actions are judged by the ordinary law. It is preferable that he take the risk of liability than that an innocent citizen should take the risk of being shot.

Whether a policeman should act as a soldier or a soldier as a policeman is a matter for those in control of such forces.[20] At the end of the day 'the Army is only the spear point. It is the shaft of the spear and the force behind it that drives the blow home.' (quoted in Townshend, 1978, p. 206).

NOTES

1. Following riots in a number of cities in Great Britain in the summer of 1981, police forces are now equipped with protective clothing, plastic

bullets, and C.S. gas. Anxiety about the use by police and the army of plastic bullets in Northern Ireland exists, The Times, 1 September 1981. 'The comment that the plastic bullet was developed because the rubber missile caused widespread injuries implies that it is less lethal. The fact is that the former has the same effect as a brick landing on a soldier's face if fired close to. The latter, in real terms, is comparatively ineffective but useful for routine "aggro"', G. Waggett, The Times, 7 September 1981 (letter).

2. Opinion of Law Officers (18 August, 1911) on duty of soldiers called upon to assist the police, Manual of Military Law Part II, Section V, p. 511; See Burdett v. Abbott [1812] 4 Taunt. 401. Employment of soldiers in Northern Ireland from 1969-73 demonstrated the need for greater powers of stop, search and arrest. The Northern Ireland (Emergency Provisions) Act 1973 gave soldiers greater powers than a civilian, but less than those of a police constable, in respect of these matters. See also, s. 193, Army Act 1955 (offence to obstruct a soldier in exercise of his duty).

3. Trial is by court-martial. A commanding officer may deal summarily with certain offences and may impose detention or a fine. See generally, Rowe, 'Military Justice in the British Army' 94 Military Law Review 99 (1981).

4. See also (1979) 5 Commonwealth Law Bull. 1194. The carrying of an unlicensed firearm by civilians even for the protection of others was held in R v. Porter [1973] N.I. 198 not to be unlawful. Would its use in these circumstances be prima facie a reasonable use of force in the prevention of crime?

5. For an account of the operation of martial law in Ireland in 1920 see Townshend, 1978.

6. McGonigal L.J., Reference under s. 48A of the Criminal Appeal (Northern Ireland) Act 1968 (No. 1) of 1975 (unreported) Judgment 18th Dec. 1975. See also Greenwood (1975) 'The Evil Choice' Criminal Law Review 4. Concern over the conduct of the SAS in the Iranian Embassy siege in 1980 was answered by the Attorney General in a letter to The Times, 17 February 1981. See also The Times, 23 December 1983 concerning the acquittal in October 1980 of two London police officers who had mistakenly shot a motorist.

7. Before 1967 it was necessary to distinguish clearly between a felony and a misdemeanour. Following the lapse of an hour after the reading of

a Proclamation in the Riot Act 1714, by a Justice of the Peace, misdemeanants became felons and greater force was justified by law against them. The Riot Act was repealed by the Criminal Law Act 1967, a course not approved of by Evelegh, 1978, p. 157.

8. The Committee on Featherstone Riots declared that force would be justified if it was 'necessary to protect persons or property'. Compare Smith and Hogan (1983) Criminal Law, 5th edn. at p. 328 who state, 'It can rarely, if ever, be reasonable to use deadly force merely for the protection of property'. It is therefore a moot point whether a soldier would be justified in shooting a person involved in looting property. See also R v. McKay [1957] V.R. 560. In Farrell v. Ministry of Defence (1978) (unreported) C.C.A. (N.I.), defence counsel conceded that shooting in order to prevent escape could not be justified by reference to an attempted robbery and this was accepted by Lord Diplock [1976] 2 All E.R. 937, 947. In any event s. 3(2) of the Criminal Law Act would appear to make earlier statements on the degree of force that may be used otiose though cf. Jaconelli (1980) Enacting a Bill of Rights, p. 234.

9. Reference under s. 48A Judgment 18th Dec. 1975. See also Hanna J. in Lynch v. Fitzgerald [1938] I.R. 382; Report of the Tribunal appointed to Inquire into the Events on Sunday 30th Jan. 1972, in Londonderry, The Widgery Report, H.C. 220 (1972) para. 93.

10. There is doubt whether the soldier's belief must be a reasonable one. See Lord Diplock in Reference under s. 48A [1976] 2 All E.R. 937, 947 and cf. Williams (1978) Textbook of Criminal Law, p. 442. Compare 2nd edn. (1983) at p. 137. The decision of the Divisional Court in Albert v. Lavin [1981] 1 All E.R. 628 would require the mistake to be a reasonable one if the defence is to succeed. Compare R v. Williams (1984) Crim. L.R. 163.

11. See also Reference under s. 48A [1976] 2 All E.R. 937 and Farrell v. Secretary of State for Defence [1980] 1 All E.R. 166.

12. Keighley v. Bell (1866) 4 F. & F. 763, 790, R v. Smith (1900) 17 Cape of Good Hope Supreme Court Reports which is reprinted in Keir and Lawson (1979) Cases in Constitutional Law, 6th edn., pp. 180-2. Both cases are discussed in Williams (1953) Criminal Law, pp. 389-94.

13. See also Williams (1978) Textbook of Criminal Law, p. 444 referring to the test of

reasonableness, 'as a rule for application by courts it is illusory'. He regretted that the Criminal Law Revision Committee in 1965 felt unable to give greater precision to the section. Compare 2nd edn. (1983) at p. 495.

14. McGonigal L.J. in the Court of Criminal Appeal in Northern Ireland gave approval to the Criminal Code Bill Commission 1879, Reference under s. 48A. Judgment 18th Dec. 1975, C.C.A. (N.I.). See also s. 25(4) of the Canadian Criminal Code, Can. Rev. Stat. c.C-34 (1970).

15. A majority in the Court of Criminal Appeal (N.I.) in Farrell in fact thought a duty in negligence was owed. See also Marshall v. Osmond [1983] 2 All E.R. 225.

16. Quaere whether in Farrell the deceased could be said to have appreciated the full extent of the risk that he ran. Was he sciens rather than volens to the risk of serious injury or death?

17. In Farrell, McGonigal L.J. thought that the use of excessive force was not something that the victim 'might reasonably have foreseen as the possible action that might be taken against him'. But see Beim v. Goyer (1966) 57 D.L.R. (2d) 253 (Canada) where the Court reduced the plaintiff's damages by 60 per cent.

18. See generally D. Hogg (1971) Liability of the Crown in Australia, New Zealand and United Kingdom (Melbourne, The Law Book Co.). A claim by or on behalf of a person killed or injured through criminal activity may be made under the Criminal Injury Compensation Scheme. For Northern Ireland generally, see D.S. Greer and V.A. Mitchell (1982) Compensation for Criminal Damage to Property (Univ. of Belfast).

19. In Farrell v. The U.K. (Application no. 9013/80) the European Commission held a complaint based on Article 2 by the widow of one of the men shot by soldiers to be admissible (Dec. 1982).

20. Community policing relies upon support of the population but it is also important that the Army retains popular support, Haldane, Evidence to Select Committee on Employment of Military in Cases of Disturbance H.C., paper 236 (1908) para. 143 'We want the Army to be a popular institution and not a menace to civil liberty'.

REFERENCES

Ashworth, A. (1980) 'Commentary on the Fourteenth Report of the Criminal Law Revision Committee:

Offences Against the Person, Intoxication and General Defences', *Criminal Law Review* 556

Boyle, K., Hadden, T. & Hillyard, P. (1980) *Ten Years On In Northern Ireland, The Legal Control of Political Violence*, London, Cobden Trust

Devlin, P. (1979) *The Judge*, Oxford University Press

Dicey, A.V. (1960) *Introduction to the Law of the Constitution*, 10th edn., London, Macmillan

Evelegh, R. (1978) *Peacekeeping in a Democratic Society*, London, Hurst

Green, L.C. (1976) *Superior Orders in National and International Law*, Leiden, Sijhoff

Grunis, A. (1978) 'Police Control of Demonstrations', 56 *Canadian Bar Review* 393, 417

Hughes-Morgan, D. (1977) 'Disobedience to a Lawful Military Command', 122 R.U.S.I.Jo. 9

Keijzer, N. (1978) *Military Obedience*, Leiden, Sijhoff

Kenny, C.S. (1966) *Outlines of Criminal Law*, 19th edn., Cambridge University Press

Murray, C. (1971) 'Civil Disturbance, Justifiable Homicide, and Military Law', 54 *Military Law Review* 129

Nichols, D.B. (1976) 'Untying the Soldier by Refurbishing the Common Law', *Criminal Law Review* 181

Radzinowicz, L. (1956) *History of English Criminal Law*, vol. 4, London, Sweet and Maxwell

Rowe, P.J. (1981) 'Military Justice in the British Army', 94 *Military Law Review* 99

Townshend, C. (1978) *The British Campaign in Ireland 1919-21*, Oxford University Press

Wade, E.C.S. & Phillips, G.G. (1977) *Constitutional and Administrative Law*, 9th edn., London, Longman

Wakerley, J.C. (1975) *Criminal Law Review* 186 (letter), and *The Times*, 8 June 1984

Ward, A. (1979) 'The British Army and Civil Trade Unions: A Marriage of the Incompatible?', 50 *Political Quarterly* 461

Chapter Ten

CONTEMPORARY CHALLENGES TO TRADITIONAL LIMITS ON THE ROLE OF THE MILITARY IN AMERICAN SOCIETY

Edward F. Sherman

Concern over military influence in civil affairs was reflected in the drafting of the American Constitution. Limitations intended to confine the military to its proper sphere can be found in the 'militia clauses',[1] the Third Amendment's prohibition on quartering of troops,[2] and the division of the war powers and authority over the land and naval forces between Congress and the President.[3] In addition to these explicit constitutional limitations, restrictions have been imposed on the military by administrative practice, court decisions, and statutes in order to preserve a proper 'civil-military relationship'.

Invocation of the ideal of the 'citizen-soldier', condemnation of a standing army, and concern that military power be narrowly restricted were once staples of American political thought. Benjamin F. Butler, a former Secretary of War, told the West Point Dialectic Society in 1839 that 'the genius of our political institutions and the settled convictions of our people, forbid the maintenance among us, of large standing armies ..., as productive of needless expenditure; injurious to the habits and morals of the people; and dangerous to public liberty'. 'The military profession', he went on, would never acquire 'the commanding influence which belongs to it in many other countries', but would be 'kept within narrow limits, and in constant subordination to the civil power' (Cunliffe, 1968: p. 129). Fifty years later John A. Logan (a Civil War general, US Senator, and Vice Presidential candidate) wrote in his book The Volunteer Soldier of America that civilian soldiers are the backbone of America and professional armies are undemocratic, un-American, and unnecessary.

Despite such continued expressions of orthodoxy, the military role has fluctuated considerably throughout American history. Periods of defence build-up and wars, in which military influence was extended to a wider range of functions, have often been followed by cutbacks in forces and, at times, by periods of reaction resulting in a shrinking of military influence. Since the end of World War II, however, when the United States failed to return to a peacetime force, the military has enjoyed mammoth budgets and unparalleled influence in Washington. The Vietnam War brought virulent attacks on the military and a modest cutback in budget and forces when the war ended, but the military has weathered those strains and stands today with its power little diminished since its zenith in World War II.

There is a growing tendency in American society today to accept the size, power, and resources of the military as a given and to look to it as a ready source for meeting non-military needs. The military has a manpower, equipment, and readiness capability which far exceed those of any other institution in society, whether it be state and city governments, other federal agencies, business and professional groups, or corporations and conglomerates. The military's efficiency, which derives in part from the 'separate society' standards of discipline it is allowed to maintain, also give it a special edge in dealing with certain societal problems.

Two developments over the past decade help to demonstrate a trend towards testing the outer boundaries of traditional limits on the role of the military in American society. They reflect both the importance of the military's large budget and plethora of resources and the effectiveness of its being allowed to deny its personnel individual and societal rights taken for granted in civilian society. These developments are: an erosion of the limitations imposed by the Posse Comitatus Act (and arguably by the Constitution) on the role of the military in enforcing laws in the civilian sphere; and the successful rejection of liberalizing movements in military personnel matters, especially in the areas of free speech and unionization.

EROSION OF LIMITATIONS ON THE ROLE OF THE MILITARY IN ENFORCING CIVILIAN LAWS

Because of the structure of the Constitution and the subsequent development of statutes and judicial precedents, the legality of using the military to enforce civilian laws must be analyzed in two different contexts. The first concerns the power of the President, as opposed to Congress, to intervene with military force in civilian matters. The Constitution (Art. I, sec. 8) gives Congress the broad power to raise, support, and make rules for governing and regulating the armed forces (clauses 12-14), to call up the militia to execute the laws (clause 15), and to make laws 'necessary and proper' for exercising its powers (clause 18). Although various Presidents, most recently Presidents Johnson and Nixon, have claimed inherent power to use the military to execute the laws, that doctrine has been severely challenged, particularly where the President's action is inconsistent with legislation specifically regulating that area or with express congressional limitations on Presidential action (see <u>Youngstown Sheet & Tube Co. v. Sawyer</u>, 343 U.S. 579 (1952)). Thus, except where the President acts to protect federal property or insure fulfillment of federal duties, his power is circumscribed by limitations contained in the statutes governing use of troops in emergency situations. A number of Presidential uses of troops have raised questions as to conformity to those limitations - ranging from the strike situations of the late nineteenth and early twentieth centuries to the dissent demonstrations and activities of the Vietnam War era - but Presidents have hastened to justify them as short-term emergencies in which paramount federal interests are at stake. This issue has been intensively discussed elsewhere, and since it more properly concerns the issue of separation of powers than of the civil-military relationship, it will not be further explored here. (For further discussion of the above see Note, 1973, Jacobs, Chapter 7, Engdahl, 1974, 1971, and citations therein.)

The second context for analyzing the propriety of military involvement in enforcing the laws concerns use of the military without direct Presidential authorization. Here the legal or constitutional issue is not separation of powers between Congress and the President, but the proper role of the armed forces in American society. Unlike the former issue, the basic legal guidelines for this context are not primarily constitutional. Its contours derive, at best, from emanations of a number of constitutional provisions already referred to, dealing with such specific matters as quartering of troops, calling-up of the militia, and war-making.

During the first ninety years of the republic, there was no clear constitutional or legal barrier to use of federal troops to enforce the laws, either state or federal. There was, of course, a notion that the primary function of the federal armed forces was to protect the nation from aggression from abroad, or, in very special cases, from rebellion and internal disorder. Indeed, hostility to a standing army reflected a widespread belief that troops had no place in the ordinary enforcement of the laws. But there was no absolute prohibition on troops being used to enforce the laws. Thus in 1792, Congress authorized the use of militia to serve as a <u>posse comitatus</u>, that is, persons whom a sheriff or marshal may call for assistance (Meeks, 1975, p. 90, n. 69).[4] It is to be noted, however, that it was the militia, and not the regular forces, who could be called; the militia were not considered to present the same kind of danger to the civilian sphere as the regular army since it was governed by state law, was made up of all able-bodied males of a certain age taken from the local community, and possessed such democratic aspects in some states as election of officers and the right to a civilian trial for offenses.

In 1854, the first widespread practice of using federal troops to enforce civilian laws occurred when the army began to assist in catching and returning slaves as required by the Fugitive Slave Act.[5] This was heavily criticized in the north, laying the groundwork for its later willingness to forbid the practice under the very different circumstances of Reconstruction. The Civil War witnessed broad use of troops to execute the laws, not only in occupied southern states but also in border states where civil disorder was prevalent. After the war, federal marshals and officers, as well as local sheriffs, frequently called on federal troops for assistance for such purposes as discovering and destroying stills violating the federal revenue laws,[6] suppressing labor disputes (7 Cong. Rec. 3581 (1878) (remarks of Mr Kimmel)), and enforcing Reconstruction policies, including protecting former slaves and Reconstruction governments and insuring against voter coercion and fraud (Davis, 1914; Sefton, 1967, p. 228) (7 Cong. Rec. 3850, 4185 and 4240 (remarks of Sens. Southard, Merrimon and Kernan)). The disputed 1876 presidential election resulted in charges by southerners of misuse of troops in enforcing election laws, leading to an understanding with President-elect Rutherford B.

Hayes that troops would be removed from the south and setting the stage for the passage of the Posse Comitatus Act of 1878 (see Meeks, 1975, pp. 88-100; Furman, 1965, p. 349; Woodward, 1966, p. 175).

Posse Comitatus Act of 1878
The Posse Comitatus Act was first proposed by Congressman William Kimmel of Maryland to forbid the use of any part of the land and naval forces as a posse comitatus or to execute the laws (7 Cong. Rec. 3586). Congressman J. Proctor Knott of Kentucky added provisions making its violation a crime, and the term 'army' was substituted for 'land and naval forces', apparently only because it was an amendment to the army appropriations bill and thus could not properly affect the navy in the form in which it was passed (Furman, 1960, p. 349). The bill's sponsors and many supporters were southerners who saw it as curbing the uses to which troops were put during Reconstruction. But the debates also indicate broader purposes, with speakers referring to other historical uses and abuses of troops (see above). Congressman Robertson of Louisiana, who spoke immediately before the act was voted on, cited intimidation of black voters by soldiers riding past polling places 'in the uniform of the United States troops and with their cartridge-boxes and arms' (7 Cong. Rec. 3852).

No one has ever been criminally prosecuted under the Posse Comitatus Act, and until the last several decades it has rarely been the subject of judicial comment. Nevertheless, the Act has had an effect. An Attorney-General opinion in the year of its passage stated that troops could not be used in aid of internal revenue collectors faced with armed resistance in Arkansas (16 Op. Att'y Gen. 162 (1878)). 1881 opinions forbade aid to federal marshals in arresting persons who had robbed a federal employee of government reclamation works on the Tennessee River (17 id. 71) and in apprehending the 'Cow Boys', a gang of bandits, in the Arizona Territory (id. 242). Thus the Act was strictly construed as prohibiting recourse to the benefits which superior military resources could bring to law enforcement, even in the difficult circumstances of the frontier.

In recent years, the courts have become involved in interpreting and applying the Act. It clearly prohibits military participation in enforcing any civilian law, whether local, state, or federal (Meeks, 1975, pp. 103-20). It does not, however, apply to non-law enforcement activities such as military aid in natural disasters or in protecting property and lives immediately after disasters and emergency situations where civilian services are unavailable (id., pp. 127-8). It applies to a broad range of military assistance, including not only active participation of troops in arresting, searching, or seizing, but also to investigation of criminal activities, surveillance for the purpose of discovering criminal activity, pursuit of alleged criminals, advising of civilian law enforcement officials as to specific law enforcement activities, and confining of arrested criminals (id., pp. 110-24).

A 1961 federal district court opinion, Wrynn v. United States (200 F. Supp. 457 (E.D.N.Y.)), reflected increasing pressure to allow law enforcement agencies to use certain devices of modern technology possessed by the military by virtue of its large budget for research and development, equipment, and personnel. A county sheriff and local police who were searching for two escapees from the county penal farm called a nearby Air Force base and asked for assistance. The base sent a helicopter which was directed by the police on the ground and later by two police officers who came aboard. As the helicopter was landing, it hit a small tree, injuring a bystander who sued the Air Force under the Federal Tort Claims Act. Ironically, a strict interpretation of the Posse Comitatus Act was used as the basis for getting the Air Force off the hook. The judge determined that use of the helicopter in the search violated the Act; thus its crew was not acting within the scope of employment, and the United States was not liable.

Civil disturbances involving the American Indian Movement at Wounded Knee, South Dakota, in 1973 presented a further situation for testing the Posse Comitatus Act when superior military technology and resources are provided to civil law enforcement officials. The Department of Defense sent an army colonel to observe and advise as to whether the President should order in federal troops. However, he went beyond the role of observer, becoming an active advisor to the federal marshals and officials, obtaining large quantities of military materiel and equipment 'on loan' (including armored personnel carriers, protective vests, rifles, flares, and ammunition), and directing the placement of equipment. Other military personnel came with the equipment, providing training for the civilian officials in its use and maintenance and conducting reconnaissance flights. Indians, who were charged with interfering with federal officers engaged in the lawful performance of their duties, alleged that the Posse Comitatus Act had been violated, warranting dismissal of the charges. In United States v. Banks (383 F. Supp. 368 (D.S.D. 1974)), the court dismissed the charges, finding that participation of members of the military in such acts as repairing armored personnel carriers violated the Act. In United States v. Jaramillo (380 F. Supp. 1375 (D. Neb. 1974), appeal dismissed, 510 F. 2d 808 (8th Cir. 1975)), the court acquitted the defendants on the ground that the prosecution could not prove beyond a reasonable doubt that the civilian authorities had acted 'lawfully' in light of the participation of military personnel. The court observed that 'it is the use of military personnel, not materiel, which is proscribed' (p. 1376). The same judge later dismissed indictments against nine other persons charged with the same offenses.

A different result was reached by another judge in a Wounded Knee prosecution, United States v. Red Feather (392 F. Supp. 916 (D.S.D. 1975)). He granted a government motion to forbid the defendants from introducing evidence of military involvement. He reasoned that the aid provided by the mechanics and pilots and the advice given by the colonel constituted only a 'passive role' in civil law enforcement and that only active involvement, as in participating in searches, seizures, or arrests, would violate the Act. Passive roles were said to include (pp. 924-5):

> the mere presence of military personnel under orders to report the necessity for military intervention ..., advice or recommendations given to civilian law enforcement officers by military personnel on tactics or logistics, presence of military personnel to train local law enforcement officials on the proper use of such materiel or equipment and to maintain such materiel or equipment; aerial photographic reconnaissance flights and other like activities.

However, there is serious doubt as to the correctness of the Red Feather interpretation. Major Meeks, in an article in the Military Law Review, commented that 'the decisions in Jaramillo and Banks more accurately reflect the legislative intent behind the Act' (Meeks, 1975, p. 122). A 'passive role' exception, as suggested in Red Feather, would allow military personnel to become partners in civil law enforcement operations, providing advice, surveillance, and maintenance of equipment, only stopping short of actual physical participation in any final arrest, seizure, or search. This would not serve the policy objectives embodied in the Act of preventing undue military influence over civilian law enforcement and of avoiding making a national constabulary out of the armed forces.

Cases applying the Posse Comitatus Act where there is only indirect military aid to civil law enforcement have developed an exception called the 'military purpose doctrine'. If the primary purpose of the military's acts is to meet legitimate military needs and missions, there is no violation of the Act even though the civil officials receive some incidental benefit. An example would be the investigation and arrest of a serviceman, who also committed a civilian crime, by military police officers investigating a violation of the Uniform Code of Military Justice (see id., pp. 124-6). Sharing of information obtained by military personnel in the course of military functions is probably the most important aspect of this doctrine. The military may provide civilian authorities with information obtained, for example, from investigating an on-post traffic accident or a violation of the UCMJ by a service member, or from conducting military flights or boat patrols. The military activity must, however, itself be proper, lawful, and authorized. An example of gross violation of this principle occurred in the late 1960s in connection with military surveillance of political activities, a violation whose cause has never really been corrected or eliminated by congress or the courts.

Each branch of the armed services has its own criminal investigation and military intelligence corps, but their activities are generally restricted to military personnel and such matters as security clearances and UCMJ violations. However, in 1967 the army began to investigate civilians who had no relationship to the army on the grounds that it needed intelligence information in case troops were used in civil disturbances, as they had been in the July ghetto riots in Detroit (see Jacobs, 1978). Military intelligence units around the country adapted to spying on civilians, some 1,200 field investigators under the army intelligence command at Fort Holabird, Maryland, taking primary responsibility. The persons to be watched were loosely defined as those 'who might be involved in civil disturbance situations'. Some commanders had a special interest in radical groups, some in peace and civil rights organizations, and some in politicians like Senators William Fulbright and Adlai Stevenson III. Agents infiltrated radical and civil rights groups, took pictures of people attending peace rallies, and even had a disguised TV news van at the 1968 Democratic convention. Data banks were set up at Fort Holabird, Fort Monroe, Virginia, and Fort Hood, Texas, to store the information. Other services also expanded their intelligence activities to include civilian surveillance, and at some places like the Colorado Springs area (which contains a number of air force installations and a large army post), military agents were so numerous that they often made up a good part of the audience at peace demonstrations and of membership in radical groups.

These activities were first made public in January 1970 in a <u>Washington Monthly</u> article by a former army intelligence officer, Christopher H. Pyle (see Pyle, 1974). The Army admitted some of the activities, but said they had been drastically curtailed and that the data banks would be destroyed. The American Civil Liberties Union, claiming that surveillance and other activities were continuing, filed federal suits in Chicago and Washington D.C. on behalf of individuals and organizations subjected to surveillance. In December 1970, a startled federal court in Chicago heard testimony from John M. O'Brien, a former army intelligence agent in the Chicago field office, that surveillance had continued in violation of higher directives and had included a number of senators, congressmen and governors.

These revelations led to hearings by the Senate Judiciary Subcommittee on Constitutional Rights, chaired by Senator Sam Ervin of North Carolina. Although the Secretary of Defense issued orders that surveillance, spying and maintenance of dossiers on civilians be stopped, and that existing dossiers be destroyed, doubts were expressed as to the efficacy of such orders. When the hearings were completed, Senator Ervin introduced a bill to impose strict limitations over military surveillance and intelligence gathering (see Baskir, 1974; see also, Schwarz, 1977; Church Committee Report, 1976). However, the bill languished in committee, and by 1975, when Senator Ervin had retired from the

Senate, there was little interest in the congress in imposing such legislative controls on the military. Thus protections today against a recurrence of such violations depend primarily upon the orders of the Secretary of Defense.

The law suits also failed to provide a judicial remedy against military intelligence abuses. The Supreme Court, in a majority opinion by Chief Justice Burger in Laird v. Tatum (408 U.S. 1 (1972)), held that the plaintiffs lacked standing, finding that they had not shown any direct injury and that mere knowledge of military investigative activity which might be broader than necessary fell short of a 'chilling' of their First Amendment rights. However, the opinion did contain a strong statement indicating aversion to 'any military intrusion into civilian affairs' (p. 15). The court seemed to be issuing a warning to the military (p. 16):

> Indeed, when presented with claims of judicially cognizable injury resulting from military intrusion into the civilian sector, federal courts are fully empowered to consider claims of those asserting such injury; there is nothing in our Nation's history, or in this Court's decided cases, including our holding today, that can properly be seen as giving any indication that actual or threatened injury by reason of unlawful activities of the military would go unnoticed or unremedied.

This dictum suggests a constitutional dimension to improper 'military intrusion into civilian affairs'. The army surveillance program did not violate the Posse Comitatus Act because there was no attempt to use the army to enforce civilian laws; rather it was a case of the military intruding into the civilian sphere for its own reasons and purposes. Tatum suggested that the court would find a cause of action and a remedy for such conduct if the right case was presented. It also represented for the first time an expression by the Supreme Court that, as other courts have stated (see United States v. Walden, 490 F. 2d 372 (4th Cir.), cert. denied, 416 U.S. 983 (1974)), the principle of military non-intervention into civilian affairs embodied in the Posse Comitatus Act is of constitutional dimensions. Exactly what those dimensions are, however, was not explored, and, as seen when Congress undertook to amend the Act in 1981, there is continuing dispute over what is constitutionally required.

1981 Amendments to the Posse Comitatus Act

In May 1981 the Senate Armed Services Committee reported out a bill authorizing some $50 million more than the previous year's budget for the Department of Defense (S. 814, 97th Cong., 1st Sess.). Senator Tower, committee chair, said it reflected 'the urgency our committee assigns to the requirement of modernizing, improving, and enhancing the readiness of our Nation's strategic and general-purpose forces' (Cong. Rec. S4885 (May 12, 1981)). Tucked away in one part of this money authorization bill was the first significant amendment of the Posse Comitatus Act in a hundred years. The bill expressly authorized the military to provide law enforcement officials (federal, state, and local) with <u>information</u> collected during the normal course of <u>military</u> operations, <u>equipment or facilities</u>, and <u>military personnel to train</u> civilians in the operation of the equipment. It was provided that the Secretary of Defense would issue regulations insuring that such assistance did not impair military preparedness nor permit the direct participation of military personnel in searches and seizures, arrests, or similar activities.

The primary impetus for this legislation was a desire to tap into military resources and manpower to aid in interdicting the importation and distribution of drugs. A subsidiary purpose was to aid federal customs and immigration officials in their duties. When the bill was reported out of the House Armed Services Committee, several significant alterations were made. It contained amendments proposed by Congressman Charles Bennett of Florida authorizing a much larger role for the military: the Secretary of Defense could assign military personnel to assist in drug seizures and arrests so long as civilian authorities were in ultimate control and the mission could not succeed without military assistance (H.R. 3519, 97th Cong., 1st Sess., sec. 908, subsec. 375. See remarks of Mr Bennett, Cong. Rec. H4056-4058 (8 July 1981)).

Arguably, the original Senate bill provisions were only codifications of what was already permitted under the Posse Comitatus Act. If <u>collection and disclosure of information</u> were limited to <u>military operations</u>, this would satisfy the 'military purpose doctrine' (see Meeks, 1975, pp. 124-6). Thus information about boat or plane sightings or other activity relating to drug, customs, or immigration violations picked up by routine military reconnaissance could be shared with civilian law enforcement. The military would not, however, be allowed to undertake special reconnaissance missions primarily to discover violations of civilian laws. Loan of military equipment, without military operators or maintenance, was upheld in several Wounded Knee cases, although one has to wonder whether the Posse Comitatus Act was intended to allow transfer of millions, perhaps billions, of dollars worth of military equipment when Congress could instead appropriate funds for the civilian federal agencies to obtain their own equipment. The Senate bill did state that the Department of Defense could condition its aid on reimbursement, but the sheer volume of the transferred equipment still raises questions as to undue dependence of civilian law enforcement upon military resources.[7] The loan of military personnel to train in the use of equipment was also upheld in the Wounded Knee cases, although other Posse Comitatus Act precedents suggest that training must be for general educational purposes and not in relation to specific law enforcement operations (see id., pp. 120-1). However, the additional House Armed Services Committee provisions for military participation in drug seizures and arrests clearly violated existing Posse Comitatus Act precedents and raised questions of unconstitutional involvement of the military in civilian affairs.

The bill was debated extensively on the floor of the House of Representatives on July 8, 14, and 15, 1981 (Cong. Rec. H4056-4067 (July 8, 1981), H4280-4309 (July 14, 1981), H4329-4337 (July 15 1981)). An amendment was proposed by Congressman White of Texas to forbid use of military equipment in the land area of the US, except for monitoring and communicating with air and sea traffic (id., H4061, H4288-4289, H4294). White expressed the concern that military personnel have no special training in law enforcement and that 'the mere presence of uniformed troops on an unguarded border, traditionally unguarded, will raise several international protests' (id., H4061). He also voiced the objection that it was a bad precedent to cut the budget of civilian agencies (the Drug Administration and Coast Guard budgets had previously been cut) and then rely on superior military resources to make up the difference. 'A budget-searching administration', he said, 'might use troops and cut back customs and border patrol' resulting in 'an erosion of surveillance and narcotics control' (id., H4062).

The White amendment passed. However, another inconsistent amendment, proposed by Congressman Shaw of Florida, also passed by a healthy 60 vote margin (id., H4304, H4330). Although it did not go so far as the Bennett provisions allowing military seizures and arrests anywhere on land or sea, the Shaw amendment permitted military seizures and arrests if outside the US land area. Its opponents expressed the concern that congressmen were afraid to go on record against a bill which supported the 'war on drugs' (id., H4333). Congressman Hertel of Michigan noted the irony 'that when this House has cut the Coast Guard budget, when one of the primary duties of the Coast Guard is to interdict this type of illegal traffic, here we are saying, "Now, the Army and the Navy should do the job that is charged to the Coast Guard"' (id.).

Congressman Conyers of Michigan saw more basic concerns in the entire proposal to amend the Posse Comitatus Act. Pointing to military intelligence abuses after the 1967 Detroit riots, he urged that constitutional principles were at stake and that the amendment portended expanded military intervention into civilian affairs (id., H4300, H4307. Congressman Seiberling of Ohio invoked the 1970 Kent State incident as an example of improper use of the military to enforce civil law: id., H4067, H4285). Congressman Dellums of California agreed, commenting that 'we have never allowed ourselves to see law enforcement agents in military uniforms - never' (id., H4308). Congressman Bennett, however, maintained that there was no constitutional issue and 'we have made a mystique' out of the Posse Comitatus Act which was no more than a specific prohibition on the kind of carpetbagger misuse of troops employed in Reconstruction (id., H4294-4296). He stated that Congress had to face up to 'the tremendous problem in our country' of drug importation and distribution which cannot be stopped by civilian agencies alone.

The version of the bill finally passed by the Senate forbade all military participation in searches, seizures and arrests, and the Conference Committee appointed to resolve the differences between the bills passed by the two chambers adopted this provision (id., H7992-7993 (3 November 1981)). It also adopted the White amendment, but modified to (1) allow operation of equipment by military personnel only in monitoring and communicating with air and sea traffic and (2) allow use of equipment outside the US land area only in an 'emergency' defined as arising when the size or scope of suspected criminal activity poses a serious threat to US interests and when law enforcement would be seriously impaired without military assistance (10 U.S.C.A. sec. 374 (West Supp. 1981)).

The Department of Defense, in its directive implementing the 1981 amendments (No. 5525.5, DOD Cooperation with Civilian Law Enforcement Officials (22 March 1982)), left open the door for avoiding the equipment limitations through use of the Navy. The directive reserves the right of the Secretary of Defense to approve use of Navy and Marine Corps personnel in interdicting civilian vessels (id., encl. (4), sec. C.2). The theory seems to be that the 1981 amendments state that they should not be construed to limit the authority of the executive branch in using military equipment and personnel for civilian law enforcement purposes 'beyond that provided by law prior to the enactment of this chapter' (10 U.S.C.A. sec. 378. See Hilton, 1983, p. 5 for discussion of the justification of this position). The Navy and Marine Corps have never been covered by the Posse Comitatus Act, although they have voluntarily adopted its provisions by regulation.[8] However, this position raises questions, both as to whether the Constitution applies restraints similar to the Posse Comitatus Act to the Navy and Marine Corps and whether the 1981 amendments, written with the use of ships in mind, were not actually intended to apply at least to the equipment limitations to the Navy.[9] Any future decision by the Department of Defense to use ships in violation of the 1981 equipment limitations seems likely to give rise to litigation.

The story of the 1981 amendments to the Posse Comitatus Act indicates how fragile is the legal protection accorded the principle of military non-involvement in civilian law enforcement in America. An emasculation of the Act through the Bennett provisions for direct military participation in seizures and arrests anywhere on land or sea was indeed rejected. But the Shaw amendment permitting seizures and arrests outside the US land area passed in the House and was only avoided by the Senate version prevailing in the Conference Committee. Critical to that result was the fact that the Department of Defense had originally opposed the amendments as likely to result in a raid on its resources and did not favor the more sweeping proposals.[10] One must wonder about Congress' willingness to uphold the non-involvement principle had the military wanted to undertake the activity. One bright note is that the length and tenor of the debates in the House indicated an awareness that it was dealing with an important national policy, perhaps of constitutional dimensions. The ultimate compromise resulting in a modest expansion of the military role indicates the attractiveness of military resources and manpower in a tight budget era and may portend further attempts to use those resources in civil law enforcement in the future.

REJECTION OF LIBERALIZING MOVEMENTS IN MILITARY PERSONNEL MATTERS, ESPECIALLY FREE SPEECH AND UNIONIZATION

The military's competitive edge in such civilian matters as law enforcement, interdiction of drugs, intelligence gathering, disaster relief, flood and environmental control, and community projects, comes in part from its disciplinarian atmosphere. Presumably because the military can demand more from its personnel and give them less in terms of individual freedoms, it can operate more efficiently. This thesis, of course, is subject to debate. As shown in the Vietnam War period, discontent fuelled by overly disciplinarian policies can undermine morale and efficiency. Since the beginning of the Vietnam War, the military has made progress in responding to individual discontents, but the post-Vietnam War period has witnessed substantial retrenchment on liberalizing policies. The military's recent experience in according, and then cutting back on, individual liberties and in heavy-handed squelching the movement for unionization indicates that the old ways still persist.

Military Freedoms

Training has been one of the most traditional and unchanging aspects of military life. The methods used today are not markedly different from those of World War II. Recruits are subjected to physical hardship, stressful situations and enforced obedience. Military administrators freely admit that the process is intended to disrupt civilian patterns of response, replace individual gratifications with group goals, inculcate unquestioning acceptance of authority, and develop conformity to proper military attitudes and conduct.

After World War II there were so many complaints about military training and discipline that a board, headed by General James Doolittle, was appointed to look into the matter. After holding hearings and considering thousands of letters, the board called for a complete overhaul of the military personnel system. 'There is a need for a new philosophy in the military order', it said, 'a policy of treatment of men, especially in the "ranks", in terms of advanced concepts of social thinking. The present system does not permit full recognition of the dignities of man' (Doolittle Report, 1946, p. 25). The Doolittle Report quickly drew fire from career personnel, and its proposals were almost entirely rejected.

In the summer of 1969, the military broke for the first time with its traditional disciplinary policies. Oddly enough, the Marine Corps was the initiator. After a summer of serious racial unrest at bases around the world, the Marine Corps commandant issued a directive (<u>N.Y. Times</u>, 4 September 1969, p. 39) which granted blacks such concessions as wearing Afro haircuts (if not more than 3 inches on top and neatly trimmed), having 'soul' music in service clubs, and giving the Black Power clenched fist salute to one another. The other services quickly made similar concessions.

The new haircut rule was startling, for a shaved head or close cut was the very symbol for many career military of good order and obedience. Once the concession had been made to blacks, it was difficult to withhold it from whites. Thus, in May 1970, the Army issued new regulations permitting moustaches (beards and goatees are still forbidden) and sideburns down to the top of the ear lobe, and stating that excessively short haircuts are 'degrading or de-personalizing' (Dept. of Army Message 072249Z, May 1971).

Once the haircut tradition was broken, other demands of discipline that had little more than tradition to justify them were brought into question. The man who led the attack was Admiral Elmo R. Zumwalt Jr. Appointed Chief of Naval Operations in 1970, Zumwalt began issuing directives, quickly labelled 'Z-grams', which set the old 'Mickey Mouse' demands of discipline on their ears. Z-grams approved beer-vending machines in enlisted men's barracks and alcohol in individual rooms, eased provisions for overnight passes, permitted motorcycles on Naval bases, established 'hard rock' enlisted men's clubs, and ordered that sailors should not have to wait in line more than fifteen minutes for anything.[11]

The Army, not to be caught lagging, issued its own iconoclastic regulations. Practices synonymous with good order and discipline - early reveille,

prohibition of beer in barracks, bed check, tight
'pass' restrictions - were suddenly gone from Army
life. Meanwhile, experimental basic training programs were undertaken at Fort Ord, California, and
other posts, the notion being that recruits should
be treated with dignity, addressed as 'soldier'
rather than 'dud' or 'eight-ball', and be safe from
hazing, harassment or mass punishment. Increasingly, personnel were housed in rooms rather than
communal barracks.[12]

By the mid-1970s these reforms had fallen into
disfavor with commanders. Increased drug problems
were seen as a principal manifestation of the
liberalization. A roll-back of privileges and
civilianizing policies has occurred, accomplished
primarily by individual commanders. Although some
of the trappings remain - such as the individual
rooms available in some enlisted quarters - many of
the traditional military disciplinary policies have
been reinstated. Today mandatory urinalysis testing
for drugs and sweeping drug and contraband inspections are a part of every service member's daily
life.[13]

The Military Unionization Movement
The military's handling of the unionization movement
is a trenchant example of the rejection of civilianization. The spectre of unionization was first
raised in 1967 when ex-Private Andy Stapp, who had
been court-martialled and finally discharged for his
anti-war activities (see also Stapp v. Resor, 314 F.
Supp. 47 (S.D.N.Y. 1970)), organized the American
Servicemen's Union. The ASU claimed recognition as
bargaining agent for all GIs, making demands ranging
from the right of free political association to
election of officers, 'an end to saluting and sirring of officers', and 'the right to disobey illegal
and immoral orders' (Stapp, 1970, pp. 88-91). With
its marxist tone, it never had broad appeal, but
some commanders were concerned enough to threaten
court-martial for unlawful conspiracy if their men
joined it or associated with its members (id., pp.
100, 134-6). In 1969, an Army directive conceded
that 'in view of the constitutional right to freedom
of association, it is unlikely that mere membership
in a servicemen's union can constitutionally be prohibited', but warned that commanders were not authorized to recognize a servicemen's union (Department
of the Army, Guidance on Dissent, para. 5.c).

A month later, Secretary of the Army Resor
testified before a congressional committee that 'We

are not going to allow unions in the Army',[14] and a variety of official actions, running from reassignment and discharge of union activists to programs designed to eliminate the desire for unionization, were undertaken (id., pp. 133-43). A First Army directive advised: 'The key is to remove the motivation to join a collective bargaining unit by convincing the soldier that those in positions of authority have a direct interest in his welfare and morale. Commanders should make themselves available to soldiers to hear their complaints and should take immediate and positive actions within the limits of their authority to remedy reasonable complaints'. Recommended were councils 'to ferret out problems' and 'publicize the commander's interest in the morale, welfare and spirit of his command', review of local regulations to insure 'they contain nothing repugnant to a man's dignity' and emphasis upon positive leadership.[15]

The threat of unionization became more real in 1976 when the 325,000-member American Federation of Government Employees (AFGE) union voted to amend its constitution to permit recruitment of members of the armed forces (Washington Post, 25 September 1976). A union report stated that since there was no authority to conduct collective bargaining, it would restrict its activities to other means of representation such as legal assistance, lobbying, and monitoring of defense policies bearing on military members' welfare.[16] It saw a variety of collective bargaining models as possible if the law were changed, including separate unions for officers, enlisted personnel, and civilian employees, and voluntarily agreed to accept the obligation not to strike.

In response to the AFGE proposal, Senators Thurmond (Republican, South Carolina) and Stennis (Democrat, Mississippi) introduced bills to make it a federal crime for a union to enroll, solicit, or encourage service personnel to join; for service personnel to encourage others to join, to join themselves, or to support any activity intended to focus on changes in pay or working conditions; and for any Department of Defense official to negotiate or collectively bargain with a labor organization.[17] Although the AFGE voted in a referendum not to pursue military organizing,[18] the Thurmond bill, with slight modifications, was passed by Congress in late 1978 (S. 274, 95th Cong., 1st Sess., as amended, P.L. 95-610 (8 November 1978)). Meanwhile, the Department of Defense and services had issued regulations making a variety of membership and organizational activities offenses punishable by court-martial.[19]

These statutory and regulatory prohibitions in a democratic society raise issues both of sound public policy and constitutionality. These issues are highlighted by the fact that most of the United States' Western European allies today permit membership in military unions and union activity, and in some cases allow a form of collective bargaining. The Netherlands is the best example of official tolerance of military unions (Jörg, 1983). The VVDM was founded in 1966 and in 1976 represented about 60% of the non-career enlisted men in the Dutch armed forces, charging them a dollar-a-month dues. Although the army is under no legal duty to bargain collectively, it has negotiated with the VVDM as to such matters as pay and related working conditions. A Dutch-based sociologist has described the VVDM as a 'sizeable, well-led, and remarkably well-organized conscript union, with a "professional" administrative apparatus and a more or less accepted position in the national military establishment' (Teitler, 1976, p. 518). Originally a product of reformist impulses in the 1960s, the VVDM has become more establishment-minded as time has passed, now demonstrating, according to Teitler (id., p. 528), considerable 'concern for more cordial relationships with the middle cadres' of NCOs and officers. A more radical rival organization (BVD), which had once partially infiltrated the VVDM, takes a heavily class-based ideological approach but has little force or importance today. The VVDM reflects concern over more than 'bread and butter issues', and its philosophy continues to be that the Dutch military (made up of personnel drafted for 14-month tours under a universal military training plan) should reflect 'democratic' principles and not become isolated from the rest of society. There is no right to strike, but the VVDM has conducted off-post demonstrations and concerted actions in the barracks such as refusing to eat in the soldiers' mess and submission of petitions to commanders.

Sweden, athough it has the longest history of military unions in Europe (the warrant officer's union was founded in 1907, the NCOs' in 1925, and the officers' in 1921), only permits unions for these three groups and not for enlisted men. This restriction may arise from the fact that under the Swedish universal conscription system, most enlisted men only serve about six months on active duty.

However, conscripts do meet each year to make a concerted group effort to influence conditions in the service and look into complaints as to such matters as duty assignments, promotions, and efficiency reports. In 1965, the three professional unions were granted the same bargaining rights as possessed by civil servants in Sweden. The military must bargain with them as to 'negotiable questions', which chiefly involve economic issues as to pay, hours, and working conditions, but not as to discretionary matters such as task assignments. In assessing the success of their bargaining, a Swedish sociologist notes that pay levels, previously rather low, have been raised and inequality between ranks reduced; the right to use leisure time as the individual wishes has been established; housing and equipment have been improved; and integration of the three grades has been achieved, including mess halls and other activities. Military unions, like other unions, have a right to strike, although it has never been used. However, a special tribunal made up of representatives of the parties, called the Civil Servants Board, may decide that any action, including a strike, is dangerous to society and, pursuant to complex limitations, may prohibit it (see Brickman, 1976, pp. 536-7).

West Germany permits government negotiation with representatives of military personnel, although the most successful organization is an establishment-oriented association which some might call a 'company union'. Shortly after the re-establishment of the Bundeswehr, the Federal Armed Forces Association (Deutsche Bundeswehr-Verband) was formed to represent the vocational, social, and economic interests of military personnel. It now has a membership of almost 200,000, 40,000 of which are officers (out of an armed force of 495,000). About a hundred members are detached from their units to conduct Association business, negotiating with the government on such matters as pay, working conditions, and grievances, but lacking the right to strike. In the mid-1960s the organized union movement decided to organize within the military, and the Public Services, Transport and Traffic Union (OTV) began to sign up service personnel. It initially met with resistance from the military, but in 1966 was given the right to recruit members in barracks, a move which resulted in the retirement of three high-ranking generals in protest. It now has about 4,000 military members, including several generals. (See Fleckenstein, 1976, p. 506; see also

'Drive to Organize G.I.s Picks up Steam', U.S. News & World Rpt., 28 March 1977).

In Austria, a 1967 statute permits unionization of career personnel, with the same unions serving both military and civilian employees. There is no right to collectively bargain or strike, but the military is required to consult with the union as to a variety of matters. In Denmark, a number of unions have signed up service personnel and negotiate with the Danish military. Almost all officers belong to one union, and draftees elect 'conscripted privates' representatives' who sit on a board for negotiations with the Ministry of Defense (see Kosinski, 1972, p. 56; Sullivan, 1969). In Belgium, associations represent officers and enlisted personnel in dealing with the government as to pay and working conditions, and since 1975, military personnel may also join trade unions (Werner, 1976, pp. 483-6). France forbids service personnel from joining unions, although providing for 'commission consultatives' in each unit by which representatives from all ranks consult with the commander on such matters as assignments, promotions, and discipline (Mandeville, 1976, p. 549).

Given these practices, it is appropriate to ask why such severe prohibitions on union membership and activity are necessary in the United States and, by implication, the United Kingdom. Following a discussion of the principal concerns expressed about military unions - their economic impact on the defense budget and their effect on military discipline and order - we will turn to a consideration of the constitutional issues involved in the American prohibitions.

The Economic Concern. The economic concern is related to doubts about the financial viability of the American volunteer armed forces. Close to a third of the Defense Department's budget now goes for pay and pensions (House Doc. No. 98-3, 98th Cong., 1st Sess., p. 9-5), and unionization raises fears of pressure for higher pay (see McCubbin, Dahl and Hunter, 1976). And yet, few would urge a return to the sub-standard pay scales prevailing in the lower enlisted ranks prior to the replacement of the draft by the volunteer military in 1973, which contributed to low morale, a high incidence of barracks theft and larceny of government property, and the shameful necessity for many military families to go on the welfare roles (id.). The pay rise brought by the volunteer military, which amounted to a 193%

increase in the lowest enlisted grade between 1964 and 1973 ('The New-Look Army', Newsweek, 28 March 1977, p. 23), was an essential step towards both efficiency and social justice.

One culprit in the swollen military personnel costs today is the high retirement benefits enjoyed by career officers and NCOs. The military pension program - permitting retirement at half pay after 20 years or at three-quarters pay after 30 years - is one of the most generous in the world (Goldich, 1983). When military pay was notoriously low and life expectancy shorter, early retirement was justifiable as an inducement and reward, but the possibility of half-pay retirement at the age of 38 is today an inordinate drain on the public treasury. But if Congress revises the military pension system, it will have to do so over the lobbying efforts of the powerful associations of active duty, reserve, and retired officers and NCOs.[20] In fact, the effectiveness of these organizations in representing the interests of career personnel is itself a motive for unionization among the enlisted ranks.

It is difficult to predict the impact of unionization on military pay, but it seems unlikely that, in the present economic climate, unions would be able to deliver much of a pay increase. Given the fact that most enlisted men are in their teens or early 20s, and that, even under the revised GI education bill, the military provides two dollars for every one the individual contributes for educational benefits (up to $5,400) (38 U.S.C. sec. 1622), present military pay scales do not seem unfair. Like other public employee unions, a military union would undoubtedly find that Congress' control over appropriation of funds imposes severe constraints upon its ability to extract higher wages through collective bargaining.

Fear of Work Stoppages or Strikes. Even if service unions were forbidden by law to strike and to engage in collective bargaining over wages and working conditions (as are public employee unions in a number of states), there is still a fear that the very existence of the organization would encourage work stoppages or strikes. Columnist Victor Riesel's syndicated comments are typical of these concerns:

> How can militants on some bases be controlled? What would the union do if a local military union executive committee, which called a strike in peacetime, were sentenced to the

stockade or brig? Officials of teachers', transport and other civilian unions have been jailed for defying a court order. What would happen on a military base if a court-martial sentenced AFGE leaders for a year? Would there be retaliatory job action? Would one of America's vital bases be crippled by slowdowns or 'work by the rules'? ... The mere signing of union cards spurts militancy into young rank and filers. (<u>Louisville Courier Journal</u>, 15 March, 1977)

No one can be sure that a military union would not try to strike even if it were legally forbidden, or that its members would not attempt illegal activities. Despite the attempts of the AFGE to allay fears by limiting its objectives, it is legitimate to wonder whether any union can be trusted to abide by limitations on its activities, whether self-imposed or statutory. Despite no-strike clauses and laws, public employee unions have sometimes struck. Can the nation risk the possibility of a strike or slowdown which reduces military efficiency? That is not an easy question for union supporters because no categorical assurance can be given. However, such possibilities exist even without union membership, as witness the work stoppages by sailors aboard the <u>U.S.S. Midway</u> in 1974 and the <u>S.S. Sterrett</u> in 1975 (Cortright, 'Organizing the Military: the Unions Want to Join You', <u>Nation</u>, 21 February 1976, p. 208). Unions at least offer formal mechanisms for processing grievances and defusing the anger and frustrations that seem endemic in the American armed forces today. A collective bargaining representative, with a professional staff to provide assistance as to grievances and work-related problems, could offer a reasonable means of curbing alienation stemming from real or imagined injustices and from lack of confidence in a system in which enlisted personnel have little participation in personnel policies.

The history of government employees' unions does not bear out predictions of a high degree of militancy or corruption. There have been unlawful strikes, but unions have had difficulty in holding public support when they engaged in them (see Usery, 1976, pp. 6-9; Comment, 1976, pp. 937-45). There is an additional constraint on unlawful resort to strike by a military union. Military personnel are subject to the Uniform Code of Military Justice (UCMJ) and their failure to come to work or do their jobs properly can result in court-martial for AWOL, mutiny or disobedience. Thus there is legal authority to jail and prosecute both union leaders and members who conduct an illegal strike (61 Stat. 140 (1947), 29 U.S.C. sec. 158(b)(4)). The risk that union power would be used to defy the law cannot be discounted, but, as in Sweden where strikes have never occurred despite their legality, it seems remote.

Displacement of Command Mechanisms for Grievance Resolution. What unionization does offer is more effective representation of enlisted personnel within the military establishment as to such matters as work conditions and grievances. In comparison to western European enlisted personnel, the American soldier has little role in determining personnel and work condition policies and no effective means of processing grievances. The kinds of unit councils, military ombudsmen's offices, and shop steward structures which provide counterbalances to command authority in European armed forces are unknown in the US (see Krendel, 1977). Frustration, hostility, and alienation often result from the service person's powerlessness in the face of an unyielding, or perhaps merely neglectful, bureaucracy which seems to have no pressure points. The extent of the problem was brought home by the findings of President Ford's clemency program for deserters in 1974-75 which found that a considerable percentage of desertions was due to the indifference of officers and non-commissioned officers to individual problems and needs.[21]

The inspector general system is the traditional method of dealing with grievances in the Army, and there are similar structures in the other services (see AR 20-1 (August 1968); SECNAV 5430.57). An inspector general is an officer appointed by the commanding officer to investigate complaints and grievances. Inspector generals have been notably ineffective in disposing of grievances for a variety of reasons, including the fact that they are often older career officers closely identified with the command, lack independent authority, possess inadequate investigatory powers, and are often assigned the position only as an additional duty. As Major James A. Badami has written in a thesis for the US Army Judge Advocate General School, 'regardless of how objective the I.G. may attempt to be, he is perceived by some soldiers to be nothing more than a tool of the commander' (Badami, 1973, p. 72).

Chaplains also provide a possible avenue for assistance, but they too lack the authority and often the willingness to provide an effective channel for redress of grievances, particularly those challenging the actions of the commander or his subordinates.

The principal institutionalized source for the airing of grievances is an 'Article 138 complaint'. Article 138 of the UCMJ provides that a written complaint against a superior will be forwarded to higher authority for investigation and evaluation. In reality, Article 138 complaints have rarely succeeded, which many enlisted men believe is a reflection of the unwillingness of superiors to rule against their subordinate officers or NCOs. Both because of the well-known low rate of success and the risk of being marked for informal harassment, Article 138 is little used for redress of grievances (id., p. 73).

The American military has experimented with servicemen's councils but has been unwilling to give them any authority. The Army, for example, encouraged commanders in the post-World War II period to establish 'GI Councils', later called Enlisted Men's Councils and Jr. Officer's Councils, which would work within the chain of command to bring to the commander's attention problems affecting health, morale, or discipline. But they were appointed, and resorted to, solely at commanders' discretion and were advisory only. By 1970, active councils only existed in a few units (see Army Times, 17 January 1973, p. 43).

Racial tension in the military led to the establishment in the Army and Air Force in 1973 of 'Race Relations Councils' and 'Equal Opportunity Staff Officers' (AR 600-31 (26 July 1973)). These were also generally appointed by commanders and lacked independent authority, but they developed, at least in some units, into the first structures to offer meaningful official response to grievances (Brown, 1977). In the Army's European command, which had some of the most serious racial troubles, regulations required that the councils meet at least monthly at the battalion level, and at least quarterly at the brigade level, that their minutes be posted throughout the command and be forwarded to the next highest commander, and that commanders formally respond to council suggestions within five days (USAREUR Supp. 1 to AR 600-21 (14 March 1975), para. 21.d). Although their purview was limited to racial discrimination, some councils swept in other grievances and, after the influx of women into the military, expanded their coverage to sex discrimination as well. But today, with the air of crisis gone, their effectiveness depends largely upon the interest and tolerance of the commander,[22] and the Navy and Marine Corps have not reflected the same interest in encouraging enlisted involvement in dealing with discrimination.

    The controversial question is whether allowing unions to play some role in grievance resolution would undercut commanders' disciplinary power to insure order and discipline. The traditional military position is uncompromising; General Dwight Eisenhower expressed it in 1948 in opposing restrictions on commanders' control of court-martial functions, stating that 'division of command responsibility' is unthinkable, and responsibility 'cannot be as separate as it is in our own democratic government'.[23] In fact, the military did adjust to the dilution of commander control over various court-martial functions (which occurred with the 1950 UCMJ), and the changes have arguably resulted in better justice and higher morale (see Sherman, 1970; Morgan, 1965). But permitting a degree of independence from commanders in formal court-martials may be a very different matter from enabling an enlisted man to obtain assistance from a union and to require the command to participate in a complex grievance proceeding. Kenneth Blaylock, President of the AFGE, discounted this fear. Asked how the military could maintain discipline if officers have to deal with shop stewards, he responded:

> They're not going to have to deal with shop stewards in the foxhole. You can look at the other public employees in this country - fire fighters, policemen. When there's a fire going on and the captain tells them, 'Get in this building and go to floor so and so', they don't challenge that. Those things are excluded from the scope of bargaining. But when they get back to the station and the captain says, 'By the way, Joe, we're changing your shift and you're going to start working third shift', he says, 'No, the contract says I get two days' notice except under these conditions'.[24]

    There would be an inevitable displacement of some authority held by commanders if unions assumed a role in processing grievances. But would this mean a diminution of morale, discipline, and loyalty to the command? It is important here, as in other areas in which service personnel seek to achieve closer parity with civilians, to recognize the change which has taken place in the military since World War II. The movement towards less authoritarian methods of control and towards greater use of consultation and persuasion in the military has brought it closer to contemporary managerial models (see Janowitz, 1960, 1967; Moskos, 1970, 1977; Lovell and Kronenberg, 1974; Blair and Phillips, 1983). Although obedience and discipline are still requisites, they are no longer thought of as absolutes deriving from the unquestioned authority of an officer to demand unthinking compliance.[25] This is not to say that obedience is not critical in the armed forces, but that the process by which an officer commands response is much more complex than the traditional popular notion of absolute obedience.[26]

Central to fears of unionization is the feeling it will result in divided authority and loyalty which is incompatible with the need for quick reaction. The role of loyalty in achieving military efficiency is a complicated matter. No doubt respect for and trust in a superior makes it easier to carry out his orders, but we now have serious doubts that absolute loyalty to abstract causes or uncritical devotion to superiors has much to do with good military performance. General Marshall's view (1947) that closeness between peers as 'groups of friends' is the most significant factor in battlefield motivation is now widely accepted. By producing a greater sense of solidarity with fellow workers, unionization could strengthen, rather than weaken, the peer-group bond. Of course, harm could be done if union affiliation resulted in serious alienation from superiors. But it is not at all clear that identification with a union for support as to perquisites of employment need undercut the sense of duty and responsibility which the military seeks to inculcate in its personnel. For example, it no longer seems strange to see policemen and firemen who support a union position contrary to that of their employer nevertheless putting their lives on the line during duty hours.[27]

John Keegan, whose 1976 study, The Face of Battle, is a valuable contribution to our understanding of military motivation, noted (p. 318) that '[t]oday, in the late twentieth century, there exists also a considerable congruence between the technology of civilian and military life'. Modern industry, he found, teaches people 'habits of order, obedience and uniform behavior which the embryo armies of the sixteenth century could not expect to find in any of their doltish recruits' (id., p. 319). Despite this congruence of civilian and military technology, Keegan saw a 'divergence between the facts of everyday and of battlefield existence' due to such factors as the impersonalization of battle, the deliberate infliction of cruelty, and the necessary role of coercion (id., p. 320). These irrational qualities of battle provide justification for the authoritarian structure and rigid discipline imposed on armed forces. And yet no one is quite sure that such irrationality can only be adequately dealt with by severely limiting independence of choice. Norman F. Dixon, in his 1976 book, On the Psychology of Military Incompetence, presented the thesis that as to 'the very characteristics which are demanded by war - the ability to tolerate uncertainty, spontaneity of thought and action, having a mind open to the receipt of novel, and perhaps threatening information - are the antithesis of those possessed by people attracted to the controls and orderliness of militarism' (Dixon, 1976, p. 194). Contemporary motivation research suggests that many of those same characteristics of flexibility and open-mindedness are also desirable in lower-ranking personnel, at least in some proper balance with orderliness and obedience, and that a top-heavy system of authority with demands for single-minded loyalty can stymie individual initiative.

Keegan reached the conclusion that the young today 'are increasingly unwilling to serve as conscripts in armies they see as ornamental' and that battle as we once knew it 'has already abolished itself' (Keegan, 1976, p. 336). Unionization would seem to be a product, rather than a cause, of this development. It obviously cannot remove from the military experience the requirement that men must 'show each other the iron face of war' (id.), but insofar as it could bring grievances over working conditions a regularity of process and a promise of fairness based on principles of industrial democracy generally accepted in our culture, it may be an acceptable model for a democratic armed force.

Constitutionality of Prohibitions on Union Membership and Activity. The 1978 statute outlawing military unions and prohibiting a variety of union activities has not been subjected to constitutional challenge in the courts. Several cases in which individual service members sought unsuccessfully to come within the narrow guidelines for permissible activity have not resulted in suits. Although the interest of organized labor in military unionizing is currently dead, and there seems little ferment within the military for pursuing the now-dangerous course of undertaking union activity, it must still be appreciated that serious constitutional issues are raised by the prohibitions. The day may yet come when a congressional re-evaluation of the wisdom of those policies will take place or when service members or organizations will challenge them in court.

It is clearly constitutional to forbid the military from negotiating or collective-bargaining with any group or in prohibiting such obviously disruptive and illegal activity as strikes, slow-downs, or work stoppages.[28] But membership and recruiting activities are not so obviously inimical to the military mission, and their prohibition runs into direct conflict with the First Amendment right of association and free speech.

Prohibition on Membership
The statute makes it unlawful to be a member ('knowing of the activities or objectives' of the organization) in any 'military labor organization' (10 U.S.C. sec. 976(b)(1)(a)).[29] Since it is constitutionally permissible to prohibit recognition of a service union for collective bargaining or grievance representation, an appropriate means of enforcing that prohibition is to make it a crime knowingly to join and be active in an organization that attempts to coerce others to recognize a union in violation of the law (accomplished by id., sec. 976(a)(2) and (b)). But the statute's ban goes farther. It not only forbids membership in an organization which attempts to induce officials to bargain with or to recognize it, but also in one which engages in any 'concerted action' to induce 'any change' with respect to terms or conditions of employment (id., at sec. 976(a)(2)(c)). This is broad enough to include not only traditional labor unions whose objective is bargaining and representation, but any group which attempts to assist service members in approaching officials concerning complaints or undertaking a 'concerted action' (conceivably a petitioning campaign, a newspaper advertisement, or any form of publicity)[30] directed at getting the government to make 'any change' with respect to terms or conditions of service. This

would seem to include, for example, an informal association formed by a group of military doctors to try to improve military medical conditions or a civil liberties or legal assistance organization which attempted to have discussions with officials or to take some form of 'concerted action' relating to its proposals.

The freedom of speech guaranteed by the First Amendment clearly includes the right of employees to associate to further their economic and social goals. The Supreme Court stated in NAACP v. Alabama ex rel. Patterson (357 U.S. 449, 460-61 (1958)):

> It is beyond debate that freedom to engage in association for the advancement of beliefs and ideas is an inseparable aspect of the 'liberty' assured by the Due Process Clause of the Fourteenth Amendment, which embraces freedom of speech. Of course, it is immaterial whether the beliefs sought to be advanced by association pertain to political, economic, religious or cultural matters, and state action which may have the effect of curtailing the freedom to associate is subject to the closest scrutiny.

Freedom of association has also been applied to recognize in public employees a right to join and participate in the activities of a labor union, as well as in other organizations devoted to providing information, lobbying, legal assistance, or pressuring on their behalf.[31]

The constitutional precedents governing the right of association closest to the military situation are those involving police and firemen. In 1976, the Supreme Court affirmed without opinion a federal district court decision holding unconstitutional both a Police Board Rule prohibiting police officers from organizing or joining a union and a state statute which exempted from the right of public employees to join a union, 'police, deputy sheriffs, state highway patrolmen, Missouri National Guard', and university and public school teachers (Vorbeck v. McNeal, 407 F. Supp. 733 (E.D.Mo. 1976), aff'd 96 S.Ct. 3160 (1976)). The lower court had found 'no compelling reason for denying certain persons membership in organizations solely because of their status as policemen where there is no showing that the organizations are detrimental to the sui generis and paramilitary nature of police departments' (id., p. 738).

The constitutional justification for banning membership in a 'military labor organization' rests on the 'separate society' rationale of the Levy line of cases. The Supreme Court stated in its 1974 decision Parker v. Levy that 'the military is, by necessity, a specialized society separate from civilian society', going on to uphold lesser standards of specificity in the military criminal code (417 U.S. 733 (1974)). The 'separate society' rationale has since been invoked to uphold a regulation banning speeches and demonstrations of a 'partisan political nature' on post (Greer v. Spock, 424 U.S. 828 (1976)) and forbidding distribution on post of petitions to public officials without the commander's approval (Brown v. Glines, 444 U.S. 348 (1980)). 'Military personnel must be ready to perform their duty whenever the occasion arises', the court said, and the military must be able to 'insist upon respect for duty and a discipline without counterpart in civilian life' and to 'possess substantial discretion over its internal discipline' (id., at 354, 357).

The statement of congressional findings accompanying the Thurmond bill stated that 'control, discipline, and prompt and unquestioning obedience to lawful orders are essential', and that 'the processes of conventional collective bargaining and labor negotiation cannot and should not be applied to the United States military organization'. It added that 'unionization of the Armed Forces is incompatible with the military chain of command, undermines the role, authority, and position of the commander, and could have the unfavorable and divisive effect of creating adversary relationships' (S.274, 95th Cong., 1st Sess. (1977), sec. 1(1)-(5). The same findings were contained in S.997, 95th Cong., 1st Sess. (1977)).

However, there was no hard evidence in the congressional hearings to support this conclusion, and the contrary experience in police-firemen unions and West European countries which accord military unions a variety of rights indicates otherwise. But the testimony from high ranking officers and officials was unequivocal in its contention that the command structure would be undermined. The thesis underlying the membership ban, although never quite articulated in the hearings, seems to be that the very act of joining an organization which attempts to induce changes in terms and conditions of service (although by lawful means) is subversive of the loyalty a service member owes to the command structure and that the combined effect of such membership poses a tacit threat to command authority.[32]

The possibility that service members would be more prone to engage in strikes, disruption, disobedience of orders, or other unlawful acts because of organizational membership is certainly a legitimate military concern. But the causal connection between commission of such illegal acts and membership in an organization which simply advocates working for change within the law is tenuous. There is no question that loyalty to superiors can make it easier to respond favorably to orders. But contemporary soldiers are members of many groups - political, religious, social, economic - which command their loyalties in varying degrees and sometimes take positions contrary to those of the official military. Modern man is often compartmentalized in his loyalties and roles, and there seems little reason to believe that service members' identification with an organization as to certain economic interests need undercut their sense of duty. The argument that the very existence of an organization committed to ultimate change of the laws as to bargaining and grievance representation imports a threat to the military lacks empirical support.

The Levy line of cases does recognize that the unique need for discipline and obedience in the military justifies considerable limitations on service members' constitutional rights. But the deviations from constitutional standards upheld in those cases involved statutory or regulatory schemes found to accord equivalent safeguards for constitutional rights.[33] It takes much squeezing to fit the absolute ban on union membership into the Levy rationale.[34] Several constitutional law experts testified that an absolute ban on union-type organizational membership raised constitutional issues.[35] In an attempt to avoid such problems, a Department of Defense (DOD) Directive has limited the membership ban to organizations found by the Service Secretary to present a 'clear danger to discipline, loyalty, or obedience to lawful orders' (DOD Dir. 1354.1, supra note 19, at para. E(4)a).[36] The prohibition was further limited by guidelines instructing the Secretary to consider an organization's history, operations, and involvement in prohibited conduct before determining that it poses a clear danger (id., Appendix 'Guidelines'). Thus an individual can only be personally liable if he was aware that the organization was banned and nevertheless continued as an active member with intent to promote the conduct on which the banning was based (id., para. E(4)b). These provisions seem to reduce the sweep of the ban so as to avoid the overbreadth problems in the statute.[37] Nevertheless, the more sweeping statutory ban remains on the books, apparently overriding the somewhat more limited Defense Department Directive. And the legal issue still remains as to whether the prohibition on membership, as opposed to more limited prohibitions of unlawful conduct itself, constitutes an unconstitutional failure to use less-restrictive alternatives.

Prohibition on Organizing Activities
The membership ban was augmented in both the statute and DOD Directive by prohibitions on organizing, recruiting, and related activities.[38] The DOD Directive attempted to avoid the constitutional problems which arise from the broad statutory prohibition by only forbidding 'collective job-related action' 'defined as activity by two or more persons that is intended to, and does, interfere with performance of a military duty assignment' (id., E, 2, Appendix, 'Definition', at B). Interference with duty is obviously a legitimate ground for forbidding conduct, but this provision still has troubling First Amendment implications. There is no definition of interference with duty, leaving open the possibility that minor derelictions of a highly subjective nature - such as failing to have one's footlocker in prescribed order, not meeting neatness standards, or poor attitude - could be attributed to organizational activities.[39] Given command hostility, any First Amendment activities which might be interpreted as 'organizational' would be a risky business, and the prudent person will avoid them entirely. The big losers are likely to be the kind of ad hoc groups that have formed in the past over a particular issue or problem (such as a group organized by military doctors to try to improve medical facilities), which can have a useful role in providing information about and discussion of underlying dissatisfactions. It is also not encouraging to think of the surveillance, employment of undercover agents and informers, and use of the subpoena power against organizations that could be resorted to by the military to enforce the organizational activity ban.

The directive also prohibits 'recruitment efforts' on post on behalf of any organization which proposes to or holds itself out as proposing to engage in negotiations or collective bargaining or to represent military members to the chain of command with respect to terms or conditions of service when it would interfere with the chain of command.[40] The prohibition seems broad enough to forbid recruiting on behalf of an organization which only advocates representation of or collective bargaining for service personnel if and when permitted by law. A letter from the General Counsel of the Department of Defense stated that merely 'advocating a change in the law' is not intended to be prohibited, but it did not indicate whether recruiting activities on behalf of an organization which only proposes to provide representation to the extent allowed by law is permissible.[41]

The prohibition on organizational activity on post was justified in part by the Defense Department by citing the Supreme Court's approval of a ban on union organizing rights in prisons in Jones v. North Carolina Prisoners' Labor Union, Inc. (433 U.S. 119 (1977)). The Court in Jones found the concern of prison officials that 'a prisoners' labor union was itself fraught with potential dangers' was not unreasonable. It stressed that prisoners had 'violated one or more criminal laws established by society for its orderly governance' and had demonstrated a propensity for unlawful, and often violent, conduct (id., at 126-129). There are similarities between a military post and a prison since both require a regimented environment, but a military post today seems far more analagous to schools, police departments, and places of public employment. Service personnel are not convicted criminals with proven anti-social tendencies, and given the voluntary nature of military service today and the liberality of pass and other privileges, one cannot posit the same kind of inherent danger from union activity as in a prison where physical restraint is necessary.

In a 1972 decision, Healy v. James (408 U.S. 169 (1972)), the Supreme Court held that non-recognition of a student group at a state college abridged the members' First Amendment rights because it denied them use of a formal meeting place on campus and access to bulletin boards and the school newspaper. Like service personnel, students have no right to collective bargaining or other prerogatives under the labor laws, but are entitled under the First Amendment to reasonable opportunity for discussion of public issues. Like the situation in Healy, there is normally no reasonable alternative for public discussion of issues on military posts. Furthermore, 'command-sponsored or authorized advisory councils, committees, or organizations' (which are likely to give a one-sided command point-of-view) are specifically excepted under both the statute and directive (10 U.S.C. sec. 976(e)).

The favoritism given 'authorized' organizations such as the Association of the US Army, Air Force Association, and Navy League[42] is contrary to the <u>Greer v. Spock</u> decision's emphasis on 'even-handed' application and raises equal protection issues.[43] The Defense Department maintains there is no favoritism since these organizations do not 'propose' to represent service personnel. But they do perform some of the same functions as unions, lobbying in the interests of their largely career-military membership, presenting programs to Congress and the military, consulting with military officials, and conducting recruiting and organizing activities on post. Their consultation with high-ranking military officials, most of whom are association members, is sometimes close to the kind of representation that labor unions provide in negotiation and collective bargaining. The fact that these associations represent service personnel, but do it <u>sub rosa</u>, should not make a difference for First Amendment purposes. Probably the most significant difference between the two from commanders' point of view is that the associations are generally supportive of military policy and are therefore unlikely to resort to the sort of pressure tactics used by union-type organizations. But, in fact, the associations are capable of their own kind of pressure tactics, cashing in their debts and using their influence when needed. It is difficult to believe that the First Amendment can be satisfied by such favoritism for a 'company union' because the military finds its objectives and methods more compatible.

The broad prohibitions of the statute and the more-finely crafted restrictions of the directive have not been subjected to constitutional test, and, indeed, the penalties are so severe and the monitoring capacity of the military so effective that test cases may not soon arise. The lopsided vote by which the statute passed the Congress indicates a strong sentiment in this country against military unionization. It also reflects a strongly-held societal view that service personnel live by a different code and the military is not just another government bureaucracy whose labor-management relations can be determined through the adversary process in a market-place system of negotiation and collective bargaining. But the prohibitions have swept up many other speech and associational activities with a broad brush. It seems unlikely that such restrictive provisions can entirely pass constitutional muster.

CONCLUSION

The balance in the American civil-military relationship has subtly tipped towards the military side in the decade following the end of the Vietnam War. The military, with its enormous advantage in terms of budget and resources, is increasingly looked to for assistance in traditionally civilian areas. The 1981 amendment to the Posse Comitatus Act was a modest move in that direction, but should raise warning signals as to further encroachments. Likewise, the military's foray into civilian intelligence gathering was finally terminated after congressional prodding, but limitations on such activity in the future rest largely on the sufferance of the defense establishment.

Meanwhile, there has been a return by the military, after a brief liberalization at the end of the Vietnam War, to traditional patterns of training and discipline. The post-World War II movement toward less authoritarian methods of control has not been extended to permit greater recognition of individual rights. The sweeping ban on organizational activity imposed in response to union activity further enlarges the gulf between military and civilian life. It also magnifies the difference between the American military and that of most of its European allies who allow greater individual diversity in the interests of preserving democratic values. The European experience suggests that limitations on organizational and speech activity might not be the most effective way to deal with underlying morale and discipline problems. Even more troubling is the impact such restrictive measures have upon the nature and values of the military and its attendant role in a democratic society.

That these encroachments of the military have been relatively modest and, in most cases, have been accompanied by debate is a sign that the civil-military relationship is still a matter of public concern. In a period of continuing military build-up, it is critical that each change be carefully monitored and considered to insure that the balance, so important to a democratic society, is not lost.

NOTES

1. Congress is empowered 'To provide for organizing, arming, and disciplining, the Militia, and for governing such Part of them as may be employed in the Service of the United States, reserving to the States respectively, the appointment of the Officers, and the Authority of training Militia according to the discipline prescribed by Congress', U.S. CONST. art. I, sec. 8, cl. 16, and 'To provide for calling forth the Militia to execute the Laws of the Union, suppress Insurrections and repel Invasions', id., art. I, sec. 8, cl. 15.

2. 'No soldier shall, in time of peace be quartered in any house, without the consent of the owner, nor in time of war, but in a manner to be prescribed by law', U.S. CONST., 3d amend.

3. U.S. CONST., art. II, sec. 2, cl. 1 provides 'The President shall be Commander in Chief of the Army and Navy of the United States, and of the Militia of the several States, when called into the actual Service of the United States ...' Art. I, sec. 8, cls. 11-14 give Congress the power 'To declare War ... To raise and support Armies, but no Appropriation of Money to that Use shall be for a longer Term than two Years; To Provide and maintain a Navy; To make Rules for the Government and Regulation of the land and naval Forces'.

4. W. Blackstone, I Commentaries 332 (1765), defines posse comitatus as all those over the age of 15 upon whom a sheriff could call for assistance in preventing civil disorder.

5. Op. Att'y Gen. 466 (1854); Message of President Fillmore to Congress, in 5 J. Richardson, A Compilation of the Messages and Papers of the Presidents 1789-1897 101 (1897).

6. See 7 Cong. Rec. 4248 (1878) (remarks of Senator Hill), 3581 (1878) (remarks of Mr Kimmel); N.Y. Times, 13 January 1871, p. 3, col. 2, 14 January 1871, p. 3, col. 2; High, 1969; Note, 1973, p. 142.

7. The Report of the Committee on the Judiciary To Accompany H.R. 3519, Department of Defense Authorization Act, 1982 (Rept. 97-71, Part 2, June 12, 1981) did state: 'The Committee does not, however, intend the military to become the routine supplier of basic equipment for civilian law enforcement agencies. Under existing practices,

co-operation regarding equipment loans and other dispositions generally fall into two categories ... older, less useful military equipment [and] the occasional loan of sophisticated equipment for a short time to accomplish the objective of a particular mission.'

8. SECNAVINST 5400.12 (17 Jan. 1969); Op. JAGN 1965/5184, 23 July 1965; Op. JAGN 1973/1508, 26 Feb. 1973. A 1968 Department of Defense Directive, DOD Dir. 3025.1 (June 8, 1968), stated: 'Although the Navy and Marine Corps are not expressly included within the provisions, the Posse Comitatus Act is regarded as national policy applicable to all military services of the United States'. United States v. Walden, 490 F. 2d 372 (4th Cir. 1968) concerned the use of three Marines by the Treasury Department as undercover agents posing as purchasers of weapons from the defendants' gun shop. The court found this a violation of the Navy regulation which, it stated, reflected the congressional intent underlying the Posse Comitatus Act.

9. Compare Meeks, 1975, pp. 100-103 indicating little doubt that the original proposal was meant to be applicable to all services with Hilton, 1983, p. 5, suggesting that the Navy may avoid the equipment limitations.

10. See Letter from Lee I. Dogoloff, Associate Director for Drug Policy, Domestic Policy Staff, the White House, to Cong. Lester Wolff, dated April 30, 1980, and enclosures: Cong. Rec. H4291-4292, H4299 (14 July 1981).

11. See 'Humanizing the U.S. Military', Time, 21 December 1970, p. 16.

12. Id. at 16; 'Westmoreland Mutes Reveille Bugler', N.Y. Times, 9 December 1970, p. 1, col. 5.

13. The Court of Military Appeals held in United States v. Ruiz, 23 USCMA 181, 48 CMR 797 (1974) that the UCMJ prohibition on self-incrimination prevented the military from taking adverse criminal or administrative action against a private who refused to furnish a urine sample two weeks after being sent to a detoxification center for suspected drug usage. However, in later cases the court considerably limited the self-incrimination protection as to forced taking of 'bodily fluids' specimens. United States v. Armstrong, 9 M.J. 374 (1980). In 1981 the Deputy Secretary of Defense issued a memorandum authorizing a mandatory urinalysis program, thereafter implemented by the services. See Maizel (1982) 'Urinalysis: Search and Seizure Aspects', 14 The Advocate 402; Wiesner

(1983) 'Urinalysis: Defense Approaches', 15 The Advocate 114.

14. Hearings on Military Posture and Legislation to Authorize Appropriations during the Fiscal year 1970 for Procurement of Aircraft, Missiles, Naval Vessels, and Tracked Combat Vehicles, Research Development, Test and Evaluation for the Armed Forces, etc. 91st Cong., 1st Sess., Part II at 3823 (1969).

15. Letter, AHABB-SI, Subject: American Servicemen's Union-Introduction of Subversive Literature at Army Installations, Dept. of Army, HQ, First U.S. Army, 24 March, 1969, printed in The Bond, publication of the ASU, 'Help Us to Organize for Justice'.

16. 'Union Chiefs Vote to Open Rolls to Military', Army Times, 5 July 1976, at 2, col. 1. See also 'Union Plans '76 Drive to Represent Servicemen', Wall Street Journal, 27 June 1975, p. 30, col. 1.

17. S. 3079, H.R. 12526, 12691, 13608, 94th Cong., 2d Sess. (1976); S. 274, 95th Cong., 1st Sess. (1977) (Thurmond); S. 997, 95th Cong., 1st Sess. (1977) (Stennis).

18. House Rpt. No. 95-894, Part 1, in Legislative History of P.L. 95-610, 6 U.S. Code Cong. and Admin. News 7575, 7578 (1978).

19. DOD Dir. 1354.1 (6 Oct. 1977, 32 C.F.R. sec. 143); see also AR 600-80, Relationships with Organizations which Seek to Represent Members of the Army in Negotiation or Collective Bargaining (3 January 1978).

20. For example, the Association of the U.S. Army, Air Force Association, Navy League, Fleet Reserve Association, Retired Officers Association, Reserve Officers Association, Veterans of Foreign Wars, and American Legion.

21. A Defense Department review board under President Ford's clemency program found a constant complaint that:

> the non-commissioned officers over him not only did not help but in some cases intentionally or unintentionally blocked his way from going to higher authority to obtain help. In other cases, alleged indifferences on the part of unit officers to listen to or be aware of his problems frustrated the individual. Often, a promise to look into the matter or to help resolve a problem apparently was not followed through ...

L. Baskir & W. Strauss (1977) Chance and Circumstance: The Draft, the War and the Vietnam Generation, p. 118.

22. Captain John S. Brown, a brigade EEO officer in Germany from 1973 to 1975, concluded that the position could evolve into a broader role: 'Technically I was to confine myself to race relations issues, but the boundary was too difficult to draw, a connection with discrimination (even if superficial) could always be made, and the concept of the operation was to restore confidence in brigade grievance machinery' (Brown, 1977, p. 32).

23. Quoted in Letter from N.Y. State Bar Association to Committee on Military Justice, 29 January 1949, p. 4, in VI Papers of Professor Edmund Morgan on the UCMJ, on file in Treasure Room, Harvard Law School Library.

24. Statement of Kenneth Blaylock, in U.S. News & World Rpt., 28 March 1977, reprinted in 123 Cong. Rec. S. 5103 (29 March 1977).

25. Modern military leadership techniques have moved away from the older notion that, as John Keegan (1976) has written of the Battle of Waterloo, the 'motive power' of troops and 'the solidarity of groups' only 'derive from the influence of those who lead and those who manipulate; in the case of armies, from the officers'. Military training doctrine now favours persuasion over authoritarian domination as more likely to instill high initiative and morale. See Office of the Deputy Chief of Staff for Personnel and the United States Military Academy, Proceedings for the Junior Officer Leadership Workshop on Contemporary Problems (1972).

26. The Nuremberg and related cases also challenged the notion that absolute obedience is required of a soldier. See 'Einsatzgruppen Case', XI Trials of War Criminals 470, quoted in U.S. v. Kinder, 14 CMR 742, 776 (AFBR 1953):

> The obedience of a soldier is not the obedience of an automaton. A soldier is a reasoning agent. He does not respond, and is not expected to respond, like a piece of machinery. It is a fallacy of widespread consumption that a soldier is required to do everything his superior officer orders him to do.

27. There is a high degree of unionization among the paramilitary - police, firefighters, and prison guards - in the U.S. See, for example, 'Chicago Police Take Fraternal Step', N.Y. Times,

11 November 1980, p. 3E, col. 4 (officers under the rank of sergeant voted 82% for unionizing despite 'no-union' drive of city administration). The form of unionization in these forces has been shaped so as to preserve a high degree of authority in supervisors, despite a union role in grievance presentation and/or collective bargaining. See, Schmertz (1975) 'New York City Fire Department Under the New York City Collective Bargaining Law', 3 Hofstra L. Rev. 605, 609-10, 626-32.

28. Lontine v. Van Cleave, 483 F. 2d 966 (10th Cir. 1973); Cook County Police Assoc. v. City of Harvey, 289 N.E. 2d 226 (1972) (no right to collective bargaining or grievance procedure without enabling legislation or agreement); Beauboenf v. Delgado College, 428 F. 2d 470 (5th Cir. 1970); Firefighters Local 574 v. Floyd, 170 S.E. 2d 394 (1969) (no right to use concerted activity to compel employer to recognize or bargain with union).

29. 'Military labor organization' is defined as an organization that engages or attempts to engage in: (a) negotiating or bargaining with officers or officials concerning terms or conditions of service; (b) representing service members before officers or officials in connection with a grievance or complaint arising out of terms or conditions of service; or (c) striking, picketing, marching, demonstrating, or any other similar form of concerted action directed against the government and intended to induce officers or officials to (i) negotiate or bargain concerning terms or conditions of service, (ii) recognize an organization as a representative of service members in connection with complaints and grievances arising out of terms or conditions of service, or (iii) make any change with respect to terms or conditions of service.

30. The statutory language, 'striking, picketing, marching, demonstrating, or any other similar form of concerted action', arguably limits 'concerted action' to the more activist qualities of the specific words which precede it. However, the House Committee report explaining the substitution of this language for prior language ('a strike or other concerted action') said it was intended 'to specify the other activities which are also prohibited'. Union Organization - Armed Forces - Prohibition; House Rpt. No. 95-894 - Part 1, 6 U.S. Code Cong. and Admin. News 7575, 7576 (1978) (emphasis added). Thus the language seems broad enough to cover a mere publicity campaign if it involved organizational or any form of group activity.

31. *AFSCME v. Woodward* 406 F. 2d 137 (8th Cir. 1969); *McLaughlin v. Tilendis*, 398 F. 2d 287 (7th Cir. 1968); *Vorbeck v. McNeal*, 407 F. Supp. 733 (E.D. Mo. 1976); *Melton v. City of Atlanta*, 324 F. Supp. 315 (N.D. Ga. 1971); *Atkins v. City of Charlotte*, 296 F. Supp. 1068 (W.D.N.C. 1969).

32. Similar objections were made to unionization of public employees. The National Labor Relations Act of 1935 excluded employees of federal, state, or local governments from coverage in the belief that public service demands undivided loyalty and that representation of government workers would give unions a dangerous hold on the nation. B. Hart (1961) *Collective Bargaining in the Federal Civil Service* 36, 170-71. However, in 1961, President Kennedy appointed a task force which recommended recognition of federal employee unions. Executive Order 10988, issued on 17 January 1962, established a federal policy permitting recognition of employee organizations as bargaining representatives, but withholding the right to strike and authorizing advisory arbitration as the last resort in a negotiated grievance procedure. 3 C.F.R. sec. 521. A high percentage of federal employees have now been unionized. A 1967 review by a committee appointed by President Johnson noted substantial benefits from unionization including improved communications, increased participation by employees in determination of working conditions, and greater continuity in the labor-management relationship. Usery (1970) 'Labor Management Relations in the Federal Service and the New Executive Order 11491', 4 *Ga. L. Rev.* 724.

Similar developments have taken place in regard to state and local government employees as increasing numbers of states and cities have passed enabling legislation to permit collective bargaining. Union membership of state and local government employees grew from 2.5 million in 1968 to 4.7 million (or 51.5% of the total) in 1974. 11,600 out of 78,000 government bodies engaged in collective bargaining or confer-and-discuss sessions with unions. Fishgold (1976) 'Dispute Resolution in the Public Sector: the Role of FMCS', 27 *Labor L. J.* 731, 732.

33. *Parker v. Levy*, 417 U.S. 733 (1974), found that the 'general articles', due to military case law and administrative gloss, had materially reduced the defect of vagueness and overbreadth; *Middendorf v. Henry*, 425 U.S. 25 (1976) found that the summary court-martial, without a right to counsel, provided adequate procedural protections for a disciplinary

proceeding lacking serious consequences; and <u>Brown v. Glines</u>, 444 U.S. 348 (1980), found that the detailed prior restraint procedures for distribution of literature insured timely and fair consideration of First Amendment rights. Only <u>Greer v. Spock</u>, 424 U.S. 828 (1976), upheld an absolute ban, and that was only as to partisan political activity on post, still leaving unregulated a broad range of political activities both by and directed at service members.

34. A relevant factor in assessing the constitutionality of the restrictions on organizational activity is whether there are less restrictive alternatives which satisfy the legitimate interests of the services. In a thesis for the Army JAG School, Major James A. Badami concluded that unionization 'would serve the best interests of the individual military man and of the United States'. He recommended use of administrative machinery already in existence for collective bargaining by civilian federal employees, with certain restrictions applicable only to the military. There would be absolute prohibitions on work slowdowns, strikes, and interference with the military mission. He favored a separate union for each division or comparable-sized unit, with subdivisions for officers, senior NCOs and enlisted men, thus preventing the growth of a union with service-wide jurisdiction and the mingling of the three rank groups. Representatives from each rank would be elected annually and would set policy for the professional union administrators they hired (Badami, 1973, p. 64).

35. Former Solicitor General Erwin Griswold observed that the bill's 'broad prohibition' on membership in civilian unions that do not assert the right to collective bargaining is 'far broader than the Committee's actual concern and cannot be justified by the danger of military strikes', <u>Unionization of the Armed Forces: Hearings before the Comm. on Armed Services U.S. Senate on S. 274 and S. 997</u>, 95th Cong., 1st Sess. 389 (1977). He found it not 'self-evident' that Congress can restrict abstract advocacy of organizing the military for collective bargaining, although such advocacy might be banned on military bases because of 'the obvious need for bases to be free to conduct their training and other duties without undue disturbances and by the large concentration of military personnel on a base', <u>id</u>. at 389-399.

Professor Charles A. Wright concluded that Congress could prohibit membership in a union that supports, advocates, or asserts the right of service members to strike, but was doubtful that it could constitutionally prohibit membership in a labor organization based on a claim of inherent danger to discipline and effectiveness. 'To the extent to which others soliciting for private causes are barred' from posts, he believed that 'union organizers could be barred'. However, since 'military bases are not prisons, and soldiers, sailors, and airmen are hardly prisoners', the <u>Jones v. North Carolina Prisoners' Labor Union, Inc.</u> case dealing with solicitation in the prison context would 'not clearly answer questions about solicitation of union membership in the military', <u>id</u>. at 417.

36. The 'clear danger' must arise 'because' the organization or any person acting on its behalf engages in any act prohibited by the directive or violates, conspires to violate, solicits, or aids and abets a violation of specified UCMJ articles relating to obedience and discipline.

37. Attorneys who participated in the drafting of the directive expressed the following concern over an absolute membership ban: 'Perhaps the most effective roadblock to unionization of the armed forces would be an across-the-board prohibition on union membership. The likelihood of incurring a substantial fine or imprisonment for mere membership could deter enthusiasm for collective activities and would make organizing very difficult. Such a prohibition, however, faces substantial First Amendment hurdles, whether it is measured against some form of clear and present danger test or whether an interest balancing approach is used' (Siemer, Hut and Drake, 1977, p. 36).

38. The statute imposes the more sweeping prohibition. It makes it unlawful to enroll or solicit service members for membership, or to attempt to organize or participate in or use government property for a strike, picketing, march, demonstration, or similar form of 'concerted action' directed against the government to induce bargaining, recognition for grievance representation, or making 'any change' with respect to terms or conditions of service. 10 U.S.C. sec. 976(c)(1), (2), and (4). This would conceivably cover a 'bull session' at which suggestions for getting the government to make 'any change' in terms of conditions of service are discussed.

39. Interference with duty is not limited to offenses under the UCMJ or even to the broader categories of 'unfitness' or 'unsuitability' in job performance which can be the basis of an

administrative discharge. Thus there seems nothing to prevent a court-martial from determining that an alleged 'collective job-related action' interfered with duty because of its impact upon an individual's morale or proper attitudes.

40. 'Recruiting efforts' are defined as 'a demonstration, meeting, march, speechmaking, protest, picketing, leafleting, or other similar activity ... for the purpose of forming, recruiting members for or soliciting money or services for an organization'. DOD Dir. 1354.1, *supra* note 19, at para. E(3)a. Also prohibited is 'any activity on any part of a military installation, including but not limited to individual contacts or the posting for public display of any poster, handbill or other writing, if that activity or the material displayed constitutes or includes an invitation to collectively engage in an act prohibited by this Directive', *id*. at para. E(e)b.

41. Letter from Deanne C. Siemer, General Counsel of the DOD, to Jay A. Miller, Assoc. Dir. of ACLU (28 October 1977), at p. 2: 'We see nothing in the language of the regulation that would go so far [as to prohibit membership in an organization that proposes to engage in negotiation or collective bargaining if and when the law permitted it]. The regulation specifies the activities that are prohibited, and advocating a change in the law is not one of them'.

42. See note 20, *supra*. Although voluntary and supported by dues from the members, these organizations often enjoy a quasi-official status on military installations, with meetings announced in bulletins, being accorded on-post meeting places, and having unofficial access to commanders and other officials.

43. Although *Greer v. Spock*, 424 U.S. 828 (1976) upheld an absolute ban on partisan political activity on post, it only covered demonstrative political activity and not mere discussion of issues. Several justices were persuaded by the ready availability of other sources of communication such as TV, radio, newspaper, magazines, mail, and off-post rallies and meetings. And the court emphasized that the ban on political activity was 'even-handed', applying to all groups, parties and ideologies.

REFERENCES

Badami, J. (1973) 'Servicemen's Unions: Constitutional, Desirable, Practical' (unpublished

Advanced Course thesis in U.S. Army JAG School, Charlottesville, Virginia)
Baskir, L. (1974) 'Reflections on the Senate Investigation of Army Surveillance', 49 Indiana Law Journal 618
Blair, J. & Phillips, R. (1983) 'Job Satisfaction Among Youth in Military and Civilian Work Settings', 9 Armed Forces and Society 555
Brickman, A. (1976) 'Military Trade Unionism in Sweden', 2 Armed Forces and Society 529
Brown, J.S. (1977) 'Para-legal Aspects of the Equal Opportunity Staff Officer, U.S. Army, Europe (USAREUR)' (unpublished paper for M.A. thesis, Indiana University, Bloomington, Indiana)
Church Committee Report (1976) Final Report of the Select Committee to Study Governmental Operations with Respect to Intelligence Activities, 94th Cong., 2d Sess., Sen. Rept. No. 94-755
Comment (1976) 'Public Employee Legislation: An Emerging Paradox, Impact and Opportunity', 13 San Diego Law Review 931
Cunliffe, M. (1968) Soldiers and Civilians: the Martial Spirit in America, 1775-1865, Boston, Little Brown
Davis, W. (1914) 'The Federal Reconstruction Acts', in Studies in Southern History and Politics, New York, Columbia University Press, p. 205
Dixon, N. (1976) On the Psychology of Military Incompetence, New York, Basic Books
Doolittle Report (1946) Senate Doc. No. 196, 79th Cong., 2d Sess.
Engdahl, D. (1971) 'Soldiers, Riots and Revolution: the Law and History of Military Troops in Civil Disorders' 57 Ia. Law Review 1
────────────── (1974) 'The New Civil Disturbance Regulations: The Threat of Military Intervention', 49 Indiana Law Journal 581
Fleckenstein, B. (1976) 'The Military and Labor Organizations in Germany', 2 Armed Forces and Society 495
Furman, H. (1960) 'Restrictions upon Use of the Army Imposed by the Posse Comitatus Act', 7 Military Law Review 85
Goldich, R. (1983) 'Military Nondisability Retirement "Reform", 1969-1979: Analysis and Reality', 10 Armed Forces and Society 59
High, J. (1969) 'The Marine Corps and Crowd Control', in R. Higham (ed.), Bayonets in the Streets, Lawrence, University Press of Kansas, p. 119
Hilton, R. (1983) 'Recent Developments Relating to

the Posse Comitatus Act', <u>The Army Lawyer</u> 1
Jacobs, B. (1978) 'Overview of National Political Intelligence', 55 <u>Journal of Urban Law</u> 853
Janowitz, M. (1960) <u>The Professional Soldier</u>, Glencoe, Illinois, Free Press
―――――――― (ed.) (1967) <u>The New Military</u>, New York, Science Editions
Jörg, N. (1983) 'Organisational Change and Fundamental Rights in the Dutch Army: 1966-1976', 7 <u>Contemporary Crises</u> 183
Keegan, J. (1976), <u>The Face of Battle</u>, New York, Viking Press; London, Jonathan Cape
Kosinski, F. (1972) 'The Right to Organize the Military' (unpublished LL.M. thesis, George Washington Law School)
Krendel, E. (1977) 'European Military Unions', in E. Krendel & B. Samoff (eds.) <u>Unionizing the Armed Forces</u>, Philadelphia, University of Pennsylvania Press, pp. 135-56
Logan, J. (1887) <u>The Volunteer Soldier of America</u>, Chicago, R.S. Peale
Lovell, J. & Kronenberg, P. (1974) <u>New Civil-Military Relations: the Agonies of Adjustment to Post-Vietnam Realities</u>, New Brunswick, N.J., Transaction Books
McCubbin, H., Dahl, B. & Hunter, E. (eds.) (1976) <u>Families in the Military System</u> (Vol. 9, Sage Series on Armed Forces and Society), Beverly Hills, California, Sage
Mandeville, L. (1976) 'Syndicalism and the French Military System', 2 <u>Armed Forces and Society</u> 539
Marshall, S. (1947) <u>Men Against Fire</u>, New York, William Morrow
Meeks, C. (1975) 'Illegal Law Enforcement: Aiding Civil Authorities in Violation of the Posse Comitatus Act' 70 <u>Military Law Review</u> 83
Morgan, E. (1965) 'The Background of the Uniform Code of Military Justice', 28 <u>Military Law Review</u> 17
Moskos, C. (1970) <u>The American Enlisted Man: the Rank and File in Today's Military</u>, New York, Russell Sage Foundation
―――――――― (1977) 'From Institution to Occupation: Trends in Military Organization', 4 <u>Armed Forces & Society</u> 41
Note (1973) 'Honored in the Breech: Presidential Authority to Execute the Laws with Military Force', 83 <u>Yale Law Journal</u> 130
Pyle, C. (1974) 'Spies Without Masters: The Army Still Watches', 1 <u>Civ. Lib. Review</u> 38

Schwarz, F. (1977) 'Intelligence Activities and the Rights of Americans', 32 The Record of the Assoc. of the Bar of the City of N.Y. 43

Sefton, J. (1967) The United States Army and Reconstruction, 1865-1877, Baton Rouge, Louisiana State University Press

Sherman, E. (1970) 'The Civilianization of Military Law', 22 Maine Law Review 3

Siemer, D., Hut, A. & Drake, G. (1977) 'Prohibition on Military Unionization: A Constitutional Appraisal', 78 Military Law Review 1

Stapp, A. (1970) Up Against the Brass, New York, Simon Schuster

Sullivan, D. (1969) 'Soldiers in Unions - Protected First Amendment Rights?', 20 Labor Law Journal 581

Teitler, G. (1976) 'The Successful Case of Military Unionization in the Netherlands', 2 Armed Forces and Society 517

Usery, W. (1976) 'Bargaining in the Public Sector: Problems, Progress and Prospects', 1 Oklahoma City U. Law Review 1

Werner, V. (1976) 'Syndicalism in the Belgian Armed Forces', 2 Armed Forces and Society 477

Woodward, C. (1966) Reunion and Reaction, Boston, Little Brown

Chapter Eleven

MILITARY INTERVENTION IN DEMOCRATIC SOCIETIES: THE ROLE OF LAW

Christopher J. Whelan

In democratic societies, the domestic use of the military raises constitutional, legal and political questions of the most fundamental kind. In the words of Edmund Burke (1815, p. 17) 'An armed disciplined body is in its essence dangerous to Liberty: undisciplined, it is ruinous to Society'. In the modern era, the military has a 'manpower, equipment and readiness capability which far exceeds those of any institution in society' (Sherman, p. 217). With new calls being made upon it, the military is now being used for a wide variety of domestic purposes and an elaborate contingency planning machinery exists in many countries to coordinate and prepare for intervention. This, however, may threaten some of the most cherished principles of democratic society.

Most commentators who have evaluated the practice and potential of the domestic military role have done so in terms of what may be called a 'rhetoric of legality', the fundamental constitutional and legal principles which form the ideology of a democratic society. Thus, many chapters of this book have described ways in which the practice of military intervention 'deviates' from the role which that rhetoric proposes. Against this yardstick, commentators have argued that the scales have been weighted too heavily in favour of the state (see, for example, Jacobs, Chapter 7; Bennett and Ryan, Chapter 8) or against the military (Evelegh, 1978); and that the legal foundations for military intervention have at best been ambiguous (id.; Bennett and Ryan, Chapter 8) or at worst 'shaky' (Greer, 1983, p. 583) or 'faulty' (Engdahl, Chapter 1).

The objective of this chapter is to offer new perspectives on the practice of military intervention in Great Britain and the United States and on the role of the law in its accomplishment. The idea which will be explored, one that was first developed in the field of British criminal justice by McBarnet (1981), is that deviation from the rhetoric may be institutionalised in the law itself. To test this proposition requires an empirical investigation of the rhetoric of legality, the practice of military intervention and of the role of law. The questions raised are, how far does the rhetoric accord with the detail of the law and with the use made of the law in practice; how far does the law control military intervention and protect civil liberties and how far does it deviate from its own rhetoric actually to facilitate military intervention? By concentrating upon the detailed structure of the law, the way it is framed, the procedures under which it operates and the controls for which it provides, rather than the rhetoric, the full scope of legitimate military intervention can be established. In particular, attention will be given to the ways in which the law has been <u>used</u> when the military have intervened.

RHETORIC OF LEGALITY

Over the centuries and on each side of the Atlantic, domestic use of the military has provided the impetus for major constitutional reforms. (For a description of the law and practice of military intervention in British constitutional history, see Clode, 1869.) Fear and suspicion of military abuses by the monarchy led first to the establishment of political and constitutional controls. Subsequent apprehension of public disorder together with the perceived need to use the military in other circumstances has in turn led to re-assessments of the rhetoric of legality.

Many commentators (such as Engdahl, Chapter 1, 1971; Greer, 1983) have described how various English kings used military force in defiance both of Parliament and of the pledge in Magna Carta that no man would be taken, imprisoned or destroyed except 'by the law of the land'. In the sixteenth century, the Tudors claimed and used prerogative powers to intervene domestically by way of 'martial law', which, they asserted, allowed them on grounds of purported necessity, to use the military domestically and to suspend or supersede ordinary law and its processes, including Magna Carta (Engdahl,

p. 6). In this way, the monarchs quartered troops in private houses, exacted 'ship' money or other forced loans, carried out summary trials with punishments and suppressed civil disorders (id.). The establishment of a permanent standing army in the seventeenth century and its increased use, superseding regular civil officials, in a civil order role 'was widely seen in government circles as providing the army with a foot in the door of national politics which parliamentarians preferred to keep firmly closed against military intrusion' (Greer, 1983, p. 579). In the Middle Ages, internal disorder had been dealt with by 'local' representatives of the Crown, such as sheriffs and magistrates, through the posse comitatus, a contingent of able-bodied free men. These had later been superseded by the local feudal aristocracy through their militia and yeomanry. Neither method of dealing with disorder had posed a threat to parliamentary government. But the combination of an increased use of the military in apparent defiance of the law and of the establishment of a permanent army conceived of 'as an instrument of the Crown and of monarchial absolutism in general, provoked one of the most important constitutional upheavals in the history of the nation' (id., p. 580). Parliament, in its enactment of the Petition of Right in 1628, declared the 'martial law' prerogative of the Crown to be unconstitutional and against Magna Carta. Continued use of the military by Charles I, despite the Petition of Right, 'helped precipitate the civil war which commenced in 1642' (Engdahl, p. 6). Parliament, after the restoration of the monarchy, reaffirmed its rejection of the martial law prerogative in the first declaration of the Bill of Rights 1688: 'That the pretended power of suspending of laws, or the execution of laws, by royal authority without consent of Parliament is illegal'. From this history emerged the firm constitutional principle that the military is subservient to parliamentary authority; its very existence in peacetime to be lawful must be with the consent of Parliament (Bill of Rights, Art. 9).

Virtually identical royal abuse in the Colonies led to the establishment of similar principles in the United States. Rather than use magistrates, the traditional posse or the process of civilian law, the King had used British troops to suppress disorders. This led to clashes between troops and colonists (Engdahl, p. 7). According to the Declaration of Independence (clause 14) the King had 'affected to render the military independent of and superior to the Civil Power' (Engdahl, p. 7). The 'due process' clause of the Fifth Amendment of the Constitution was 'conditioned in major part by fear of domestic use of the national military force' for which the Constitution had itself provided (id.). Thus, according to Engdahl (id.) 'This repudiation of military intervention in domestic law enforcement is the bedrock of due process upon which American government was built'. Other constitutional provisions, such as the militia clauses (Art. I, sec. 8, cls. 15, 16) and the division of war powers and authority over the land and naval forces between Congress and the President (Art. II, sec. 2, cls. 1, 11-14), also attempt to 'preserve a proper "civil-military relationship"' (Sherman, p. 216) from which Congressional control can be inferred. In addition, the third amendment prohibits the peacetime quartering of troops without the houseowner's consent.

Despite this, however, Presidents have subsequently claimed and invoked inherent executive powers not dissimilar to the royal prerogative. During the Civil War, Lincoln had 13,000 people arrested and detained by military authority in the loyal North; during the process of 'reconstruction', Grant also freely used the army. In the opinion of Attorney General Edward Bates in 1861, the doctrine of separation of powers placed this power 'beyond judicial or legislative restraint' (Engdahl, p. 14); the requirement that the military be subordinate to the civil power was retained by the fact that the President as Commander-in-Chief was a 'civil magistrate not a military chief' (id., quoting Bates). This thesis, however, was rejected and denounced by courts in several cases and by the Supreme Court in Ex parte Milligan (71 U.S. 2 (1866)). The notion of extra-statutory, inherent powers was also rejected by Congress in the Posse Comitatus Act 1878 (see Sherman, Chapter 10; see also, Youngstown Sheet & Tube Co. v. Sawyer, 343 U.S. 579 (1952)). This reaffirmed the principle that recourse to military resources in civilian law enforcement, whether local, state or federal, was prohibited:

> it shall not be lawful to employ any part of the Army of the United States as a posse comitatus, or otherwise, for the purpose of executing the laws, except in such cases and under such circumstances as such employment of said force may be expressly authorized by the Constitution or by act of Congress. (Act of

June 18, 1878, ch. 263, sec. 15; 20 Stat. 145, 152)

In both Great Britain and the United States therefore, use of the military in domestic law enforcement is repudiated in the rhetoric of constitutional law. In this form of law, the principles of military subservience to civil authority and to 'due process of law' is uncompromising.

In both countries, foundations for military intervention have subsequently been laid which, in terms of these strict constitutional principles, have been characterised respectively as 'shaky' (Greer, 1983, p. 583) and 'faulty' (Engdahl, Chapter 1). For the most part, however, these foundations reflect an equally clear rhetoric of legality: in times of grave emergency, as a matter of last resort and on grounds of necessity, strict constitutional principles may have to give way and the military may be used to deal with the emergency.

In Britain, the increase in the frequency and scale of disturbances in the late eighteenth and nineteenth centuries led to a restoration of 'local' control of military intervention by the magistracy. A new 'common law' was developed, based initially on the 'soldier as citizen' doctrine enunciated by Lord Mansfield (see Engdahl, Chapter 1; Greer, 1983, pp. 581-2). Any citizen, including a soldier, could be called upon to aid the civil power in maintaining the peace (<u>R. v. Kennett</u> (1781) 5 Car. & P. 282; <u>Burdett v. Abbot</u> (1812) 4 Taunt. 401; <u>Redford v. Birley</u> (1822) 3 Stark. 76); and magistrates could be guilty of a common law misdemeanour if they failed to call on the army if the circumstances so demanded (Greer, 1983, p. 585). According to Greer (<u>id</u>., p. 583)

> Civil libertarian reservations about the increasing use of the army in riots seems to have been overwhelmed by the general establishment view that what was good for the maintenance of public order was desirable and, therefore, legal. The fear of disorder had by this stage largely replaced the spectre of military intervention in civil affairs as the <u>bête noir</u> of the status quo.

The common law principles are clearly stated, however: the military can aid the civil power 'when it is necessary to do so ... but not otherwise' (Manual of Military Law, 1968, Part II, Section V, para. 3), 'to maintain peace and public order' or, 'in very exceptional circumstances for grave and sudden emergencies' (Queen's Regulations for the Army 1975, J11.002) or when the disturbance is 'grave enough to be beyond the power of the police to suppress' (Manual of Military Law, para. 1). The rhetoric of the common law was summed up by Haldane, Secretary of State for War, in 1908:

> We demur to being called out except in the last and most perilous necessity ... we are called out illegally if we are called out in any circumstances which admit of being dealt with by a force less menacing than a military force necessarily is ... the civil authority ... has no power to call out the military unless they cannot get on without the military. They ought to do it by civil aid if they can. (Minutes of Evidence, Parliamentary Select Committee, the Employment of Military in Cases of Disturbance, H.C. Parl. Papers (1908), paras. 103, 104, 152; pp. 11, 12, 17)

As Sir Robert Mark has observed (p. 89), there has emerged 'a firm and deepening conviction, shared by soldiers, police and public alike that the army has no part to play in Great Britain in matters of political and industrial dispute not involving the overthrow of lawful government by force'.

As a result of this, images of political neutrality and subservience to the civil authority, whether local or central, have been retained and now permeate the general military and police literature (see, for example, Logan, 1887; Finer, 1962, 1976; Huntington, 1957; Otley, 1968; Cunliffe, 1968) particularly in relation to the military role in public order (Bramall, Chapter 3; Perkins, 1973). Thus, according to Mark, troops, having been called out in aid of the police (under the procedure outlined in Chapter 4) 'could not take action, other than reconnaissance, unless asked to do so by the chief police officer in command of the police district' (Report, 1978).

Statutory authority under the Emergency Powers Acts 1964 and 1920 for military intervention in industrial disputes is similarly phrased. The 1964 Act (s. 2) empowers the Defence Council to authorise use of service personnel to do 'urgent work of national importance'. Under the 1920 Act (s. 1(1)), troops can be used following a proclamation of emergency where it appears to the government that the 'essentials of life' of at least a substantial portion of the community are being threatened (see generally, Whelan, Chapter 6). A notion of military neutrality when intervening in trade disputes or to quell industrial unrest has thus developed. Paragraph 7 of the Manual of Military Law states:

> The merits or demerits of such disputes or unrest are of no concern whatsoever to soldiers, who are solely concerned with the duty and obligation common to all citizens of assisting the civil authority in the maintenance of law and order, and in these situations their principal duty will be the protection of persons and property.

Indeed, paragraph 31 states that:

> It is a principle of the employment of troops in civil tasks that the employer should not thereby obtain labour more cheaply than he would by employing civilians in the normal way. The employer is therefore charged for soldiers at the recognised civil rate by a procedure set out in Defence Council Instructions.[1]

In the United States, judicial expressions and some statutory language reflect very closely the constitutional rhetoric of due process. In 1866, the Supreme Court regarded the enforcement of laws by military means as an alternative to civilian measures to be impermissible per se even in times of stress (Ex parte Milligan, 71 U.S. 2; see Engdahl, Chapter 1). Congress, in 1878, also rejected use of the army in order to execute the laws unless 'expressly authorized by the Constitution or by act of Congress' (Posse Comitatus Act 1878, ch. 263, sec. 15; 20 Stat. 145, 152). Congress has acted to grant the President power to use armed forces in situations not dissimilar to the British common law: in order to suppress insurrections against State government (10 U.S.C. sec. 331), or unlawful obstructions, combinations, assemblages or rebellion against the authority of the United States which makes it impracticable to enforce the laws by the ordinary course of judicial proceedings (id., sec. 332), or any insurrection, domestic violence, unlawful combination or conspiracy if it threatens constitutional rights and state authorities are unable, fail or refuse to protect those rights or if it opposes the execution of the laws or impedes the course of justice (id., sec. 333).

Furthermore, the three sets of Civil Disturbance Regulations made since 1968 (and discussed by Engdahl, Chapter 1), which claim various authority existing for military intervention, do so in terms of dealing with serious threats. The military may be used to assist in preventing loss of life or destruction of property and in restoring government functioning and public order when sudden and unexpected civil disturbances, disasters or calamities seriously endanger life and property to the extent that local authorities are unable to control the situations (32 C.F.R. sec. 215.4(c)(1)(i) (1981)); and in protecting Federal property and Federal governmental functions when the need exists and duly constituted local authorities are unable or decline to provide adequate protection (id., (ii)).

Recently-enacted statutory authority for military assistance in law enforcement is also carefully circumscribed. Under the Defense Department Authorization Act of 1982 (P.L. 97-86, 95 Stat. 1115) military assistance may be made 'in emergency circumstances' for enforcing specified federal immigration, customs and drug laws, and the Defence Department may make available, following a 'cabinet-level request', any equipment for law enforcement purposes 'outside the land area of the United States' (see now, 10 U.S.C. secs. 371-378).

Engdahl has criticised the interpretation which has been placed upon many of these provisions. To the extent that they contravene the constitutional standards he has argued forcefully that they 'could not survive judicial scrutiny if historic due process principles were applied' (Engdahl, pp. 14, 15, 17, 19). Thus, the constitutional rhetoric rejects the idea that 10 U.S.C. sec. 331 can be invoked to deal with riots or disorders not amounting to insurrections (a 'prevalent misconception': id., p. 9); that the use in 10 U.S.C. sec. 332 of the term 'impracticability' instead of 'necessity' is not warranted (id., p. 15); and the interpretation of 10 U.S.C. sec. 333 that the military can be invoked other than as a last resort (id., pp. 10-19). He criticises some of the regulations also: C.F.R. sec. 215(4)(c)(1)(i) and (ii) are reminiscent of claims of inherent executive prerogative authority and both retaliate against the provisions of the Posse Comitatus Act (id., pp. 19-31). In short, he argues (p. 3) that these foundations for military intervention have 'no footing on the bedrock of our law'.

THE PRACTICE OF MILITARY INTERVENTION IN BRITAIN AND
THE UNITED STATES

The military have been used for an extremely wide variety of tasks. What emerges from a review of these is that the principles which underlie the practice of military intervention contrast sharply with the rhetoric of legality outlined above.
It is only one hundred years since the Secretary of State for War laid down 'the effective support of the civil power in all parts of the UK' as the first principal requirement from the British army (Jeffery, p. 53). Such wholesale potential intervention, despite the establishment of the metropolitan police in 1829 and of several provincial forces later, became a reality as the military frequently came to the rescue of the police during nineteenth century riots and demonstrations (Blake, 1979, pp. 52-54). Indeed, between 1869 and 1908, the military intervened in at least twenty-four disturbances and on two occasions had been ordered to fire (Parliamentary Select Committee, The Employment of Military in Cases of Disturbance, H.C. Parl. Papers (1908), 236, vol. vii, p. 365).
During the Featherstone disturbances in 1893, a crowd of around three hundred had attempted to enter Ackton Hall colliery. Numbers grew as the military prepared to intervene. Colliery buildings were set alight and wrecked. The Riot Act was read, but before the statutory one-hour dispersal time limit had passed, troops attempted to clear the colliery yard. Stones were thrown at the troops who responded by opening fire and charging with bayonets fixed. Four people were killed before further military forces were brought in. The Committee of Inquiry which examined the circumstances of the shooting (a jury having earlier disagreed) declared that the military not only had the legal right, but had the obligation to judge for themselves whether to open fire regardless of the statutory time limited: 'The necessary prevention of such outrage on person and property justifies the guardians of the peace in the employment against a riotous crowd of even deadly weapons'. The troops in these riots, then, were not legally liable: 'The reason is that the soldier who fired has done nothing except what was his strict legal duty ... their action was necessary ... it follows that the action of the troops was justified by law' (Report of the Commission on the Featherstone Riots, Parl. Papers (1893-4), C.7234, vol. xviii).

Widespread and forceful military intervention occurred also in a host of other collieries in this dispute (Mesborough, Barnsley, Chesterfield, E. Derbyshire, N. Staffordshire, Llanelli, Sheffield, Nottingham and the Midlands), and again to combat industrial disorder in the syndicalist era, most notably at Tonypandy, Liverpool and Llanelli, in 1910 and 1911. At Tonypandy in 1910, the Chief Constable requested military aid, only later informing the civil government (H.C. Deb., Vol. 21, col. 228). The response of Winston Churchill, then Home Secretary, and Haldane, Secretary of State for War, was to send 270 metropolitan police officers instead; and to despatch General Sir Nevil Macready to take charge both of troops and police at Tonypandy. Macready thereupon took full charge and responsibility. He determined when to move troops to troubled areas (id., cols. 229-30) and he applied 'a hitherto untried policy for dealing with disturbances consequent upon labour disputes' (Macready, 1924, p. 154).

Further military intervention and elaborate contingency planning occurred in the docks and railway strikes and civil disturbances in 1911. In Liverpool, the military successfully escorted carts of perishable goods past strikers. But prison vans containing men sentenced for offences during disturbances were attacked, and the troops escorting them opened fire and two men were killed (although who shot them was left in some doubt). This military action again was totally exonerated at the subsequent inquests (see Blake, 1979, pp. 109 et seq.).

In 1911, Churchill used the military to break a national railway strike. This was achieved by military protection of strikebreakers providing a limited service of essential supplies and by extensive contingency planning, including the establishment of a central organisation and a regional structure. In this strike 'practically the whole of the troops in Great Britain were on duty' (Macready, 1924, p. 163). Once again, military intervention and deaths went together, this time in Llanelli. Two men were killed, one in his own back garden. At the inquest, it was again stated that force used was such as necessary to ensure the free passage of trains and that it did not have to be authorised by a magistrate. According to Winston Churchill, in protecting blackleg workers, the military authorities were granted 'full discretionary powers to move troops along the lines of railways to such points as may enable them to safeguard as far as possible the ordinary working of all necessary traffic' (H.C. Deb., Vol. 29, col. 2285). Local authorities, however, were often not involved in the requisitioning of troops. Indeed, on occasion, despite local civil authorities' rejection of the need for military aid, Winston Churchill, following requests for aid from local trade associations or railway companies, and the military authorities determined that the military should be used (Blake, 1979, pp. 128-130). In answer to charges of taking 'illegal or extra constitutional action', Churchill replied 'The military authorities always enjoy power to move troops in their own country ... whenever it is found to be convenient or necessary' (H.C. Deb., Vol. 29, col. 2286). He described the regulation that restricts use of troops in disorderly cases until requisitioned by local authorities as only 'for the convenience of the War Office and generally of the Government, and has in these circumstances necessarily been abrogated in order to enable the military authorities to discharge the duties with which at this juncture they were officially charged' (id.).

The Emergency Powers Acts 1920 and 1964 have provided legal authority to use the military as 'substitute labour' in industrial disputes (see Whelan, Chapter 6). They have been invoked in a wide range of circumstances. Greatest use of the military under the 1920 Act was made in the General Strike of 1926, in which troops, with machine guns, armoured cars and drums beating, escorted food convoys through dockers' picket lines. According to Blake (1979), the armed forces in 1926 were regarded by government as perhaps the most vital element of its anti-strike, anti-revolutionary vanguard. Prominent army officers were privy to ministerial discussions regarding the formulation, organization and deployment of the anti-strike machinery. Among the committees established was the Supply and Transport Committee, which had earlier been called the Industrial Unrest Committee and the Strike Committee (see Jeffery and Hennessy, 1983).

Under the 1920 Act, Parliament must be kept informed of every proclamation of emergency and regulation made. This has not led, however, to any significant discussion or amendment. The Act has been invoked, arguably, in circumstances not covered by the statute's definition of emergency. Thus, it is questionable whether the use of service personnel to protect a government's statutory incomes policy and the balance of payments in a merchant seamen's strike (1966), or to proclaim an emergency because tramwaymen and busmen strike in London (1924) or 15,000 dockers in London (1949) or in three ports (1948) go on strike, were responses to threats to the 'essentials of life of a substantial portion of the community'. It is equally questionable whether these descriptions accurately portray the reasons for military intervention. However, since the definition is interpreted almost exclusively by government there can be virtually no accountability.

A similar case can be made in respect of the Emergency Powers Act 1964. The use of the military to stoke Buckingham Palace boilers during a strike by Ministry of Works employees (1948), to protect a government non-statutory incomes policy (1977-78), to remove garbage in Tower Hamlets (1970) and Glasgow (1975) or to provide firecover in Glasgow (1973) may or may not be reasonable interpretations of 'urgent work of national importance'. The legal authority for such intervention was, however, the 1964 Act and the defence regulation which preceded it. It is clear that the Defence Council, a body comprising senior politicians, civil servants and military commanders, alone has to determine the meaning of that phrase and by its very nature it is not required to give reasons publicly nor open itself up to any kind of legal challenge. It exercises very wide discretion and, without having to consult Parliament, it can take the crucial decision to employ troops 'almost by stealth' (Jeffery and Hennessy, 1983, p. 266). The result has been that since 1970, and with very little public debate, the military have been involved in twenty-seven disputes, twenty-two since 1975.

There has been a long history of military involvement in industrial disputes and in the associated unrest in the United States also. Following the Civil War, troops were used to suppress labour disputes. State militia and National Guard intervention continued well into the twentieth century. Military force was often used to break strikes. In the railroad strike in 1877, 45,000 militiamen were called up; 100 strikers were killed and several hundred wounded (Jacobs, pp. 130-1). Between 1877 and 1892, at least 30 per cent of the militia's active duty assignments involved strikes (Riker, 1957, p. 55, quoted in Jacobs, p. 131). In the 1894 Pullman strike, President Cleveland sent in federal troops to 'preserve order' despite protests from the state governor.

In terms of military replacement of civilian private sector labour, while the practice was not uncommon earlier this century, all such deployments 'appear to have been linked to military or national defense activities' (Jacobs, p. 131). In terms of public sector employees, before 1970, the State Guard had been used only in the 1919 Boston police strike. As Jacobs shows however, following the development of public sector unionism in the 1960s, and the growing union militancy in the 1970s, between 1970 and 1981, military forces have been used as replacements for striking public employees on forty-seven occasions. In the five year period from mid-1976 to mid-1981, they were used on thirty-one occasions. Federal troops have been used in the 1970 postal and the 1981 air traffic controllers strikes; National Guardsmen have been used mainly as substitute firemen, police, prison guards and mental health attendants. 30,000 troops and Guardsmen were used in the 1970 strike, and 12,000 Guardsmen in the prison guards dispute in New York in 1979.

Despite the constitutional, statutory and judicial rhetoric, the military have also been used in a wide range of law enforcement and public order circumstances. Before the Civil War, they were used to assist in controlling and capturing slaves (Sherman, p. 219). During the War, Union troops were regularly used, superseding civilian officials 'to suppress civil disorders, seizing and confining civilians suspected of supporting the Confederacy' (Engdahl, p. 2). Despite judicial rejection of the authority claimed by the President to justify this intervention (id.), the military were again used in the process of reconstruction. Thousands of local officials and six state governors were ousted; the army purged state legislatures and laws were set aside or modified by military decree (id., p. 17). In addition, federal troops assisted marshals and local sheriffs to discover and destroy stills (Sherman, p. 219).

In the 1960s, the military were not only used in the urban riots, but, in order to prepare for such intervention, military intelligence units conducted surveillance of civilians engaged in political activities (radical, peace and civil rights groups) and of some senators, governors and congressmen. Military personnel infiltrated those groups and established several data banks (see Sherman, pp. 223-4). On several occasions in the 1960s, presidents had to call in the armed forces (and 'federalise' the state National Guard) to enforce desegregation laws in southern states, often to overcome the local use of the National Guard to prevent the enforcement of the ruling in Brown v. Board of Education of Topeka (347 U.S. 483 (1959)) (see Weiner, 1969). At the Wounded Knee disturbance in 1973, armoured personnel manned by civilians replaced civilian vehicles at roadblocks; military personnel acted as observers and advisers and coordinated logistics; photographic reconnaissance flights were made; troops were placed on alert and prepositioned (although never actually used); large quantities of military material and equipment were 'loaned' for which use civilians were trained and contingency plans were drafted in case federal military intervention would be ordered by the President (Engdahl, pp. 35-7; Sherman, pp. 221-3; see also United States v. Red Feather, 392 F. Supp. 916 (D.S.D. 1975)). In a law enforcement role, marines have acted as undercover agents for the Treasury Department in a federal firearms violation investigation (United States v. Walden, 490 F. 2d 372 (4th Cir. 1974); military criminal investigators have assisted the police (Burns v. State, 473 S.W. 2d 19 (Tex. Crim. App. 1971); and an Air Force helicopter crew have been used to search for an escaped civilian prisoner (Wrynn v. U.S., 200 F. Supp. 457 (E.D.N.Y. 1961).

Of greater significance even than these examples of intervention is the potential for intervention expressed in new codes of regulations. Regulations made in 1972 assert (32 C.F.R. sec. 215.4(c)(i)) and 1982 regulations repeat that the right to use military force is based upon 'the inherent legal rights of the U.S. Government ... to ensure the preservation of public order and the carrying out of governmental operations ... by force if necessary'. As Engdahl comments (p. 29): 'the boldly defiant thrust of the latest regulations is simply that the executive will use military force whenever the executive deems it expedient to do so, congressional prohibitions notwithstanding'.

Furthermore, the statutory authority contained in 10 U.S.C. secs. 331-33 has, as noted earlier, been widely interpreted to include power to use the military in disturbances not amounting to insurrection (sec. 331), and despite the presence of civilian alternatives (sec. 333; see Engdahl, pp. 9-19). Thus, in 1957, the Attorney General asserted that secs. 332 and 333 authorised the use of troops in a school integration crisis (Engdahl, p. 45).

The executive has also relied upon a host of other statutes to justify use of the military. The Economy Act of 1932 was cited to authorise use of military personnel to keep the mail moving in 1934 and 1970, and again in the Wounded Knee disturbance in 1973. The Federal Aviation Act of 1958 was cited in the air traffic controllers' strike in 1981. Moreover, in <u>In re Debs</u> (158 U.S. 564, 582 (1895)), the Supreme Court stated that 'If the emergency arises, the army of the nation, and all its militia, are at the service of the nation to compel obedience to its laws'. Although the emergency in that case arguably referred to an insurrection (Engdahl, p. 45) there is nothing to prevent the executive acting upon its own initiative on this basis.

The military on both sides of the Atlantic have engaged in a variety of other 'miscellaneous' tasks, whose legality has, on occasion, been even more confused. At one end of the spectrum has been the use, worldwide, of the military to protect internal security and to combat terrorism. Some examples would include the Quebec Liberation Front kidnapping in 1970; manoeuvres at London Heathrow Airport in 1974 and 1978; security at the Montreal Olympics in 1976; the 1978 Hilton Hotel bombing in Australia; and the Iranian London Embassy siege in 1980. At the other end of the spectrum the military have also been used for more 'mundane' tasks. In the United States a fleet of eleven military jets (each costing $742 an hour of the Pentagon's budget) was used to bring senators to Washington D.C. for a vote on a gasoline tax measure (and to overcome a filibuster), and then return them to their home states (<u>Time</u>, 3 January 1983). Service personnel have also been used to assist in traffic control at county fairs and to augment District of Columbia police when foreign dignitaries visited the White House. In Great Britain, military tasks have included laying wire netting in public parks on which cars could park during a railwaymen's dispute (1982), digging up the garden of a murder suspect (<u>The Times</u>, 10 February 1984) and 'housing' police involved in miners' picket duty (1984). Their possible use in running the city of Liverpool if council workers had gone on strike was not discounted by Whitehall officials in 1984 (<u>Sunday Times</u>, 19 February). The literal effect of laws and regulations in both countries therefore is not only to expand the potential for military intervention beyond that for which the rhetoric of legality allows but to do so at the expense of the rhetoric itself. Indeed, even the principle of military subservience to the civil power is, in both countries, contradicted in the detail of the law.

Military Subservience to the Civil Power
In Great Britain, although there is no legal difference between soldiers and other citizens in respect of their duty to come to the aid of the civil power when so requested (Charge to the Bristol Grand Jury (1832) 5 C. & P. 261) there is 'in cases of disturbance where the civil authority has not asked for help' (Manual of Military Law, 1968, Part II, Section V, para. 3) and 'in very exceptional circumstances for grave and sudden emergencies' (Queen's Regulations for the Army 1975, J11.002) which have arisen 'a duty to take action which is not laid upon other citizens, except magistrates and peace officers' (para. 3). In such circumstances the commander is to act on his own responsibility (J11.002). Moreover, even in less dire situations, the military commander must judge for himself whether aid to the civil power is indeed necessary (paras. 3, 4), and whether use of force is justified (para. 5) despite contrary directions from the civil authority (para. 3; see, Whelan, pp. 120-4). There is at least one precedent for a military commander exercising independent judgment in these circumstances. In 1908, Haldane reported to the Select Committee on 'Employment of Military in Cases of Disturbance (Parl. Papers, H.C. 236, vol. vii, p. 3651) that a military commander, with the concurrence of the Chief Constable of Hampshire, refused a request from the mayor of Winchester to use his troops to deal with rioters (see Bramall, pp. 82-3).

Thus, although Mark has stated (p. 91) that should military aid be sought by the police today 'There is no question of one service coming under command of the other', Bramall is historically more correct in his analysis that 'in a real breakdown of order ... once called in, command would then devolve to the military commanding officer' (p. 74). As Jeffery has observed (p. 58) 'when the army is called in actively to support the government, both the responsibility and, perhaps more significantly, the initiative for action may shift away from civilians to soldiers themselves'.

In the United States, under 32 C.F.R. sec. 215 (4)(c)(1)(i), military force may be used

> to prevent loss of life or wanton destruction of property, and to restore government functioning and public order when sudden and unexpected civil disturbances, disasters, or calamities seriously endanger life and property and disrupt normal governmental functions to

such an extent that duly constituted local authorities are unable to control the situations.

Yet, it is clear that federal military intervention may occur in a state without a request from that state, and the judgment as to whether the state can control the situation may even be made by military officials. The discretion to invoke the 'inherent legal rights of the U.S. Government' is not reserved to the President. Although the President will 'normally' issue an Executive Order directing the Secretary of Defense to provide for the restoration of law and order in a specific state or locality, in cases of 'sudden and unexpected emergencies ... which require that immediate action be taken', no civilian higher than the Secretary or Under Secretary of the Army need be involved in the decision. He is fully responsible, as 'Executive Agent' for the Department of Defense, for the deployment of the military in civil disturbances. Moreover, the operational command structure provides for a Steering Committee, comprising military officers, Defense Department officials and the Deputy Attorney General of the United States, to advise and assist the Executive Agent. Actual operational control, however, is exercised by designated task force commanders; and planning, coordination and direction is the responsibility of a 'Directorate of Military Support' with a joint service staff under the Chief of Staff, U.S. Army. As Engdahl observes (p. 33):

> the 'emergency authority' justification for military intervention, which is the most extraordinary and far-reaching power asserted by the new Civil Disturbance Regulations, may be invoked and implemented by the military itself with only a modicum (if even that) of civilian involvement.

Having adjudged that local officials are out of control, the military is given a 'free hand to "restore governmental functioning and public order ..."' (id., p. 20). Indeed, since the military can respond not only to actual but also to potential emergencies, it can prepare in advance for contingencies as yet unstipulated in states or localities as yet undesignated. If the military units involved are no larger than a battalion in size, they may be prepositioned without presidential approval whenever a potential need might be perceived.

This discussion would be merely hypothetical were it not for the existence in both countries of a contingency planning machinery to facilitate intervention. It is this which turns potential use of the military into practical reality.

Contingency Planning
In the United States, to facilitate prepositioning and independent military action 'an established Pentagon machinery of intelligence and planning is constantly in operation, watching for occasions for intervention to arise' (id., p. 35). As mentioned earlier, intelligence gathering occurred following the urban disorders of the 1960s. Civil rights, peace and radical groups were the subject of military surveillance and infiltration; also subjected to surveillance were senators, congressmen and governors. In case troops should be required, the military collected information in advance.

In Britain, government contingency planning for major industrial disputes has been characterised by Jeffery and Hennessy (1983, p. 220) as the 'hidden history of British industrial relations'. It has become part of the 'seamless robe' of modern British administration, a 'hidden factor in the equation of State power versus labour power' (id., p. vi).

In both countries, such contingency planning is shrouded in secrecy. To the extent that the objectives of such planning accord with the rhetoric of legality, there can be little justification for this 'almost melodramatic air of secrecy' (Josiah Wedgwood, quoted id., p. 267). However, as Jeffery and Hennessy observe of the British Civil Contingencies Unit (id., p. 268), governments do have 'very good cause to be circumspect if it is also a political weapon' and those authors regard as 'disturbing' the lack of trade union involvement in contemporary contingency planning (id.).

There is, moreover, more than a suspicion that contingency planning is not simply a matter of 'protecting the public interest', but may also be a matter of politics. In 1920, a Cabinet-approved scheme for recruiting volunteer labour was prepared for distribution to chairmen and clerks of local authorities, but, 'in view of the political complexion of certain local authorities' (the Labour Party had in 1919 gained control of a number of boroughs) it was decided that authorities generally 'should not be given their instructions until the actual emergency' (quoted id., p. 41). The supervision of this scheme developed into a central

Supply and Transport Executive and later into a department 'known for purposes of disguise' (<u>id</u>., p. 42) as the 'Supply Department'. The department also had a pseudonymous telegraphic address (<u>id</u>., p. 54). Similar political sensitivities led ministers and departments to treat the Supply and Transport Organisation, when no major industrial dispute seemed imminent, 'like a species of departmental pariah' (<u>id</u>., p. 45).

More recently, in 1981, a Department of Health and Social Security circular which described finalised contingency plans for military intervention in an ambulance drivers' dispute was leaked. The circular, which was sent to health service administrators, stated that

> The security of these documents is paramount. You are in possession of military plans which are highly sensitive. Any disclosure of information contained in these plans would be <u>extremely damaging to government's industrial relations policy</u>. (<u>The Times</u>, 20 January 1981)

If use of troops is part of the government's industrial relations policy then, in a democratic society, even if it is a 'sensitive matter', it is questionable whether it should amount almost to a 'state secret'. Similarly, one would expect in a government consultation paper which discussed at length the problem of protecting the community against potentially damaging industrial action some reference to a main instrument in recent years of achieving that - the use of troops. Yet the Green Paper on Trade Union Immunities published in 1981 (Cmnd. 8128) did not discuss the Emergency Powers Act 1964 nor the regulations which could be made under the Emergency Powers Act 1920, either of which would authorise the intervention of service personnel. Despite its conclusion (para. 338) that 'This is a sensitive and difficult area in which arguments of fundamental principle and practice must be carefully weighed', use of the military was excluded from its own discussion. In other words, the document cast the debate in terms of the rhetoric of legality, and ignored the reality which the law itself posits.

A further consequence of this characteristic government secrecy is that

> when any element of emergency planning was made public, it was generally at the height of an

industrial crisis, at precisely the time when Parliament and public opinion was least able dispassionately to weigh-up either its short-term merits or long-term consequences. Such was the case with the Emergency Powers Bill' [of 1920] (Jeffery and Hennessy, 1983, pp. 53-4).

More recent examples of this are regulations made in 1980 (Motor Vehicles (Drivers' Licences) (Amendment) (2) Regulation, and Heavy Goods Vehicle (Drivers' Licences) (Amendment)). These enabled service drivers under the age of 21 to drive heavy vehicles without a special licence and receive full legal protection for so doing. While these regulations were made as a direct response to the threat of firemen to engage in one-day strikes in 1980, they are permanent measures, and will enable troops to drive heavy goods vehicles, such as petrol tankers, in other disputes, without proclaiming a state of emergency and having to consult parliament. Indeed, young drivers have undergone training courses at the Ordnance Corps Apprentice School in Surrey; and the Home Office has made 'Green Goddess' fire engines available for service training (The Times, 18 November 1980), having spent £1.7 million refurbishing them (id., 11 November 1980).

The paradox is well illustrated by events in 1946. While the government was proposing to repeal the Trade Disputes Act 1927, which had declared general strikes to be illegal, it was at the same time preparing contingency plans for defeating a general strike should one occur (Jeffery and Hennessy, 1983, p. 152). While attention is paid to the rhetoric of legality contained in the form of statutory principles, in reality departures from the rhetoric are being achieved in the detail of the law.

That these matters are of fundamental democratic importance is further illustrated by recent events in Britain. In the lengthy miners' strike in 1984, the government publicly played a 'back-seat' role, leaving the two sides of the mining industry to 'fight it out'. It is only the shroud of secrecy surrounding government contingency planning that has allowed the government to succeed in that role. Contingency planning by the Thatcher government has been augmented substantially since it came to power in 1979 on the basis of a secret report, prepared by a small group, chaired by Lord Carrington, which predicted a government defeat in any confrontation with the unions (The Times, 18 April 1978). By the time of the 1984 dispute a highly developed and detailed secret plan, drawn up in 1981, prepared and costed options for buying time if the mineworkers stopped coal supplies to power stations and other essential industries. The strategy reportedly included bigger coal stocks at power stations, measures to replenish supplies by using private road hauliers and an increase in coal imports and oil burning (The Times, 30 May 1984), together with 'picketing-breaking by mobile police squads' (Sunday Times, 28 May 1978). While the statutory and constitutional principles remain permanently enshrined, the original decision to use the military, which depends 'to a very great extent ... on political circumstances' (Jeffery, p. 64) is made in secret by the Defence Council, by the executive or by the military themselves none of which need to consult Parliament.

There can be no doubt about the threat which an abuse of the military role can pose to any democratic society. It is but a short step for a government to treat the exercise of constitutional rights by citizens as threats to the state; the exercise of civil liberties as undermining the institutions in society; and the expression of grievances by way of industrial action as a challenge to government policy. According to Blake (1979, pp. 257-8), Sir Frank Kitson, has concluded that should the police or civil authorities be unable to cope with breakdowns in public order 'the army will become directly involved in the rendering of political advice, the performance of civilian functions, the formulation of civil policy, and the maintenance of civil order'. In these circumstances, Kitson elsewhere (1971) set out an 'agenda' by which the army could execute its functions: providing essential services; civil population control; reinforcing and superseding the police force; carrying out psychological operations and intelligence-gathering; responsibility for general political strategy and civil/political policy-making based on joint civil/ military command systems and, if necessary, military assumption of total responsibility for counter-insurgent operations if civilian authorities proved unable to respond adequately (see generally, Bunyan, 1977, Chapter 7).

Kitson's ideas of military involvement have been integrated into training courses for high-ranking officers at the Royal College of Defence Studies, the School of Infantry at Warminster, Camberley Staff College and other institutions (see

Blake, 1979, pp. 273-8). Kitson became Commandant at Camberley and was later appointed Deputy Commander UK Land Forces. Bramall also has outlined (p. 74) the 'peripheral roles' and 'background services' which the military could provide in its public order role:

> helicopters, bomb disposal, special lighting, night vision, which would help the police get on with the job. And then, at the other end of the spectrum, the sporadic armed terrorist attacks or hijacking which are international or eccentric in character ...

Sherman too has raised the question of how far, following the 1981 amendments to the Posse Comitatus Act, civilian law enforcement agencies in the United States may become unduly dependent upon military resources in relation to drug, customs or immigration violations. The 'story' of the amendments, which he relates in Chapter 10,

> indicates how fragile is the legal protection accorded the principle of military non-involvement in civilian law enforcement in America ... The ultimate compromise resulting in a modest expansion of the military role indicates the attractiveness of military resources and manpower in a tight budget era and may portend further attempts to use those resources in civil law enforcement in the future. (pp. 229-30)

Moreover, increasing use of the military in civilian affairs is bound to lead to their performing further tasks simply because they have already become involved. Thus, in the 1979 British ambulance drivers dispute, service personnel not only drove ambulances, but they were also involved in the simple removal of an ambulance and van whose tyres had been slashed and which were blocking a hospital entrance (Guardian, Daily Telegraph, 2 February 1979, p. 1).

While the contingency planners and the military have prepared to respond to subversion and insurrection, their preparations themselves facilitate intervention which threatens democracy. While Kitson has argued (1977, p. 39) that subversion 'can involve the use of political and economic pressures, strikes, protest murders and propaganda', how can we know whether or not other agencies, such as the Special Branch, which exist to defend the realm against subversion or, in the United States, the National Security Agency see such a threat in every strike and protest march? Such agencies have access to the most modern technology; they can store vast amounts of information on 'subversives' in very expensive police intelligence computers (<u>The Times</u>, 26 February 1979); and links with army communications systems can easily be forged. Such intelligence information is used by contingency planners both for the threats posed by industrial action as well as those posed by terrorists (Hennessy, Chapter 5). Moreover, the shroud of secrecy has, on occasion, led to abuse (see Bamford, 1982; Engdahl, Chapter 1) or to questionable operations such as intercepting copies of TUC telegrams in the General Strike (Jeffery and Hennessy, 1983, p. 109).

Contingency planning of this kind hardly reflects the rhetoric of legality; but then, neither does the practice and potential of military intervention. Yet it is in the substance and structure of the law that such planning and intervention are provided; the law itself subverts the rhetoric. While this observation is important in itself, the contradictions in the law need to be explained. How is it possible for the military to play such a role within a democratic society and yet the constitutional and democratic principles remain in being?

THE ROLE OF LAW IN DEMOCRATIC SOCIETIES

While 'congenital secrecy' (<u>id</u>., p. 267) can be viewed as a deliberate means of precluding public discussion of government plans to use the military, the failure to question the feeble legal and political controls is explained more by the way the form of law in this area obstructs useful and clear analysis. The detail of the law is ambiguous, artificial and contradictory. Calls for greater clarity in the law (Evelegh, 1978; Bennett and Ryan, p. 193; Jeffery and Hennessy, 1983, p. 266; Greer, 1983, p. 598), for more openness in the debate (Jacobs, p. 154) and in policy (Jeffery and Hennessy, 1983, p. 268) fail to recognise that a gap between the rhetoric of legality and the practical operation of the law is the inevitable consequence of the form of law in this area.

At one extreme, the law is kept totally secret. Thus, in the United States, the largest secret intelligence agency, the National Security Agency, was created by an executive order signed by

President Truman in 1952. Despite the fact that the Agency has been used in violation of the constitutional rights of Americans (by 'eavesdropping' within the United States), that executive order remains secret even after thirty years (see Bamford, 1982). In Britain, various publications, such as Defence Council Instructions, 'Land Operations Volume III', 'Internal Security Doctrine and Instructions', and even 'Military Aid to the Civil Community in Routine Situations', to which the military would refer when aiding civil authorities are all 'restricted' and unavailable for public scrutiny.

Alternatively the law, while not secret per se, may be in its essence totally unreviewable. This is the case with the British royal prerogative powers which will apply in situations not otherwise dealt with under statute (Burmah Oil Co. Ltd. v. Lord Advocate [1965] A.C. 101). Royal prerogative powers are enormous in scope; their exercise is not reviewable by the courts; and they remain in the hands of the government. In the words of Bennett and Ryan (p. 186) the prerogative power of central government to control disorder 'is a dangerous mystery unwarranted in a democratic society'. Moreover, the myth that the Queen's Regulations are merely administrative guidelines and not a source of legal authority (Jeffery and Hennessy, 1983, pp. 242-3; NALGO, 1984, p. 4) needs to be exposed. They are issued under royal prerogative power, and the Queen commands that they be 'strictly observed on all occasions' (Prologue to the Queens Regulations for the Army 1975). The paradox, however, is that although strict observance is mandated, the Regulations recognise that 'necessary and self-evident exceptions' exist (id.). Accordingly, commanders at all levels are left, somewhat equivocally, with the instruction that their actions be 'guided and directed by the spirit and intention of these Regulations' (id.).

On both sides of the Atlantic, the law encourages governments to act first, to engage in secret contingency planning and ultimately to use the military while enabling them to avoid open debate. It is no coincidence that there currently exists in the United States a 'nonpolicy' regarding use of military forces as replacements in strikes (Jacobs, p. 153). The ambiguity in the laws and regulations makes it difficult to ascertain, for example, the authority for use of federal troops in the 1970 postal strike. President Nixon declared the strike to be a national emergency, and implicitly relied upon his power to execute the laws (U.S. Const. Art. II, sec. 3 and 10 U.S.C., sec. 3500). Jacobs has questioned whether use of federal troops was justified without the regular forces' prior failure to execute the laws. However, the judgment is to be exercised by the President. Just as courts are unlikely to 'second-guess the governor' (Jacobs, p. 140) in deploying troops, judicial review of Presidential deployment is unlikely to prevent such deployment. As Jacobs observes (id., pp. 138, 140) 'Following it to its logical conclusion, ... [t]he authority to execute the laws could be transformed into a charter for military rule ... Read broadly, this formulation could justify the use of troops in any illegal public employee strike'. Indeed, many state constitutions and statutes grant broad discretionary gubernatorial authority to activate the National Guard (id., pp. 141-2), making judicial challenge unlikely. Moreover, there is 'a strong tradition of judicial non-involvement in executive decisions involving deployment of the militia' (id., p. 162, n. 28). A majority of the Supreme Court in Laird v. Tatum (408 U.S. 1 (1972)), despite strong reaffirmation of the rhetoric that military intrusion into civilian affairs was traditionally and strongly resisted by Americans (id., p. 15), refused to hear complaints that intelligence-gathering 'chilled' their First Amendment rights. Moreover, there have been no criminal prosecutions under the Posse Comitatus Act (Sherman, p. 220) and it is abundantly clear that few legal constraints exist to prevent military intervention; indeed, the form of law actually facilitates it. The practical consequence of this is that the potential intervention of the military has often become an 'implicit factor' in collective bargaining (Jacobs, pp. 48-9). Indeed, the prepositioning of the military in 1979, when Montana prison guards threatened to strike, or the preparations to mobilize 100,000 military personnel when postal workers in 1981 so threatened (id., p. 162, n. 29, p. 164, n. 37) may not only 'chill' collective bargaining, it also calls into question the extent to which the military are in fact used as a last resort.

In Britain too, elastic phrases such as 'emergency', 'essentials of life' and 'urgent work of national importance', the content of which are determined exclusively by the government or the Defence Council, cannot in practice be invoked by 'victims' of military intervention or constrain the executive. Thus, much of the discussion by Greer to show 'demonstrably false' the view that the military may have a legal duty to intervene without, or even in defiance of, Cabinet direction[3] is irrelevant in practice since, as he also recognizes, the law takes a form which effectively precludes any redress against exactly such an eventuality (Greer, 1983, p. 597).

On other occasions, and at the other extreme, the law is used specifically to destroy the rhetoric. In the United States, while Grant recognized that much of the Reconstruction legislation was undoubtedly unconstitutional, he hoped that the laws enacted would 'serve their purpose before the question of constitutionality could be submitted to the judiciary and a decision obtained' (see Engdahl, p. 17). In Britain, governments have been willing to act first, without clear legal authority, and, if necessary, obtain an indemnity afterwards. This occurred in Great Britain in the 1920 miners' strike. Ministers decided that they should use servicemen in civilian tasks in reliance upon inherent powers of doubtful legality. In the words of Jeffery and Hennessy (1983, p. 53), it was 'more expedient to break, rather than make, law'. In the 1949 docks emergency also, the 'disciplinary powers' which the Port Emergency Committee, established by emergency regulations made under the 1920 Act, were given to exercise, along with other provisions of the dock labour scheme, were of doubtful legal enforceability. The attitude of government to this was clearly stated by the Attorney General, Sir Hartley Shawcross:

> I do not think that matters ... I have advised that this risk should be taken and that the Regulations should cover matters on which action is required without undue regard to the niceties of the law. In an emergency the Government may have, in matters admitting of legal doubt, to act first and argue about the doubts later, if necessary obtaining an indemnification Act. (quoted in Jeffery and Hennessy, 1983, p. 206)

In other words, ambiguity in the law can serve to enhance a government's freedom of action: 'The end clearly justified the means' (id.).

This approach to legality can also be seen in the attitude of governments to other emergency regulations, made under the Emergency Powers Act 1920, the legality of which had been doubted in the

1930s. The Home Secretary, Sir Herbert Samuel, recommended that such regulations, which had provided for distribution of food and coal in 1926, should continue to be made: 'if the Regulations were challenged it would be during an emergency and the challenge would not be well received by the House of Commons so that the conditions for getting amending legislation would be more favourable' (quoted id., p. 141). The amending legislation, of course, would be to achieve an identical outcome (in this case, of enabling administrative duties to be performed during an emergency by local authorities).

It is also possible to view this approach as one which the form of law facilitates. By imposing ambiguous and weak ex post controls, by allowing secrecy and preventing scrutiny of government action, the law itself provides the basis for intervention. It thus becomes possible, regarding the use of force, for the Manual of Military Law (para. 26) to reassure soldiers that

> the last word as far as civil [as opposed to military] pains and penalties are concerned rests with a jury, who may be relied upon to make liberal allowances for the difficulties of persons so circumstanced, and to err, if they do err, on the side of leniency, when it appears that an official, even if his action has proved excessive, acted honestly to the best of his judgment.

Similarly, during the General Strike in 1926, the government announced through the media that:

> All ranks of the Armed Forces of the Crown are hereby notified that any action which they may find is necessary to take in an honest endeavour to aid the Civil Power will receive, both now and afterwards, the full support of His Majesty's Government. (see Blake, 1979, p. 205)

Blake regarded this as 'an indemnity to the troops to take "any action" they might deem necessary to maintain order' (id.). Accountability of this kind means that actions can be taken and rationalisations made later. Even if an individual is later found to have gone beyond the limits, the general pattern of behaviour remains secure: that is, a broad degree of freedom of choice and action and of political initiative is retained.

Thus, the equivocal treatment of service personnel accused of overreaching or using excessive force (Jeffery, pp. 56-7) is not the result of corrupt or partisan adjudication, but the inevitable consequence of a post hoc system of control. Use of the military thus provides government with a powerful and flexible weapon. If there has been a moderating influence on government in Britain it has not been the law, the rhetoric of legality or the courts; it has been the permanent civil servants who have been in charge of contingency planning and the military themselves (Jeffery and Hennessy, 1983, p. 264). The rhetoric of legality cannot destroy the foundations of military intervention which the law actually provides. Thus, not only is the 'will of Congress not always respected by the executive branch' (Engdahl, p. 26), that will is sometimes rejected or sidestepped. Widespread military intervention can be facilitated without breaking the law.

The form of law in this area is a combination of case law, government regulation, inherent executive prerogative, secret planning and military autonomy. Such a loosely-knit amalgam cannot control government; rather it allows its interests in industrial relations and law enforcement to be accommodated without difficulty. Public discussion and private planning are kept very much apart. What begins as private disagreement can easily be redefined to bring it within the scope of 'emergency' or 'last resort' procedures, and outside the scope of the rhetoric; 'political and economic pressures, strikes, protest marches and propaganda' become redefined as 'subversion' (Kitson, 1977, p. 39); government 'neutrality' can thereby be preserved. In public, governments on both sides of the Atlantic use the military in industrial disputes when the 'public' or 'national' interest, or when the 'survival of a government based on law' (President Nixon, quoted in Jacobs, p. 137), is threatened. But, while eulogising the rhetoric, the law in fact allows and protects the making of private political decisions. The statutory principles appear clear and limited, yet the law actually provides for the wide use of troops, without consulting Parliament, managed by way of contingency planning, civil-military coordination and secrecy. In this form, the goal of certainty can never be realised. It is upon the form of law, therefore, that public debate ought to be focussed, and it is within this framework that the law and practice of military intervention in democratic societies must be considered.

NOTES
1. According to Winston Churchill in 1919, using soldiers to take sides with the employer in a trade dispute would be 'a monstrous invasion of the liberty of the subject, and would be a very unfair, if not illegal order to give to the soldier'. (H.C. Deb., Vol. 116, col. 1511).
2. It is probably erroneous of Greer to posit that 'local' requisitioning necessarily contravenes the principle of 'ministerial responsibility and is accordingly unlawful today'. Parliament, in the Army Reserve Act 1950, s. 10, provided for both governmental and local (justice of the peace) power to requisition army reserves to aid the civil power in the preservation of public peace. It can be argued by analogy that a similar duality of legal authority exists for requisitioning the regular army.
3. Citing Luther v. Bordon, 48 U.S. (7 How.) 115 (1845); Gilligan v. Morgan, 413 U.S. 1 (1973). See also, Monarch Ins. Co. of Ohio v. District of Columbia, 353 F. Supp. 1249 (D.D.C. 1973): 'presidential discretion in exercising these powers [to quell disorder] granted in the Constitution and in the implementing statutes is not subject to judicial review' (William B. Jones, district judge). But see Sterling v. Constantin, 287 U.S. 378 (1932) regarding a governor's discretion.

REFERENCES

Bamford, J. (1982) The Puzzle Palace, New York, Houghton Mifflin
Blake, J. (1979) 'Civil Disorder in Britain 1910-39: the Role of Civil Government and Military Authority' (unpublished Ph.D., Univ. of Sussex)
Bunyan, T. (1977) The History and Practice of the Political Police in Britain, London, Quartet
Burke, E. (1815) Works, Vol. V, London, Rivington
Clode, C.M. (1869) The Military Forces of the Crown: Their Administration and Government, London
Cunliffe, M. (1968) Soldiers and Civilians: the Martial Spirit in America, 1775-1865, Boston, Little Brown
Engdahl, D. (1971) 'Soldiers, Riots and Revolution: the Law and History of Military Troops in Civil Disorders', 57 Iowa Law Review 1
Evelegh, R. (1978) Peacekeeping a Democratic Society, London, Hurst
Finer, S.E. (1962) (1976) The Men on Horseback, 1st edn., London, Pall Mall Press; Peregrine Books
Greer, S.C. (1983) 'Military Intervention in Civil

Disturbances: the Legal Basis Reconsidered', Public Law 573

Huntington, S. (1957) *The Soldier and the State: the Theory and the Practice of Civil-Military Relations*, Cambridge, Harvard University Press

Jeffery, K. & Hennessy, P. (1983) *States of Emergency*, London, Routledge & Kegan Paul

Kitson, F. (1971) *Low Intensity Operations*, London, Faber & Faber

────────── (1977) *A Bunch of Five*, London, Faber & Faber

Logan, J. (1887) *The Volunteer Soldier of America*, Chicago, R.S. Peale

McBarnet, D. (1981) *Conviction: Law, the State, and the Construction of Justice*, London, Macmillan

Macready, General Sir N. (1924) *Annals of an Active Life*, Vol. 1, London, Hutchinson

NALGO (1984) *Government Activities Against Trade Unions*, London, NALGO

Otley, C. (1968) 'Militarism and Social Affiliations of the British Army Elite', in J. Van Doorn, *Armed Forces and Society*, Paris and The Hague, Mouton

Perkins, Brig. K. (1973) 'Soldiers or Policemen?', 45 *British Army Review* 7

Report to the Minister for Administrative Services on the Organisation of Police Resources in the Commonwealth Area and other Related Matters (1978), Canberra, Australian Government and Printing Service

Riker, W. (1957) *Soldiers in the States: the Role of the National Guard in American Democracy*, Washington D.C., Public Affairs Press

Weiner, Colonel F.B. (1969) 'Martial Law Today', 55 *American Bar Association Journal* 723

NOTES ON CONTRIBUTORS

GEOFFREY J. BENNETT is Lecturer in Law at the University of Leeds. In 1983-4, he was Visiting Associate Professor, University of Louisville, Kentucky. He has written several articles relating to use of the military in public order situations.
FIELD MARSHAL SIR EDWIN BRAMALL GCB OBE MC is Chief of the Defence Staff. He was formerly a Fellow of the Royal Society of Arts.
DAVID E. ENGDAHL is Professor of Law at the University of Puget Sound School of Law in Tacoma, Washington. Professor Engdahl has published numerous articles on legal questions of military intervention and has been directly involved in civil litigation arising out of the use of the military.
PETER HENNESSY is a leader writer with The Times and produces its weekly 'Whitehall Brief' column. In 1983-4, he was a Visiting Lecturer in Politics at Strathclyde University. He is about to join the Policy Studies Institute. He has co-authored several books including States of Emergency (London, Routledge & Kegan Paul, 1983).
JAMES B. JACOBS is Professor of Law and Director, Center for Research in Crime and Justice, at New York University. His articles on the socio-legal dimensions in civil/military relations have appeared in Armed Forces and Society and, with some new essays, will appear in New Dimensions in Civil Military Relations (Transaction Press, 1985).
KEITH JEFFERY is Lecturer in History and Politics at the Ulster Polytechnic (now merged into the University of Ulster). He is the author of The British Army and the Crisis of Empire, 1918-22 (Manchester, 1984) and co-author of States of Emergency (London, Routledge & Kegan Paul, 1983).
SIR ROBERT MARK is a former Metropolitan Police Commissioner. He is the author of Policing a

Perplexed Society (London, Allen & Unwin, 1977) and In the Office of Constable (London, Collins, 1978).

PETER ROWE is Senior Lecturer in Law, University of Liverpool. He was Director of Legal Studies, Cayman Islands, 1982-4. He has written several articles relating to military affairs, as well as books on Health and Safety at Work (London, Sweet & Maxwell, 1980) and Evidence and Procedure in the Magistrates' Court (London, Oyez Longman, 1982).

CHRISTOPHER L. RYAN is Lecturer in Law, University of Liverpool. He has written several articles and co-authored several books.

EDWARD SHERMAN is Angus Wynne Professor of Law at the University of Texas at Austin. He is the co-editor of a casebook, The Military in American Society (New York, Matthew Bender, 1979), and has written numerous articles on military law. Professor Sherman has engaged in much litigation involving the civil rights of military personnel.

CHRISTOPHER J. WHELAN is Research Officer at the Centre for Socio-Legal Studies, Wolfson College, Oxford. In 1982-3 he was Visiting Professor of Law at the University of Texas at Austin. In 1985 he will hold the Strom Thurmond Distinguished Visiting Chair at the University of South Carolina Law School. Dr Whelan has published extensively on the role of the military in industrial disputes.

LIST OF CASES

AFSCME v. Woodward, 406 F. 2d 137 (8th Cir. 1969). 257
Albert v. Lavin [1981] 2 W.L.R. 955. 124, 189, 198, 213
Ashton v. Turner [1980] 2 All E.R. 870. 209
Atkins v. City of Charlotte, 296 F. Supp. 1068 (W.D.N.C. 1969). 257
Attorney General v. De Keyser's Hotel [1920] A.C. 508. 187
Attorney General for Northern Ireland's Reference No. 1 of 1975 see Reference

Beatty v. Gilbanks (1882) 9 Q.B.D. 308. 173, 176
Beauboenf v. Delgado College, 428 F. 2d 470 (5th Cir. 1970). 256
Beckwith v. Bean, 98 U.S. 266 (1879). 44
Beim v. Goyer (1966) 57 D.L.R. (2d) 253. 214
Bowles v. Bank of England [1913] 1 Ch. 57. 193
Brown v. Board of Education of Topeka, 347 U.S. 483 (1959). 277
Brown v. Glines, 444 U.S. 348 (1980). 246, 258
Burdett v. Abbott (1812) 4 Taunt. 401. 212, 268
Burmah Oil Co. Ltd. v. Lord Advocate [1965] A.C. 101. 287
Burns v. Edmen [1970] 2 Q.B. 541. 209
Burns v. State, 473 S.W. 2d 19 (Tex. Crim. App. 1971). 277
Button v. DPP [1966] A.C. 591. 176

Chandler v. DPP [1962] 3 W.L.R. 694. 186
Charge to the Bristol Grand Jury (1832) 5 C. & P. 261. 121, 189, 279
Cook County Police Assoc. v. City of Harvey, 289 N.E. 2d 226 (1972). 256
Coward v. Baddeley (1859) 4 H. & N. 478. 171-2

In re Debs, 158 U.S. 564 (1895). 21, 45, 278
Devlin v. Armstrong [1971] N.I.R. 13. 176
Doherty v. Ministry of Defence (unreported, House of
  Lords, 1980). 208-09
Duncan v. Jones [1936] 1 K.B. 218. 174

Edinburgh and Dalkeith Railway v. Wanchope (1842) 8
  C.C. & F. 710. 195
In re Egan, 8 F. Cas. 367 (No. 4303) (C.C.N.D.N.Y.,
  1866). 17, 18, 43
Ellen Street Estates Ltd. v. Minister of Health
  [1934] 1 K.B. 590. 195

Farrell v. Secretary of State for Defence [1980] 1
  All E.R. 166. 202, 205, 207, 208, 210, 213, 214
Field v. Metropolitan Police Receiver [1907] 2 K.B.
  853. 175, 176
Firefighters Local 574 v. Floyd, 170 S.E. 2d 394
  (1969). 256
Fitzgerald v. Muldoon and others [1976] N.Z.L.R.
  619. 183

Georgia v. Stanton, 73 U.S. 50 (1867). 18
Gilligan v. Morgan, 413 U.S. 1 (1973). 162, 292
Greer v. Spock, 424 U.S. 828 (1976). 246, 250, 258,
  260
Griffin v. Wilcox, 21 Ind. 370 (1863). 43, 44

Healy v. James, 408 U.S. 169 (1972). 249
Hubbard v. Pitt [1975] 3 All E.R. 1. 194
Humphries v. Connor (1864) 17 Ir.C.L.R. 1. 174

Ireland v. United Kingdom, Eur. Court H.R., Series
  A. Judgment of Jan. 18th, 1978. 211

Johnson v. Jones, 44 Ill. 142, 92 Am. Dec. 159
  (1867). 43, 44
Jones v. North Carolina Prisoners' Labor Union,
  Inc., 433 U.S. 119 (1977). 249, 259

Kamara v. DPP [1974] A.C. 104. 172
Keighley v. Bell (1866) 4 F. & F. 763. 213
Kinder v. U.S., 14 C.M.R. 742 (1954). 205

Laird v. Tatum, 408 U.S. 1 (1972). 1, 43, 225, 288
Laker Airways Ltd. v. Department of Trade [1977] 2
  All E.R. 182. 187
Lamont et al. v. Haig et al., Civil Action No.
  81-5048 (D.C.S.D.). 50
Lane v. Holloway [1967] 3 All E.R. 129. 210
Langford (1842) Car. & M. 602. 176

Lansbury v. Riley [1914] 3 K.B. 229. 194
Lewis v. Arnold (1830) 4 C. & P. 354. 172
Lontine v. Van Cleave, 483 F. 2d 966 (10th Cir. 1973). 256
Luther v. Bordon, 48 U.S. (7 How.) 115 (1845). 162, 292
Lynch v. Fitzgerald [1938] I.R. 382. 207, 213

Malone v. Commissioner of Police of the Metropolis (No. 2) [1979] 2 All E.R. 620. 194, 210
Manual v. Attorney General [1982] 3 All E.R. 822. 195
Marshall v. Osmond [1983] 2 All E.R. 225. 214
Ex parte McCardle, 73 U.S. 318 (1867). 18
Ex parte McCardle, 74 U.S. 506 (1869). 18
McGuigan v. Ministry of Defence [1982] 19 N.I.J.B. 207
McLaughlin v. Tilendis, 398 F. 2d 287 (7th Cir. 1968). 257
McLoughlin v. Green, 50 Miss. 453 (1874). 18
Melton v. City of Atlanta, 324 F. Supp. 315 (N.D. Ga. 1971). 257
Ex parte Merryman, 17 F. Cas. 144 (No. 9847) (C.C.D.Md. 1861). 42
Ex parte Milligan, 71 U.S. 2 (1866). 1, 2, 14, 17, 34, 42, 267, 270
Milligan v. Hovey, 17 F. Cas. 380 (C.C.D.Ind. 1871). 43, 44
Mississippi v. Johnson, 71 U.S. 475 (1866). 18
Middendorf v. Henry, 425 U.S. 25 (1976). 257
Mitchell v. Clark, 110 U.S. 633 (1884). 44
Monarch Ins. Co. of Ohio v. District of Columbia, 353 F. Supp. 1249 (D.D.C. 1973). 292
Murphy v. Culhane [1976] 3 W.L.R. 458. 209

NAACP v. Alabama ex rel. Patterson, 357 U.S. 449 (1958). 245
Nashville v. Cooper, 73 U.S. 247 (1867). 44
Nixon v. Sirica, 487 F. & M. 700 (D.C. Cir. 1973). 193

O'Kelly v. Harvey (1883) 15 Cox. C.C. 435. 173

Padfield v. Minister of Agriculture [1968] 1 All E.R. 694. 187
Parker v. Levy, 417 U.S. 733 (1974). 246, 247, 257

R v. Allen [1921] 2 I.R. 241. 183
R v. Atkinson (1869) 11 Cox. C.C. 330. 173, 179
R v. Bohun and Temperley (unreported, Judgment 4th July 1979). 203, 205, 208

R v. Brodribb (1816) 6 C. & P. 575. 172
R v. Brown (1841) Car. & M. 314. 189, 190, 195-6, 198
R v. Caird and Others [1970] 54 Cr. App. R. 499. 172
R v. Chief Constable of the Devon and Cornwall Constabulary, ex parte CEGB [1981] 3 All E.R. 826. 168-9, 194
R v. Coney (1882) 8 Q.B.D. 534. 173, 194
R v. Dammaree (1710) 15 State Tr. 521. 170
R v. Dytham [1979] 3 W.L.R. 467. 189, 199
R v. Farnill (1982) Crim. L.R. 38. 177
R v. Foxford [1974] N.I. 181. 201
R v. Fursey (1833) 6 C. & P. 81, 172 Eng. Rep. 1155. 178
R v. Howell [1981] 3 All E.R. 383. 194
R v. Hunt (1820) 1 St. Tr. N.S. 171
R v. Kennett (1781) 5 C. & P. 282, 172 Eng. Rep. 976. 43, 124, 194, 268
R v. Lemon [1979] A.C. 617. 171
R v. Light (1857) D. & B. 332. 172
R v. McKay [1957] V.R. 560. 213
R v. Macnaughton [1975] N.I. 203. 202, 205
R v. Metropolitan Police Commissioner, ex parte Blackburn [1968] 2 Q.B. 118. 169, 193
R v. Pinney (1832) 5 C. & P. 254, 172 Eng. Rep. 962, 3 St. Tr. 11, 3 B. & Ad. 947. 43, 124, 194
R v. Porter [1973] N.I. 198. 212
R v. Sharp and Johnson [1957] 1 Q.B. 552. 176
R v. Smith (1900) 17 Cape of Good Hope Supreme Court Reports. 213
R v. Strickland [1921] 2 I.R. 317. 183
R v. Taylor (1940). 204
R v. Thomas (1816) 4 M. & S. 441. 204, 206
R v. Trainer (1864) 4 F. & F. 105. 204
R v. Vincent (1839) 3 St. Tr. N.S. 1037. 172, 175
R v. Williams (1984) Crim. L.R. 163. 213
Raymond v. Thomas, 91 U.S. 712 (1876). 44
Redford v. Birley (1822) 3 Stark. 76. 268
Reference under s. 48A of the Criminal Appeal (Northern Ireland) Act 1968 (No. 1 of 1975) [1976] 2 All E.R. 937, [1977] A.C. 105. 189, 198, 201-02, 205, 206, 212, 213, 214

S v. The United Kingdom, application No. 10044/82, European Commission on Human Rights. 181-2
Scheuer v. Rhodes, 416 U.S. 232 (1974). 1
Ex parte Siebold, 100 U.S. 371 (1879). 45
Stapp v. Resor, 314 F. Supp. 47 (S.D.N.Y. 1970). 232
State v. Coit, 8 Ohio Dec. 62 (C.P. 1897). 46

Sterling v. Constantin, 287 U.S. 378 (1932). 292

Taylor v. DPP [1973] 57 Cr. App. R. 915. 176
Town Investments Ltd. v. Secretary of State for the Environment [1977] 1 All E.R. 813. 195

United States v. Armstrong, 9 M.J. 374 (1980). 253
United States v. Banks, 383 F. Supp. 368 (D.S.D. 1974). 49, 222
United States v. Casper, 541 F. 2d 1275 (8th Cir. 1976), cert. denied, 430 U.S. 970 (1977). 50
United States v. Jaramillo, 380 F. Supp. 1375 (D. Neb. 1975) appeal dismissed, 510 F. 2d 808 (8th Cir. 1975). 49, 222
United States v. Kinder, 14 CMR 742 (AFBR 1953). 255
United States v. McArthur, 419 F. Supp. 186 (D.N.D. 1975), aff'd on other grounds sub nom. 50
United States v. Red Feather, 392 F. Supp. 916 (D.S.D. 1975). 50, 222, 223, 277
United States v. Ruiz, 25 USCMA 181, 48 CMR 797 (1974). 253
United States v. Walden, 490 F. 2d 372 (4th Cir. 1974) cert. denied 416 U.S. 983 (1974). 46, 225, 253, 277

Vorbeck v. McNeal, 407 F. Supp. 733 (E.D.Mo. 1976) aff'd 96 S. Ct. 3160 (1976). 245, 257

Wise v. Dunning (1902) 1 K.B. 167. 194
Woolmington v. DPP [1935] A.C. 462. 177
Wrynn v. United States, 200 F. Supp. 457 (E.D.N.Y. 1961). 47, 221, 277

Youngstown Sheet & Tube Co. v. Sawyer, 343 U.S. 79 (1952). 21, 28, 138, 159, 218, 267

LIST OF STATUTES

Administration of Justice Act 1774 7
Air Force Act 1955 115
Armed Forces Reserve Act 1952 160
Army Act 1955 115, 184-5, 198, 205-06, 212
Army Appropriation Act 1878 23
Army Reserve Act 1950 195, 292

Bill of Rights 1688-9 6, 184-6, 187, 193, 266

City of London Police Act 1839 174
Civil Rights Act 1866 16, 18, 48
Conspiracy and Protection of Property Act 1875 170
Criminal Attempts Act 1981 181
Criminal Damages Act 1971 174
Criminal Law Act 1967 73, 80, 178, 182, 194, 195, 199-211, 213
Criminal Law Act 1977 170, 174

Defence of the Realm Acts 1914-5 195
Defence (Transfer of Functions) Act 1964 115
Defense Department Authorization Act 1982 25
Dick Act 1903 147

Economy Act 1932 36-7, 278
Emergency Powers Act 1920 94, 98, 107, 117-20, 128, 170, 195, 269-70, 274, 282-3, 289
Emergency Powers Act 1964 71, 94, 107, 114-16, 117, 119, 120, 170, 195, 269, 274-5, 282
Emergency Powers (Defence) Acts 1939-40 195
Enforcement Act 1870 18, 23

Federal Aviation Act 1958 155, 278
Fugitive Slave Act 219

Highways Act 1980 168, 174

Incitement to Disaffection Act 1934 60

Industrial Relations Act 1971   99, 118

Judiciary Act 1789   11

Ku Klux Klan Act 1871   16, 18-19

Magistrates Court Act 1952   174
Magna Carta   5, 6, 40, 41, 265-6
Metropolitan Police Act 1829   52, 174
Military Reconstruction Act 1867   16, 17

National Defense Act 1916   164
National Emergency Act 1976   158
National Labor Relations Act 1935   257
Northern Ireland (Emergency Provisions) Act 1973
    198, 202, 212

Offences Against the Person Act 1861   174

Petition of Right 1628   6, 7, 41, 266
Police Act 1964   85, 174
Posse Comitatus Act 1878   19, 23-28, 29, 31, 34, 37,
    38, 47, 49, 138-9, 156, 159-60, 161, 217,
    220-30, 251, 253, 267-8, 270, 271, 285, 288
Public Order Act 1936   168, 174

Race Relations Act 1964   174
Race Relations Act 1976   168, 174
Reserve Forces Act 1966   195
Riot Act 1411   9
Riot Act 1714   6-7, 9, 41, 91, 178-80, 190-1, 213,
    272
Riot (Damages) Act 1886   171

Seditious Meetings Act 1817   174
Shipping Offences Act 1793   174
Statute of Treasons, see Treason Act 1351
Statute of Winchester   11

Taft-Hartley Act 1947   153, 159
Town and Country Planning Act 1971   169
Town Police Clauses Act 1847   168, 174
Trade Disputes Act 1927   283
Treason Act 1351   170, 174
Treason Act 1702   174, 194
Treason Act 1795   174, 194
Treason Act 1945   174
Treason Felony Act 1848   174, 194
Tumultuous Petitioning Act 1661   174

Vagrancy Act 1824   174, 181

NAME INDEX

Alderson, J. 166, 188, 190, 196
Alioto, J. 152
Altgeld, Gov. 131
Anderson, Sir J. 125
Ashworth, A. 206, 214
Attlee, C. 97-8, 100

Badami, J.A. 239, 258, 260
Baldwin, S. 54, 96, 97
Balfour, A.J. 62
Bamford, J. 286, 287, 292
Barber, A. 99
Baskir, L. 224, 255, 261
Bates, E. 2, 13, 14, 267
Benewick, R. 52, 67
Bennett, C. 226, 228, 229
Bennett, G.J. 183, 196, 264, 286, 287
Bishop, Brig. R. 100, 103, 108
Blackman, J.L. 131, 155, 164
Blackstone, W. 7, 9, 41, 50, 252
Blair, J. 242, 261
Blake, J. 53, 67, 272, 273-4, 284, 285, 290, 292
Blaylock, K. 241, 255
Bowden, T. 52, 55, 67
Boyle, K. 201, 215
Bramall, Sir E. 122, 124, 166, 190, 197, 269, 279, 285

Brickman, A. 235, 261
Brittan, L. 108
Brooke, H. 115
Brown, J.S. 240, 255, 261
Brownell, Attorney General 45
Buchanan, J. 13
Budd, T. 100, 108
Bunyan, T. 52, 67, 128, 284, 292
Burke, E. 264
Butler, B.F. 216
Byrne, J. 152

Callaghan, J. 94-5, 101, 103
Cameron, Lord 87
Campbell, J. 43
Carey, H. 135
Carr, R. 119
Carrington, Lord 95, 106, 284
Carter, J. 158
Champion, Lord 119
Chapman, B. 52, 67
Charles I 6, 7, 38, 266
Churchill, R. 53, 67
Churchill, W. 56, 76, 123, 273-4, 292
Chuter Ede, J. 98
Clark, Attorney General 43
Cleveland, Pres. 131, 275
Clode, C.M. 265

Clutterbuck, R. 84
Coffey, K.J. 147, 164
Coke, E. 7, 41
Commager, H.S. 50
Conyers, Cong. 228
Coolidge, C. 132
Corwin, E.S. 138, 164
Courtney, Sir W. 75
Cousins, B. 102
Creighton, W.B. 111, 129
Crick, B. 52, 67
Critchley, T.A. 52, 67, 84
Cromwell, O. 88
Cunliffe, M. 216, 261, 269

Dahl, B. 236, 262
Davis, W. 219, 261
Dellums, Cong. 228
de Lury, J. 163
de Smith, S.A. 57, 60, 67, 183, 184, 186, 196
Devlin, Lord P. 206, 215
Dicey, A.V. 183, 187, 195, 196, 200, 215
Dixon, N.F. 243, 261
Dogoloff, L.I. 253
Doolittle, J. 230-1
Drake, G. 259, 262
Draper, Col. G. 185
Dulles, F.R. 130, 164
Dyer, Gen. 56-7, 58, 62, 80, 195

Edward II 5
Effron, A. 159
Ehrlichman, J. 161
Eisenhower, D. 160, 241
Engdahl, D.E. 3, 9, 11, 12, 39, 46, 50, 156, 160, 164, 218, 261, 264, 265-8, 270, 271, 276, 277, 278, 280, 286, 289, 291
Ennals, D. 119
Ervin, S. 224
Evelegh, R. 57, 67, 123, 166, 177, 179, 191, 193, 196, 200, 201, 206, 213, 215, 264, 286

Fawcett, J.E. 167, 196
Fergusson, Sir J. 58, 67
Finer, S.E. 269
Fishgold, H. 257
Fleckenstein, B. 235, 261
Ford, G. 239, 254
Ford, W. 7, 50
Fraser, M. 66
Friendly, A. 88
Fulbright, W. 224
Furman, H.W.C. 160, 220, 261

Gaitskell, H. 98, 103
Gandhi, M.K. 56
Genkel, W.D. 151, 164
George II 7, 41
Gilbert, M. 66
Goldich, R. 237, 261
Goodall, D. 108
Grant, U.S. 17, 22, 23, 24, 25, 34, 45, 138, 267, 289
Green, L.C. 204, 215
Greenwood, C. 212
Greer, D.S. 214
Greer, S.C. 124, 191-2, 196, 264, 265, 266, 268, 286, 289, 292
Griswold, E. 258
Grunis, A. 198, 215
Gwynn, Sir C.W. 65, 182, 196

Hadden, T. 201, 215
Haig, Sir D. 63
Haldane, R. 80, 82, 198, 214, 269, 273, 279
Hale, M. 5, 6, 7, 9, 41, 50
Hamilton, A. 4-5, 40
Hampton, C. 194
Hanson, L. 103
Hardie, K. 60
Hart, B. 257
Hayes, R.B. 22, 45, 219-20
Heath, E. 95, 98, 100, 101, 106, 109
Hennessy, P. 54, 67, 94,

96, 109, 112, 117, 127, 128, 129, 274, 275, 281, 283, 286, 287, 289, 291
Henry II 11
Henry III 11
Herbert, Col. 81
Hertel, Cong. 228
Heuston, R.F.V. 186-7, 196
High, J. 252, 261
Hillyard, P. 201, 215
Hilton, R. 229, 253, 261
Hofstadter, R. 130, 164
Hogan, B. 194, 213
Hogg, Q. (Lord Hailsham) 118
Hogg, D. 214
Hudson, I. 102
Hughes-Morgan, D. 204, 215
Hunt, Sir J. 100
Hunter, E. 236, 262
Huntington, S. 269
Hurd, D. 98-9
Hut, A. 259, 262

Jacobs, B. 223, 261
Jacobs, J.B. 135, 143, 144, 164, 165, 218, 264, 275-6, 286, 287-8, 291
Jaconelli, J. 167, 196, 213
James I 6, 41
Janowitz, M. 242, 262
Jeffrey, K. 54, 55, 58, 67, 94, 96, 109, 117, 123, 128, 129, 272, 274, 275, 279, 281, 283, 284, 286, 287, 289, 291
Jellicoe, Lord 100
Jenkins, R. 127
Jennings, Sir W.I. 187-8, 196
John, King 5
Johnson, A. 15, 17
Johnson, L.B. 2, 218, 257
Jones, Sir E. 119
Jones, T. 62, 67

Jones, W. 4, 50
Jörg, N. 234, 262
Jourdain, H.F.N. 66
Judge, T. 162

Keegan, J. 242-3, 255, 262
Keijzer, N. 204, 215
Keir, D.L. 183, 188, 196, 213
Kennedy, J.F. 257
Kenny, C.S. 205, 215
Kernan, Sen. 219
Kilfeather, T.P. 66
Kimmel, W. 219, 220
King, T. 108
Kitson, Sir F. 284-5, 291
Knott, J.P. 220
Knutsford, Lord 75
Kosinski, F. 236, 262
Krendel, E. 239, 262
Kronenberg, P. 242, 262

Law, N. 102
Lawson, F.H. 183, 196, 213
Lazarus, P. 102
Leuchtenburg, W. 50
Lieber, G. 22, 23, 34, 45, 50
Lincoln, A. 13, 17, 267
Lindsay, J. 148, 151
Lloyd George, D. 58, 60, 95, 96, 109
Logan, J.A. 216, 262, 269
Lovell, J. 242, 262
Lowell, C. 39, 40, 41, 43, 50

McBarnet, D. 265, 293
McCardle, D. 53, 67
McCubbin, H. 236, 262
Macready, Sir N. 124, 273
Madison, J. 4-5, 40, 41
Mandeville, L. 236, 262
Mann, T. 60
Mansfield, Lord Chief Justice 8, 11-14, 24,

305

43, 46, 198, 268
Mark, Sir R. 75, 124, 126-7, 269, 279
Marshall, G. 120, 121, 123, 125, 126, 129, 145, 165
Marshall, S. 242, 262
Maudling, R. 109
Maxwell, Sir A. 96-7, 99
Meany, G. 163
Meeks, C. 36, 39, 50, 160, 219, 220, 222-3, 226, 253, 262
Merrimon, Sen. 219
Merrymen, J. 42
Miller, J.A. 260
Mitchell, V.A. 214
Morgan, E. 241, 255, 262
Morison, S.E. 17, 50
Morris, G.S. 112, 117, 120, 126, 128, 129
Moscos, C. 242, 262
Mosley, Sir O. 78, 168
Mottram, R. 104
Murray, C. 197, 205, 215

Neville-Jones, D. 103
Nichols, D.B. 200, 204, 215
Nixon, R. 2, 3, 135-9, 155, 156-61, 163, 218, 287, 291

O'Brien, J.M. 224
Ocheltree, K. 151, 165
Otley, C.B. 59, 67, 269

Parnell, C.S. 173
Peel, Sir R. 52, 77
Perkins, Brig. K. 166, 196, 269
Peterson, A.A. 148, 165
Phillips, G.G. 197, 215
Phillips, R. 242, 261
Pollock, S. 66
Powell, E. 166
Priddle, R. 102
Pye, A.K. 39, 40, 41, 43, 50
Pyle, C.H. 224, 262
Pym, F. 107

Radzinowicz, L. 197, 215
Reagan, R. 155
Rehnquist, W.H. 49, 140, 161
Resor, Secretary for the Army 232-3
Retsky, H. 143, 164
Richard II 5
Richardson, J. 13, 50
Riesel, V. 237
Riker, W. 131, 147, 165, 275
Robertson, Cong. 220
Rockefeller, N. 152
Rodgers, W. 94-5, 96, 101
Rowe, P. 170, 183, 196, 208, 212, 215
Russell, F. 132, 165
Russell, Lord 61, 67
Ryan, C.L. 264, 286, 287

Salmond, Sir J.W. 194
Samoff, B. 262
Samuel, Sir H. 290
Scargill, A. 99, 100
Scarman, Lord 167, 180-1, 196
Schmertz, E.J. 256
Schwarz, F. 224, 262
Sefton, J. 219, 262
Seiberling, J.R. 47, 228
Sewill, B. 99
Shaw, Cong. 227-8
Shaw, W. 154
Shawcross, Sir H. 289
Sherman, E. 241, 262, 264, 267, 276, 277, 285, 288
Siemer, D.C. 159, 259, 260, 262
Smillie, R. 96
Smith, J.C. 194, 213
Smith, T. 52, 67
Soskice, F. 115
Southard, Sen. 219
Stapp, A. 232, 263
Stennis, Sen. 233
Stephen, D. 102
Stevenson III, A. 224
Strauss, W. 255

Sullivan, D. 236, 263
Swisher, C. 42

Taney, Chief Justice 41-2
Teitler, G. 234, 263
Thatcher, M. 95, 103, 106, 107, 108, 284
Thurmond, S. 233, 246
Tilden, S.J. 22
Tillotson, Brig. M. 102
Tower, Sen. 226
Townshend, C.J.N. 62, 67, 211, 212, 215
Truman, H. 287

Usery, W. 238, 257, 263

Wade, E.C.S. 197, 215
Wade-Gery, R. 102, 103, 108
Waggett, G. 212
Wake, M. 102
Wakerley, J.C. 199, 215
Wallace, M. 130, 164
Ward, A. 210, 215
Wedgwood, Col. J. 119, 281
Weiner, Col. F.B. 277, 293

Wellington, Duke of 77
Werner, V. 236, 263
Wheeler-Bennett, J.W. 125, 129
Whelan, C.J. 117, 129, 144, 165, 270, 274, 279
White, Cong. 227, 228
Whitelaw, W. (now Lord) 103, 107, 108, 180
Williams, D.G.T. 213
Wilson, H. 99, 101, 118
Wilson, Sir H. 58, 60, 61, 63
Wilson, J.Q. 145, 165
Wise, E. 178, 196
Wolff, L. 253
Woodward, C. 220, 263
Wright, C.A. 258
Wulf, M.L. 154
Wurf, J. 163

Young, T. 60, 67

Zimmer, L. 135, 144, 164, 165
Zumwalt, E.R. 231

SUBJECT INDEX

Aberfan tip disaster 71, 72
affray 171, 174, 176-7, 182, 195
Amritsar Massacre 56-7, 80, 195

Balcombe Street 75, 93
Black and Tans see police
Blackshirts 56, see also Sir Oswald Mosley
Bloody Sunday 93, 211
Bolshevism see revolution
breach of the peace 142, 168, 169, 171-4, 181, 189-91, 194, 196, 198

Civil Constabulary Reserve see police
Civil Contingencies Unit (CCU) 95-108, 281
Civil War
    American 2, 9, 10, 14, 16, 34, 38, 48, 219, 267, 275, 276
    English 6, 266
    Kansas 9
contingency planning 85-109, 110, 124, 137, 264, 273, 277, 280-7, 291
Crown
    defined 195
Curragh incident (1914) 58, 61

Declaration of Independence 7, 266-7
Defence Council 114, 115-6, 120, 125, 269-70, 275, 284, 288
desuetude 171, 176
Dorr Rebellion (1842) 9
due process 3-8, 14, 15, 19, 21, 28, 34, 38, 39, 41, 42, 46, 245, 267, 268, 270, 271

Easter Rising (1916) 62
European Commission on Human Rights 181-2, 211, 214
European Convention on Human Rights 167, 181-2, 210-11

Featherstone riots see riot
Federalist papers 4, 40
force 53, 54-5, 57, 62-4, 74, 78-81, 87-8, 89, 121-2, 130, 179, 181, 182-3, 193, 195, 197-215, 269, 272-4, 277, 279, 290-1
    Yellow card 74, 203, 204, 205, 207
    see also Criminal Law Act (1967)
freedman 16

Garden House Hotel
  Affair 172
General Strike (1926)
  51, 54, 56, 61, 63,
  64, 96, 100, 123, 125,
  274, 286, 290
Gordon riots 11, 43,
  180, 194, 206
Grosvenor Square 77, 191

indemnity 183-4, 200, 289
industrial disputes see
  strikes
insurgents see insurrection
insurrection 2, 4, 7,
  8-9, 10, 13, 15, 18,
  23, 24, 34, 35, 37,
  40, 44, 45, 46, 48,
  51, 62, 70, 74, 76,
  78, 83, 137, 139,
  141-2, 160, 170-1,
  182, 188, 203, 210,
  252, 270, 271, 277,
  278, 284, 285, 286
intelligence-gathering
  33, 59, 102, 103, 200,
  223-5, 228, 230, 251,
  276, 281, 288
  in Northern Ireland
    70-1, 83
  see also surveillance
Iranian embassy siege
  (1980) 65, 212, 278
Ireland 51, 52, 53, 58,
  61-2, 197, 200, 212,
  see also Northern
  Ireland
Irish Republican Army
  65, 71, 75, 201

Lod Airport 74

magistrates 3, 4, 14,
  121-3, 124, 125, 126,
  127, 266, 267, 268,
  273, 279
Magna Carta 5, 6, 40, 41,
  265-6
Mansfield doctrine see
  Lord Mansfield

Manual of Military Law
  80, 114, 120-3, 170,
  171, 173, 189, 195,
  204, 205, 212, 268,
  269, 270, 279, 290
marshals 11-15, 18, 31,
  44, 45, 219, 220, 221,
  276
martial law 6, 7, 11,
  16, 41-2, 43, 57, 62,
  183-4, 186, 200, 212,
  265-6, see also
  prerogative powers
military
  aid to the civil
    community 64-5, 73,
    114-6, 120
  aid to the civil
    ministries 65, 73,
    117-20
  aid to the civil power
    51-67, 73-84, 85-93,
    120-4, 125-7,
    170-93, 268-9,
    272-4, 279, 290, 292
  disaffection 60-1
  freedoms 230-2
  intervention in industrial disputes
    94-165, 269-70,
    274-6, 287-8, 291,
    292
  public order role
    87-89, 110, 166-96,
    265-9, 270-4, 276-7,
    279-80, 284-5
  social class 59-60
  use of force 53, 62-4
  see also natural disasters, unionization
militia 7, 8, 10, 12,
  15, 17, 42, 45, 46,
  77, 130-1, 136, 141-2,
  147, 154, 162, 216,
  218, 219, 252, 266-7,
  275, 278, 288
  Bill 8-9, 10, 42-3
Mogadishu 75

National Council for
  Civil Liberties 82

309

National Guard 35, 42,
  92, 130, 131, 132,
  134-5, 136, 139-40,
  142, 143-52, 154, 160,
  161, 162, 163, 275-6,
  288
National Security Agency
  287-8
natural disasters 65,
  70, 89, 120, 141-2,
  148, 192, 221, 230
Northern Ireland 62, 65,
  69, 70-1, 72, 75-9, 82,
  83, 87-8, 111, 112,
  176, 179, 181, 197,
  199, 201-3, 207,
  209-11, 212, see also
  Ireland

Operation Motorman 77

Peasants' Revolt (1381)
  5
picketing 76, 99, 100,
  101, 106, 108, 123,
  124, 127, 274, 278, 284
police 54, 68
  Black and Tans 62
  Civil Constabulary
    Reserve 56
  compared with army 52
  coordination with
    army 69-70, 72-3,
    74, 75, 84, 85-93,
    122, 124-7, 188-93,
    197-8, 269, 273, 279,
    285
  historical roots in
    Britain 52, 77
  in Ireland 61-2
  in Northern Ireland 71,
    72, 79
  public order role 85-7
  role in strikes 112,
    124-8
  Royal Military 65
  Special Constabulary
    55, 56, 62, 64
  strike (1918) 54, 56
  strike (1919) 54-5, 56,
    65, 79-80

strike (1919) (Boston)
  132, 276
strike (1976) (US)
  151-2
see also third forces
posse comitatus 3, 4, 5,
  7, 9, 11, 12, 13, 14,
  15, 16, 18, 23, 24,
  31, 40, 43, 44, 46,
  47, 60, 191, 219, 220,
  252, 266, see also
  Posse Comitatus Act
  (1878)
prerogative powers 3, 6,
  7, 8, 11, 14, 19, 21,
  23-5, 28, 29, 34, 40,
  41, 45, 115, 120, 122-
  3, 136-7, 156-7, 184,
  186-8, 191, 218, 265-
  7, 271, 277, 287, 291

Queens Regulations for
  the Army (1975) 114,
  120, 122-3, 192, 269,
  279, 287

Reconstruction 2, 16-19,
  22, 34, 38, 39, 219,
  220, 228, 267, 276,
  289
Red Lion Square 76
revolution 51, 54, 60,
  64
  Bolshevism 54
  Russian 54
riot 4, 6, 9, 20, 34,
  37, 44, 62, 64, 76,
  89, 108, 121, 141-2,
  144, 160, 166, 170-2,
  174, 175-82, 193, 195,
  203, 210, 268, 271,
  272, 279
  Bristol (1831) 194-5
  control 78, 83
  Featherstone colliery
    (1893) 52-3, 197,
    213, 272
  Kent State 228
  Mosley 78
  Northern Ireland 71
  urban 19, 43, 145,

163, 197, 211, 223, 228, 276, 281
see Gordon riots, Riot Act 1714
rout 171, 174, 181, 182
royal prerogative see prerogative powers

Saltley coke depot 76, 99, 100, 101, 108, 109, 123
Scheveningen prison 75
secrecy 114, 281-4, 286-91
Secret Service 19, 30-1, see also intelligence gathering, surveillance
separation of powers 14, 21, 153, 218, 267
Shay's Rebellion (1786-7) 9
Special Air Service 65, 75, 212
Special Branch 285
strikes
　air traffic control (1977) 124; (1979) 119, 124, 125-6; (1981) 134, 135, 155, 276, 278
　ambulance drivers (1979) 285; (1981) 112, 125-6, 281; (1982) 112, 125-6
　civil servants (1981) 127
　docks (1911) 273; (1945) 98, 128; (1948) 98, 118, 119, 275; (1949) 98, 118, 119, 275, 289; (1950) 98; (1972) 116
　electricity supply 103-6; (1950) 98, 103-4; (1970) 98, 99; (1977) 105
　firemen 144, 151, 152; (1977-8) 71, 72-3, 101, 112, 119, 124, 128, 144-5, 275;

(1978) (US) 148; (1980) 152, 283
　Glasgow
　　dustmen (1975) 71, 91, 113, 116, 275;
　　firemen (1973) 71, 72, 113, 275;
　　general (1919) 63
　health service (1982) 127
　industrial civil servants (1978) (1981) 116
　loggers (1917-18) 131
　London
　　dustmen (1970) 113, 116, 275; social workers (1979) 126; tramwaymen and busmen (1924) 118, 275
　longshoremen (1863) 131
　machinists (1941) 131
　meat-handlers (1947) 98
　mental health attendants (1968) 151
　military intervention in 110-65
　miners 106; (1910) 53, 273; (1911) 53; (1920) 65, 289; (1921) 55, 65; (1926) 119; (1972) 99, 101; (1973-4) 101; (1984) 109, 127, 278, 283-4
　Ministry of Works (1948) 116, 275
　NGA (1983) 108
　petrol tanker drivers (1953) 94, 109
　police 145, 151, 152; (1918) 54, 56; (1919) 54-5, 56, 65, 79-80; (1919) (Boston) 132, 276; (1975) (US) 151-2
　postal (1934) 278; (1970) 130, 134, 135-40, 143-4, 146,

311

148, 155-60, 163, 276, 278, 287-8; (1981) 164, 288; (1981) (Canada) 157
prison officers 128, 151, 152, 162; (1973) 152; (1979) 135, 146, 148, 276, 288
Pullman Strike (1894) 19, 45, 131, 275, see also In re Debs
railway (1877) 130-1, 275; (1911) 122, 123, 273-4; (1919) 55; (1921) 65; (1955) 98; (1982) 108, 113, 278
road hauliers (1979) 94-5, 101
sanitation workers (1968) 148, 152
seamen (1960) 116; (1966) 98, 113, 118, 119, 274
ship-repair (1944) 131
social workers (1967) 151
transit workers (1980) 143
truckers (1974) 131
Ulster Workers Council 72
water (1981) 107; (1983) 107-8, 124-5
see also General Strike (1926)
Supply and Transport Organisation 97, 274, 282

surveillance 27, 30, 221, 223-5, 227, 248, 276, 281, see also intelligence-gathering
Sydney Street 75-6

Territorial Army 107
terrorism 48, 64, 69-71, 74, 76, 83, 89-90, 91, 120, 125, 199, 201, 202, 208, 209, 278, 285, 286
third forces 55-6, 92
treason 170-1, see also Treason Acts
Trade Union Immunities, Green Paper (1981) 282
Triple Alliance 96, 109
tumult 142

unionization 210, 217, 230, 232-51, 255-60
Austria 236
Belgium 236
Denmark 236
France 236
Netherlands 234
Sweden 234-5, 239
West Germany 235
unlawful assembly 10-11, 20, 170-5, 181, 182, 195, 203

Whiskey Rebellion (1794) 9
Wounded Knee 3, 35-7, 221-2, 227, 277, 278

For Product Safety Concerns and Information please contact our EU representative GPSR@taylorandfrancis.com
Taylor & Francis Verlag GmbH, Kaufingerstraße 24, 80331 München, Germany

www.ingramcontent.com/pod-product-compliance
Lightning Source LLC
Chambersburg PA
CBHW071343290426
44108CB00014B/1426